DATABASE MANAGEMENT SYSTEM

NIRUPMA PATHAK
M.Tech. **(CS & Engg.)**
Assistant Professor,
Department of Computer Application,
Lal Bahadur Shastri Institute of Management and Development Studies,
LUCKNOW.

Himalaya Publishing House
ISO 9001:2015 CERTIFIED

First Edition : 2008
Reprint : 2011
Reprint : 2017
Reprint : 2024

Published by : Mrs. Meena Pandey
for **HIMALAYA PUBLISHING HOUSE PVT. LTD.,**
"Ramdoot", Dr. Bhalerao Marg, Girgaon, Mumbai - 400 004.
Phone: 022-23860170, 23863863; **Fax:** 022-23877178
E-mail: himpub@bharatmail.co.in; **Website:** www.himpub.com

Branch Offices :

New Delhi : "Pooja Apartments", 4-B, Murari Lal Street, Ansari Road, Darya Ganj, New Delhi - 110 002.
Phone: 011-23270392, 23278631; Fax: 011-23256286

Nagpur : Kundanlal Chandak Industrial Estate, Ghat Road, Nagpur - 440 018.
Phone: 0712-2721215, 2721216

Bengaluru : Plot No. 91-33, 2nd Main Road, Seshadripuram, Behind Nataraja Theatre, Bengaluru - 560 020.
Phone: 080-41138821; Mobile: 09379847017, 09379847005

Hyderabad : No. 3-4-184, Lingampally, Besides Raghavendra Swamy Matham, Kachiguda, Hyderabad - 500 027.
Phone: 040-27560041, 27550139

Chennai : No. 34/44, Motilal Street, T. Nagar, Chennai - 600 017. Mobile: 09380460419

Pune : "Laksha" Apartment, First Floor, No. 527, Mehunpura, Shaniwarpeth (Near Prabhat Theatre), Pune - 411 030.
Phone: 020-24496323, 24496333; Mobile: 09370579333

Cuttack : Plot No. 5F-755/4, Sector-9, CDA Markat Nagar, Cuttack - 753 014, Odisha. Mobile: 09338746007

Kolkata : 3, S.M. Bose Road, Near Gate No. 5, Agarpara Railway Station, North 24 Parganas, West Bengal - 700 109. Mobile: 09674536325

Printed at : Geetanjali Press Pvt. Ltd., Nagpur. On behalf of HPH (P).

Preface

The primary objective of **"DATABASE MANAGEMENT SYSTEM"** is to provide materials that not only introduce the student to the field of computer science but also acquaint the student with specific issues related with Information Technology industry, I wrote this book in recognition of the ever-growing importance of information and the unique challenges faced information Technology Industry. In order to remain ahead of others competitors, Industries are taking the advantage of information. Information is playing a major role in all the spheres. Whether it is Information Technology Industry, Banking Sector, Phasma Industry, Education Sector, Automobile Industry etc. This is an era of Information, the entire world is globalised and it has become global village and single society just after the revolution of IT that lead to easy access of Information.

This book introduced the basic concept needed for designing, using and implementing Database Systems and applications (along with its practical applications). The object of this book is to provide as much as tecnical detail as possible specially to the beginners who would like to learn Database Management System in the graduate level. However, we hope that this book would also be useful for the database management courses of masters degree as reference.

Modern database management provides sound, clear and current coverage of the concepts, skills and issues, depicts new applications needed to cope with an expanding organisational data resource.

Nirupma Pathak

Acknowledgement

We are extremly thankful to our dear students as the interaction with them helped us in understanding their needs.

First of all, I am thankful to all the authors whose journals, papers and books were referred while preparing the content of this book.

I express my profound thanks to Dr. Sunil Kumar (Director), LBSIMDS, Lucknow as he has been a source of inspiration for such creative work and initiatives.

I convey my heartfelt thanks to Dr. Subhash Chandra (Director) MLRSM, Lucknow, Mr. Pawan Tripathi, (PRO), U.P. Technical University, Lucknow, Ms. Anshum Srivastava (H.O.D), Master of Computer Application, LBSIMDS, Lucknow, Mr. Pramod Bhatnagar (Reader), LBSIMDS, Lucknow, Mr. Praveen Sachan (Reader), LBSIMDS, 'Lucknow, Dr. Syed Haider Ali (Reader),. LBSIMPS, Lacknow and also thankful heartly thanks to my colleagues for their unending efforts, encouragement, guidance and continuous support during the preparation of this book.

I am sincerely grateful to my family, specially my parents Mrs. and Mr. Devi Prasad Pathak, beloved Brothers Abhishek Pathak. (DBA), RTO Office, Mirzapur Akhilesh Pathak, Ashutosh Pathak and Ashish Pathak, sisters Anupama Pathak, Archana Pathak and Rachana Pathak for their good wishes, love moral support and vocal on couragement and without them this manuscript would not have been completed successfully. I also gratify them for abiding me ever and anon to come to grips with all ups and downs of life.

I deeply express my heartful thanks to Himalaya Publishing House, New Delhi for publishing this book in such a beautiful get up and well in time last but not the least, all praise, laud and honour to great Almighty God for His amazing grace and guidance.

Nirupma Pathak
nirupmapathak@gmail.com

Contents

UNIT 1

UNIT 2

Unit 3

Unit 4

Unit 5

Unit 6

ABOUT THE AUTHOR

Nirupma Pathak, Assistant Professor, Department of Computer Application, Lal Bahadur Shastri Institute of Management and Development Studies, Lucknow, has done her B. Tech (CS & Engg.) and then M. Tech (CS & and Engg.) from U.P. Technical University. She has specialized in Database Management System Software Engineering, Enterprise Resource Planning and theory of Automata and formal languages.

Here area of resourch work is Software Engineering Models. She has published seven research papers and presented ten papers.

ABOUT THIS BOOK

This book attempts to bring under one cover the entire revised syllabus prescribed by the U.P. Technical University for the B.Tech (CS & Engg.), B. Tech (IT), BCA, MCA, BBA, MBA(IT) Course in Database Management System. The book has been written to cover the syllabus of other Indian Universities PG and UG Courses. The book has been written in a lucid manner to facilitate understanding Extremely well organized and lucidly written book with an approach to explain the concepts in communicable languages.

Inspite of my best care, it is quite possible that some errors, printing mistakes might have crept in. I shall be thankful if the same is brought to my notice suggestions for further improvement will be highly appeciated.

UNIT — ONE

Chapter 1 Introduction

Chapter Outline

- An Overview of Database Management System
- Database System vs. File System
- Database System Concepts Architecture
- Data Models
- Schema and Instances
- Data Independence
- Database Language and Interfaces
- Data Definitions Language
- Data Manipulation Language (DML)
- Overall Database Structure
- DBMS Users

AN OVERVIEW OF DATABASE MANAGEMENT SYSTEM

DBMS can divide the term into two parts one is database and other is management system.

1. Database

A database is a collection of related information stored so that it is available to many users for different purposes.

Fundamental of Database : (1) Field (2) Record (3) File (4) Database (5) Key field

1. Field. The smallest piece of meaningful information in a file is called a data item or field.

NAME	LOCALITY	CITY	STATE	PINCODE

(Fields or Dataitem)

2. **Record.** The collection of related fields is called a record.

1. Ram	118, Shamina Road	LKO	UP	226003

3. **File.** File is the collection of all related records.

Field Name

NAME	LOCALITY	CITY	STATE	PIN CODE
1. Ram	198, Shamina Road	LKO	U.P	226003
2. Sita	108, Mohan Road	Allahabad	U.P.	211001

Record 1 — Field contents (LOCALITY), Field contents (STATE)

Record 2

4. **Database.** Database is a collection of interrelated files.

5. **Key Field.** The key field in a record is a unique dataitem which is used to identify the record for the purpose of accessing and manipulating database.

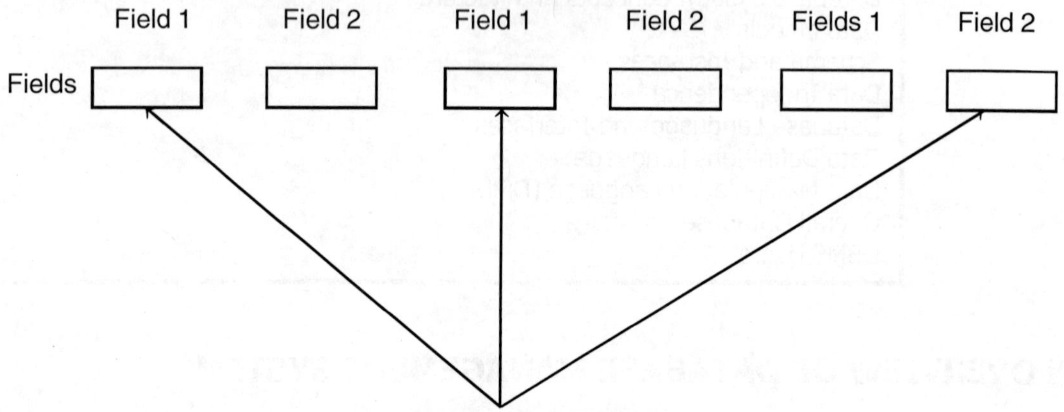

Relating Key Fields

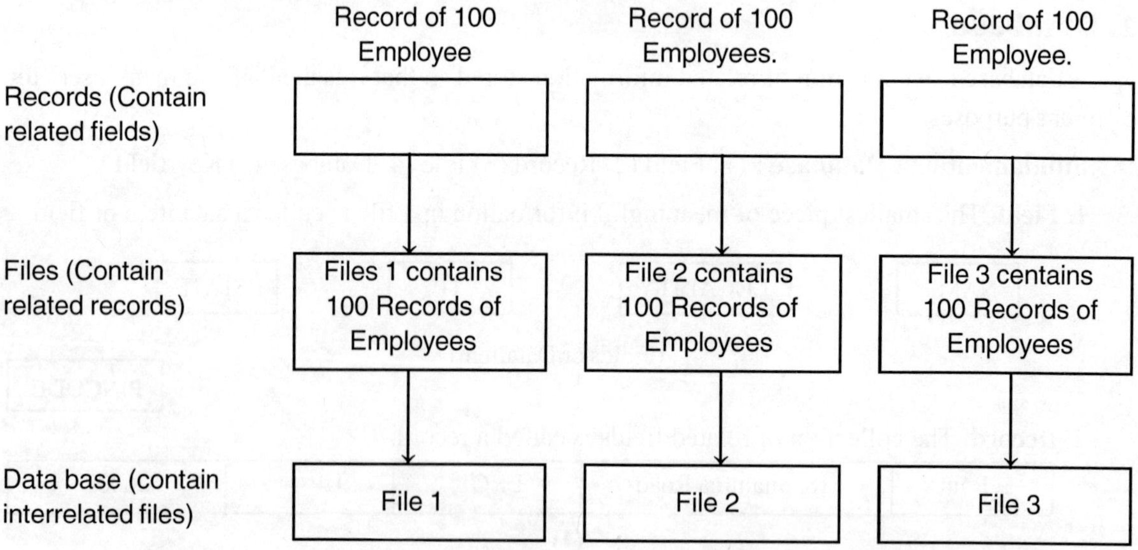

2. Management System

Management System is a collection of programs that enables users to create and maintain the database.

So "A DBMS is a collection of interrelated files and a set of programs that allow users to access and modify these files. The system hides contain details of how the data is stored and maintained."

Advantages of DBMS

1. Redundancy and Inconsistency can be Reduced. In traditional file system, if same database is to be used by multiple applications then we have to create the separate file for each application which gives a considerable duplicity in the stored data resulting wastage of minor space.

But in DBMS, DBA (Database Administrator) has the centralized control of the data. DBMS allows the sharing of data under its control by any number of applications

2. Data Independence. DBMS allows the Data Independence at two level, physical Data Independence base and logical Data Independence .

Data Independence is one of the main advantage of DBMS.

The ability to modify a schema definition in one level without affecting a schema definition in the next higher level is called data independence.

1. **Physical Data Independence :** PDI (Physical Data Independence) is the ability to modify the physical schema without causing application programs to be rewritten.
2. **Logical Data Independence :** LDI (Logical Data Independence) is the ability to modify the conceptual schema without causing application program to be rewritten.

3. Efficient Data Access. A DBMS provides so many techniques to store and retrieve the data efficiently.

Disadvantages of DBMS

1. Problems associated with centralization
2. Cost of software and hardware incurred in the application of DBMS is its major disadvantages.
3. Complexity of backup and recovery.

DATABASE SYSTEM VS. FILE SYSTEM

File Processing System	*Database System*
1. In file processing system, the system stores permanent records in various files. Application programs are need to extract records from and add records to appropriate files. As time passes new files and corresponding application programs are added to the system.	1. In the database system, there exists a collection of interrelated files and a set of application programs to acess and modify these files. Details of Data storage and maintenance are hidden from the users.
2. Supported by conventional operating systems such as MSDOS.	2. A database system may be generated automatically or it may be computerized.
3. Since the files and application programs are created by different programmers over a long period of time, data in files is likely to get repeated. Redundancy can lead to inconsistency that is the various copies of the same data may certain different information.	3. A database system so designed does not involve to problem of data redundancy or inconsistency

DATABASE SYSTEM CONCEPTS ARCHITECTURE

It gives three types of level

1. Internal Schema (Physical level)

The lowest level of abstraction describes how the data are actually stored.

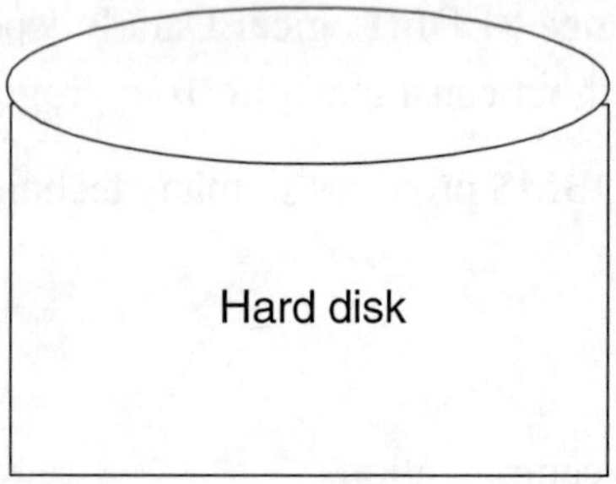

2. Logical Level (Conceptual Schema)

The next higher level of absraction describes data stored. What data are stored in the database and what relationship exists among those data.

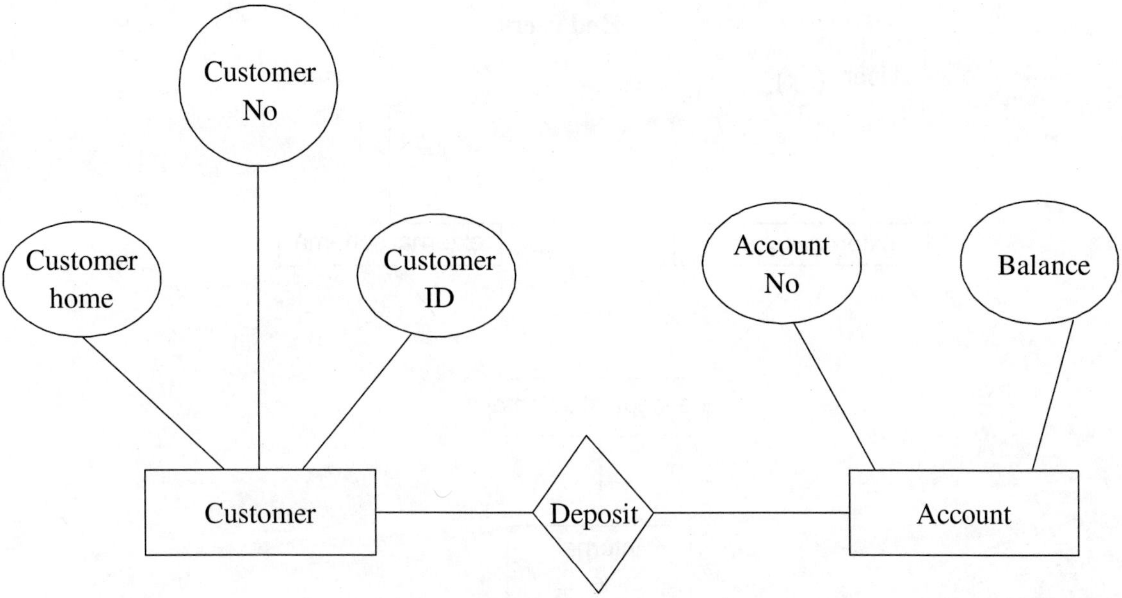

Logical level (Conceptual schema)

3. External Schema (View Level)

1. The highest level of abstraction describes only part of the entire database. Schemas are not change frequently. The overall logical design of the database is called database schema.

2. Schemas are changed infrequently. Data changes over time as information is inserted and deleted. The collection of information stored in the database at a particular moment is called instance of database.

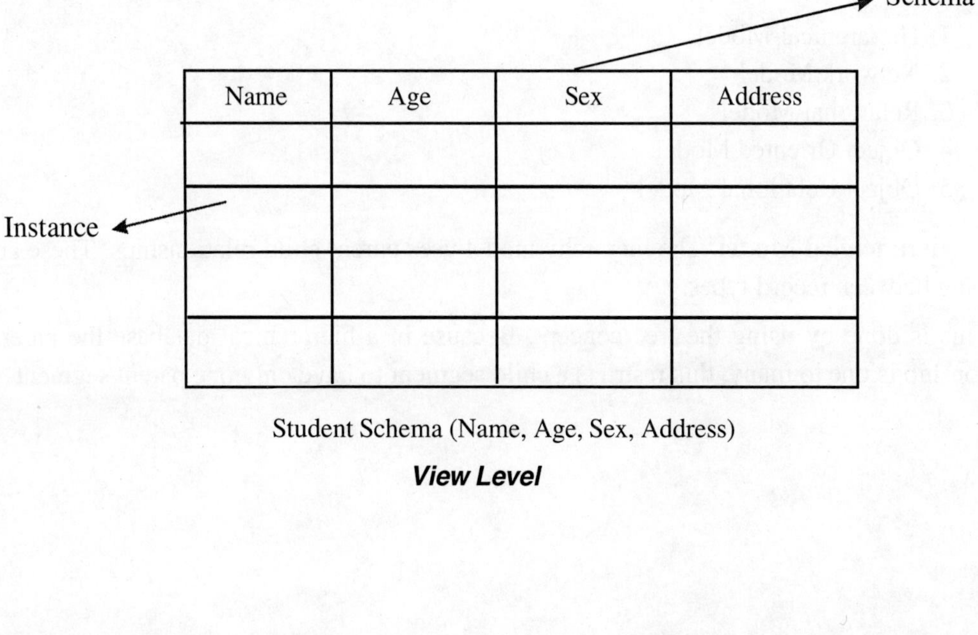

Student Schema (Name, Age, Sex, Address)

View Level

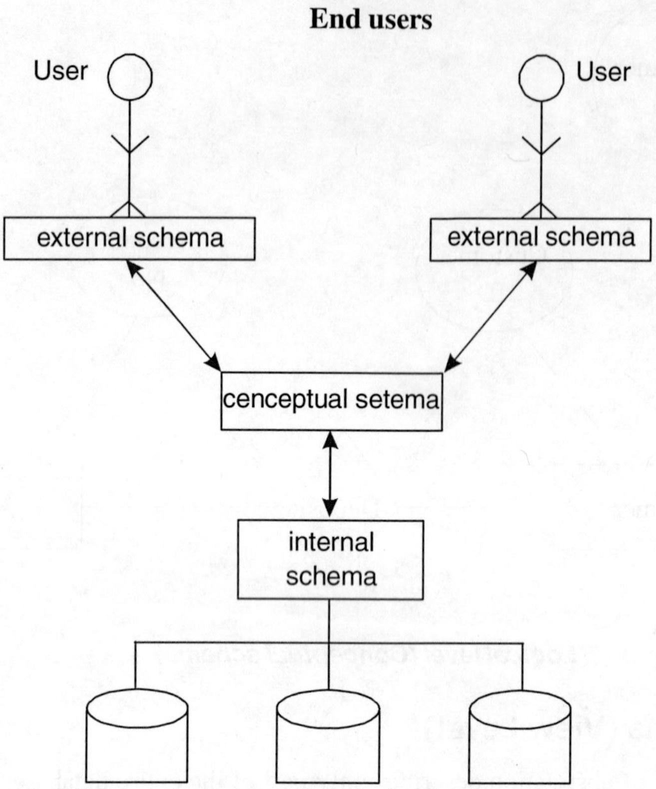

Three level architecture of DBMS

DATA MODELS

A data model is collection of conceptual tools for describing data their relationships, data semantics and consistency constraints :

1. Hierarchical Model
2. Network Model
3. Relational Model
4. Object Oriented Model
5. Object Relational Model

1. **Hieranchical Model.** The hierarchy model uses parent child relationships. These are 1 : N mapping between record types.

This is done by using the tree concept. Because in a hierarchical database the parent child relationship is one to many, this restricts a child segment to have only one parent segment.

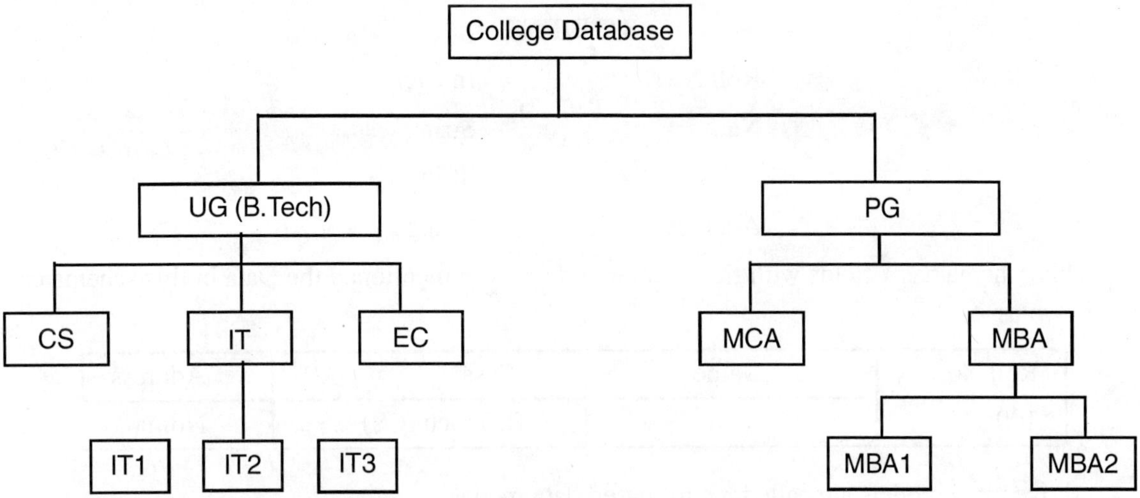

Hierarchical Model Representation

2. Network model : In hierarchical model in can not have more than one parent per child, which may be necessary for some application so, the Network model permitted the modeling of many to many relationships in data.

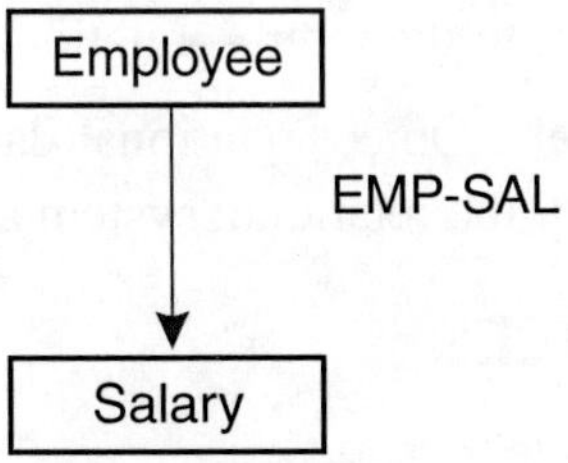

Network Representation

The Network model can be graphically represented as follows :

A labeled rectangle represents that corresponding entity or record type. A arrow represents the set type, which denotes the relationship between the owner record type and member record. The arrow direction in the owner record type to the member record type. In Figure two record types. Employee and salary and the set type EMP-SAL with employee as the owner type salary as the member record type.

3. Relational Model. In relational model the data and the relations among them are represented by a collection of tables. A table is a collection of records and each record in a table contains the same fields.

A description of data in terms of a Data model is called a schema.

Database may be stored in a relation with the following schema.

STUDENT

Roll No.	Integer
Name	String
Class	String
Address	String

This schema has 4 fields with field names and types as mentioned the Data in this schema can be shown as

Roll No	Name	Class	Address
100	Ram	B. Teach (CS)	Noida

Above three models are called record based data model.

4. **Object Oriented Model :** Object DBMS add database functionality to object programming languages. Object DBMS extend the schematics of the C++ and JAVA object programming Languages to provide full features database programming capability. The object programming language gives one to one mapping. This one to one mapping object programming language to database objects has two benefits over other storage approaches. It provides high performance management of objects and it enables better management to the inter —relationships between objects.

5. **Object Relational Model :** Object relational database management systems (ORDBMS) add new object storage capability the relational system at the core of modern information system.

SCHEMA AND INSTANCES

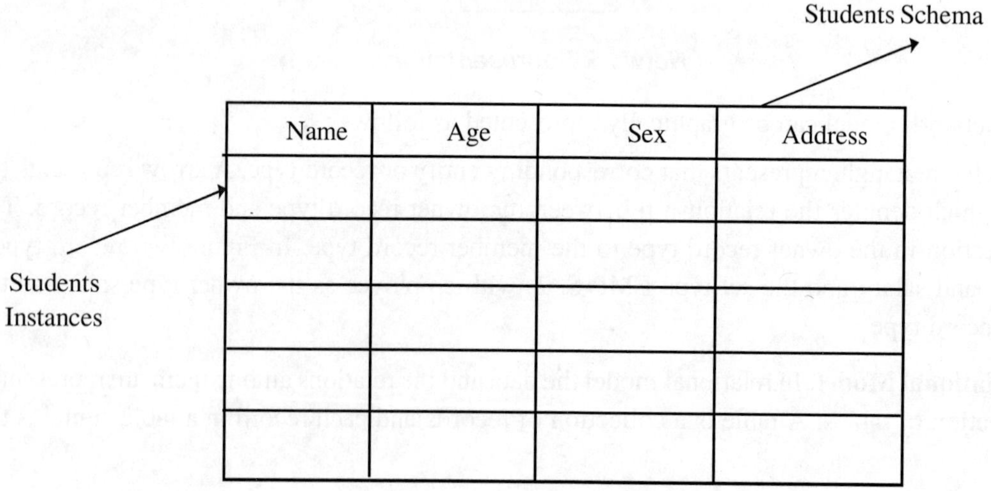

Schemas are not change frequently. The overall logical design of the database is called the **database schema**. Schemas are changed in frequently data changes over time as information is inserted and deleted. The collection of information stored in the database at a particular moment is called **instance of database.**

DATA INDEPENDENCE — ADVANTAGE OF DBMS

DATA LANGUAGE AND INTERFACES

1. DBMS languages

1. DDL (Data Definition Language)
2. SDL (Storage Definition Language)
3. VDL (View Definition Language)
4. DML (Data Manipulation Language)

- High Level or Non Procedural DML (HL or NPDML)
  - is called record at a time DML
- Low Level or Procedural DML (LL or PDML)
  - is called set at a – time or set oriented DMLs.

1. DDL is used by the DBA and by database designers to define both schemas (conceptual and internal)
2. SDL is used to specify the internal schema.
3. VDL to specify user views and their mappings to the Conceptual Schema.
4. In DML manipulations include retrieval, insertion deletion and modification of the data.
5. A HL or NPDML can be used on at own to specify complex database operations.
6. ALL or PDML must be embedded in a general purpose programming language. A query in a high level PML often specifies which data to retrieve rather them how to retrieve it, hence such languages are also called **declarative.**

2. DBMS interfaces

User friendly interfaces for interacting with the database these can also be used by casual users. User friendly interfaces provided by a DBMS may include the following :

1. **Menu-Based interfaces for Browsing.** These interfaces present the user with lists of options called menu that lead the user through the formulation of a request browsing interfaces which allow a used to look through the contents of a database is unstructured manner.

2. **Forms Based interfaces :** A form based interface displays a form to each user.

3. **Graphical user Interfaces (GUI) :** A GUI typically displays a schema to the user in diagrammatic form. Most GUIs use a pointing device.

4. **Natural language Interfaces (NLI) :** A NLI usually has its own schema which is similar to the database conceptual schema.

5. **Interfaces for Parametric users :** Parametric users, such as bank tellers, often have a small set of operations that they must perform repeatedly.

6. Interfaces for DBA : Most database systems contain privileged commands that can be used only be the DBA's staff.

7. **DDL (Data Definition Language)**. A database schema is specified by a set of definitions expressed by a special language called a DDL. The result of compilation of DDL statement is a set of tables *i.e.* stored in a special file called data dictionary or data directory.

Data dictionary means data about data.

DATA MANIPULATION LANGUAGE

DML (Data manipulation language). By data manipulation we mean

1. The retrieval of information stored in the database.
2. The insertion of new information into the database.
3. The deletion of information from the database.
4. The modification of information stored in the database.

A DML is the language that enables users to access for manipulate data as organized by the appropriated data model.

DML is two types :

1. **Procedural DML** requires a user to specify what data are needed and how to get those data, *for example* Relation Algrea.
2. **Non-procedural DML** requires a uses to specify what data are needed and have if not get those data, *for example* Relation Calculus.

OVERALL DATABASE STRUCTURE

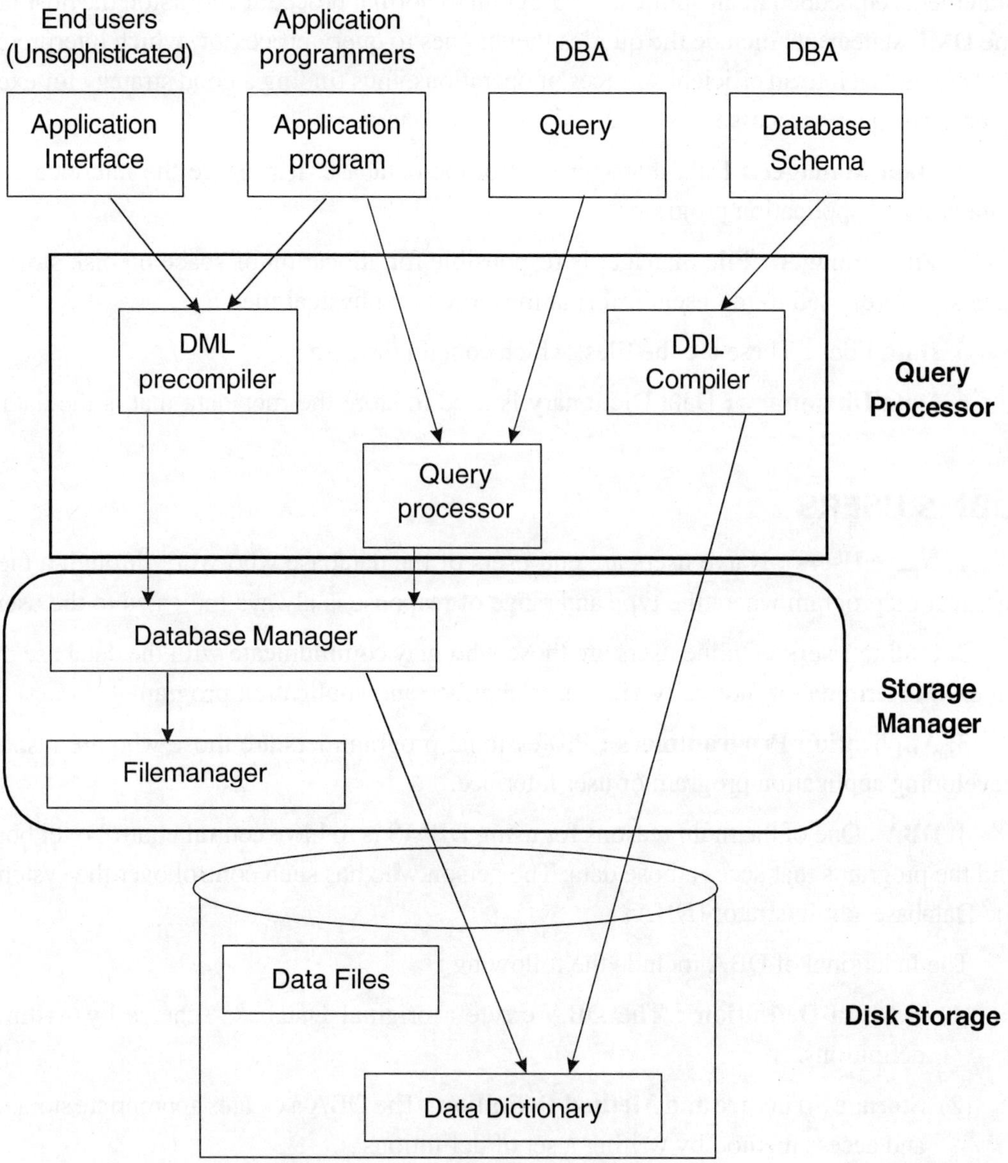

Overall System Architecture

The major components of a DBMS are as follows.

1. **DDL Compiler :** The DDL statements are sent to the DDL compiler, which converts these statements to a set of tables. These tables contain the metadata concerning the database and are in a form that can be used by other compound of the DBMS.

2. **DML Precompiler and Query Processor :** The DML pre-compiler converts the DML statements embedded in an application program to normal procedure collision the host language. If the DML statements include the queries then it goes to query processor, which interprets the query and converts it into an efficient services of operations, thus finding a good strategy for executing the query. The query processor also users the date dictionary.

3. **Data Manager :** Data manager control the database. It provide the interface between the database and application programs.

4. **File Manager :** File manager is responsible for allocation of space on disk storage and the data structures used to represent information stored on physical media.

5. **Data Files :** These are the files, which contain the data.

6. **Data Dictionary :** Data Dictionary is used to store the metadata that is the data about the data.

DBMS USERS

1. **Naive Users :** Naive users are end users of the database who work through a menu driven application program where the type and range of response is always indicated to the user.

2. **Online Users :** Online users are those who may communicate with the database directly via an on-line terminal or indirectly via a user interface and application program.

3. **Application Programmers :** Professional programmers are those who are responsible for developing application program or user interface.

4. **DBA :** One of the main reasons for using DBMS is to have central control over both the data and the programs that access those data. The person who has such control over the system is called the Database administrator (DBA).

The functional of DBA include the following :

(1) **Schema Definition :** The DBA create a original Database schema by writing a set of definitions.

(2) **Storage Structure and Method Definition :** The DBA a creates appropriate storage structure and access method by writing a set of definitions.

(3) **Granting of Authorization for Data Access :** The authorization information is kept in a special system structure.

(4) **Integrity Constraint Specification :** No. of hours an employee may work in one week may not exceed a specified limit. Such a constraint must be specified explicitly by the Database administration (DBA).

Emp. No.	Emp. Name	Attributes	No. of hours

In figure no of hours on employee may work in one week may not exceed a specified limit. Such a constraint must be specified explicitly by the Database administration (DBA).

UNIT — ONE

Chapter 2 Data Modeling Using the Entity Relationship Model

Chapter Outline

- ER model concepts
- Notation for ER diagram
- Mapping constraints
- Key concepts of Super key, Candidate key, Primary key
- Generalization
- Aggregation
- Reduction of an ER diagrams to tables
- Extended model
- Relationships of higher degree

ER (ENTITY RELATIONSHIP MODEL)

1. An **entity** is thing or object in a real world that is distinguishable from all other objects, for example-person, place

2. **Attribute :** An object or entity is characterized by its properties (or attributes)

- **Weak and Strong Entity sets :** A entity set may not have sufficiently attributes to form a primary key such an entity set is termed as weak entity set.
- An entity set that has a primary key is termed as strong entity set.

3. **Entity set.** An entity set is a set of entities of the same type that share the same properties or attributes.

- An entity is represented by a set of attributes.
- Each entity has a value for each of its attributes.
- For each attribute, there is a set of permitted values, called the domain or value set.

Every weak entity set can be converted to a strong entity set by adding appropriate and reverse is not possible.

Simple and Composite Attributes

Simple Attributes are not divided into subparts Composite Attributes, can be divided into subparts. (*i.e.* other attributes).

Customer ID	*Customer Name*	*Customer Street*	*Customer City*
1001	Ram	North	Harrison
1002	Mohan	Main	Woodside
1003	Sohan	North	Harrison

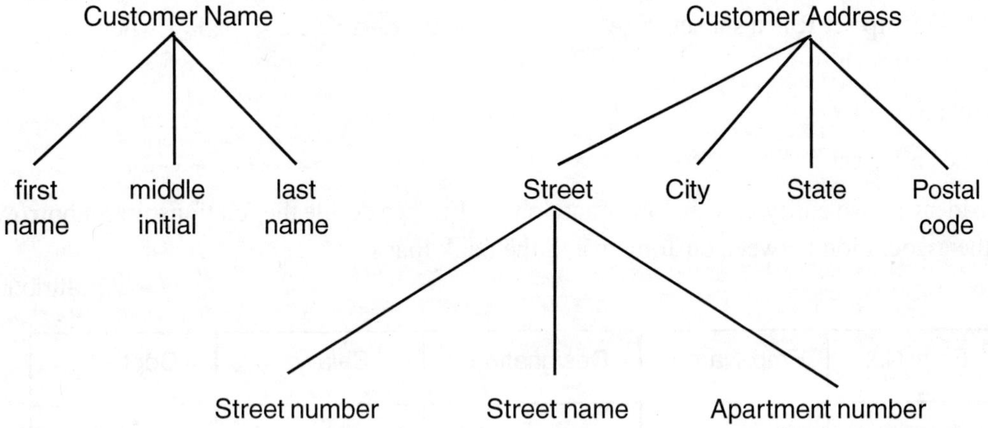

COMPOSITE ATTRIBUTES CUSTOMER NAME AND CUSTOMER ADDRESS

Single Valued and Multi Valued Attributes

The attributes all have a single value for a particular entity loan number attribute for a specific loan entity refers to only one loan number. Such attributes are said to be single valued. An employee entity set with the attribute phone number. An employee may have zero, one, or several phone numbers, and different employees may have different numbers of phones. This type of attribute is said to be multi-valved.

Derived Attribute

The value for this type of attribute can be derived from the values of other related attributes or entities.

Example : Suppose that the customer entity set has an attribute age, which indicates the customer's age. If the customer entity set also has an attribute date of birth, we can calculate age from date of birth and the current date. Thus, age is a derived attribute.

An attribute takes a null value when on entity does not have a value for it.

- A relationship is an association among several entities.

- A relationship set is a set of relationships of the same type Customer Loan

Cust. ID	*Cust. Name*	*Cust. Street*	*Cust. City*
1001	Ram	North	Harrison
1002	Mohan	Main	wood side

Loan no	*Loan value*
L – 5	1000
L-14	2000

Relationship set between Customer and Loan

This relationship specifies that Ram is a customer with loan number L – 15.

In relationship set is a mathematical relation on $n \geq 2$ entity sets. If (E_1, E_2..... E_n) are entity sets, then a relationship set R is a subset of $(e_1, e_2 - e_n) | e_1 \in E_1, e_2 \in E_2, ... e_n \in E_n\}$ where $(e_1,$ -- $e_n)$ zis a relationship.

e is relationship

E is the entity set

Consider the two entity sets customer and loan in Fig. we define the relationship set borrower to denote the association between customers and the bank loans.

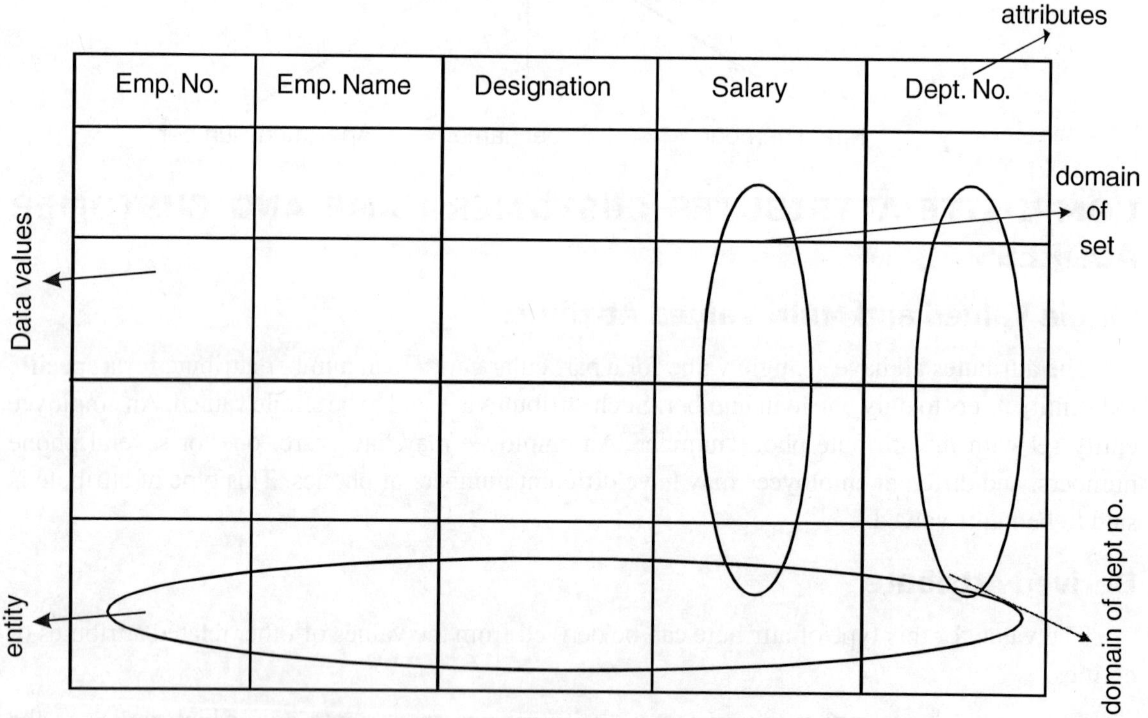

Entity set

For each attribute, there is a set of permitted values, called the domain or value set of that attribute.

- An entity is representation by a set of attributes.
- An entity type is a collection of entities that share a common definition.

NOTATION FOR ER DIAGRAM

	Symbol	Meaning
Rectangles	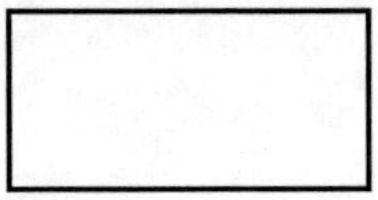	which represent entity sets
Double rectangles	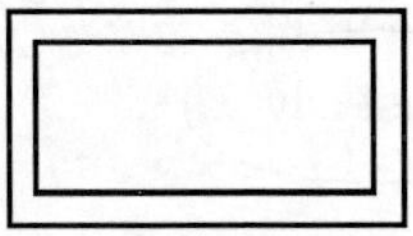	which represent weak entity sets
Diamonds which	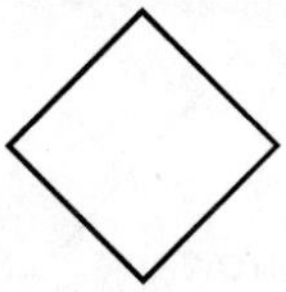	represent Relationship sets
Ellipses	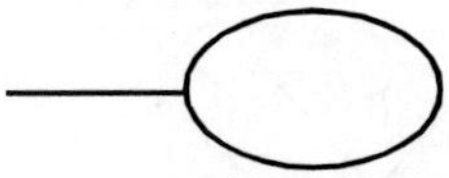	which represent attributes
Lines		which link attributes to entity sets and entity sets to relationship sets.
Ellipses with Line	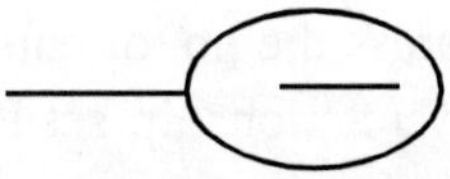	which represenet key attribute
Double Ellipses	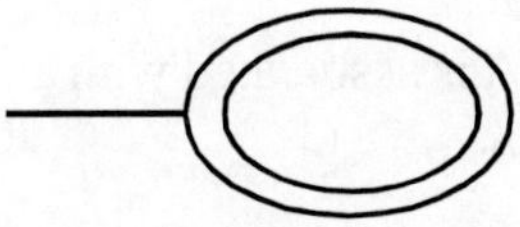	which represent multivalued attributes
Dashed ellipses double lines	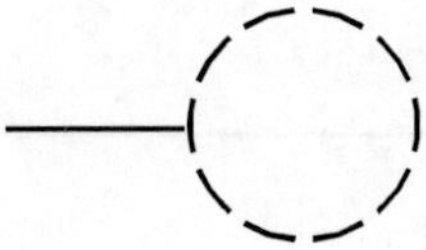	which denote derived attributes
		which indicate total participation of an entity in a relationship set.

For example

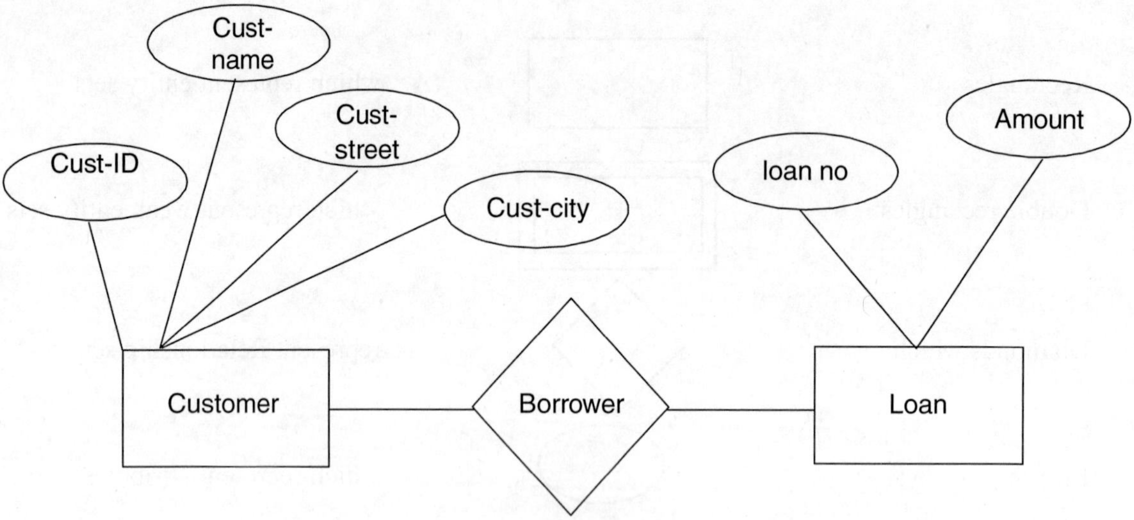

E-R diagram correspondisng to customers and loans

MAPPING CONSTRAINTS

Mapping cardinalities or constraints express the no. of entities to which another entity can be associated via a relationship set for a binary relationship set R between entity set A and B. The mapping cardinality must be one of the following :

1. One to One mapping : An entity in A is associated with almost one entity in B. And an entity in B is associated with almost an entity in A.

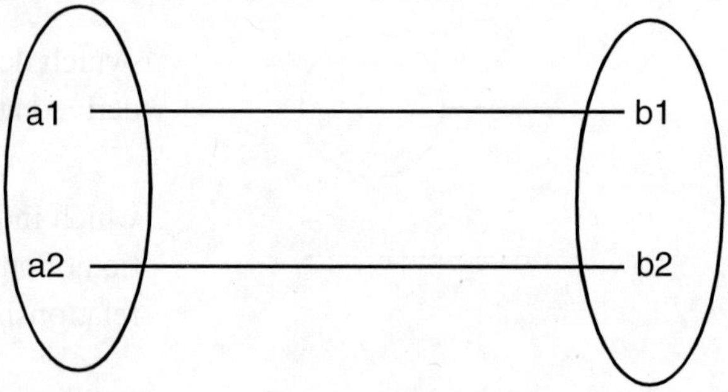

One to One

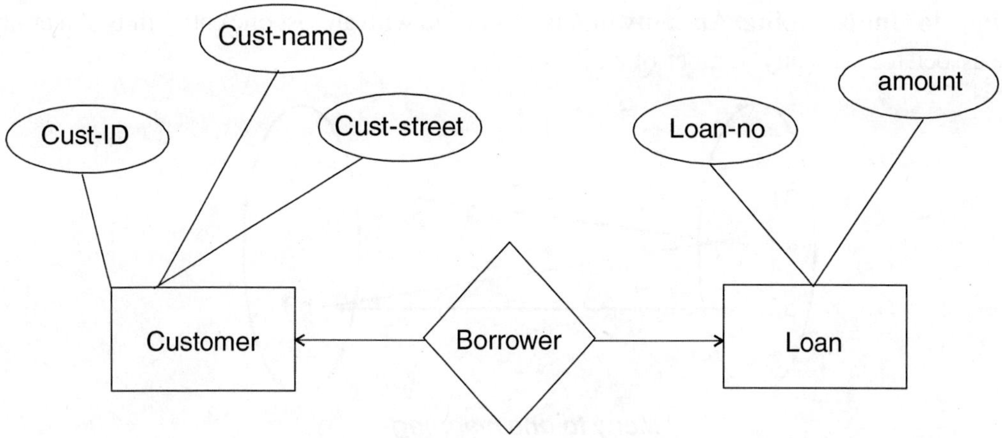

One to One mapping

2. One to Many Mapping. An entity in A is associated with any no of entities in B. An entity in B can be associated with almost one entity in A.

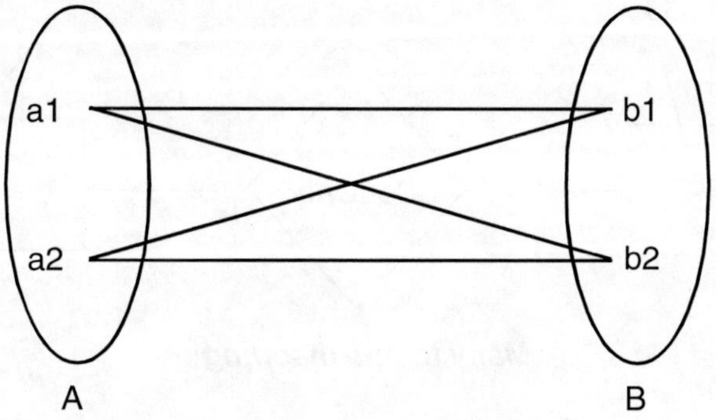

One to many mapping

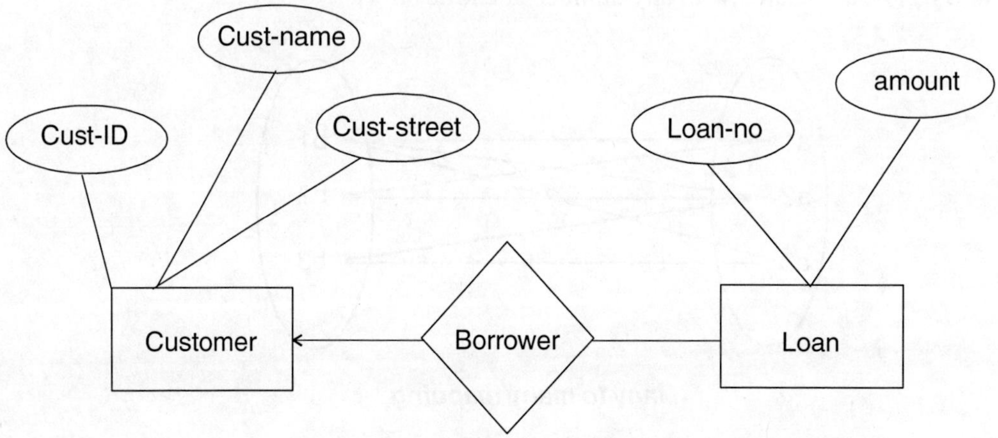

One to many mapping

3. Many to One Mapping. An entity in A is associated with almost one entity in B. An entity in B can be associated with any number of entities in A .

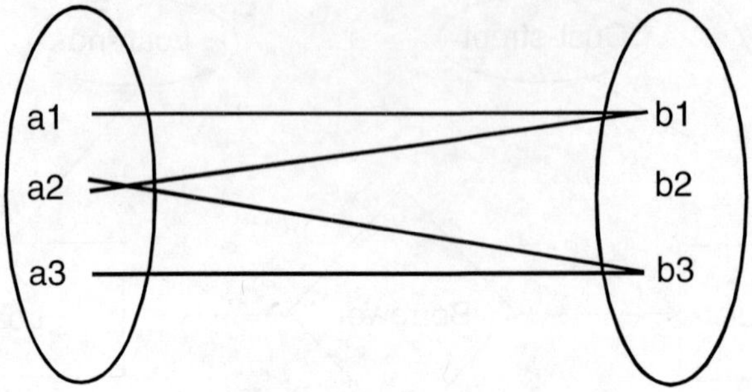

Many to one mapping

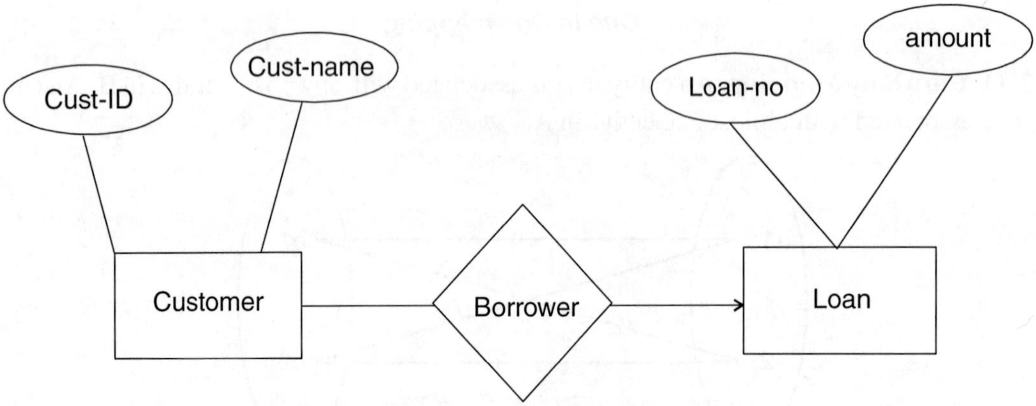

Many to one mapping

4. Many to Many Mapping. An entity in A is associated with any number of entities in B and an entity in B can be associated with any number of entities in A.

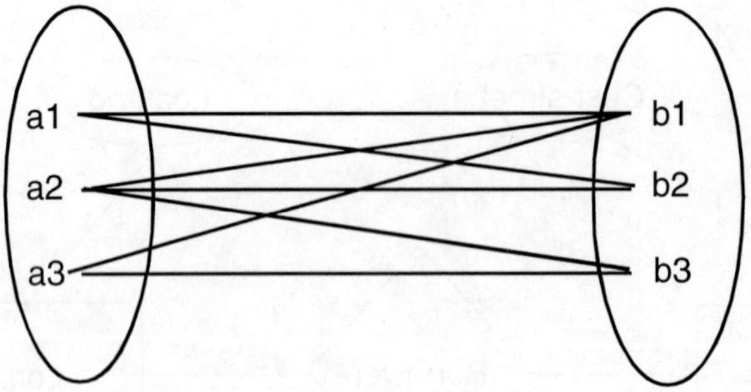

Many to many mapping

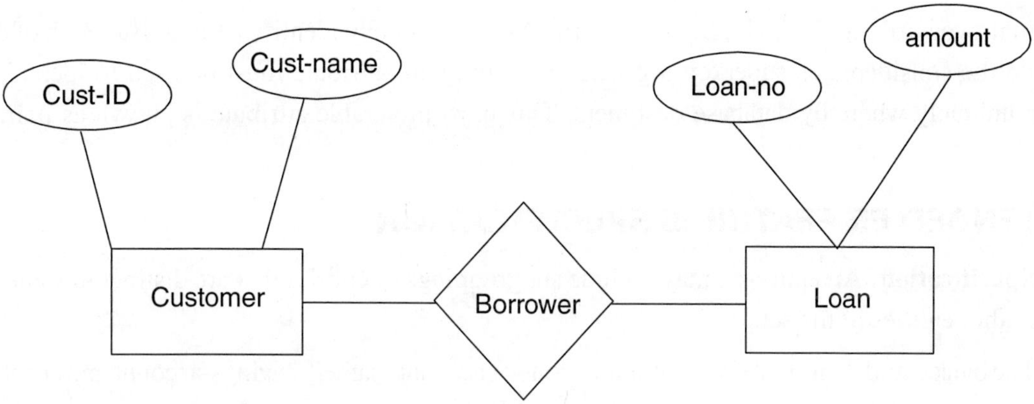

Many to many mapping

Notes : Arrow only add both side in one to one mapping, only right side in many to one mapping, only left side in one to many mapping.

KEY CONCPETS OF SUPERKEY, CANDIDATE KEY, PRIMARY KEY

Keys: It is important to able to specify how entities within a given entity set and relation ships within given relationship set are distinguished.

Superkey : A superkey is a set of one or more attributes that taken collectively allow us to identify uniquely an entity in the entity set.

For example the customer-id, attribute of the entity set customer is sufficient to distinguish one customer entity from another. Thus costumer-id is a superkey. The combination of customer-name and customer-id is a superkey for the entity set customer. The customer name attribute of customer is not a superkey because several people might have the same name. If K is a superkey then so is any superkey of K. we are often interested in superkeys for which no proper subset is a superkey. Such minimal superkeys are called **candidate key.**

Primary key : Primary key to denote a candidate key that is chosen by the database designer as the principal means of identifying entities within an entity set.

For example :

Student entity set

Roll No.	Social security No.	Father's name

In it two attributes Roll No, Social Security No can uniquely identify a thing. But Both of them can not be considered as superkey together. Thus only are attribute must be used to identify the thing uniquely where by database designers. This most preferable attribute is known as **primary key.**

EXTENDED ER FEATURES SPECIFICATION

Specification: An entity set may include subgroupings of entities that are distinct in some way from other entities in the set.

The bank could then create two specializations of account, namely savings-account and checking-accounts.

Savings account entities are described by the attribute "interest rate" where as checking account entities are described by the attributes "Overdraft amount". The process of designating subgroups within an entity set is called specializations.

The specification of account allows us we distinguish among accounts based on the type of account. The bank may offer the following three types of checking accounts.

1. A standard checking account.
2. A gold checking account
3. A senior checking account.

The specification of checking account by account type yield the following entity set.

1. Standards with attribute number checks..
2. Gold, with attributes min-balance and interest payment.
3. Senior with attribute date of birth specification is the **Top down** process.

Specification : Top down process
Generalization : Bottom up process

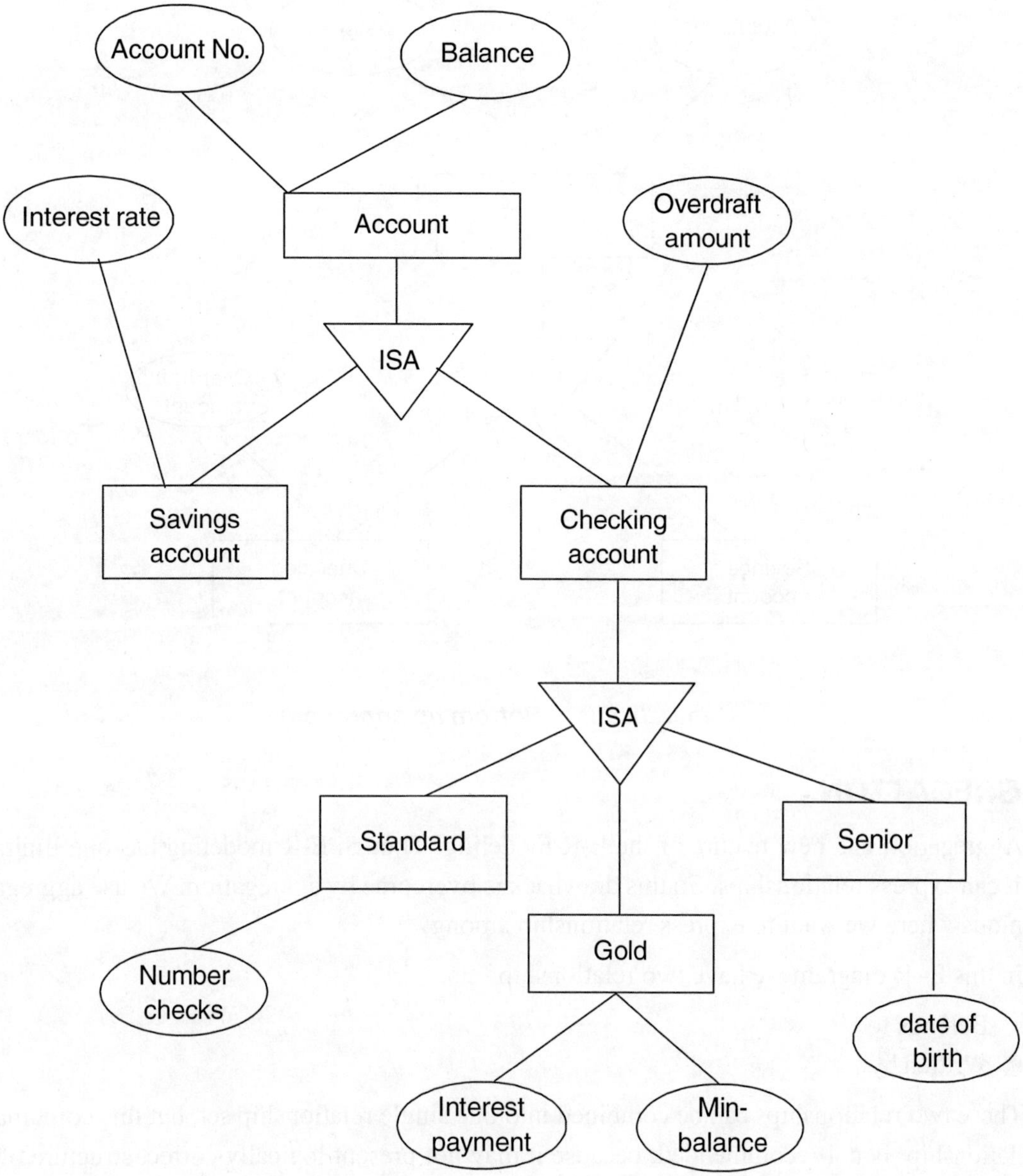

Top down approach (Specification)

Generalization : The design process may also proceed in a bottom-up manner in which multiple entity sets are synthesized into a higher level entity set on the basis of common features. The database designes may have first identified a checking account entity set units attributes overdraft amount balance-no. Acs and a savings account quantity set with the attribute interest rate account-no., balance.

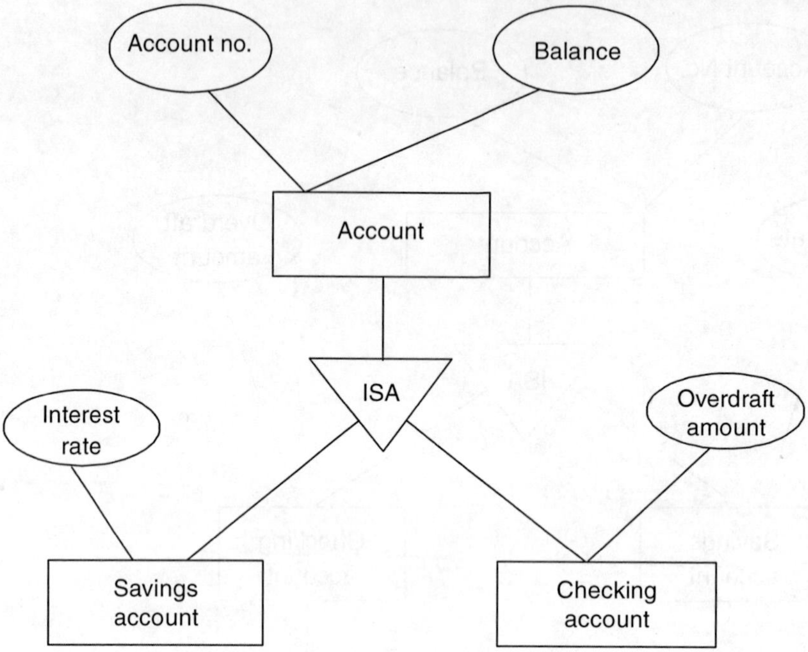

Generalization (Bottom up approach)

AGGREGATION

Aggregation is a new feature of the E-R modeling. Though E-R modeling has one limitation that it can express relationships. So this drawback is overcome by aggregation. We use aggregation technique where we want to express relationship among.

In this E- R diagram we have two relationship sets.

- Belongs to
- Written by.

These two relationships can be combined into one single relationship set, but this combination of relationship is not recommended, because it may not present logically correct structure of this schame. To present the logically correct structure of this scheme, we will use the aggregation technique.

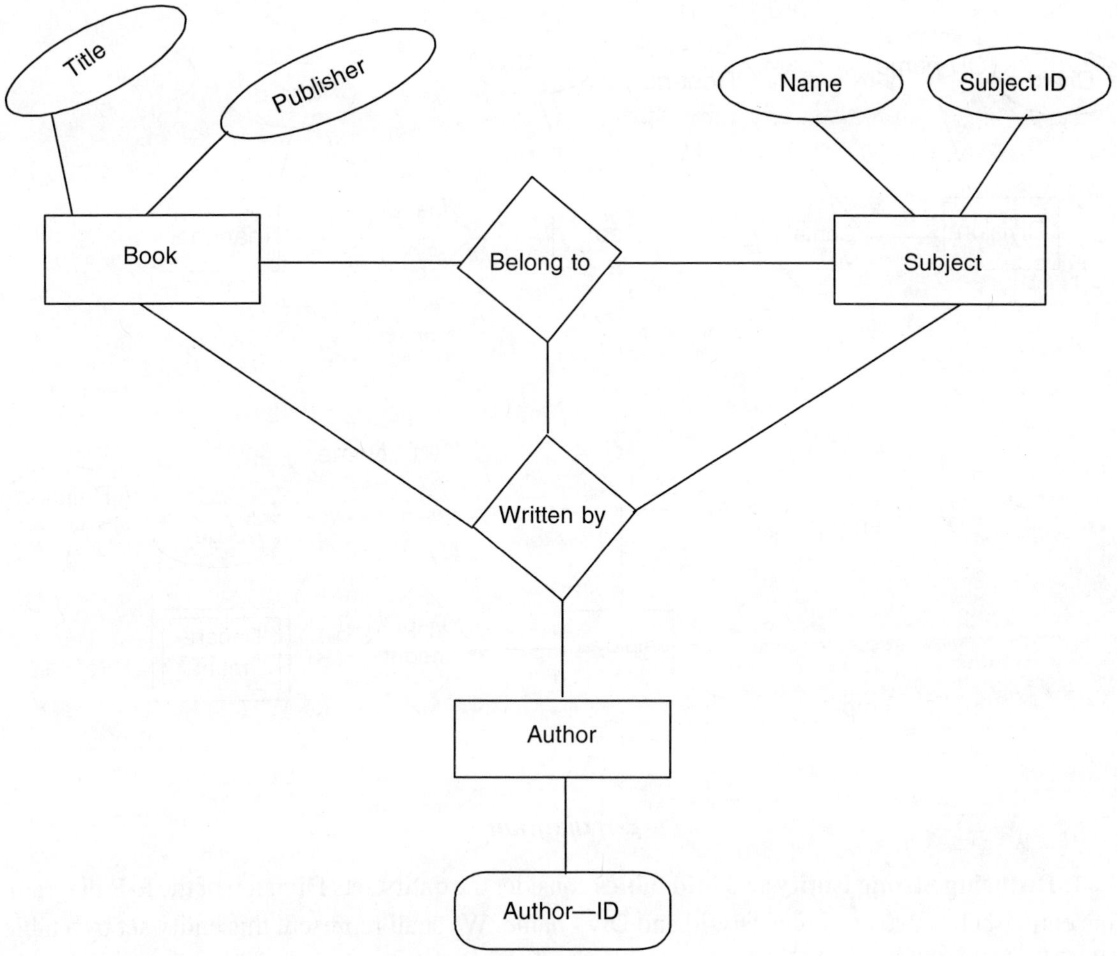

Aggregation

REDUCTION OF AN E-R DIAGRAMS TO TABLES

We convert ER diagram to tables : We can devide this ER diagram into three rections :

1. Strong Entity sets (Division, Dept. Manger, Employees)
2. Weak entity sets (Dependents)
3. Relationship sets (contains, managed – by, have, dependents – of)

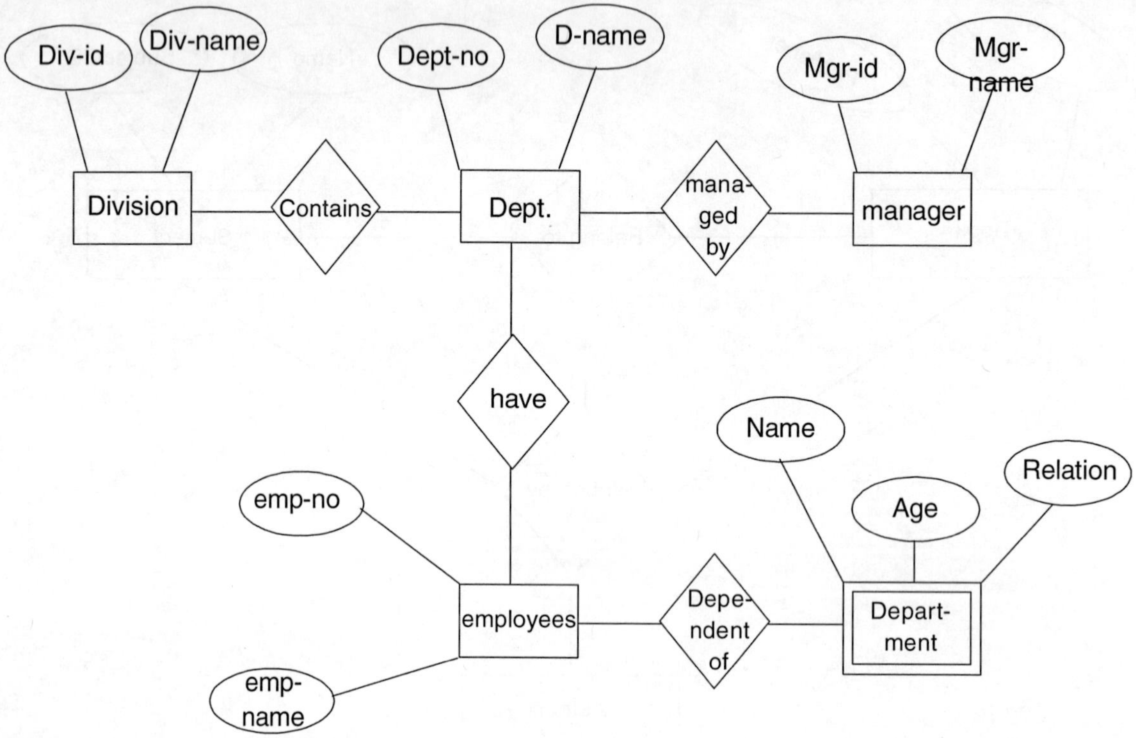

E-R diagram

1. **Reducing Strong Entity sets into tables** consider the qntity sets Division of the E-R diagram. This entity set has two attributes Div-id and Div - name. We shall represent this entity set by a table called division with two columns,

Division id	Division name
D1	Marketing Division

Division Relation

Similarly entity set 'Dept' has two id Dept - no and D- name, which will be represented by table Dept.

Dept no	D-name
DEPT 01	New Business Department
DEPT 02	Education Department

Department Relation

entity set manager also has two id, Mgr id and Mgr - name which will be replacement (by table manager)

Mgr Id	Mgr Name
MG 01	Ram
MG 02	Sohan

Manager Relation

Entity set Employee has to ID, Emp. no and Emp. name which will be represented by table employee.

Emp. No.	Emp. Name
1001	Ram
1002	Ashok
1003	Rahu
1004	Rahul

Employe Relation

2. Reducing weak entity sets into tables

In the ER diagram we have only one weak entity set depandent. This entity set has three attributes Name, Age and Relationship. The dependent is dependent on the primary key EMP – No. of entity type employee. Thus Dependent is represented by a table with your columns EMP-NO, 1 Name, Age and Relationship as shown in below fig.

EMP-No	Name	Age	Relationship
1001	Ram	10	Son
1001	Mohan	12	Son
1002	Sita	8	Daughter
1006	Ravi	11	Daughter

Dependent Relation

3. Producing Relationship sets in Tables

In E-R diagram, we have four relationship sets contains, Managed-by, Have, Dependents of

1. **Contains :** relationship set involves two entity sets dividison with primary key Div-id and Dept with primary key Dept. no 1

Div-id	Dept-no
D1	DEPT 01
D2	DEPT 02

Contains Relation

2. **Managed By:** relationship set involves two entity sets kept with primary key dept no. and manager units primary key Mgr-id

Dept no	Mgr-id
DEPT 01	Ram
PEPT 02	Mohan

Managed by Relation

3. **Have:** relationship set involves two entity sets Dept with primary key Dept and Employee with primary key Emp-no.

Dept-no	Emp-no
DEPT 01	1001
DEPT 01	1002
DET 02	1003
DL-T 02	1004

Have Relation

Lastly we shall deal with the case of relationship set dependents of, linking a weak entity set (Dependent) to its corresponding strong entity set (Employee).

EXTENDED ER MODEL (EER MODEL)

The EER models include all the modeling concepts of the ER model and the concepts of subclass, super class, specialization, and generalization.

RELATIONSHIPS OF HIGHER DEGREE

We have defined the degree of relationship type as the number of participating entity types. If there are two entity types participating in a relation then it is called a relationship type of degree two (binary), and a relationship types in called degree three (ternary) if there are three entity types participating. If there is a relationship that involves N entities is called N-ary relationship.

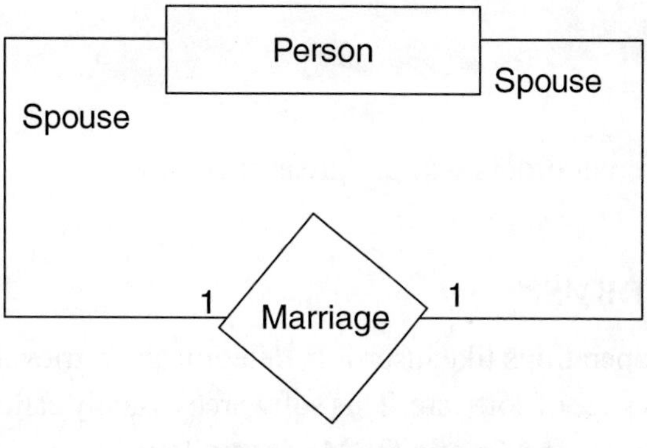

Binary relationship

In this figure a marriage for example is a relation between a man and woman that is modeled by a relationship set marriage between two instances of entities derived from the entity set person.

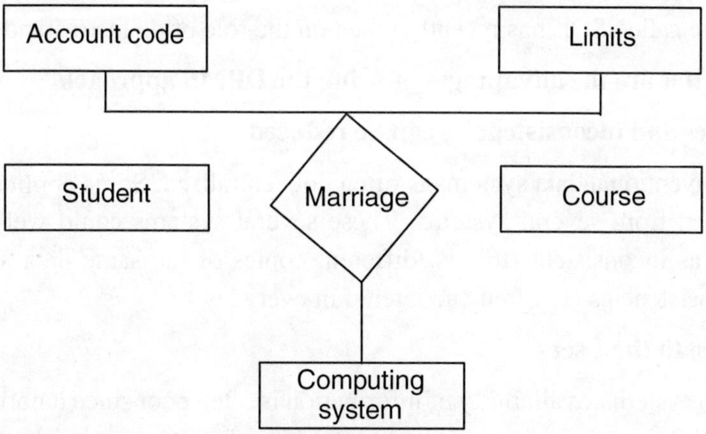

Ternary relationship

Ternary relationship involving three entities sets — Computing represents the relationship involving a student using a particular computing system to do the computations for a given course.

Example 1. What is a database?

A database is a well organized collection of data that are related in a meaningful way which can be accessed in different logical orders but are stored only once. The data in the database is therefore integrated, structured and shared.

Example 2. What are the main features of database?

The main features of data in a database are :

- It is well organized
- It is related
- It is accessable in different orders without great difficulty
- It is stored only once

Example 3. What is a DBMS?

To be able to carry out operations like insertion, deletion and retrieval, the database needs to be managed by a substantial package of software. This software is usually called a Database Management System (DBMS). The primary purpose of a DBMS is to allow a user to store, update and retrieve data in abstract terms and thus make it easy to maintain and retrieve information from a database. A DBMS relieves the user from having to know about exact physical representations of data and having to specify detailed algorithms for storing, updating and retrieving data. To provide the various facilities to different types of users, a DBMS normally provides one or more specialized programming languages often called Database Languages. Different DBMS provide different database languages although a language called SQL has recently taken on the role of de facto standard.

Example 4. What are the advantages of using the DBMS approach?

- **Redundancies and inconsistencies can be reduced**

The data in conventional data systems is often not centralised. Some applications may require data to be combined from several systems. These several systems could well have data that is redundant as well as inconsistent (that is, different copies of the same data may have different values). Date inconsistencies are often encoutered in everyday life.

- **Better service to the Users**

In conventional systems, availability of information is often poor since it normally is difficult to obtain information that the existing systems were not designed for. Once several conventional systems are combined to form one centralised data base, the availability of information and its up-to-dateness is likely to improve since the data can now be shared and the DBMS makes it easy to respond to unforeseen information requests.

Centralizing the data in a database also often means that user can obtain new and combined information that would have been impossible to obtain otherwise. Also, use of a DBMS should allow users that do not know programming to interact with the data more easily.

The ability to quickly obtain new and combined information is becoming increasingly important in an environment where various levels of governments are requiring organisations to provide more and more information about their activities. An organisation running a conventional data processing system would require new programs to be written (or the information compiled manually) to meet every new demand.

- **Flexibility of the system is improved**

Changes are often necessary to the contents of data stored in any system. These changes are more easily made in a database than in a conventional system in that these changes do not need to have any impact on application programs.

- **Cost of developing and maintaining systems is lower**

Although the initial cost of setting up of a database can be large, one normally expects the overall cost of setting up a database and developing and maintaining application programs to be lower than for similar service using conventional systems since the productivity of programmers can be substantially higher in using non-procedural languages that have been developed with modern DBMS than using procedural languages.

- **Standards can be enforced**

Since all access to the database must be through the DBMS, standards are easier to enforce. Standards may relate to the naming of the data, the format of the data, the structure of the data etc.

- **Security can be improved**

Setting up of a database makes it easier to enforce security restrictions since the data is now centralized. It is easier to control who has access to what parts of the database. However, setting up a database can also make it easier for a determined person to breach security.

- **Integrity can be improved**

Integrity may be compromised in many ways. For example, someone may make a mistake in data input and the salary of a full-time employee may be input as $4,000 rather than $40,000. A student may be shown to have borrowed books but has no enrolment. Salary of a staff member in one department may be coming out of the budget of another department.

Controls therefore must be introduced to prevent such errors to occur. However, since all data is stored only once, it is often easier to maintain integrity than in conventional systems.

- **Enterprise requirements can be identified**

All enterprises have sections and departments and each of these units often consider the work of their unit as the most important and therefore consider their needs as the most important. Once a database has been set up with centralised control, it will be necessary to identify enterprise requirements and to balance the needs of competing units. It may become necessary to ignore some requests for information if they conflict with higher priority needs of the enterprise.

- **Data model must be developed**

Perhaps the most important advantage of setting up a database system is the requirement that an overall data model for the enterprise be built. In conventional systems, it is more likely that files will be designed as needs of particular applications demand. The overall view is often not considered. Building an overall view of the enterprise data, although often an expensive exercise, is usually very cost–effective in the long term.

Example 5. What are the disadvantages of using the DBMS approach?

A database system generally provides on-line access to the database for many user. In contrast, a conventional system is often designed to meet a specific need and therefore generally provides access to only a small number of user. Because of the larger number of users accessing the data when a database is used, the enterprise may involve additional risks as compared to a conventional data processing system in the following areas :

- **Confidentiality, Privacy and Security**

When information is centralised and is made available to users from remote locations, the possibilities of abuse are often more than in a conventional data processing system. To reduce the chances of unauthorised users accessing sensitive information, it is necessary to take technical, administrative and, possible, legal measures.

Most databases store valuable information that must be protected against deliberate trespass and destruction.

- **Data Quality**

Since the database is accessible to user remotely, adequate controls are needed to control users updating data and to control data quality. With increased number of user accessing data directly, there are enormous opportunities for user to damage the data. Unless there are suitable controls, the data quality may be compromised.

- **Data Integrity**

Since a large number of users could be using a database concurrently, technical safeguards are necessary to ensure that the data remain correct during operation. The main threat to data integrity comes from several different users attempting to update the same data at the same time. The database therefore needs to be protected against inadvertent changes by the users.

- **Enterprise Vulnerability**

Centralising all data of an enterprise in one database may mean that the database becomes an indispensable resource. The survival of the enterprise may depend on reliable information being available from its database. The enterprise therefore becomes vulnerable to the destruction of the database or to unauthorised modification of the database.

- **The Cost of using a DBMS**

Conventional data processing systems are typically designed to run a number of well-defined, preplanned processes, Such systems are often "tuned" to run efficiently for the processes that they were designed for. Although the conventional systems are usually fairly inflexible in that new applications may be difficult to implement and or expensive to run, they are usually very efficient for the applications they are designed for.

The database approach on the other hand provides a flexible alternative where new applications can be developed relatively inexpensively. The flexible approach is not without its costs and one of these costs is the additional cost of running applications that the conventional system was designed for. Using standardised software is almost always less machine efficient than specialised software.

Example 6. What are the main components of a DBMS?

A database management system is a complex piece of software that usually consists of a number of modules. The DBMS may be considered as an agent that allows communication between the various types of users with the physical database and the operating system without the users being aware of every detail of how it is done. To enable the DBMS to fulfil its tasks, the database management system must maintain information about the data itself that is stored in the system. This information would normally include what data is stored, how it is stored, who has access to what parts of it and so on.

A database management system is often used by two different type of users. Firstly, there are users who pose ad hoc queries and updates, which are usually executed only once. Then there are users that use canned programs that are installed on the system by application programmers. These programs language are often used repeatedly. The database system must provide query language and an embedded host language to meet the needs of these two types of users.

In addition, a DBMS provides facilities for

1. describing the database, when a database is being set up
2. authorization specification and checking
3. access path selection
4. logging and recovery
5. and many more.

Example 7. Would a DBMS designed for use on a PC by a single user also have the same components?

Such systems generally do not need facilities like concurrency control and logging and recover. Such systems therefore can be significantly smaller than multi-user database systems.

Example 8. What are the responsibilities of a DBA?

Usually a person (or a group of persons) centrally located, with an overall view of the database, is needed to keep the database running smoothly. Such a person is called the Database Administrator (DBA)

The DBA would normally have a large number of tasks related to maintaining and managing the database. These tasks would include the following :

• **Deciding and Loading the Database Contents —** The DBA in consultation with senior management is normally responsible for defining the conceptual schema of the database. The DBA would also be responsible for making changes to the conceptual schema of the database if and when necessary.

• **Assisting and Approving Applications and Access —** The DBA would normally provide assistance to end-users interested in writing application programs to access the database. The DBA would also approve or disapprove access to the various parts of the database by different users.

• **Backup and Recover —** Since the database is such a valuable asset, the DBA must make all the efforts possible to ensure that the asset is not damaged or lost. This normally requires a DBA to ensure that regular backups of a database are carried out and in case of failure (or some other disaster like fire or flood), suitable recovery procedures are used to bring the database up with as little down time as possible.

Deciding Data Structures — Once the database contents have been decided, the DBA would normally make decisions regarding how data is to be stored and what indexws need to be maintained. In addition, a DBA normally monitors the performance of the DBMS and makes changes to data structures if the performance justifies them. In some cases, radical changes to the data structures may be called for.

• **Monitor Actual Usage —** The DBA monitors actual usage to ensure that policies laid down regarding use of the database are being followed. The usage information is also used for performance tuning.

Example 9. What is Database Analysis Life Cycle and explain clearly.

Data analysis is concerned with the NATURE and USE of data. It involves the identification of the data elements which are needed to support the data processing system of the organization, the placing of these elements into logical groups and the definition of the relationships between the resulting groups.

Other approaches, *e.g.* D.F.Ds and Flowcharts, have been concerned with the flow of data–dataflow methodologies. Data analysis is one of several data structure based methodologies Jackson SP/D is another.

Systems analysts often, in practice, go directly from fact finding to implementation dependent data analysis. Their assumptions about the usage of properties of and relationships between data elements are embodied directly in record and file designs and computer procedure specifications. The introduction of Database Management Systems (DBMS) has encouraged a higher or analysis, where the data elements are defined by a logical model or 'schema' (conceptual schema). When discussing the schema in the contact of a DBMS, the effects of alternative designs on the efficiency or ease of implementation is considered, *i.e.* the analysis is still somewhat implementation dependent. If we consider the data relationships, usages and properties that are important to the business without regard to their representation in a particular computerised system using particular software, we have what we are concerned with, implementationin dependent data analysis.

It is fair to ask why data analysis should be done if it is possible, in practice to go straight to a computerised system design. Data analysis is time consuming; it throws up a lot of question. Implementation may be slowed down while the answers are sought. It is more expedient to have an experienced analyst 'get on with the job' and come up with a design straight away. The main difference is that data analysis is more likely to result in a design which meets both present and future requirements, being more easily adapted to changes in the business or in the computing equipment. It can also be argued that it tends to ensure that policy questions concerning the organisations data are answered by the managers of the organisation, not by the systems analysts. Data analysis may be thought of as the 'slow and careful' approach, whereas omitting this step is 'quick and dirty'.

From another viewpoint, data analysis provides useful insights for general design principals which will benefit the trainee analyst even if he finally settles for a 'quick and dirty' solution.

The development of techniques of data analysis have helped to understand the structure and meaning of data in organisations. Data analysis techniques can be used as the first step of extrapolating the complexities of the real world into a model that can be held on a computer and be accessed by many users. The data can be gathered by conventional methods such a interviewing people in the organisation and studying documents. The facts can be represented as objects of interest. There are a number of documentation tools available for data analysis, such as entityrelationship diagrams. These are useful aids to communication, help to ensure that the work is carried out in a thorough manner, and ease the mapping processes that follow data analysis. Some of the documents can be used as source documents for the data dictionary.

In data analysis we analysis we analyse the data and build a systems representation in the form of a data model (conceptual). A conceptual data model specifies, the structure of the data and the processes which use that data.

Data Analysis = establishing the nature of data.

Functional Analysis = establishing the use of data.

However, since Data and Functional Analysis are so intermixed, we shall use the term Data Analysis to cover both.

Building a model of an organisation is not easy. The whole organisation is too large as there will be too many things to be modelled. It takes too long and does not achieve anything concrete like an information system, and managers want tangible results fairly quickly. It is therefore the task of the data analyst to model a particular view of the organisation, one which proves reasonable and accurate for most applications and uses. Data has an intrinsic structure of its own, independent of processing, reports formats etc. The data model seeks to make explicit that structure.

Data analysis was described as establishing the nature and use of data.

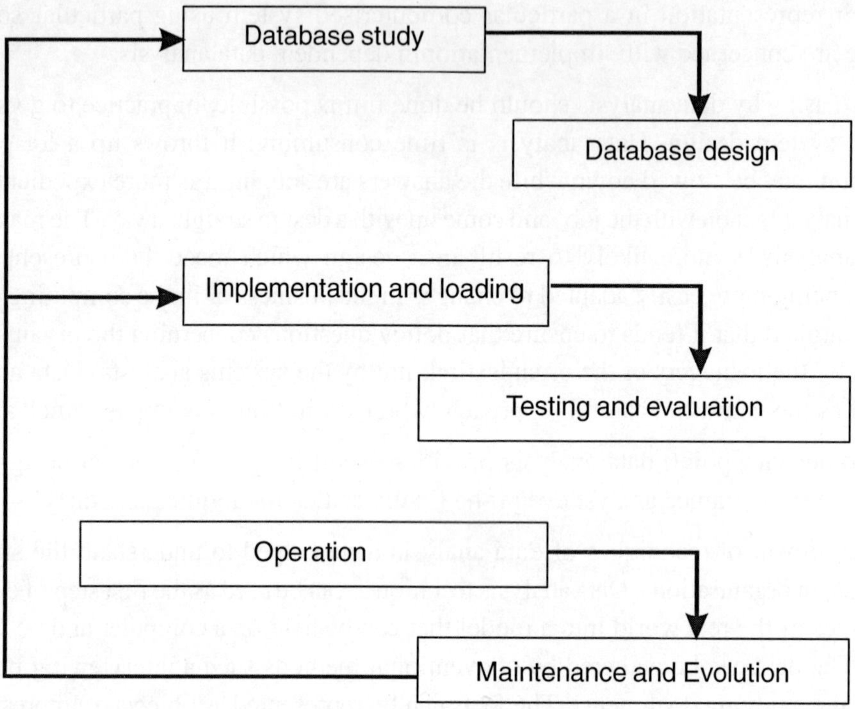

Database Analysis Life Cycle

When a database designer is approaching the problem of constructing a database system, the logical steps followed is that of the database analysis life-cycle :

- **Database study —** Here the designer creates a written specification in words for the database system to be built. This involves :
  - analysing the company situation — is it an expanding company, dynamic in its requirements, mature in nature, solid background in employee training for new internal products, etc. These have an impact on how the specification is to be viewed.
  - define problems and constraints — What is the situation currently? How does the company deal with the task which the new database is to perform. Any issues around the current method? What are the limits of the new system?
  - define objectives — What is the new database system going to have to do, and in what way must it be done. What information does the company want to store specifically, and what does it want to calculate. How will the data evolve.
  - define scope and boundaries — What is stored on this new database system, and what it

stored elsewhere. Will it interface, to another database?

- **Database Design —** Conceptual, logical, and physical design steps in taking specifications to physical implementable designs. This is looked at more closely in a moment.

- **Implementation and loading —** It is quite possible that the database is to run on a machine which as yet does not have a database management system running on it at the moment. If this is the case one must be installed on that machine. Once a DBMS has been installed, the database itself must be created within the DBMS. Finally, not all database itself must loaded with the initial data set (such as the current inventory, current staff names, current customer details, etc.).

- **Testing and evaluation —** The database, once implemented, must be tested against the specificating supplied by the client. It is also useful to test the database with the client using mock data, as clients do not always have a full understanding of what they have actually asked for! In addition, this step in the life cycle offers the chance to the designer to fune-tune the system for best performance. Finally, it is a good idea to evaluate the database in-situ, along with any linked application.

- **Operation —** This step is where the system is actually in real usage by the company.

- **Maintenance and evolution —** Designers rarely get everything perfect first time, and it may be the case that the company requests changes to fix problems with the system or to recommend enhancements or new requirements.

- Commonly development takes place without change to the database structure. In elderly systems the DB structure becomes fossilized.

Example 10. What is Three-Level Database Model and explain clearly.

Often referred to as the three-level model, this is where the design moves from a written specification taken from the real-world requirements to a physically-implementable design for a specific DBMS. The three levels commonly referred to are 'Conceptual Design', 'Data Model Mapping', and 'Physical Design'.

The specification is usually in the form of written document containing customer requirements, mock reports, screen drawings and the like, written by the client to indicate the requirements which the final system is to have. Often such data has to be collected together from a variety of internal sources to the company and then analysed to see if the requirements are necessary, correct and efficient.

Once the Database requirements have been collated, the conceptual Design phase takes the requirements and produces a high–level data model of the database structure. In this module, we use ER modelling to represent high-level data models, but there are other techniques. This model is independent of the final DBMS which the database will be installed in.

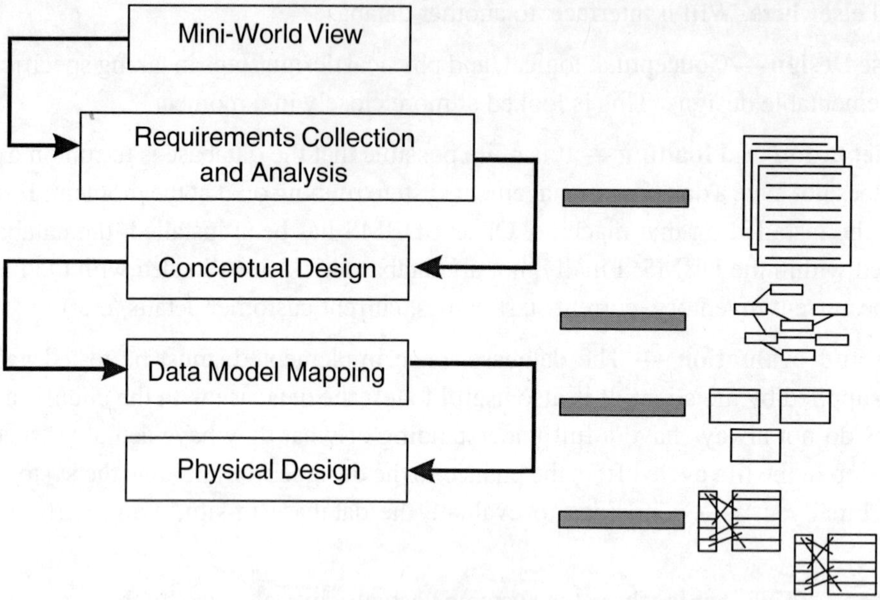

Logic behind the three level architecture

Next, the Conceptual Design phase takes the high-level date model it taken and converted into a converted into a conceptual schema, which is specific to a particular DBMS class (*e.g.* relational). For a relational system, such as Oracle, an appropriate conceptual schema would be relations.

Finally in the Physical Design phase the conceptual schema is converted into database internal structures. This is specific to a particular DBMS product.

Example 11. Write Short Note following :

- Basics
- Entities
- Attributes
- Keys
- Relationships
- Degree of a Relationship
- Replacing ternary relationships
- Cardinality
- Optionality
- Entity Sets
- Confirming Correctness

- Deriving the relationship parameters
- Redundant relationships example
- Splitting n:m Relationships
- Splitting n:m Relationships — Example
- Constructing an ER model

Basics

Entity Relationship (ER) modelling

- is a design tool
- is a graphical representation of the database system
- provides a high–level conceptual data model
- supports the user's perception of the data
- is DBMS and hardware independent
- had many variants
- is composed of entities, attributes, and relationships

Entities

- An entity is any object in the system that we want to model and store information about.
- Individual objects are called entities.
- Groups of the same type of objects are called entity types or entity sets.
- Entities are represented by rectangles (either with round or square corners)

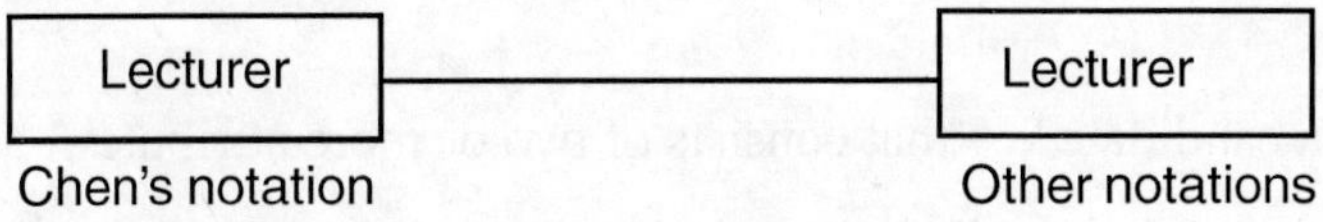

Entities

- There are two types of entities, week and strong entity types.

Attribute

- All the date relating to an entity is held in its attributes.
- An attribute is a property of an entity.
- Each attribute can have any valuc from its domain.
- Each entity within an entity type.

•Many have any number of attributes.

• Can have different attribute values than that in any other entity.

• Have the same number of attributes.

• Attributes can be.

• Simple or composite.

• Single–valued or multi-valued.

• Attributes can be shown on ER models.

• They appear inside ovals and are attached to their entity.

• Note that entity types can have a large number of attributes. If all are shown then the diagrams would be confusing. Only show an attribute if it adds information to ER diagram, or clarifies a point.

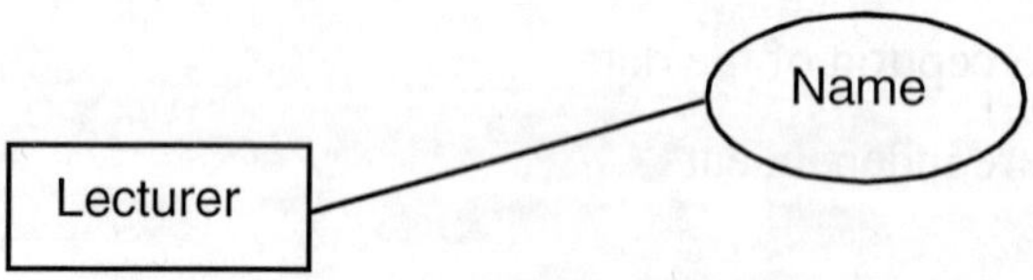

Attributes

Keys

• A key is a data item that allows us to uniquely identify individual occurrences or an entity type.

• A candidate key is an attribute or set of attributes that uniqusly identifies individual occurrences or an entity type.

• An entity type may have one or more possible candidate keys, the one which is selected is known as the primary key.

• A composite key is a candidate key that consists of two or more attributes.

• The name of each primary key attribute is underlined.

Relationships

• A *relationship type* is a meaningful association between entity types.

• A *relationship* is an association of entities where the association includes one entity from each participating entity type.

• Relationship types are represented on the ER diagram by a series of lines.

• As always, there are many notations in use today...

• In the original Chen notation, the relationship is placed inside a diamond, *e.g.* managers manage employees:

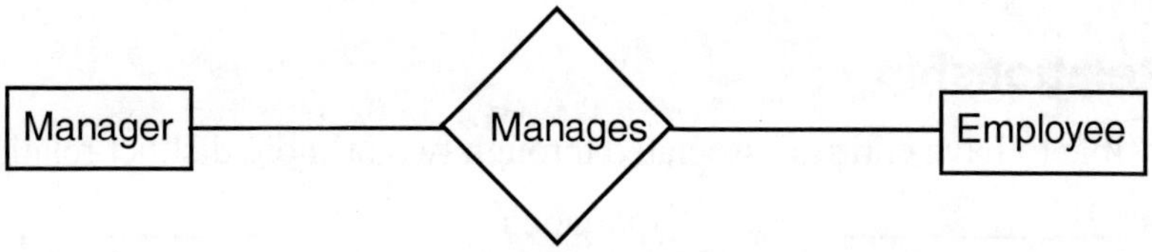

Chens notation for relationships

• For this module, we will use an alternative notation, where the relationship is a label on the line. The meaning is identical.

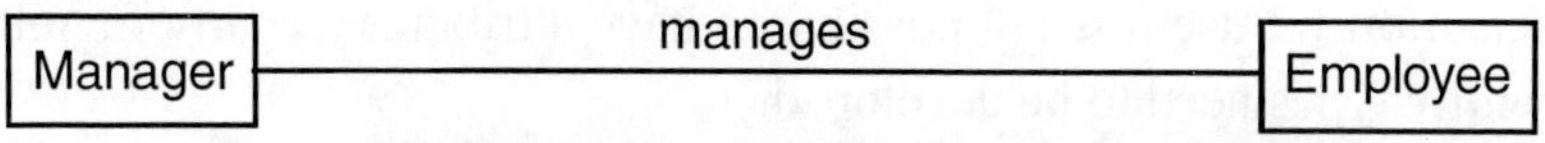

Relationship used in this Document

Degree of a Relationship

• The number of participating entities in a relationship is known as the degree of the relationship.

• If there are two entity types involved it is a binary relationship type

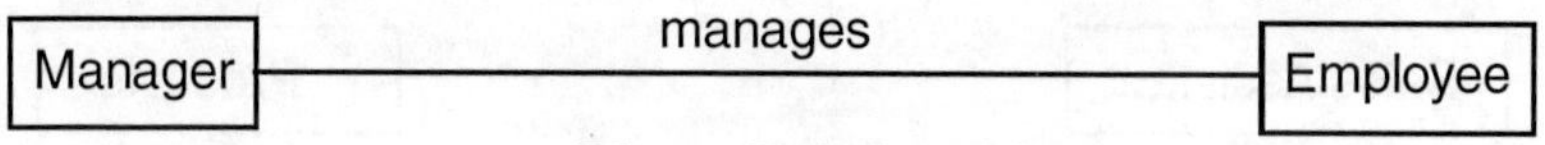

Binary Relationships

• If there are three entity types involved it is a ternary relationship type.

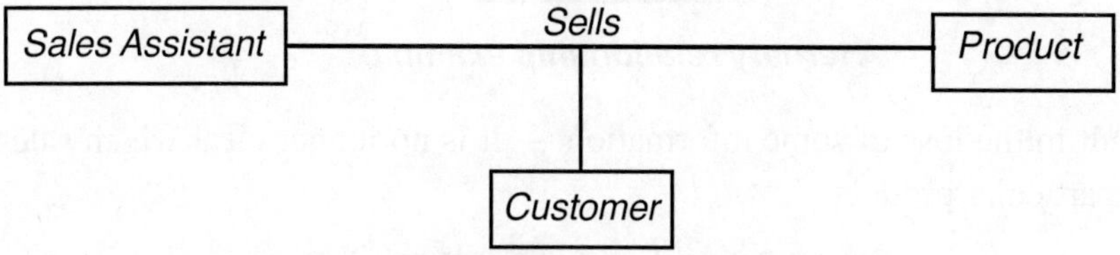

Ternary relationship

• It is possible to have a n-ary relationship (*e.g.* quaternary or unary).

• Unary relationships are also known as a *recursive* relationship.

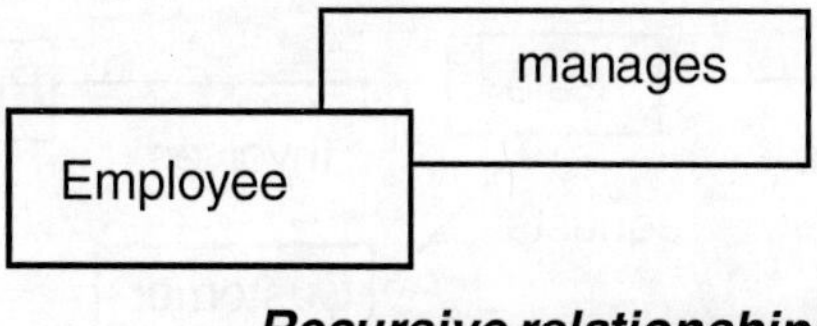

Recursive relationships

• It is a relationship where the samc entity participates more than once in different roles.

• In the example above we are saying that employees are managed by employees.

• If we wanted more information about who manages whom, we could introduce a second entity type called manager.

Degree of a Relationship

• It is also possible to have entities associated through two or more distinct relationship.

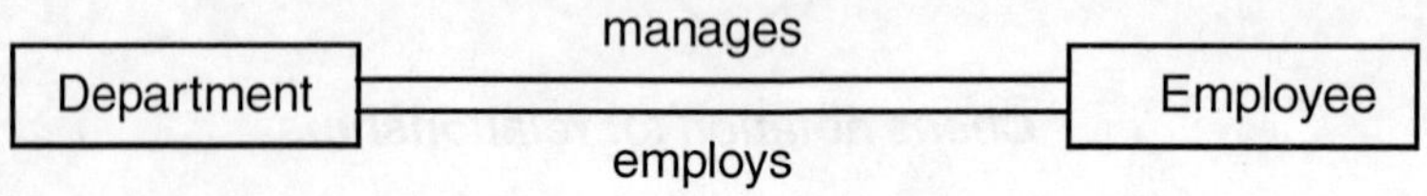

Multiple relationships

• In the representation we use it is not possible to have attributes as part of a relationship. To support this other entity types need to be developed.

Replacing ternary relationships

When ternary relationship occurs in an ER model they should always be removed before finishing the model. Sometimes the relationships can be replaced by a series of binary relationships that link pairs of the original ternary relationship.

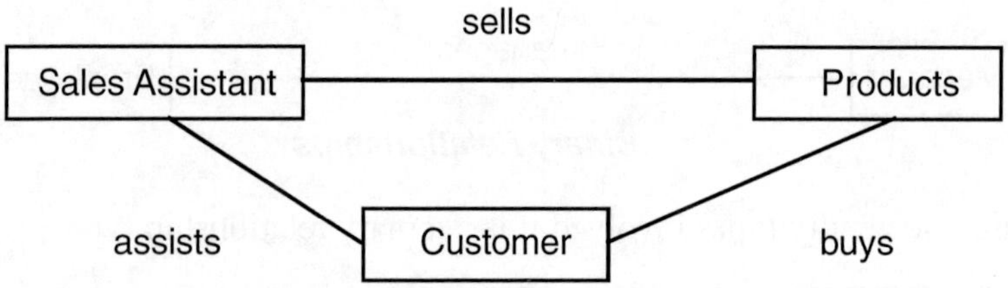

A ternary relationship example

• This can result in the loss of some information — It is no longer clear which sales assistant sold a customer a particular product.

• Try replacing the ternary relationship with an entity type and a set of binary relationships.

Relationships are usually verbs, so name the new entity type by the relationship verb rewritten as a noun.

• The relationship *sells* can become the entity type *sale.*

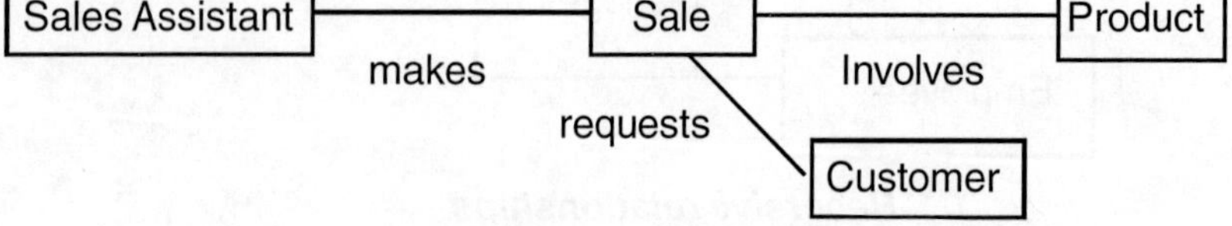

Replacing a ternary relationship

• So a sales assistant can be linked to a specific customer and both of them to the sale of particular product.

• This process also work for higher order relationships.

Cardinality

• Relationships are rarely one-to-one.

• For example, a manager usually manages more than one employee.

• This is described by the cardinality of the relationship, for which there are four possible categories.

• One to one (1:1) relationship.

• One to many (1:m) relationship.

• Many to one (m:1) relationship.

• Many to many (m:n) relationship.

• On an ER diagram, if the end of a relationship is straight, it represents 1, while a "crow's foot" and represents many.

• A one to one relationship — A man can only marry one woman and a woman can only marry one man, so it is a one to one (1 : 1) relationship.

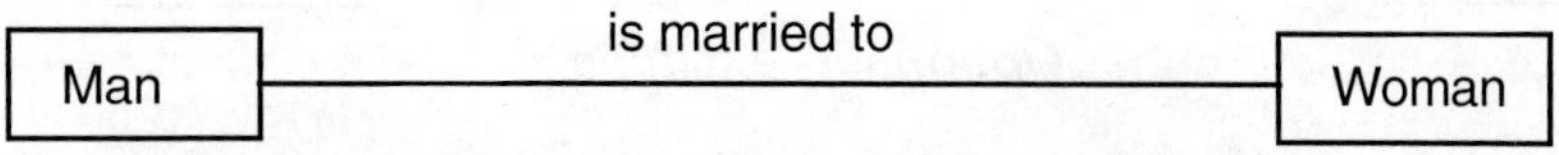

One to One relationship example

• A one to may relationship — One manager manages many employees, but each employee only has one manager, so it is a one to many (1 : n) relationship.

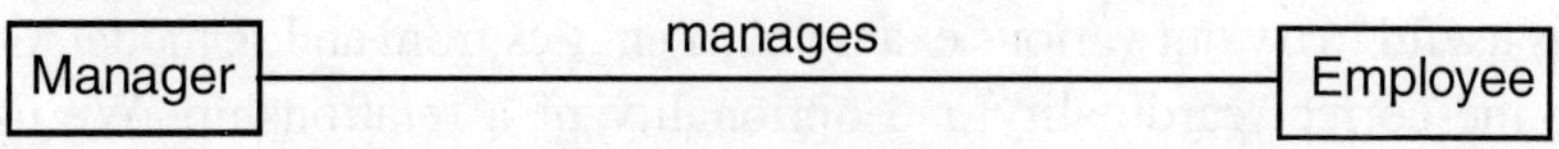

One to Many relationship example

• A many to one relationship — Many students study one course. They do not study more than one course, so it is a may to one (m : 1) relationship.

Many to One relationship example

• A many to many relationship — One lecturer teaches many students and a student is taught by many lecturers, so it is a many to many (m : n) relationship.

Many to Many relationship example

Optionality

A relationship can be optional or mandatory:

• If the relationship is mandatory.

• An entity at one end of the relationship must be related to an entity at the other end.

• The optionality can be different at each end of the relationship.

• For example, a student must be on a course. This is mandatory. To the relationship 'student studies course' is optional.

• But a course can exist before any students have enrolled. Thus the relationship 'course is _studied_by student is optional.

• To show optionality, put a circle or 'O" goes at the student end of the relationship connection.

• As the optional relationship is course is _studied_by student, and the optional part of this is the student, then the 'O' goes at the student and of the relationship connection.

Optionality example

• It is important to know the optionality because you must ensure that whenever you create a new entity it has the required mandatory links.

Entity Sets

Sometimes it is useful to try out various examples of entities from an ER model. One reason for this is to confirm the correct cardinality and optionality of a relationship. We use an 'entity set diagram' to show entity examples graphically. Consider the example of course is_studied_by student'.

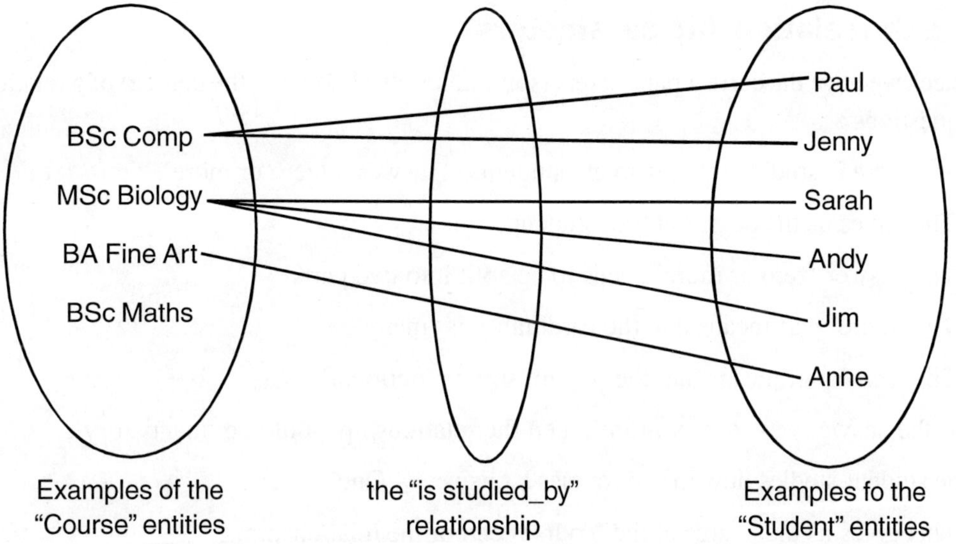

Entity set example

Confirming Correctness

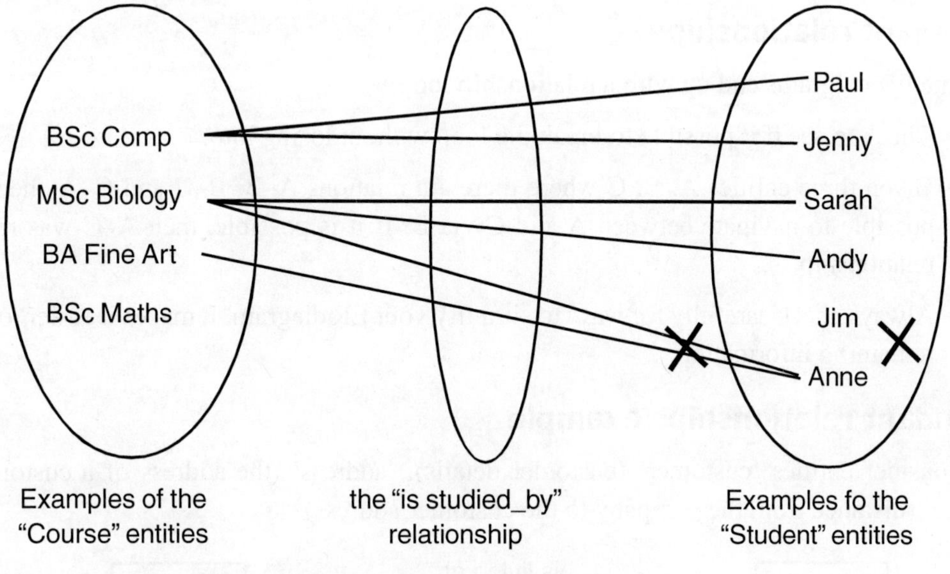

Entity set confirming errors

- Use the diagram to show all possible relationship scenarios.
- Go back to the requirements specification and check to see if they are allowed.
- If not, then put a cross through thc forbidden relationships.
- This allows you to show the cardinality and optionality of the relationship.

Deriving the relationship parameters

To check we have the correct parameters (sometimes also known as the degree) of a relationship, ask two questions :

1. One course is studied by how many students? Answer = 'zero or more'.
   - This gives us the degree at the 'student' end.
   - The answer 'zero or more' needs to be split into two parts.
   - The 'more' part means that the cardinality is 'many'.
   - The 'zero' part means that the relationship is 'optional'.
   - If the answer was 'one or more', then the relationship would be 'mandatory'.
2. One student studies how many courses? Answer = 'One'
   - This gives us the degree at the 'course' end of the relationship.
   - The answer 'one' means that the cardinality of this relationship is 1, and is 'mandatory'.
   - If the answer had been 'zero or one', then the cardinality of the relationship would have been 1, and be 'optional'.

Redundant relationships

Some ER diagrams end up with a relationship loop.

- Check to see if it possible to break the loop without losing into.
- Given three entities A, B, C where there are relations A–B, B–C and C–A check if it is possible to navigate between A and C via B. If it is possible, then A–C was redundant relationship.
- Always check carefully for ways to simplify your ER diagram. It makes it easier to read the remaining information.

Redundant relationships example

• Consider entities 'customer' (customer details), 'address' (the address of a customer) and 'distance' (distance from the company to the customer address).

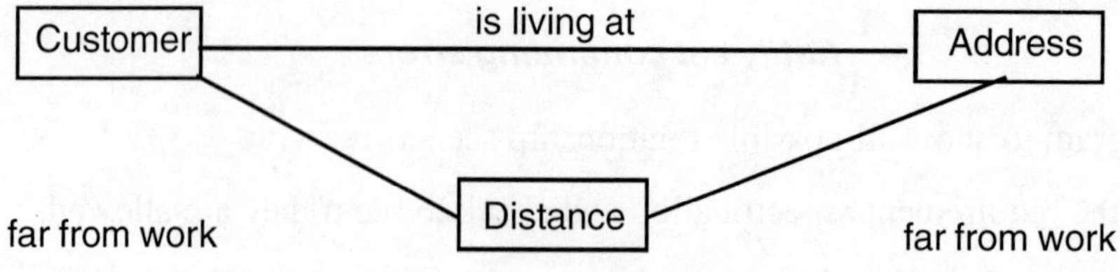

Figure: Redundant relationship

Splitting n:m Relationships

A many to many relationship in an ER model is not necessarily incorrect. They can be replaced using an intermediate entity. This should only be done where :

• The m:n relationship hides an entity

• The resulting ER diagram is easier to understand.

Splitting n:m Relationships — Example

Consider the case of a car hire company. Customer hire cars, one customer hires many card and a car is hired by many customers.

Many to many example

The many to many relationship can be broken down to reveal a 'hire' entity, which contains an attribute 'date of hire'.

Splitting the Many to Many example

Constructing an ER model

Before beginning to draw the ER model, read the requirements specification carefully. Document any assumptions you need to make.

1. Identify entities — List all potential entity types. These are the object of interest in the system. It is better to put too many entities in at this stage and them discard them later if necessary.

2. Remove duplicate entities — Ensure that they really separate entity types or just two names for the same thing.

- Also do not include the system as an entity type.
- *e.g.* if modelling a library, the entity types might be books, borrowers, etc.
- The library is the system, thus should not be an entity type.

3. List the attributes of each entity (all properties to describe the entity which are relevant to the application).

- Ensure that the entity types are really needed.
- Are any of them just attributes of another entity type?

- If so keep them as attributes and cross them off the entity list.
- Do not have attributes of one entity as attributes of another entity!

4. Mark the primary keys.
   - Which attributes uniquely identify instances of the entity type?
   - This may not be possible for some weak entities.
5. Define the relationships.
   - Examine each entity type to see its relationship to the others.
6. Describe the cardinality and optionality of the relationships.
   - Examine the constraints between participating entities.
7. Remove redundant relationships.
   - Examine the ER model for redundant relationships.

Example 12. What is the difference between DBMS and RDBMS?

1. DBMS stands for Database Managements System which is a general term for a set of software dedicated to controlling the storage of date.

RDMBS stand for Relational Database Management System. This is the most common form of DBMS. Invented by E.F. Codd, the only way to view the data is as a set of tables. Because there can be relationships between the tables, people often assume that is what the word 'relational" means. Not so. Codd was a mathematician and the word "relational" is a mathematical term from the science of set theory. It means, roughly, "based on tables".

2. DBMS includes the theoretical part that how data are stored in a table. It does not relates tables with another. While RDBMS is the procedural way that includes SQL syntax's for relating tables with another and handling datas stored in tables.

3. RDBMS is object based database management system while DBMS 2)RDBMS can maintain at many users at same time while DBMS not 2)in RDBMS is relation is more important than object itself while DBMS entity is more important.

4. The main advantage of an RDBMS is that it checks for referential integrity (relationship between related records using Foreign Keys). You can set the constraints in a RDMBS such that when a particular record is changed, related record are update/deleted automatically.

5. A database has to be persistent, meaning that the information stored in a database has to continue to exist even after the application(s) that saved and manipulated the data have ceased to run. A database also has to provide some uniform methods that are not dependent on a specific application for accessing the information that is stored inside the database.

An RDBMS is a Relational Data Base Management System. This adds the additional condition that the system supports a tabular structure for the data, with enforced relationships between the tables.

6. The difference is DBMS has no table while RCBMS has and also it describes about the relationships among the tables DBMS for small organization where RDBMS for large amount of data

7. In DBMS all the tables are treated different entities. There is no relation established among these entities. But the tables in RDBMS are dependent and the user can establish various integrity constraints on these tables so that the ultimate date used by the user remains correct.

8. In DBMS there are entity sets in the form of tables but relationship among them is not defined while in RDMBS in each entity is well defined with a relationship set so as retrieve our data fast and easy.

EXERCISE

1. What is DBMS? Describe three level schema architecture of DBMS.
2. Diffierentiate between the following :
   (*i*) Strong Entity set/ Weak entity set
   (*ii*) Logical data independence/ Physical data independence.
   (*iii*) Data definition language/ Data manipulation language.
   (*iv*) Relationship/Relationship set
3. Explain the following :
   (1) Meta data (2) DBA (3) Multivalued attribute (4) Host language (5) Concurrency (6) Data dictionary (7) Data inconsistency.
4. Advantages of Database system over normal file processing system.
5. Define the following terms:
   (*i*) Domain
   (*ii*) Attribute
   (*iii*) Relation schema
   (*iv*) Relation Instance
   (*v*) Relational Data
   (*vi*) Degree of a Relation

6. Why are tuples in a relation not ordered?
7. What are the difference between a key and super key?
8. Why do we designate one of the candidate keys of a relation to be primary key?
9. Discuss the various reasons which occurrence of Null values in Relations?
10. Discuss the entity integrity main and referential integrity constraints, why is each considered important?
11. Define the foreign key what is this concept used for?
12. What is union compatibility? Why do the Union, intersection and difference operations requires what the relation on which they are applied be union compatibility?
13. What do you understand by E-R diagram? What are graphical notations of E-R diagram? Show in a example.
14. Construct an E-R diagram for the following database :

    Employee (eno, name, address)
    Department (d_name)
    Work – in (eno, d_name)
    Item (item_no, br_name, model_no, C_prece, S_price)
    Sale (d_name, item_no)
    Suppliers (s_ name, s_address)
    Supplied by (item_no, s_name)
15. Discuss the different types of user friendly interfaces and the types of users who typically use each?
16. What are major components of DBMS? Show overall structure of DBMS?
17. What are advantages and disadvantages of DBMS ?
18. What do you mean by data models? Explain the following record based data models ?
19. Define the following terms :

    (*i*) Abstraction (*ii*) Generalization
    (*iii*) Specialization (*iv*) Aggregation
20. What are role and responsibilities of Database Administrator?
21. Explain the concept of generalization and secialization with a suitable example?

Solved Examples

Example 1. In an organisation several projects are undertaken each project can implies one or more employees each employee can work on one or more project each project is undertaken on the request of client. A client can requested for several projects each project has only one client. A project can used a number of items and a item may be used by several projects. Draw an E-R diagram.

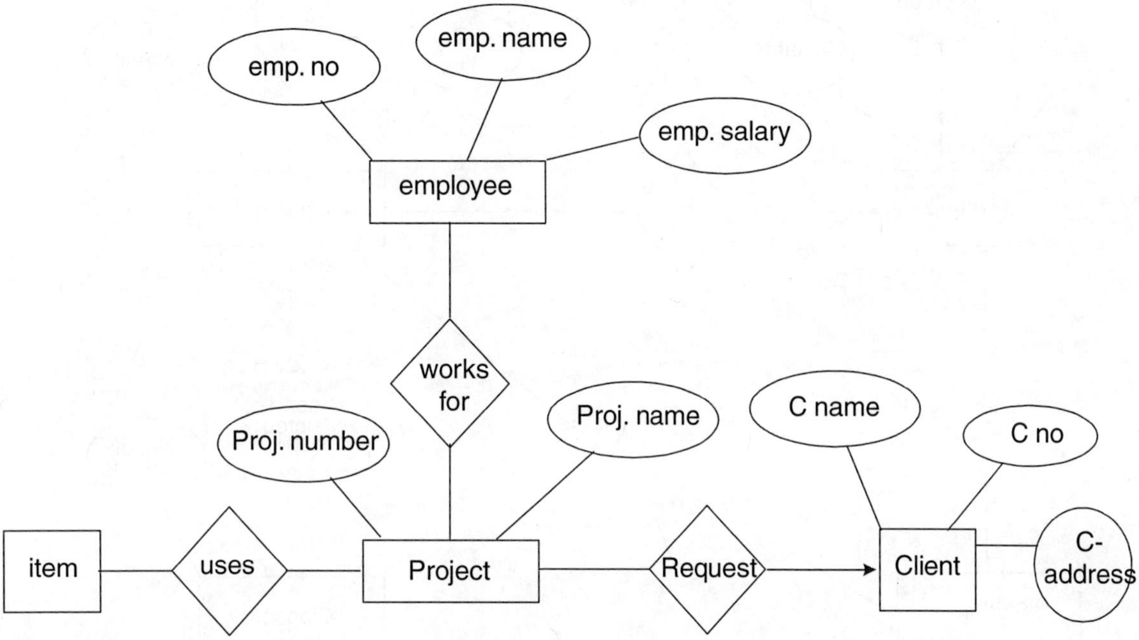

E-R diagram

Example 2. Construct a E-R diagram for a University Register Office. The office maintains data about each class indicating the instructor, the enrollment and time and the room no of the class for each student no of subjects, class is recorded document all assumptions that you make about the mapping constraints.

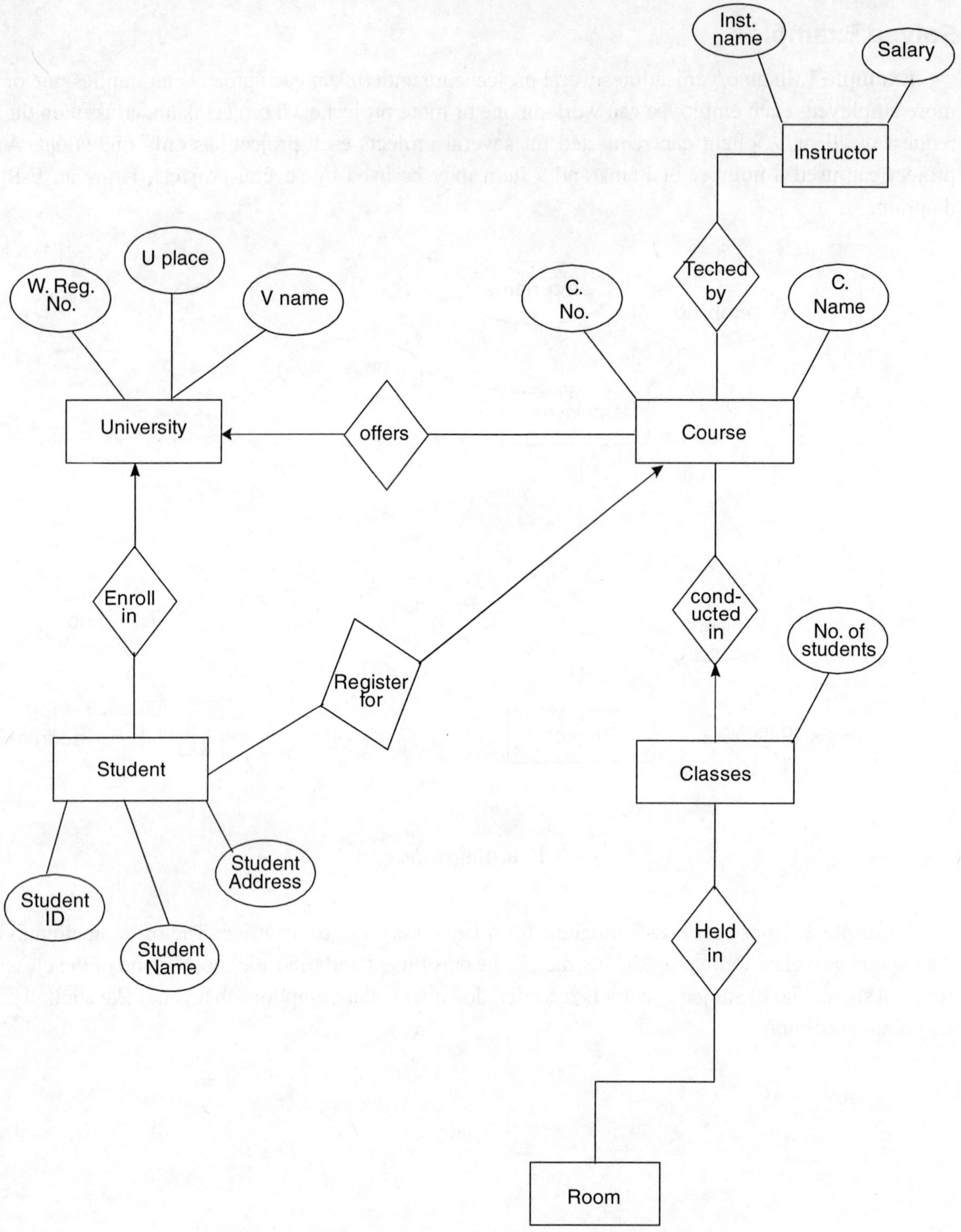
Inst. name
Salary
Instructor
Teched by
C. No.
C. Name
W. Reg. No.
U place
V name
University
offers
Course
Enroll in
Register for
cond-ucted in
No. of students
Classes
Student
Student Address
Student ID
Student Name
Held in
Room

E-R diagram

Example 3. Construct E-R diagram for a Insurance company that has the set of customers each of whom owns one or more cars each car has associated with to any number of accidents regarded.

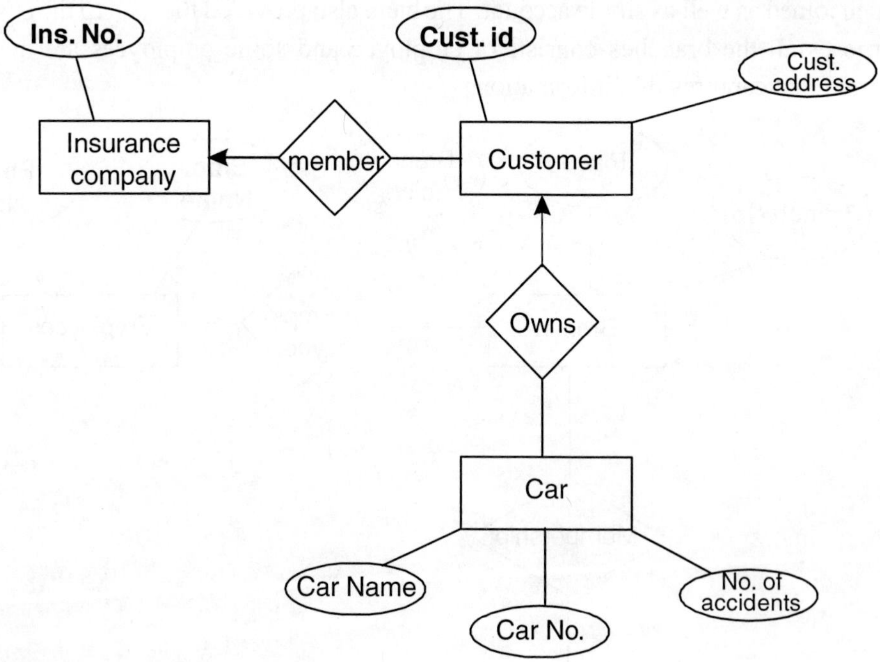

E-R diagram

Example 4. Construct an E-R diagram for a Hospital with set of medical patient and set of medical Doctor associated with each patient a log of various test and examination conduct.

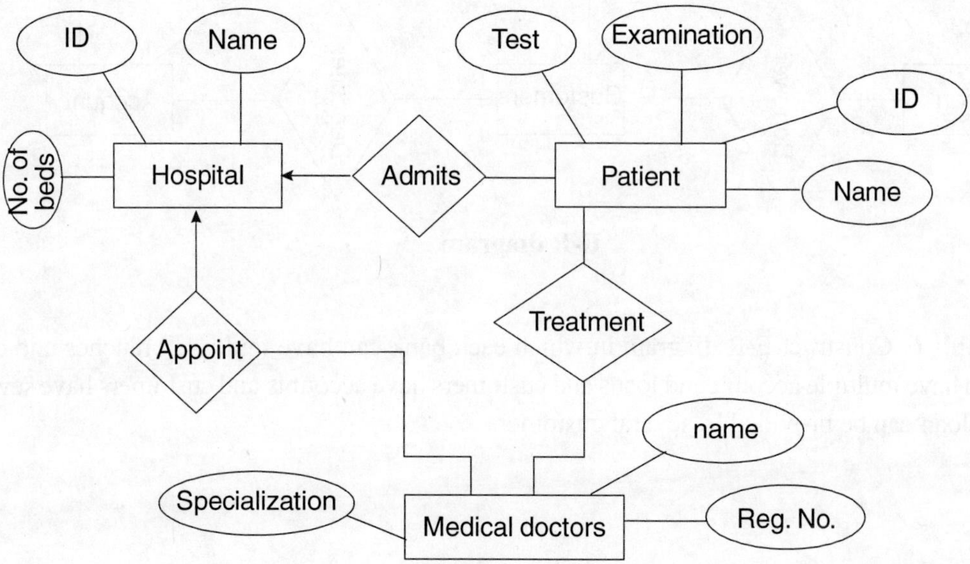

E-R diagram

Example 5. Consider the following set of requirements for a Bank Data base a large bank has several branch and different places each branch maintaines the account details of the customer. The customer may open joined as well as single account. The bank also provided the loan to the customer for different purposes all the branches consists of employee and some employees are mangers. Draw a E-R diagram that captures this information.

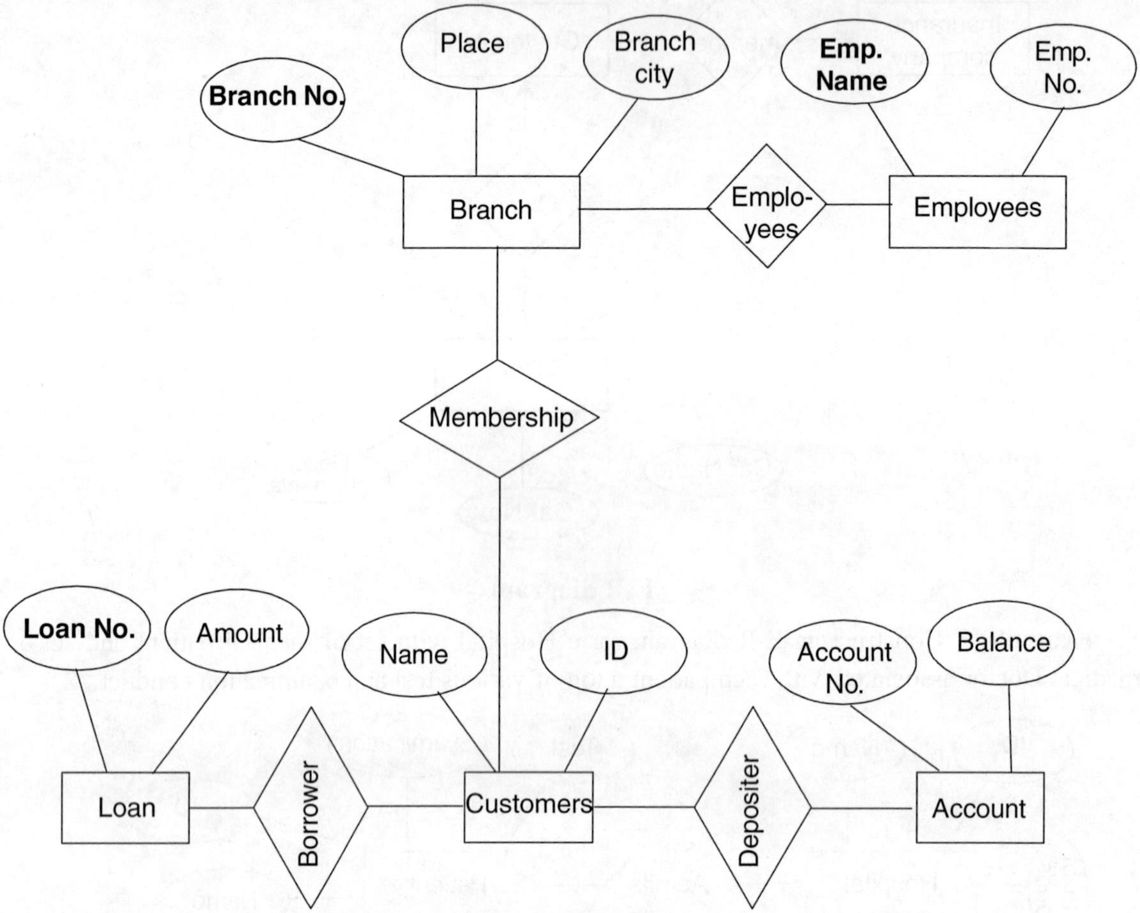

E-R diagram

Example 6. Construct E-R diagram in which each bank can have multiple branches and each branch can have multiple account and loans and customers have accounts and customers have several loans and loan can be provided to several customers.

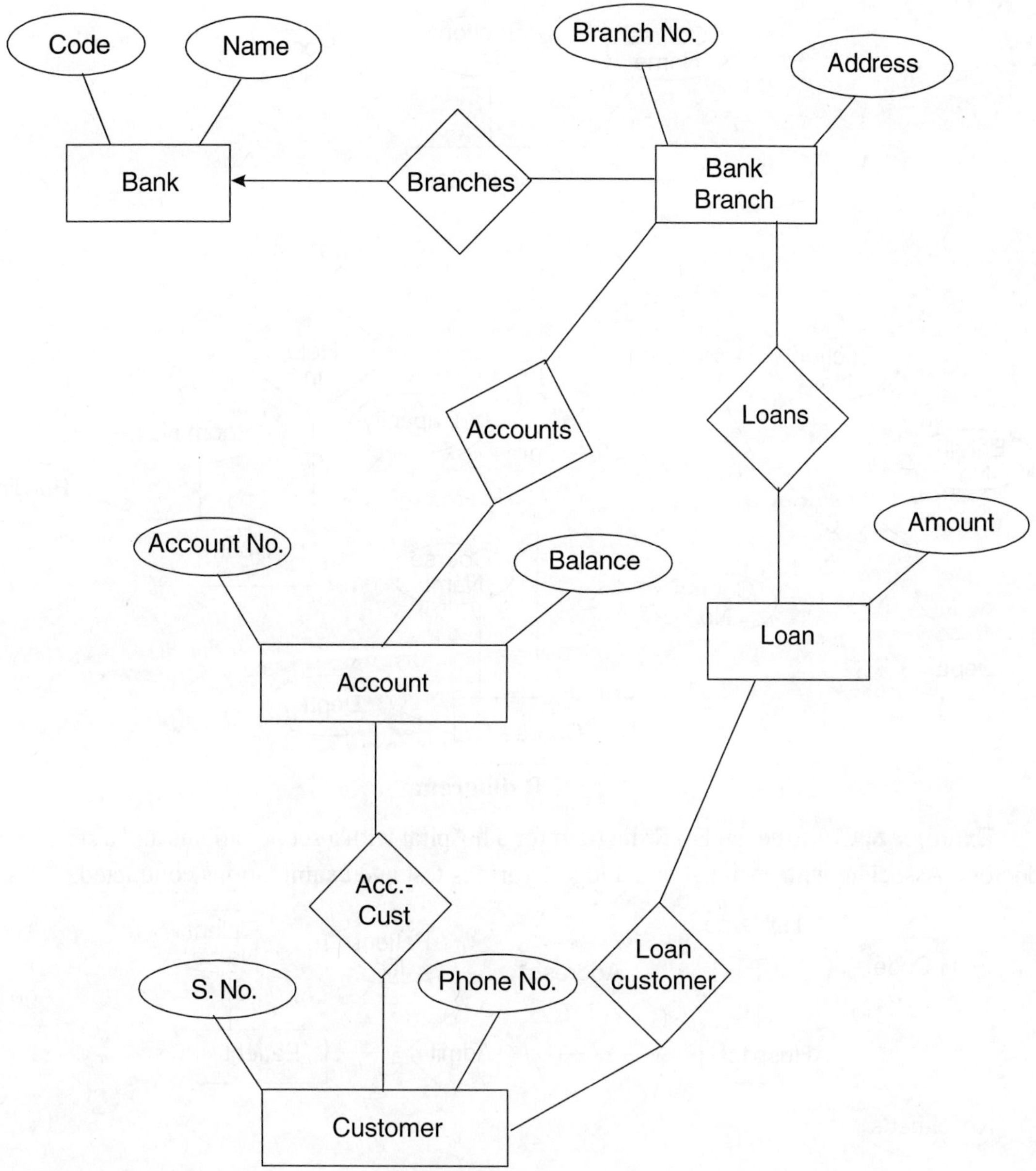

E-R diagram

Example 7. Consider the university database for the scheduling of class rooms for final examination. This database could be made as the single entity set examination with attribute course – name, section – no, room – no and time alternatively one or more additional entity set could be defined along with relationship set to replace some of the attributes of EXAM entity sets as course, with attributes name, with attributes name department and course – no section with attributes S – No and enrolment room, with attribute room – no, capacity and building show an E–R diagram illustrating the use of all three additional entity set.

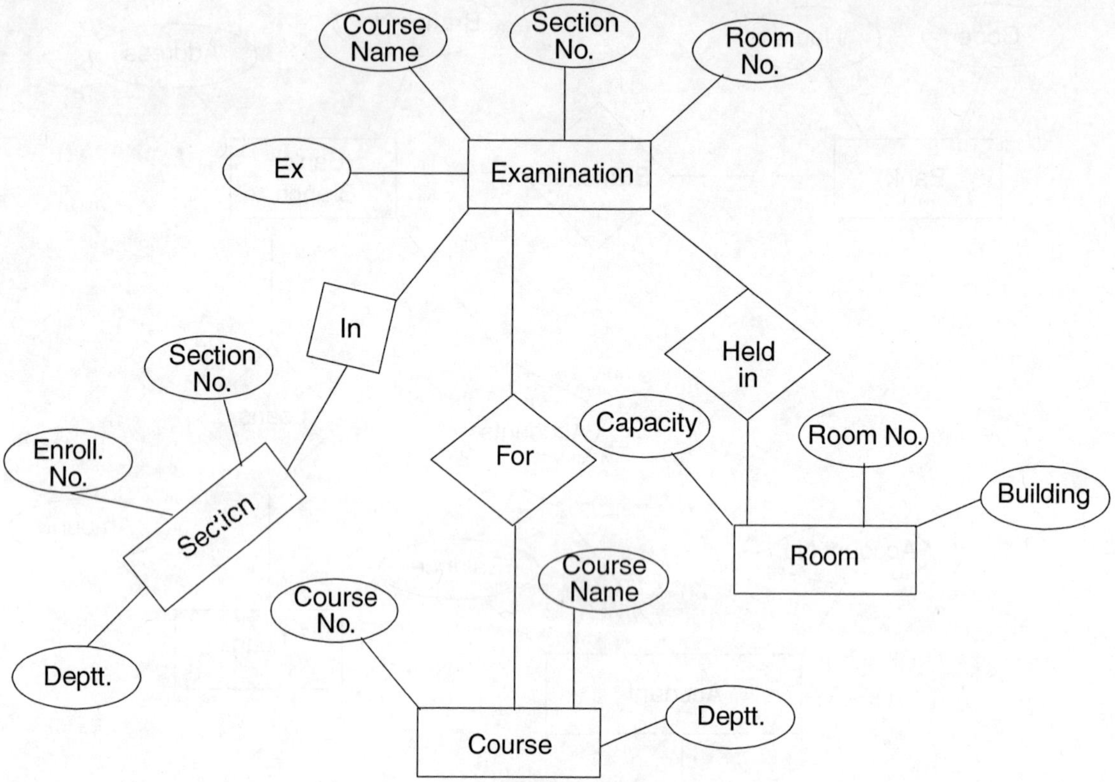

E-R diagram

Example 8. Construct an E – R diagram for a hospital with a set of patients and a set of medical doctors. Associate with each patient, a log of various test and examinations conducted.

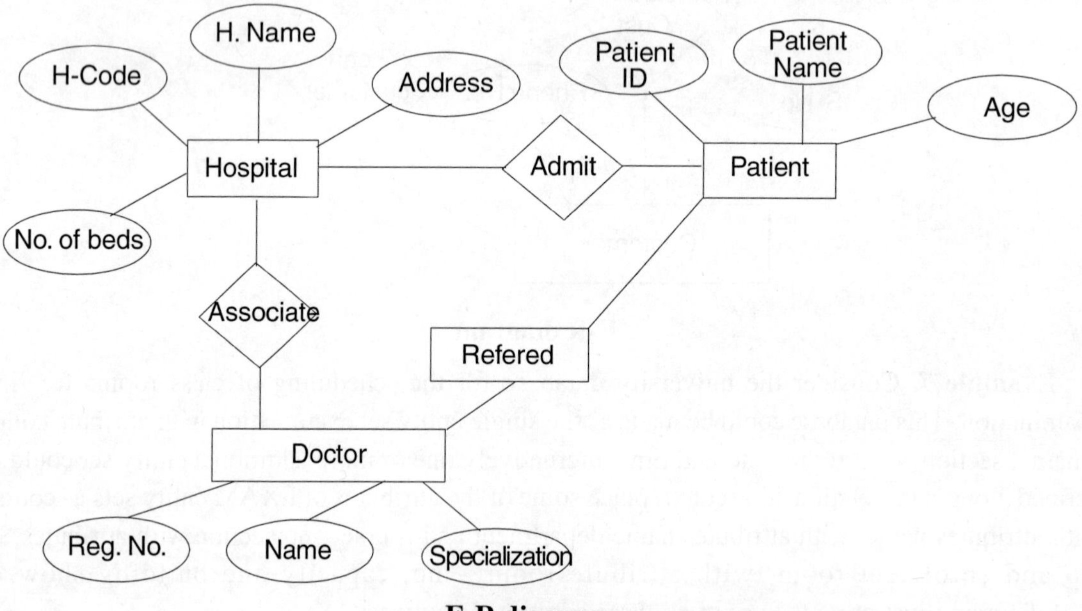

E-R diagram

Example 9. A large bank has several branches at different places. Each branch maintain the account details of the customers. The customers may open joint as well as single accounts. The bank also provides the loan to the customer for different purposes Bank keeps record of each transaction by the customer to his account. All of the branches have employees and some employees are managers draw an E-R diagram that captures this information.

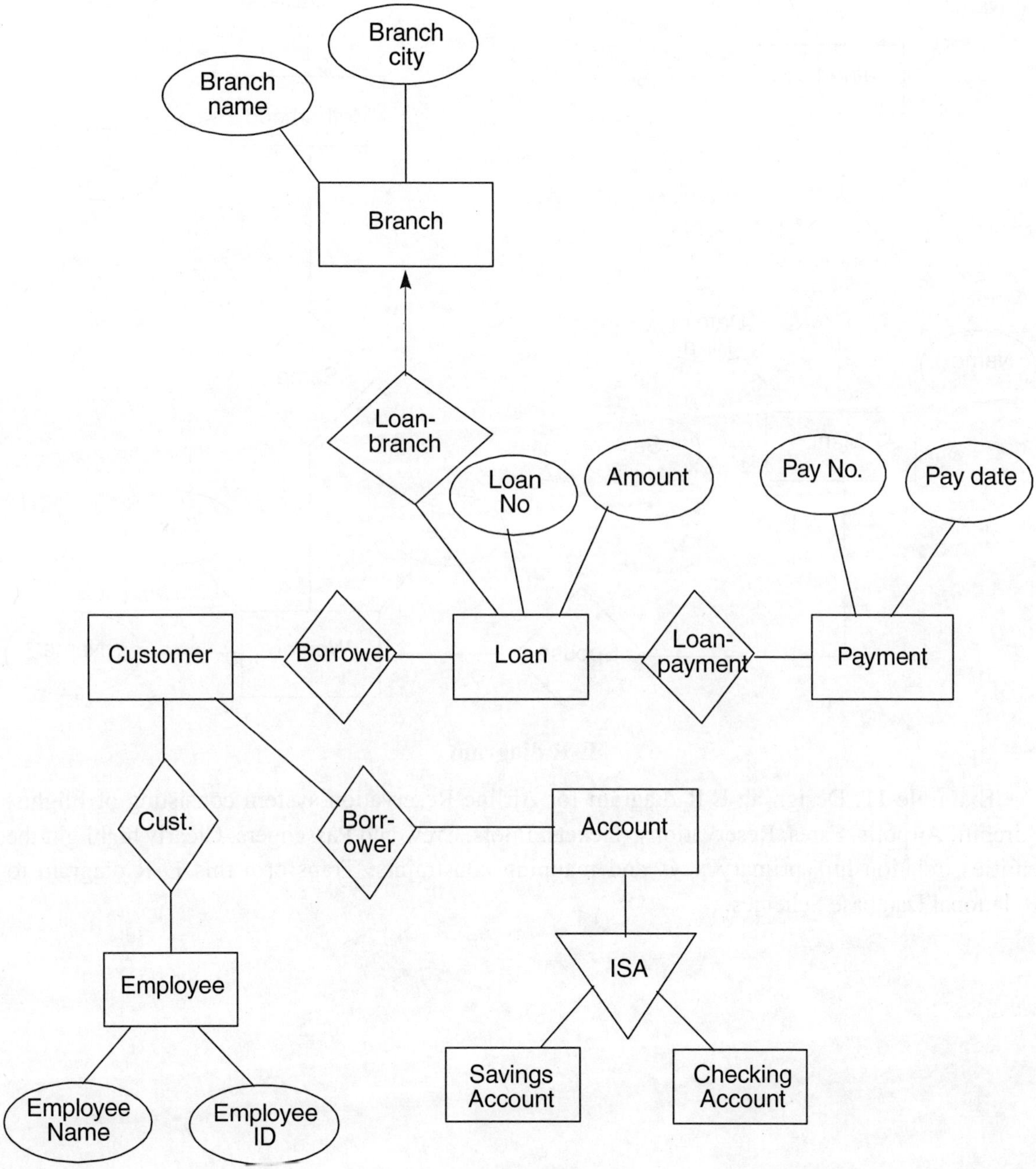

E-R diagram

Example 10. Give an entity relationship diagram for a database showing fatherhood, motherhood and spouse relationship among men and women.

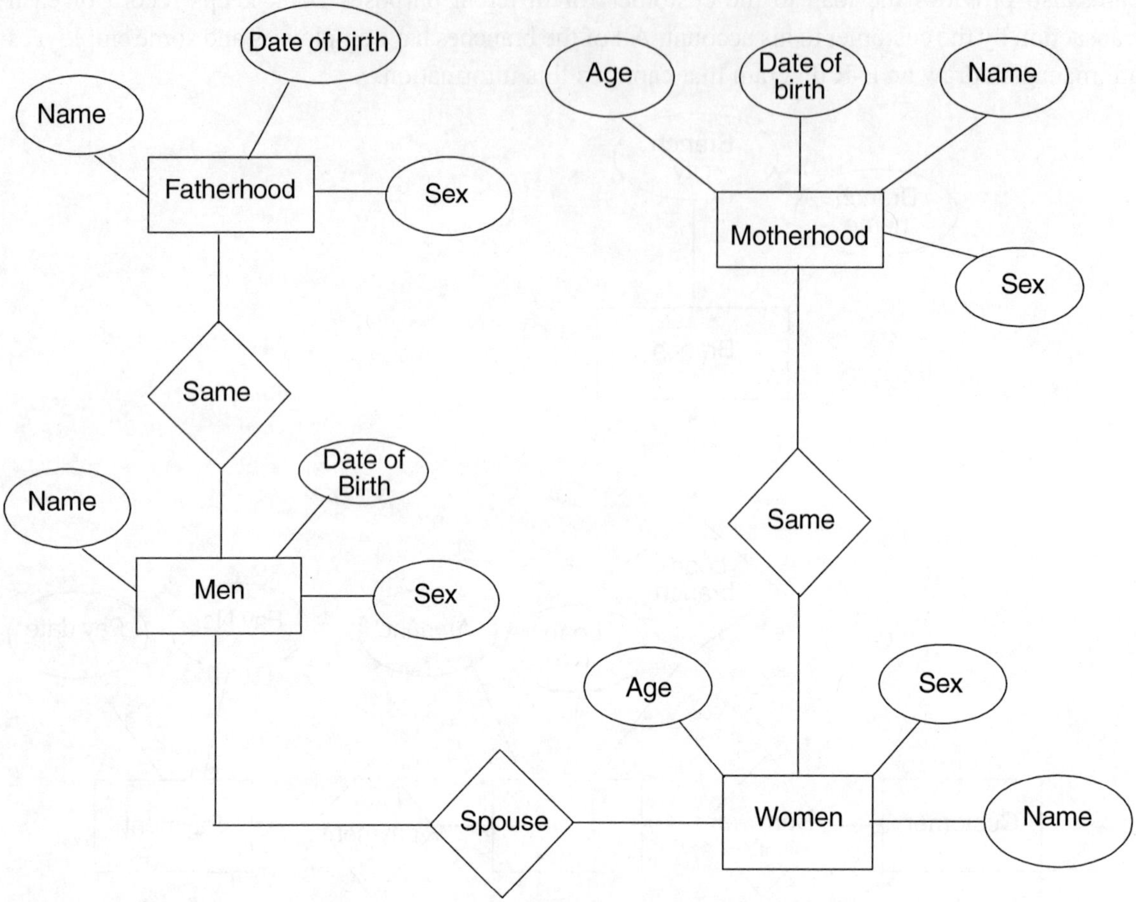

E-R diagram

Example 11. Design an E-R diagram for Airline Reservation system consisting of Flights, Aircraft, Airports, Fares, Reservations, Tickets, Pilots, Crew and Passengers. Clearly highlight the entities, relationship, primary keys and mapping constraints. Transform this E–R diagram to Relational Database Schemes.

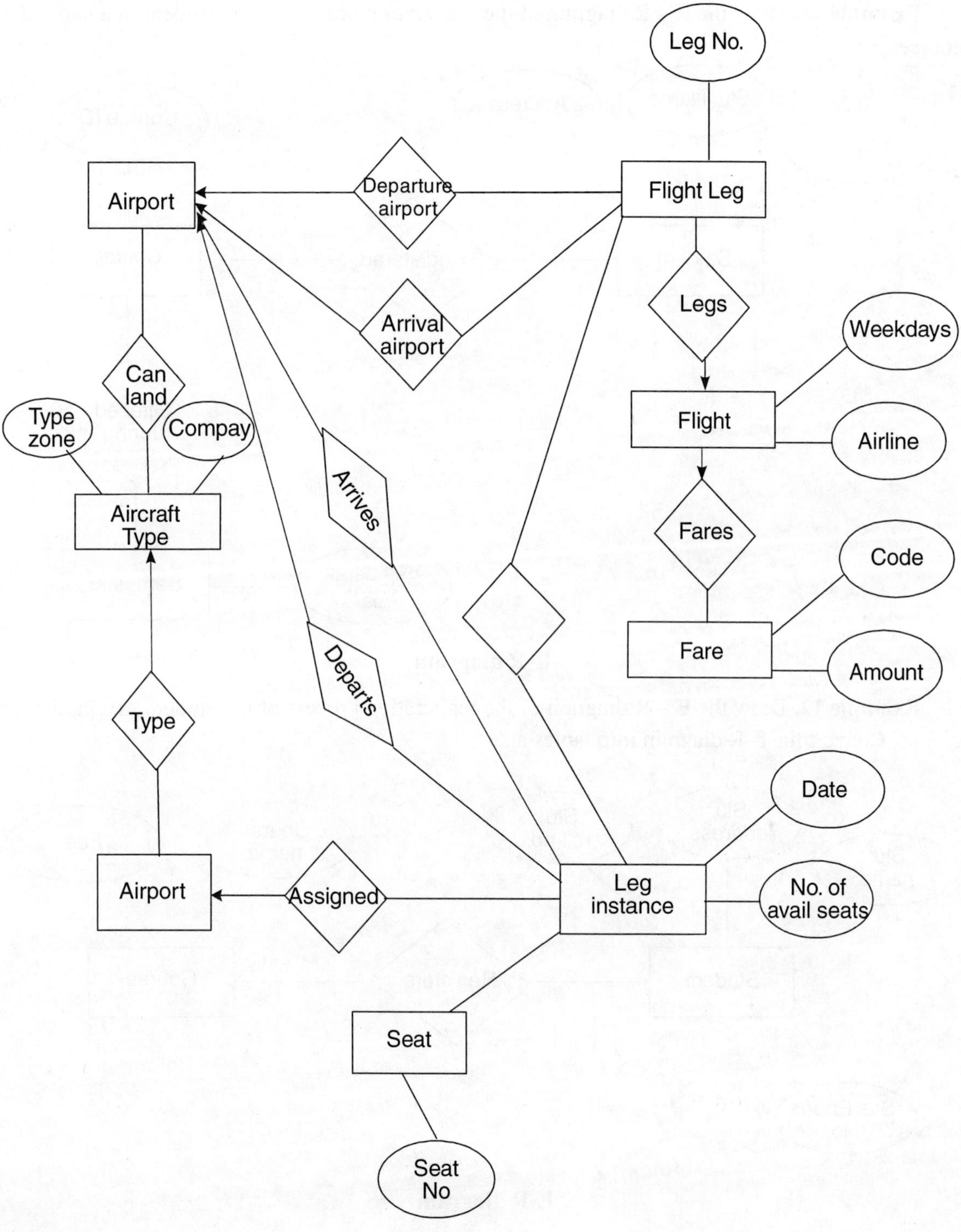
Leg No.
Airport
Departure airport
Flight Leg
Arrival airport
Legs
Weekdays
Can land
Type zone
Compay
Flight
Airline
Aircraft Type
Arrives
Fares
Code
Departs
Fare
Amount
Type
Date
Airport
Assigned
Leg instance
No. of avail seats
Seat
Seat No

E–R diagram

Example 11. Draw the E – R diagram of the registration process of the student in a particular course.

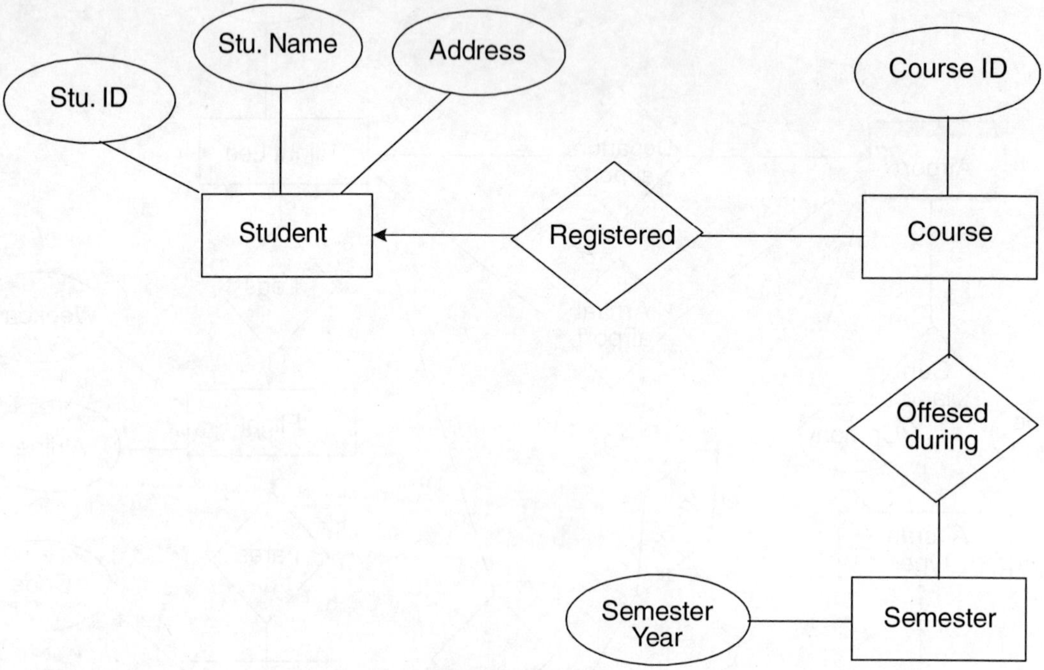

E-R diagram

Example 12. Draw the E – R diagram of the registration process of the student in a particular course. Convert the E-R diagram into tables also.

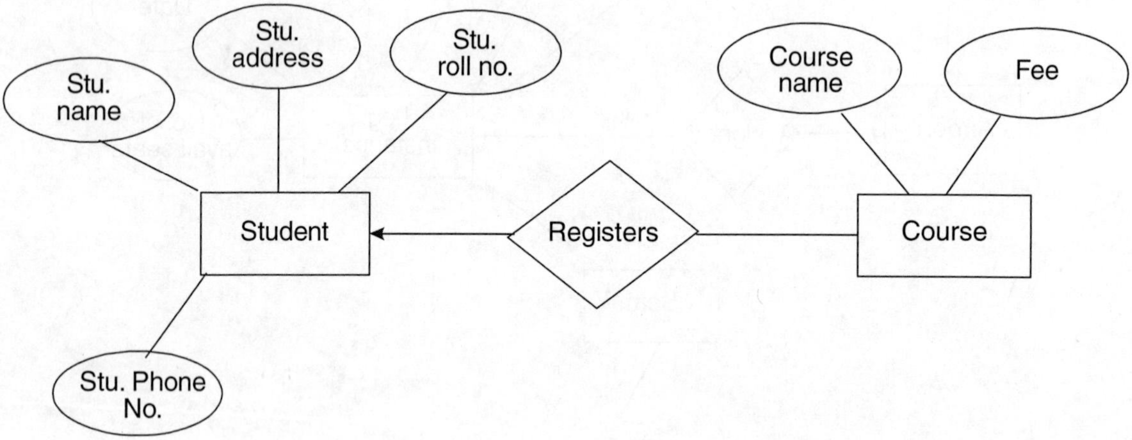

E-R diagram

Example 13. Design an E – R diagram for Banking Enterprise.

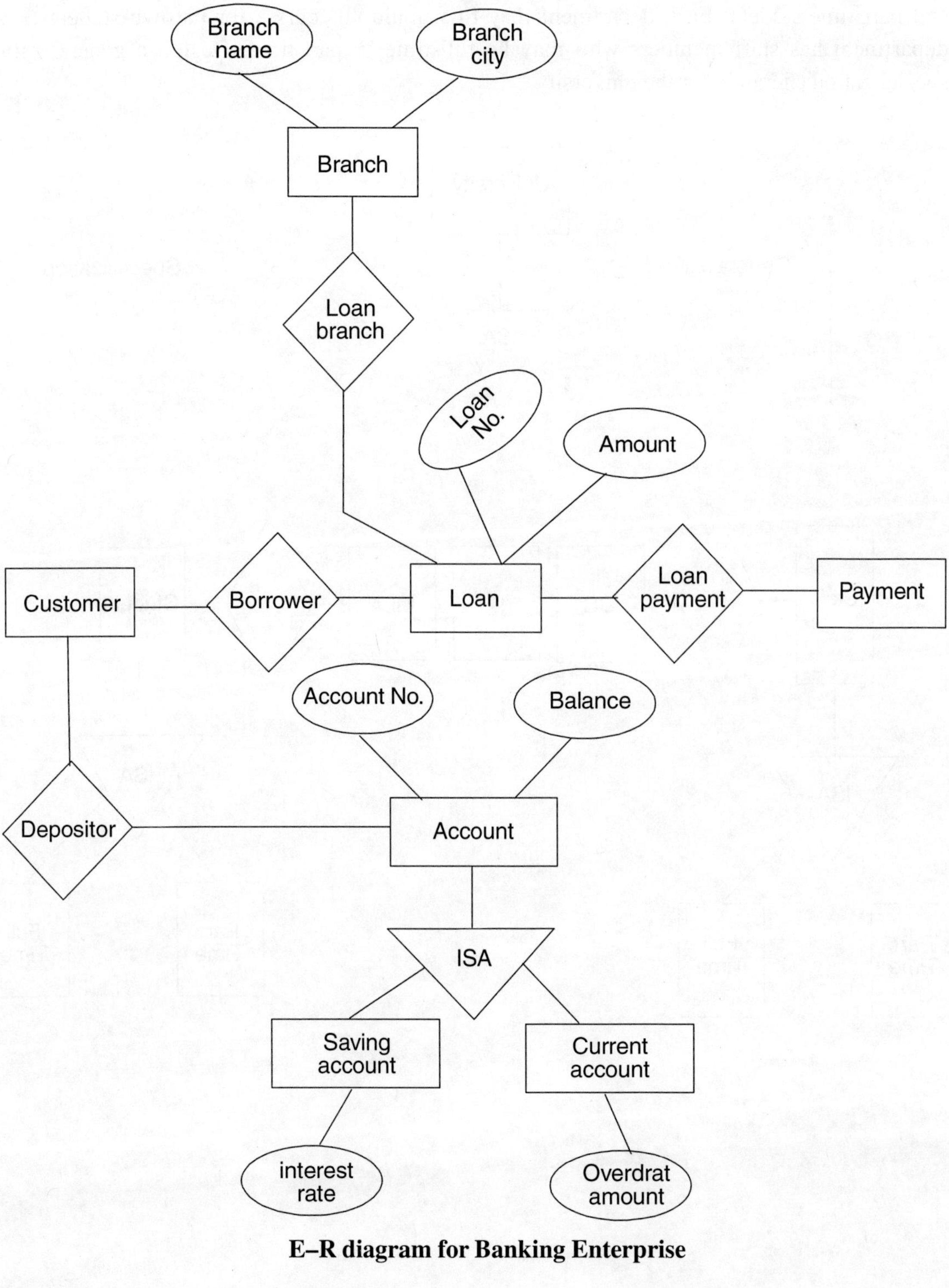

E–R diagram for Banking Enterprise

Example 14. A university has many departments – Each department may have many full – time and part time student. Each department may float multiple courses for its own students. Each department has staff members who may be full-time or part-time. Design a generalization, specialization Gierarely for the university.

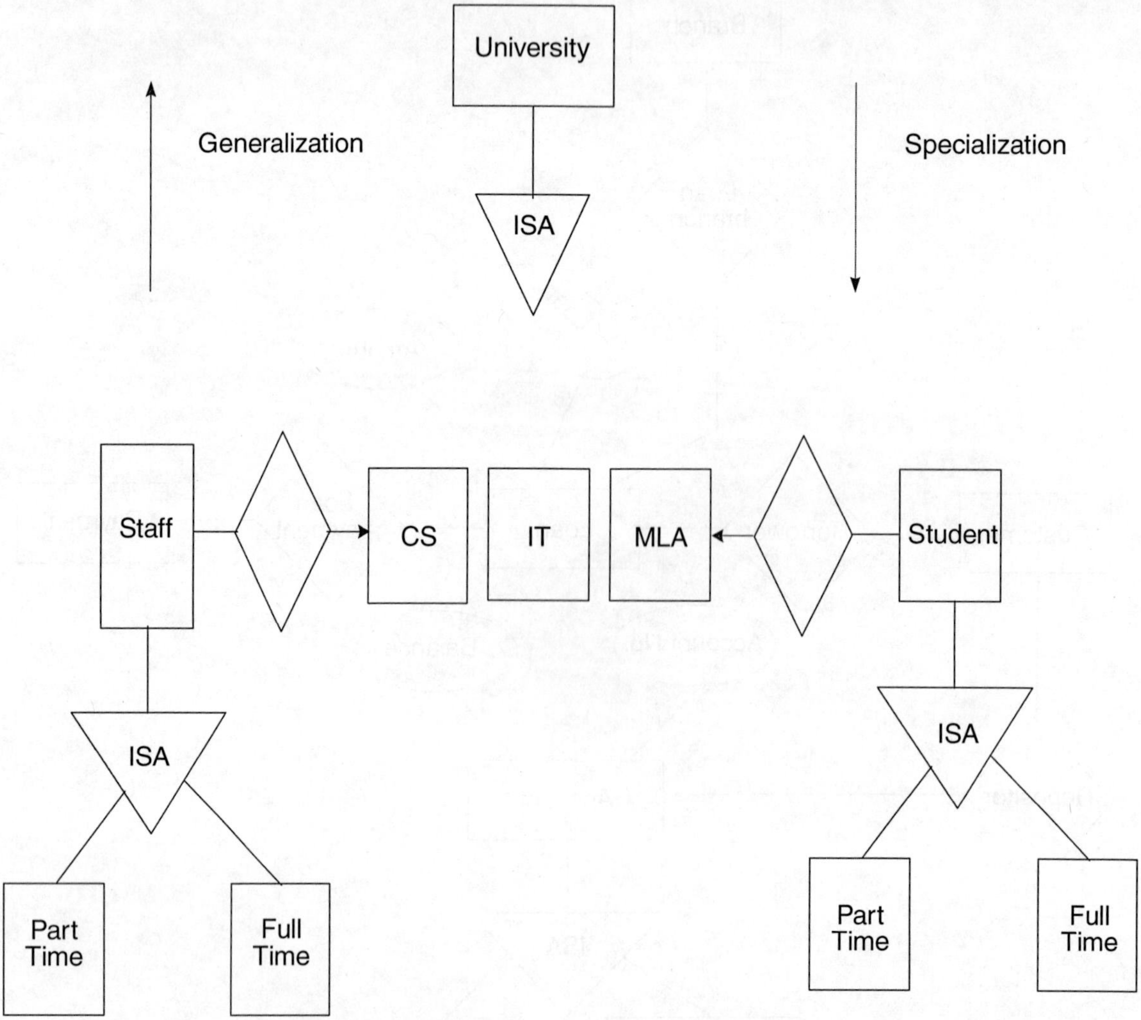

UNIT — TWO

Chapter 3

Relational Data Model and Language

Chapter Outline

Relational Data Model concepts
Integrity constraints
Entity Integrity
Referential Integrity
Keys Constraints
Domain Constraints
Relational Algebra
Relational Calculus
Tuple and Domain Calculus

RELATIONAL DATA MODEL CONCEPTS

The major advantage of this model is its simple data representation and the case with which even complex queries can be expressed. This model allows the uses to be totally unconcerned with the physical structure of data :

Codd's Rule—

1. **The information Rule :** This rule simply requires all information to be represented as data values in the lows and columns of tables.

2. **The Guaranteed Access Rule :** Every data values in a relational database should be logically accessible by specifying a combination of the table name, like primary key valves and the column name.

3. **Systematic Treatment :** The RDBMS must support NULL values to represent missing information.

4. **Active Online Catalogue based on the Relational Model :** The system catalogue is a collection of tables that the (System) DBMS maintains for its own use.

5. **The comprehensive data sub-language rule :** This rule states that the system must support as least all the following functions (1) Data Definition (2) View definition (3) Data manipulation operations (4) Security and integrity constraints (5) Transaction mgt operations.

6. **The View Updating Rule :** All views that are theoretically updateable must be updated by the system views.

7. **High level insert, update and Delete :** The DBMS must allow multiple rows to be updated. This rule states that low should be treated as sets in inserts, delete and update operations.

8. **Physical Data Independence :** Application programs must remain unimpaired when any change are mode in storage representation or access methods.

9. **Logical Data Independence :** Changes shouldn't be the user's ability to work with the data.

10. **Integrity Independence :** Integrity constraints are storable in the system catalog. The concept of data integrity requires no further explanation.

11. **Distribution Independence :** Database must allow manipulation of distribution data located on other computer systems.

12. **Non-subversion - Rule :** The non-subversion rule states that different levels of language can not subrest or by-pass the energetic rules and conditions.

In the relational model, a database is a collection of tables or relations. The columns of the table contain information about the table. The name of the column is called the attribute name. We use the term attribute and attribute name rather than column and column name to be consistent with relational database conventions. The number of attributes in a relation is called the *degree of the relation.* The Rows of the table expressed the relationships among the set of values. The Rows of a relation or a table are also called as *tuples*

Formal terms	Many Database Manuals
Relation	Table
Attribute	Column
Tuple	Row

Retational Model Terminology

The set of all possible values that an attribute may have is the domain of the atribute.

Relation name

Employee

Attributes

Tuples

ENO	ENAME	ADDRESS	SAL	DNO
1001	Ram	PRO	6000	1
1002	Mohan	PRO	6500	1
1003	Sita	Sales Person	7000	2
1004	Gita	Sales Person	7500	2

Employee Table/Relation

Properties of Relational Tables

Relational tables have six properties

1. **Values are Atomic :** This property implies that columns in a relational table are not repeating group or arrays. Hence composite and multi valued altributes are not allowed.

2. **Column Values are of the Same Kind :** In relational terms this means that all values in a column come from the same domain. A domain is a set of values, which a column may have.

3. **Each Low is Unique :** This property ensures that no two rows in a relational table are identical these is at least one column, or set of columns, the values of which uniquely identify each row in the table such columns are called primary keys.

4. **The Sequence of Columns is Insignificant :** This property states that the ordering of the columns in the relational table has no meaning columns can be retrained in any order and in various sequences. The benefit of this property is that it enables many users to share the same table without concern of how the table is organised.

5. **The Sequence of Row is Insignificant :** The main benefit is that the rows of a relational table can be retrieved in different order and sequences.

6. **Each Column has a Unique Name :** Because the sequence of columns is insignificant, columns must be referenced by name and not by position.

INTEGRITY CONSTRAINTS

An integrity constraint is the condition that can be applied on a database schema to restrict the data according to the need. If the condition is satisfied then only it can be stared in the database. There integrity contraints can be applied on the database when the DBA or end users define the database schemes.

DBMS checks these constraints when a database application is run. The purpose of there constraints is to ensure that there should not be any loss in data consistency due to change made to the database by the authorized users.

There are so many constraints/which are used to verify the validity of the data in the database.

We have two rules :

(a) Entity Integrity
(b) Referential Integrity

ENTITY INTEGRITY

Entity Integrity is concerned with the primary key values. The rows in a relation represents instances in the database of a specific real world objects or entities for example a row in employee relation represents a specific employee.

Moreover, Since all the instance of the relation are members of a mathematical set each table should be unique. To establish this uniqueness, specified column or concatenation of number of columns must certain unique values for each table in the body. Those columns are referred as Primary keys.

If there is more than one column involved in uniqueness then it is called as concatenated key or composite key.

The definition of Entity Integrity Rule. No component of the primary key in a relation allowed to accept NULL value.

REFERENTIAL INTEGRITY

This rule is concerned with the concept of the foreign keys Foreign keys are used to relate the rows in one relation to rows in another relations.

A database in which all non-null foreign keys reference actual key values in other relations give the idea referential integrity rule, which is as follows :

Let A and B be two relations where A relation is having an attribute (*s*) with primary key. Let B be having a foreign key, which refers to relation a with the same set of attributes. Then the value of the foreign key in a type in B relation must either be equal to primary key of a tuple in A relation or be entirely null. More simply we can write it as every foreign key must either be null or it must be having the same value of a primary key attribute in another relation.

KEY CONSTRIANTS

Keys are nothing but attributes which are used to uniquely identify the roux in a relation.

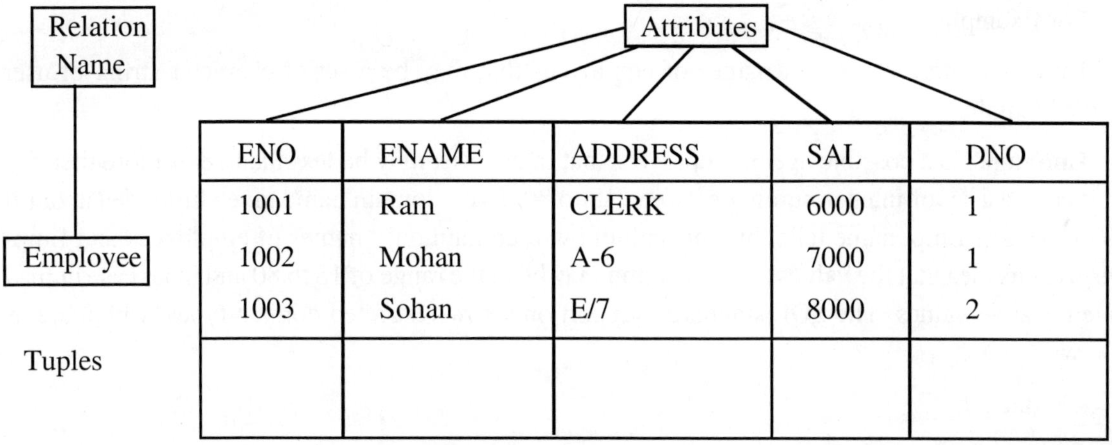

Employee Table Relation

In the figure the attribute EMPNO has this property this can be used to distinguish a rows or tuples from another rows or tuples relationships are expressed in the data values of the primary and foreign keys.

1. **Primary Key :** A primary key is a column or columns in a table whose values uniquely identify each row in a table.

In the Employee table, we might use ENAME to find a particular entry. But that column does not make a good key. Just imagine what will happen if more than one employee have same name "Ram". In most of the cases we shall create our own keys to ensure that they are unique. For example we have created EMPNO as identification number.

The relationship between the primary key and the rest of data is *one-to-one* that is each entry for a key points to exactly one employee row.

2. **Composite Key or Concatenated Keys :** In many cases, when we use more than one column as a part of the primary key. These are called Composite Keys or Concatenated Keys. We use composite keys when the table contains one to many or many-to-many relationships.

3. **Foreign Key :** A foreign key is a column or columns whose values are the same at the primary key of another table. We can think of a foreign key as a copy of primary key from another relational table. The relationship is made between two relational tables by matching the values of the foreign key in one table with the values of the primary key in another.

DOMAIN CONSTRAINTS

A domain is a collection of data that can appear in each column and the data type of every column, or to be more precise, we can call as the data type of every domain is already defined we specify the data type for data values that form a domain. The name of the domain may be specified in such away that it may interpret the data type of its domain.

For Example

Emp—Name : The set of names of employees that may be a set of character string of user defined length.

Emp age : is a possible age of employees that in no case. may be less than 18 or more then 80. So it can be a set of integer number between 18 to 80. Bach domain name gives little idea about it data type, *e.g.* Emp. name tells that this column will contain only names of employees and Emp-age gives us idea that the values of this column may be in the range of 18 to 80 and in no case ut may have negative values. The SQL standards support only fow restricted domain types, which are as follows :

- Integer
- Small Integer
- Fixed point number (with user defined precision)
- Fixed character string (with user defend length)
- Floating point numbers (with user defined precision)
- Floating point and double floating point number (with machine dependent provision). (To Read Relational Algera and Relational calculous first known about query language)

QUERY LANGUAGES

- A query language is a language through which we communicate with database. When we want to read or write something into or from existing database then we use query language we can category these query languages as either procedural query language or non-procedural query language. Relational Algebra and Relational calculus are two formal query languages.

1. Relational Algebra : Relational Algebra is a procedural language. When as Relational calculus is an non-procedural language.

Non-procedural Query Language

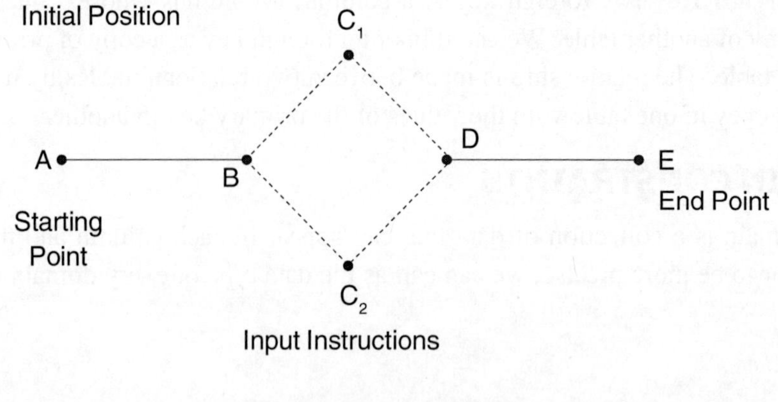

Start from point A and reach to point E (Here we have first given instructions, we have not specified how to reach point E).

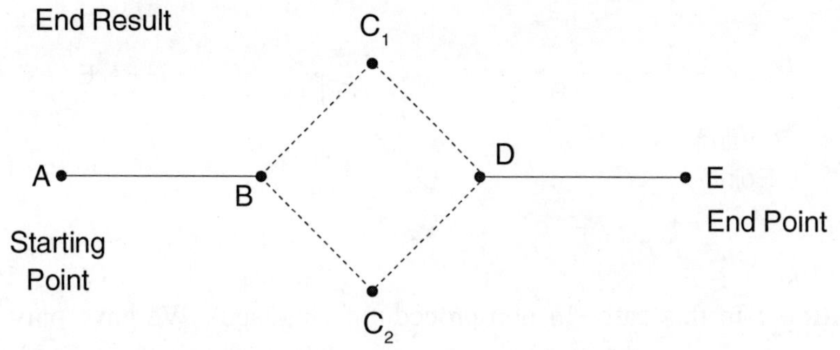

In Procedural Query Language

Case 1. Input Instructions

1. Start from point A
2. Go to point B
3. Go to point C1
4. Go to point D
5. Reach to point E.

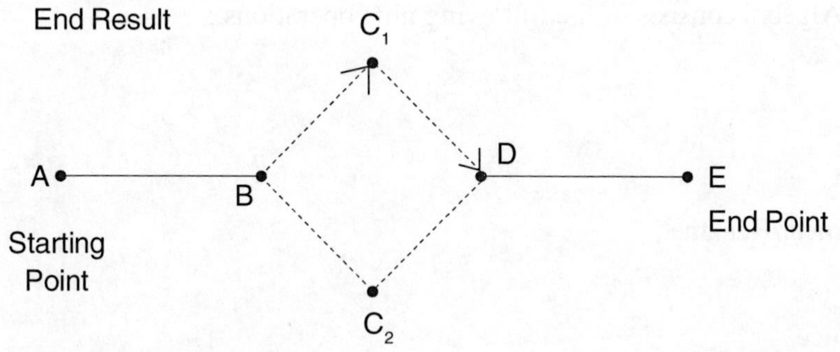

Case 2. Alternatively we may write another set of Instructions.

1. Start from point A
2. Go to point B
3. Go to point C2
4. Go to point D
5. Reach to point E

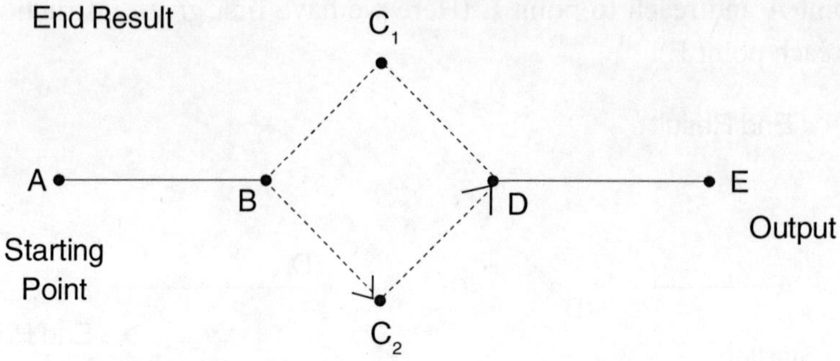

Explaination : In this case (In non-procedural language). We gave only desired output as Input. We have not mentioned how each step is to be executed in order to obtain End-result.

Conclusion : End Result is same in both cases

Explanation : On this case (In procedural language) we have given each step in order to get desired output.

Conclusion : End Result is same in both cases.

RELATIONAL ALGEBRA

Relational Algebra is one of the two query languages associated with relational model. Queries in relational algebra are composed using different operators.

Relational Algebra consists of the following nine operations :

1. Select
2. Project
3. Product
4. Assignment/Rename.
5. Unions
6. Difference
7. Intersection
8. Join
9. Divide/Division

1. **The Select Operation :** The select operation is used to create a relation from another relation by selecting only those entire rows (from the original relation) that satisfies given condition.

The EMP Relation

Emp no.	Emp name	Designation	Salary	Dept no.
1001	Akhilesh	Clerk	5000	1
1002	Ashish	Sales pers on	5500	1
1003	Sohan	Sales person	6000	2
1004	Mohan	PRO	6500	2
1005	Ram	PRO	10500	2
1006	Rahul	Manager	11000	2

The Dept Relation

Dept. No.	Dept. name	Relation
1	Account	Delhi
2	Address	Bombay

Query : Given all information for employees of Dept no 2.

σ Dept_no_“2” (Emp.)

Emp no.	Emp name	Designation	Salary	Dept no.
1003	Sohan	Sales person	6000	2
1004	Mohan	PRO	6500	2
1005	Ram	PRO	10,500	2
1006	Rahul	Manager	11000	2

Result of Dept no = “2” (Emp)

Query : Give all information for employees who are not in Dept no. 2

σ Dept_no “2” (Emp.)

Emp no.	Emp name	Designation	Salary	Dept no.
1001	Akhelesh	Clerk	5000	1
1002	Ashish	Sales person	5500	1

2. **Comparison operators**

We can also use comparison operators (>, , =, <,).

\> σ salary > 10500 (Emp.)

Emp. No	Emp. Name	Designation	Salary	Dept. No
100.6	Rahul	Manager	11,000	2

σ salary 10500 (Emp)

Emp. No	Emp. Name	Designation	Salary	Dept. No
1005	Ram	PRO	10500	2
1006	Rahul	Mager	1000	2

= σ salary 11000(Emp)

Emp. No	Emp. Name	Designation	Salary	Dept. No
1006	Rahul	Manager	11000	2

< σ salary <5500 (Emp)

Emp. No	Emp. Name	Designation	Salary	Dept. No
1001	Akhilesh	Clerk	5000	1

σ salary 5500 (Emp)

Emp. No	Emp. Name	Designation	Salary	Dept. No
1001	Akhilesh	Clerk	5,000	1
1002	Ashish	Sales person	5500	1

3. **Connectives :** We can also conbine more than one set of results using connectives, AND (Λ) and or (V).

Query : Given the information of all those employees who are in Dept no 1 and who are getting salary more than 5000.

σ (Dept - no = "1") ∧ (Salary > 5000)

Emp no.	Emp name	Designation	Salary	Dept no.
1002	Ashish	Sales person	5500	1

Result of σ (Dept - no = "1") (salary > 5000) (Emp)

Query : Give the information of all those employees who are working in Dept 1 or who are getting more than 5000 (in any department)

σ (Dept _ no = "1") (salery > 5000) (Emp)

Emp no.	Emp name	Designation	Salary	Dept no.
1001	Akhilesh	**Clerk**	5000	1
1002	Ashish	Sales Person	5500	1
1003	Sohan	Sales person	6000	2
1004	Mohan	PRO	16500	2
1005	Ram	PRO	10500	2
1006	Rahul	manager	11000	2

Result of σ Dept - no = "1" ^ salary > 5000 (EMP)

4. **The project operation** : The project operator is denoted by the Greek letter pi (π). The project operator allow us to extract desired column(s) from a relation that satisfies given condition. The basic difference between. Select and Project operator is as given below :

Select operator	Project operator
The select operator selects entire row (all columns) that sctisfies the given cendition, for example. σ Dept. no = "2" (Emp)	The project operator can select one or more than one calumn (insteed of entire row) out of row(s) that satisfaces given condition for example. π Emp. no. Emp name (σ Dept. no. = "2" (Emp.)

Select operator

σ Dept - no = "2" (Emp)

Emp no.	Emp name	Designation	Salary	Dept no.
1003	Sohan	Sales persorn	6000	2
1004	Mohan	PRO	6500	2
1005	Ram	PRO	10,500	2
1006	Rahul	Manager	1000	2

Project operator

π Exp. no. Exp. name (σ Dept. no. = "2")

ENO	Emp.No
1003	Sohan
1004	Mohan
1005	Ram
1006	Rahul

Query: Show names and designation of all employees.

π Emp. name, designation (EMP)

Emp. name	Designation
Akhilesh	**Clerk**
Ashish	Sales person
Sohan	Sales person
Mohan	PRO
Ram	PRO
Rahul	Manager

Result of ∧ Emp-name, designation (Emp.)

Query. Show Emp-name, Designation who salary is more than 10000 σ salary > 10000 (Emp.)

π Emp.–name, Designation (σ salary > 10,000) (Emp.)

Emp-name	Designation
Ram	PRO
Rahul	Manager

π Emp. name, Designation (σ salary > 10000)

5. The product operations is indicated by * or X. It is identical to mathematical operation which creates cartesian product of two sets. relation r = Dapt x Emp.

The relation scheme (Emp. sal.) for r is (Dept. Dept no., Dept. dept-name, Dept, location, Emp. Emp No, Emp. emp - Name, Emp. (location, Emp. Salary, Emp. Dept-no).

Emp. Dept. No.	Emp. Dept. Name	Emp. location	Emp. Emp. No.	Emp. Name	Emp. Designation	Emp. Salary	Emp. Dept. No.
1	Account	Delhi	1001	Akhilesh	**Clerk**	5000	1
1	Account	Delhi	1002	Ashish	Sales person	5500	1
1	Account	Delhi	1003	Sohan	Sales Person	6000	2
1	Account	Delhi	1004	Mohan	PRO	6500	2
1	Account	Delhi	1005	Ram	PRO	10,500	2
1	Account	Delhi	1006	Rohul	Manager	11000	2
2	Activies	Bombay	1001	Akilish	**Clerk**	5000	1
2	Activies	Bombay	1002	Ashish	Sales person	5500	1
2	Akhilesh	Bombay	1003	Sohan	Sales Person	6000	2
2	Akhilesh	Bombay	1004	Mohan	PRo	6500	2
2	Akhilesh	Bombay	1005	Ram	PRo	10500	
2	Akhilesh	Bombay	1006	Rahul	Manager	11000	2

Result of Dept. X Emp.

$A \times B = \{(1, 2, 3)\} \times \{2\ A\}$

$A \times B = \{(1, 2)\ (1, 4)\ (2, 2), (2, 4)\ (3, 2)\ (3, 4)\}$

Carterisan product

Qurey : Find all Employee - names for Account department and their salary.

σ dept _ name = "Account" (Dept. × Emp)

Emp. Dept. No.	Emp. Dept. Name	Emp. location	Emp. Emp. No.	Emp. Name	Emp. Designation	Emp. Salary	Emp. Dept. No.
1	Account	Delhi	1001	Akhitesh	Clerk	5000	1
1	Account	Delhi	1002	Ashih	Sales person	5500	1
1	Account	Delhi	1003	Sohan	Sales person	6000	2
1	Account	Delhi	1004	Mohan	PRD	6500	2
1	Account	Delhi	1005	Ram	PRD	10500	2
1	Account	Bombay	1006	Rahul	Manager	11000	2

Result of

Dept_name = "Account" (Dept X Emp.)

However the Emp. Dept_no may contain employees of other departments also. Dept. dept no

Employees of other departments also.

σ Dept. dept no = Emp. dept - no.

σ Dept. dept-no = Emp. dept_no (σDept_name = "Account" (Dept × Emp.)

Since we want only employee name and salary, so finally we can write.

π Emp. - name, salary (σ Dept. Dept_no= Emp. dept no (σ dept~nar = "Account" (Dept × Emp)

Emp. emp – name	Emp. salary
Akhilesh	5000
Ashish	5500

6. The (Assignment or. Rename) operation

This operator is also known as Rename operator.

Query

Find the names of all employees who are in the same Dept_no as Akhilesh

π Dept_no (Emp_name = "Akilesh" (Emp))

This type of problems are solved using Assignment/Rename operator, denoted by "P". The expression *P* × (*m*) returns relation in under the name × We shall use to rename one reference to the EMP relation and thus reference the relation twice without any ambiguity.

π Emp.Dept_no (π EMP2. Dept_no = **Emp**. Dept_no

(EMP × (π Dept. no (σEmp_name = (σEMP)))) "Akhilesh"

The result of this query is shown in

Emp-name

Akilesh

Ashish

7. **The Union Operator :** The union operation denoted by "U" combines data from two relations.

Query : Find all employees names whose salary is more than 10000 or belongs to Dept. no 1. to answer the above query we shall split it into two parts.

Find all employee names who are department no.1.

π Emp.-name (σDept_no= "1" $^{(EMP)}$). (1)

Find all employee names whose salary is more than 10,000.

π Emp._name (σ salary > 10,000$^{(EMP)}$ (2)

joining both queries OR.

(π Emp._name σ Dept_no = "1" $^{(EMP)}$) U (π Emp._name)

(σ salary > 10,000$^{(EMP)}$)

8. Difference operator : The Difference operator, denoted by – allows us to identify rows that are in one relation but not in other relation.

Emp._no.	Emp_name
1001	Akhilesh
1002	Ashish
1003	Sohan
1004	Mohan

Exp. -no	Emp_name
1001	Akhilesh
1002	Ashish
1003	Sohan
1004	Mohan

Emp. no	Exp. name
1001	Akhilesh

Query.

Find all employes names who have salary more than 5,000 but not in Dept _ no 2.

Ist step m = ⩒ (Emp-name (σsalary > 5000$^{(Emp)}$)

Emp-name
Akhilesh
Sohan
Mohan
Ram
Rahul

Second step

To find out "employees in Dept. no. "2",

n = πEmp-name σ (Dept-no-no="2"$^{(Emp)}$)

Emp-name
Sohan
Mohan
Ram
Rahul

To answer the above query m-n

Emp.-name
Ashish

9. **Intersection Operator :** The Intersection operator, indicated by "$\cap$" allows the rows that are common to two relations.

Emp. name	Emp-name	Emp-name
Ashish	Sohan	Sohan
Sohan	Mohan	Mohan
Mohan	Ram	Ram
Ram	Rahul	
Relation *r*	Relation *s*	Relation $r \cap s$.

Query : Find all employee names who have salary more than 5,000 on belong to Dept _no. for this query also we shall find correct result is two steps.

We known now to find out "employee name who have salary more than 5000"

$r = \pi$Emp_name (σsalary > 5000$^{(EMP)}$)

Emp-name
Ashish
Sohan
Mohan
Ram
Rahul

*More we also known that how to find "Employees in Dept._no2"

Emp-name
Sohan
Mohan
Ram
Rahul

S = $\wedge$ Emp-name ($^{\sigma}$Dept-no = '2'$^{[EMP]}$)

Finally, we get the correct answer

$r \cap s \rightarrow$

Emp. name
Sohan
Mohan
Ram
Rahul

10. **Join Operator:** The JOIN operation, denoted by $\bowtie$ is used to combine related tuples from two relations into single tuples.

Query : Find all employee names with department and location.

πEmp. Emp._name, Dept. Dept name, Dept. location

(σ Dept. Dept_no = Emp. Dept - no (Dept. $\bowtie$ Emp))

11. **The Divide operator:** The Divide operator denoted by "/" creates a new relation by selecting the rows in one relation that match every row in another relation.

Query : Find all Employees of department located at Delhi.

Execute this query in two steps.

First step. In first step we shall find out dept no located at Delhi.

Dept_no
1

r_1 = πDept-no (σ Location = "Delhi"(Dept))

Second step — Now find Emp. name, Dept-no pairs.

r_2 = πEmp-name, Dept-no (Emp)

Emp. name	Dept. no
Akhilesh	1
Ashish	1
Sohan	2
Mohan	2
Ram	2
Rahul	2

To give correct answer to above query we shall divide relation : answer r_1 by r_2.

Or we can also write r_1/r_2

Emp. name	Dept. no.
Akhilesh	1
Ashish	1

RELATIONAL CALCULUS

Relational Calculus uses a different approach than relational algebra, but both language are logically equivalent. Any query that can be solved by relational algebra can also be solved by relational calculus. The Relational calculus is a non-procedural query language where relational algebra is procedural query language. In non-procedural query language, the user *i.e.* not concerned with the details of how to obtain the end result, where as in procedure query language, we define each step in order to obtain the end result. In relational calculus, a query is expressed as a formula consisting variables. These is no mechanism to specify how formula should be evaluated. It is up to DBMS to transform these non-procedural queries into equivalent procedural queries.

There are two versions of relational calculus.

- **Relational Tuple calculus**
- **Relational Domain calculus.**

In **Relational Tuple calculus,** the variables represent the tuples from specified relation whereas in Relational Domain calculus, the variables represent values drawn from specified domain.

- Pepsi is a drink.
- Coke is a drink.
- Zen is a car.
- Santro is a car.

In each of above statement there is an object (*e.g.* Pepsi, Coka, Zen and Santro) and every object has certain features (*e.g.,* "drink". "car"). Features of objects which can also be called as predicate. The above statement can also he written as follows, starting with predicates and followed by objects and objects are enclosed in parenthesis.

- is a drink (Pepsi)
- is a drink (Coke)
- is a car (Santro)

Let's take one more step — omit it "is a" part from all above statements.

- Drink (Pepsi)
- Drink (Coke)
- Car (zen)
- Car (Santro)

Now if we use symbols for predicate and objects then we can represent all four statemants as:

$P(t)$

Where P is predicate, denoted by upper case letter is object, *t* is object, case letters is object, denoted by lower case letters. Objects can be known as variables or argument.

A predicate followed by its argument is called as an Atomic formula. We can obtain all above statements from function *P*(*t*)

P = Drink	Drink (Pepsi)
t = pepsi	
p = Drink	
t = Coke	Drink (Coke)
P = Car	
t = Zen	Car (Zen)
P = Car	
t = Santro	Car (Santro)

Relational Calculus, means, calculating with relations, is based on predicate calculus which is calculating with predicates. Predicate calculus is a formal language used to symbolize logical arguments in mathematics.

We can specify some logical connectors as follows.

• NOT or NEGATION	denoted by
• OR	devoted by $\vee$
• AND	denoted by $\wedge$
• IMPLICATION	denoted by $\rightarrow$

For example

Drink (Pepsi), Car (Zen) represents that "Pepsi is a drink and Zen is Car"

Quantifiers—We have two more symbols, which are known as quantifiers, which can be used in formula to make more intelligent, interesting and useful formula.

There are two styles of quantifiers

- Universal Quantifiers denoted by $\forall$
- Existential quantifiers denoted by

• **Existential Quantifiers :** Existential Quantifiers state that at least on of a particular type of thing exists. It is used to select particular rows) that satisfy given condition.

Query : Find Employee name whose salary is 5000.

Universal Quantifiers : Universal Quantifiers state that some condition applies to all or to every row of same type. It is used to provide the same functionalistic as divide function of relational algebra.

Query : Find every Employee name of Dept_no. 1

TUPLE AND DOMAIN CALCULUS

(1) Relational Tuple Calculus : When we white a relational algebra expression, we write a sequence of procedures in order to generate the result of the query. In relational tuple calculus we get the desired information, we do not write sequence of procedures for obtaining he descried information as we do in relational algebra.

write query in relational tuple

Calculcus as

$$\{t| \mathrm{P}(t)\}$$

where
- P is an expression/formula conusting of *t*
- T is set of typle variable S

The expression characterizes a set of tuples of *t* such that formula p (*t*) is true.

Query : Find employee name, Emp_no, Designation, Salary, Dept_no for employees whose salary over 10,000.

$$\{t \mid t \in \mathrm{Emp} \wedge t\,[\mathrm{salary}] > 10{,}000\}.$$

Now if we want only one attribute Emp_name

$$\{t \mid \exists \mathrm{s} \in \mathrm{Emp}\ (t\in \mathrm{Emp\_name}] = \mathrm{S}[\mathrm{Emp\_name}] \wedge \mathrm{S}[\mathrm{salary}] > 10000)\}$$

How to read this relation : A set of all tuples *t* such that exists a tuples s in relation Emp. for which the values of t and s for Emp._name attribute are equal and values for s for salary attribute is greater than 10,000.

Free and Bound variables : A tuple variable is said to be a free variable unless it is quantified by a or otherwise it is called free variable.

$$(\{t \mid t \in \mathrm{Emp} \wedge \exists\ s\ \mathrm{Dept.}\ (t[\mathrm{Dept.\ no}]=\mathrm{S}[\mathrm{Dept} = \mathrm{no.})]\}$$

In above formula *t* is free variable and *s* is bound variable and whole formula is called atomic formula.

An tuple relational calculus formula is built up out of atoms. An atom has one of following form :

Type 1

- $S \in r$ where *r* is a relation and *S* in a typle variable

Type 2 S, u are tuple variable.

• $S[x] \Xi u(y)$ x is an attribute on which S is defined y is an attribute on which u is defined Ξ is a comparison operator ($<, \leq, =, \quad , \geq \geq$).

We require that attributes x and y have domains whose members can be compared by Ξ.

Type 3

$S[x] \Xi C$ S is a typle variable X is

On attribute on what S is defined. [N] is a comparison operator C is a constant in the domain of atribute X.

Rules or building up formula using atoms

Formulacare built up from atoms using the following rules—

1. An atom is a formula
2. If P_1 in a are formula then P_1 and (P_1) are also formulae.
3. If P_1 and P_2 are formulae then $P_1 \quad P_2, P_1 \quad P_2$ and $P_1 \rightarrow P_2$ are also formulae.
4. If $P_1(S)$ is a formula where S is free tuple variable

Then : a or $\exists S \in r\,(P_1(S))$ and

$S \in r(P_1(S))$ are also formula.

It is possible to write equivalent expressions that are not identical in appearence, as was the case for relational algebra. In the tuple relational calculus these equivalences can be

(*a*) $P_1 \quad P_2$ is equivalent to $(\quad P_1 \quad P_2)$

(*b*) $t \in r(P_1(t))$ is equivalent to $E+ \in r(\quad A(t))$

(*c*) $P_1 \rightarrow P_2$ is equivalent to $P_1 \quad P_2$

(2) The Domain Relational Calculus

The Domain relational calculus formulae are also built from atom

A tuple relational calculus is expressed as $\{t \mid P(t)\}$, where as an expression in the Domain Relational calculus is expressed as:

$\{<x_1, x_2, x_3...x_n>|P(x_1, x_2,..x_n)\}$ where $x_1, x_2, x_3 x_n$ represent domain variables P represents a formula composed of atoms. (as was the case in tuple relational calculus)

An atom in the Domain Relational Calculus has one of the following forms :

(1) $<x_1, x_2, x_3...x_n> E_r$ where r is a relation on n attributes and $x_1, x_2...x_n$ are domain variables or domain constants.

(2) X Ξ C where *x* and *y* are domain variables and Ξ is comparison operator

(<, = , = , ?$_1$ >$_1$=)

(3) X Ξ C where *x* is a domain variables and C is domain variables and C is domain compatible constant Ξ is comparison operator

(<, =, =, ?$_1$>, =)

* **Rules for Building formulae from atoms—**

(1) An atom is a formula.

(2) If P_1 is a formula then P_1 and (P_1) are also formulae

(3) If P_1 and P_2 are formulae then P_1 P_2, P_1 P_2 and $P_1 \rightarrow P_2$ are also formulae.

(4) If P(*x*) is a formula where *x* is domain variable.

Then : $\exists x$ (p(*x*)) and

x (P (*x*)) are also formulae.

Query 1. Find Employee Name, Emp_no, Designation, Salary, Dept_no_for Employees salary in over 10,000.

{<*e, n, e, s,dn* >| P (*e, n, d, s, dn*) ∈ Emp S>10,000}

where *e, n, d, s, dn* represent Employee name, Emp-no$_1$ Designation salary, Dept_no respectively.

Query 2. Find Employee name whose salary is over. 10,000.

{< *e*>|∃*n, d, s, dn* (<*e, n, d, s, dn*>) ∈ Emp S> 10,000}.

Chapter 4

Introduction to SQL

Chapter Outline

CHARACTERISTICS OF SQL

SQL stands for structured query language SQL is the standard language for making queries in relational database Management packages such as SQL server, Ingers, Sybase, Oracle etc. The standard language for accessing client/server database is also SQL.

(*a*) SQL is oriented specifically around relational databases.

(*b*) SQL commands can operate on several groups of tables as single objects. Also it processes any quantity of information, retrieved from these tables, as a single unit.

(*c*) SQL allows use of temporary tables. Temporary tables are used for storing intermediate results. They are useful only for the duration the program ...... is in execution and gets deleted when the program terminates.

(*d*) SQL is well suited to a client server environment, where the DBMS resides on server and services the client's requests features such as connection management locking schemes and error diagnostics enable clients to communicate with a variety of DBMS packages.

(*e*) SQL provides a flexible transaction management. A transaction is a group of SQL statements that succeed or fail as a group. That is, if any one of the SQL statements fails, the whole transaction is aborted.

(*f*) SQL allows users to create domains as objects in a schema. The users can then declare table columns to be of domains rather than that of data types.

(*g*) SQL allows one to specify constraints, constants are rules for restricting the value that can be placed in a table column.

(*h*) Privileges can be granted or denied using SQL commands. Privileges are the rights to perform actions on database objects.

ADVANTAGES OF SQL

SQL has several simple to use commands for data processing activities. You can use for data processing activities. You can use SQL commands for the following purposes.

(*a*) Creating (defining), deleting, and medifying table structure.

(*b*) Defining the relationships between two or more tables.

(*c*) Insterting data into tables.

(d) Extracting data in meaningful ways, based on the table's defined relationships.

(*e*) Updating data. This includes maintaining the data in a database, and manipulating the stored values to keep the information current.

(*f*) Controlling a database. This includes system security and authorization which must be controlled and maintained.

SQL DATA TYPES AND LITERALS

Every field or column in a table is given a data type when a table is defined. These data types describe the kind of information which can be stored in a damain.

Since relational-database systems are based on the relationships between pieces of information ..... tubes of data must be clearly distinguished from one another, so that the appropriate processes and comparisons can be applied. In SQL this is done by assigning each field a data type that indicates the kind of values the field will contain. All the values in a given field must be of the same type.

Some of the common data types

(*a*) CHAR

(*b*) VARACHAR 2

(*c*) NUMBER

(*d*) DATE

(*e*) LONG

(*a*) **CHAR (size) :** A column defined with a CHAR datatype is allowed to store all types of characters which include letters — both upper case and lower case letters such as A, B, – Z and *a, b,* – *z*, special characters – like @ # and $, etc.

Size written in brackets after the word CHAR determine the length of data that can be stored, *i.e.*, the number of characters that can be stored in the field. Note that default 'size' is 1 and maximum size is 255.

(*b*) **VARCHAR 2 (size) :** It is similar to CHAR nut can store variable sized ...... a maximum length determined by 'size' . Maximum value the size can have is 2000 characters.

(*c*) **NUMBER (p, s) :** It is used to store variable length numeric data. The value of p determines the total number of digits possible to the left of decimal point. The second syllable S, determines the total number of digits possible the right of decimal point.

(*d*) **Date :** This type of data is used to store date and time information. Default format is DD – MM – YY.

(*e*) **Long :** Long data type stores variable length character strings containing upto 2 gigabytes size. But use of data type has got the following limitations :

(*a*) A table can not have more than one LONG type of data field.

(*b*) It cannot be indexed.

(*c*) It annot be used with SQL functions

(*d*) It cannot appear in **where, Group, By, Order By clauses.**

(*f*) **Type of SQL commands**

SQL commands can be classified into the following three types :

(*a*) Data Definition language commands

(*b*) Data manipulation language commands

(*c*) Data control language commands

(*a*) **Data Definition Language :** Data Definition language (or DDL) is a part of SSL which consists of those commands that create the objects (table, indexes, views etc.) in the database. Create. Drop, and Alter are a few commands of DDL language.

(*b*) **Data manipulation Language :** Data manipulation language (DML) is the part of SQL which consists of a set of commands that determine which values are present in the table at any given time.

DML is divided into three categories :

(*a*) Retrieving data,

(*b*) Manipulating data, and

(*c*) Updating data.

(*a*) **Retrieving Data :** Rctrieving data means getting information out of a tables. The commands for retrieving data items is **Select.**

(*b*) **Manipulating Data :** Maniputatiang data refers to the DML features that allow us to perform statistical functions on data, namely averaging and summing columns and other arithmetic functions.

(*c*) **Updating Data :** Updating data refers to inserting and deleting lows in tables and changing values in the columns.

DML has commands for dealing with retrieving, manipulating and updating a database. POL manipulation and updation, the commands are update, Insert and Delete.

(*d*) **Data Control Language :** Data control language (DCL) is another portion of SQL which allows of a security mechanism or access. It contains commands like Grant, revoke etc. These are also known as (ransaction control commands.

SQL OPERATORS AND THEIR PRECEDENCE

We need operator to do arithmetic operations such as addition, subtraction elcon column values similarly to perform relational compariscon, we need relational operators like ≥,|< =, > = , etc., SQL operators may be classified as :

- Arithmetic operators
- Relational operators

SQL have the following four arithmetic operators

(*a*) + (addition)

(*b*) – (Subtraction)

(*c*) * (Multiplication)

(*d*) / (Division)

In addition to the = , <, > and < = relational operators, SQL has the following comparison operators :

(*a*) LIKE

(*b*) IN

(*c*) BETWEEN

Precedence determines which operation will be performed first in an expression comprising of multiple operators.

Precedence of operators

Operator	Precedence
( )	HIGHEST
*/	
+ –	
< < = > > =	

Like in Between

A : **D or** **Lowest**

TABLES, VIEWS AND INDEXES

Tables, as you know, are a collection of related rows and columns describing some business processing entity such as a department, an employee a project, purchase orders etc.

A view is a logical sub-set of a table. To a user, a view will look first like, a table. But they are only images or descriptions of a table and do not store any physical data views can contain some or all of the columns of a table.

Indexes are pointers to specific rows in a table, They are logically ordered by the value of a key. For example, an index created Emp-code will store all the employees code numbers along with a pointer to the corresponding low, in a table.

QUERIES AND SUB QUERIES

Column Name	Type	Description
Dept.-Code	**Number** (2)	Unique code assigned to each department
Dept - Name	**Varchar 2(10)**	Department name
Floor	**Number** (1)	Location of the department

The **Department** table structure

(1) Create Table Command

Create table command basically defines a table name describing a set of named columns in a specified order. The syntax of the create table command.

Create table table name

(Columname datatype (Size));

for example create table for department table create table department

(**Dept-Code** number (2), Dept-name Varchar 2C (floor number (1));

(2) Insert Data Into Table

Insert into table name

(column name, column name)

Values (expression, expression);

for example insert data into department table

Insert into department

(dept_code, dept-name, floor)

Values ("1", 'NP', "2") ;

The character expressions must be enclosed in single quotes (').

(3) Select all record

Select * from table name;

(4) Selected Columns and all Rows

Select columnname, columnname from table name;

(5) Selected Rows and All columns

Select * from table name

Where search condition;

(6) Selected columns and selected Rows

Select columnname, columnname (10)

from table name where search condition;

SUBQUERIES

A subquery is a form of an SQL statement the appears inside another SQL statement. It is also termed as nested query. The statement containing a subquery is called a parent statement. The parent statement used the rows returned by the subquery.

It can be used by the following commands :

(1) To insert records in a target table

(2) To create table and insert records in the table created

(3) To update records in a target table

(4) To create views

(5) To provide values for conditions in WHERE, HAVING, IN etc. used with SELECT, UPDATE and DELETE statements.

AGGREGATE FUNCTIONS

Functions that act on a set of values are called as aggregate functions. For example, SUM, is a function which calculates the total of a set of numbers. A aggregate function returns a single result arow for a group of queries rows.

(a) AVG — syntax AVG ([**Distinct/All**]*n*)

purpose Returns average vaue of '*n'*},

ignoring null values

Exampe — **Select** AVG (Sell-price) "Average" from product – master;

(b) MIN Syntax – MIN ([**Distinct/all**]expr]

Purpose Returns minimum value of 'expr'

Example — Select MIN (bal-due) "Minimum Balance" Fron Client master;

(c) COUNT(expr) – **Syntax** – **Count** ([**Distinct/All**]expr)

Purpose Returns the number of rows where 'expr' is not null.

Example— **Select Count** (product - no) "**No** of Products" From product-mastir;

(d) MAX

Syntax **Max ([district/All]**expr)

Purpose Returns maximum value of 'expr'

(e) SUM Syntax SUM ([District/All]*n*)

Purpose Refuens sum of values of '*n*'

Example Select Sum (bal-due) Total Balance Due" From client-master.

Example SELECT SUM (bal-due) Tobal Balance Due" From chent master)

DESERT, DELETE AND UPDATE OPERATIONS INSERT OF DATA INTER TABLES

Syntax : INSERT INTO TABLENAME

(Column name, expression Column name)

Delete Operations

* *Removal of All Rows—*

Syntax : Delete From table name;

Example — Delete all rows from the table client — Master

Delete From client master

**Removal of a specified Rows—*

Syntax : **Delete From** tablename **where** search condition;

Example : Delete rows from the table client - master where the value in the bal - due field is less than 500. **Delete from** client - master where bal - due <500;

Update operations

Updating of All Rows

Syntax : **Update** tablename

Set Column name = expression, column name = expression;

Example : Give every employee a bonus of 15%. Calculate the 15% amount based on the value held in the column basic sal of the table enp-master and update the values held in the column net _ sal.

UPDATE emp _ master

Set netsal = net _ sal + basic - sal * 0.15;

Updating records conditionally

Syntax : **Update** tablename

Set column name = expression, column name = expression

Where column name = expression;

Example : Update the table client – master change the contents of the field name to 'vijay kadam' and the contents of the field address to 'SCT Jay Apartments' for the record identified by the field client – no retaining the value 'CO2000.

Update client – master

SET name 'Vijay kadam', address 1=

'SCT Jay Apartment'

Where client - no =' CO2000';

JOINS, UNIONS, INTERSECTION MINUS JOINS

Joining Multiple Tables (Equi Joins)

Sometimes we require to treat multiple tables as though they were a single entity. Then a single SQL sentence can manipulate data from all the tables. To achieve this, we have to join tables. Tables are formed on columns that have the same data type and data width in the tables.

Example : Relative the order numbers, client names and their order dates from (14) the client – master and sales – order tables. The order date should be display in 'DD/ MM/ YY' format and sorted in as clouding order.

Select orders – no, name, to_ char (order_ date, 'DD/MM/YY') "Order Date"

From sales a– order, client – master where client – master, client - no = sales – order - client - no order by to-char (order - date, 'DD/MM/YY');

Sub Queries (nested Quesies)

You can nest the SQL queries within one another. Nested query or subquery is an SQL SELECT statement inside another SELECT or action statement.

For example

Select Emp_Name From Employee

Where Dept – Code = (Select aDept – Code From Employee

Where Emp – Name = 'Amar Roy');

(i) ***Correlated Nested Queries*** **:** In correlated nested queries, the inner query is executed once for each row in the outer query. In a correlates mested query, the column value used in the inner query refers to the column value apresent in the outer query. *For example.*

Select Emp – Code, Emp – Name, Basic From Employee "E"

Where Basic> (Select Avg (Basic) from Employee

Where (Dept " Code = E. Dept – Code);

***Unions, Inter section and Minus**

The set operators **union, Intersect and Menus** can be used to combine information from several tables.

The union operator merge outputs of two or more queries into a set of row and columns. The rows and columns which are to be merged must be of the same data type.

For example : names of employee working in department 10 and 20.

Select Emp – name From Employee

Where Dupt –Code = 10

Union

Select Emp – Name From Employee

Where Dept – Code = 20

The intersect operator returns the rows that are common. For example return designations that are common to both department 20 and 30.

Select Desig from Employee

Where Dept – Code = 20

Intersect

Select Desig from employee

Where Dept - code = 30

The **Minus** operator will return the rows that are unique to the first query, *i.e.* lows which are not present in the recond query

For example, designations present in department 20, but not in department 30

Select Desig from Employee

Where Dept – Code = 20

Minus

Select Desig From Employee

Where Dept – Code = 30

(ii) Cursors in SQL : A cursor allows you to name these work areas and access their stored information. There are two types of cursors. These are;

(*a*) Implicit cursors.
(*b*) Explici cursors
(*c*) Handling cursors

(*a*) **Implicit cursors** : Implicit cursors are the cursors declared automatically by the Query processing software cursors are declared implicity for all Data Manipulation Language (DML) statements. Fo example, the results of a SELECT query is stored in an unnamed cursor by the query processing software.

(b) **Explicit cursors** : Explicit cursors are user – defined cursors declared in the EXEC -End EXEC block. These cursors can be named and manipulated through other statements within the block. Explicit cursors allow multiple rows to be processed from the query result.

(c) **Handling cursors :** Cursors are handled through the open, fetch and close statements.

(1) *Open statement :* A cursor is opened for executing a query After a cursor is opened, the rows returned by the query are available for fetching. The syntax for opening a cursor is as follows :

Open < Cursor Name >

The open statement causes the database (18) system to execute the query and to save the results within the cursor. The cursor will point to the first row of the query result.

(2) *Fetch statement :* The retrieval of lows returned by a query execution is done through the fetch statement the syntax for fetch statement is as follows :

Fetch < Cursor name > Into < variables > For each column – Value of the low returned by the query, there must be a corresponding variable in the Into list Also their data types must also be compatible.

(3) *Close statement :* A cursor can be closed using the close statement the syntax for close statement is as follows :

Close < cursor name >

For the sample query, the statement is of the following form:

EXEC SQL close c End Exec

The close statement is used to indicate the database system to delete the cursor that held the results of the query. The cursor can then be reopened if needed.

Example 1. Define Relational Algebra with Examples

From the example, one can see that for complicated cases a large amount of the answer is formed from operator names, such as PROJECT and JOIN. It is therefore commonplace to use symbolic notation to represent the operators.

- SELECT → σ (signa)
- PROJECT → π (pi)
- PRODUCT →× (pi)
- JOIN → |×| (bow–tie)
- UNION → (cup)
- INTERSECTION → ∩ (cap)
- DIFFERENCE → – (minus)
- RENAME → ρ (rho)

Usage

The symbolic operators are used as with the verbal ones. So, to find all employees in department 1:

$\text{SELECT}_{\text{dipno = 1}}(\text{employee})$

becomes $\sigma_{\text{depno = 1}}(\text{employee})$

Conditions can be combined together using ∧ (AND) and ∨ (OR). For example, all employees in department 1 called 'Smith':

$\text{SELECT}_{\text{depno = 1} \wedge \text{surname = 'Smith'}}(\text{employee})$

becomes$\sigma_{\text{depno = 1} \wedge \text{surname = 'Smith'}}(\text{employee})$

The use of the symbolic notation can lend itself to brevity. Even better, when the JOIN is a natural join, the JOIN condition may be omitted from |X| . The earlier example resulted in:

$\text{PROJECT}_{\text{dnane}}(\text{department JOIN}_{\text{depno = depno}}($

$\text{PROJECT}_{\text{depno}}(\text{employee JOIN}_{\text{depno = depno}}($

$\text{PROJECT}_{\text{dnane}}(\text{empcourse JOIN}_{\text{depno = depno}}($

$\text{PROJECT}_{\text{courseno}}(\text{SELECT}_{\text{cname = 'Futher Accounting'}}\text{Course}))))))$

becomes

π_{dname} (dempartment |×| (

π_{dname} (employee |×| (

π_{dname} (empcourse |×| (

$\pi_{courseno}$ ($\sigma_{cname = \text{'Further Accounting'}}$ Course)))))))

Rename Operator

The rename operator returns an existing relation under a new name. $\rho_A(B)$ is the relation B with its name changed to A. For example, find the employees in the same Department as employee 3.

$\rho_{emp2.surname,emp2.forenames}$ (

$\sigma_{employee.empno = 3 \wedge employee.depno = emp2.depno}$ (

employee × (σ_{emp2}employee)

)

)

Equivalence

A|×|$_c$B □ $\pi_{a1,a2,...aN}(\sigma_c(A \times B))$

• where *c* is the join condition (eg A.al = B.al),

• and a1,a2,...aN are all the attributes of A and B without repetition. c is called the join–condition, and is usually the comparison of primary and foreign key. Where there are N tables, there are usually N–1 join–conditions. In the case of a natural join, the conditions can be missed out, but otherwise missing out conditions results in a cartesian product (a common mistake to make).

Equivalences

The same relational algebraic expression can be written in many different ways. The order in which tuples appear in relations is never significant.

• $A \times B$ □ $B \times A$

• $A \cap B$ □ $B \cap A$

• A□B□B□A

• (A – B) is not the same as (B –A)

• $\sigma_{c1}(\sigma_{c2}(A))$ □ $\sigma_{c2}(\sigma_{c1}(A))$ □ $\sigma_{c1 \wedge c2}(A)$

• $\pi_{a1}(A)$ □ $\pi_{a1}(\pi_{a1,etc}(A))$

where etc. represents any other attributes of A

• many other equivalences exist.

While equivalent expressions always give the same result, some may be much easier to evaluate that others.

When any query is submitted to the DBMS, its query optimiser tries to find the most efficient equivalent expression before evaluating it.

Example 2. Define comparison Between Relational Algebra and Structured Query Language(SQL).

Comparing RA and SQL —

RELATIONAL ALGEBRA:

- is closed (the result of every expression is a relation)
- has a rigorous foundation
- has simple semantics
- is used for reasoning, query optimisation, etc.

SQL:

- is a superset of relational algebra
- has convenient formatting features, etc.
- provides aggregate functions
- has complicated semantics
- is an end–user language.

Any relational language as powerful as relational algebra is called relationally complete.

A relationally complete language can perform all basic, meaningful operations on relations.

Since SQL is a superset of relational algebra, it is also relationally complete.

Example 3. How do you implement one–to–one, one–to–many and many–to–many relationships while designing tables?

One–to–One relationship can be implemented as a single table and rarely as two tables with primary and foreign key relationships.

One–to–Many relationships are implemented by splitting the data into two tables with primary key and foreign key relationships.

Many–to–Many relationships are implemented using a junction table with junction table.

Example 4. What's the difference between a primary key and a unique key?

Both primary key and unique enforce uniqueness of the column on which they are defined. But by default primary key creates a clustered index on the column, where are unique creates a nonclustered index by default. Another major difference is that, primary key doesn't allow NULLs, but unique key allows one NULL only.

Example 5. What are user defined datatypes and when you should go for them?

User defined datatypes let you extend the base SQL Server datatypes by providing a descriptive name, and format to the database. Take for example, in your database, there is a column called Flight_Num which appears in many tables. In all these tables it should be varchar(8) In this case you could create a user defined data types called flight_num_type of varchar (8).

Example 6. Define candidate key, alternate key, composite key.

A candidate key is one that can identify each row of a table uniquely. Generally a candidate key becomes the primary key of the table. If the table has more than one candidate key, one of them will become the primary key, and the rest are called alternate keys. A key formed by combining at least two or more columns is called composite key.

Example 7. What are constraints? Explain different types of constraints.

Constraints enable the RDBMS enforce the integrity of the databse automatically, without needing you to create triggers, rule or defaults. Types of constraints: NOT NULL, CHECK UNIQUE, PRIMARY KEY, FOREIGN KEY.

For an explanation of these constraints see books online for the pages titled: "Constraints" and "CREATE TABLE", "ALTER TABLE"

Example 8. What is an index? What are the types of indexes? How many clustered.

Indexes can be created on a table? I create a separate index on each column of a table. What are the advantages and disadvantages of this approach?

Indexes in SQL Server are similar to the indexes in books. They help SQL Server retrieve the data quicker.

Indexes are of two types. Clustered indexes and non–clustered indexes. When you create a clustered index on a table, all the rows in the table are stored in the order of the clustered index key. So, there can only one clustered index per table. Non–clustered indexes have their own storage separate from the table data storage. Non–clustered indexes are stored as B–tree structures (so do clustered indexes), with the leaf level nodes having the index key and it's row located. The row located could be the RID or the Clustered index key, depending up on the absence or presence of clustered index on the table. If you create an index on each column of a table, it improves the query performance, as the query optimizer can choose from all the existing indexes to come up with an efficient execution plan. At the same time, data modification operations (such as INSERT, UPDATE, DELETE) will become slow, as every time data changes in the table, all the indexes need to be updated. Another disadvantage is that, indexes need disk space, the more indexes you have, more disk space is used.

Example 9. What are cursors? Explain different types of cursors. What are the disadvantages of cursors? How can you avoid cursors?

Cursors allow row–by–row prcessing of the resultset. Types of cursors: Static, Dynamic, Forward–only, keyset–driven. See books online for more information.

Disadvantages of cursors: Each time you fetch a row from the cursor, it results in a network roundtrip, where as a normal SELECT query makes only one rowundtrip, however large the resultset is. Cursors are also costly because they require more resources and temporary storage (results in more IO operations). Furthere, there are restrictions on the SELECT statements that can be used with some types of cursors. Most of the times, set based operations can be used instead of cursors. Here is an example:

If you have to give a flat hike to you employees using the following criteria:

Salary between 30000 and 40000 -- 5000 hike

Salary between 40000 and 55000 -- 7000 hike

Salary between 55000 and 65000 -- 9000 hike

In this situation many developer tend to use a cursor, determine each employee's salary and update his salary according to the above formula. But the same can be achieved by multiple update statements or can be combined in a single UPDATE statement as shown below:

UPDATE tbl_emp SET salary =

CASE WHEN salary BETWEEN 30000 AND 40000 THEN salary + 5000 WHEN salary BETWEEN 40000 AND 55000 THEN salary + 7000 WHEN salary BETWEEN 55000 AND 65000 THEN salary + 10000 END

Another situation in which developers tend to use cursors: You need to call a stored procedure when a column in a particular row meets certain condition. You don't have to use cursors for this. This can be achieved using WHILE loop, as long as there is a unique key to identify each row. For examples of using WHILE loop for row by row processing, check out the 'My code library' section of my site or search for WHILE.

Example 10. Write down the general syntax for a SELECT statements covering all the option.

SELECT select_list

[INTO new_table]

FROM table_source

[WHERE search_condition]

[GROUP BY group_by_expression]

[HAVING search_condition]

[ORDER BY order_expression [ASC | DESC]]

Example 11. What is a join and explain different types of joins.

Joins are used in queries to explain how different tables are related.

Joins also let you select data from a table depending upon data from another table.

Types of joins: INNER JOINs, OUTER JOINs, CROSS JOINs, OUTER JOINs are further classified as LEFT OUTER JOINS, RIGHT OUTER JOINS and FULL OUTER JOINS.

Example 12. What is a self join? Explain it with an example.

Self join is just like any other join, except that two instances of the same table will be joined into he query. Here is an example: Employees table which contains rows for normal employees as well as managers. So, to find out the managers of all the employees, you need a self join.

```
CREATE TABLE emp
(
empid into,
mgrid into,
empname char(10)
)
INSERT emp SELECT 1,2, 'Vyas'
INSERT emp SELECT 2,3, 'Mohan'
INSERT emp SELECT 3, NULL, 'Shobha'
INSERT emp SELECT 4,2, 'Shridhar'
INSERT emp SELECT 5,2, 'Sourabh'
SELECT t1.empname [Employee], t2.empname [Manager]
FROM emp t1, emp t2
WHERE t1.mgrid = t2.empid
```

Here's an advanced query using a LEFT OUTER JOIN that even returns the employees without managers (super bosses)

```
SELECT t1.empname [Employee], COALESCE (t2.empname, 'No manager')
[Manager]
FROM emp t1
LEFT OUTER JOIN
emp t2
```

ON

t1.mgrid = t2.empid

EXERCISE

1. Define the following terms:

   (*i*) Super key

   (*ii*) Candidate key

   (*iii*) Primary key

2. What is views? How view is created? What are advantage of view?
3. Define foreign key. What is the concept used for defining the foreign key? How does it play a role in join operational?
4. What do you mean by data definition in SQL? Which statements are used for this? Explains.
5. Give the system and usage of alter and drop command of data definition in SQL.
6. What do you mean by data manipulation in SQL? Which statements are used for this?
7. Write short note about relational calculus. How does tuple relational calculus differ from domains relational calculus?
8. Dr. E. F. codd has given 12 rules for the relational data model "codd's rules" explain each in detail.
9. Explain the Integrity rules with suitable examples.
10. What is Relational Algebra? Explain basic operations in relational algebra.
11. Write short note on the following :

    (*i*) Projection (π)

    (*ii*) Selection (σ)

    (*iii*) Join (∞)

Solved Examples

Example 1. Consider the following tables

	P	
A	**B**	**C**
a	b	c
b	c	a
c	a	b

	Q	
A	**B**	**C**
c	b	a
b	a	c
b	c	a

R

J

J_1

J_2

J_3

Perform the following relational algebra operations.

(*i*) P ∪ Q

(*ii*) P ∩ Q

(*iii*) P — Q and Q — P

(*iv*) P × R and Q× R

Ans.

(*i*) P ∪ Q

A	**B**	**C**
a	b	c
b	c	a
c	a	b
c	b	a
b	a	c

(*ii*) P ∩ Q

A	**B**	**C**
b	c	a

(*iii*) P — Q and Q — P

P — Q

A	B	C
a	b	c
c	a	b

Q — P

A	B	C
c	b	a
b	a	c

(*iv*) P × R and Q × R

P × R

A	B	C	J
a	b	c	J_1
a	b	c	J_2
a	b	c	J_3
b	c	a	J_1
b	c	a	J_2
b	c	a	J_3
c	a	b	J_1
c	a	b	J_2
c	a	b	J_3

Q × R

A	B	C	J
c	b	a	J_1
c	b	a	J_2
c	b	a	J_3
b	a	c	J_1
b	a	c	J_2
b	a	c	J_3
b	c	a	J_1
b	c	a	J_2
b	c	a	J_3

Example 2. Consider the following scheme —

SUPPLIER (SUPPLIERID, SUPPLIER – NAME, SUPPLIER _ ADDRESS)

PARTS (PART _ ID, PART _ NAME, COLOR)

CATALOG (SUPPLIER _ ID, PART _ ID, COST)

Write the following queries in Relational Algebra and SQL.

(*a*) Find the name of the suppliers who supply yellow parts.

(*b*) Find the name of suppliers who supply both Blue and Green Parts.

(*c*) Find the name of suppliers who supply all parts.

Ans. SQL statements:

(*a*) Select Supp _ name

from supplier, parts, catalog

Where supplier. supp _ id = catalog. Supp – id

AND parts. part _ id = catalog. part _ id

AND parts color = 'YELLOW',

(*b*) Select supp _ name

from supplies, parts, catalog

Where supplier. supp _ id = catalog. supp – id

AND parts. part _ id = catalog. part _ id

AND part. color = 'BLUE',

INTERSECT

Select supp _ name

from supplier, parts, catalog

Where supplier. supp _ id = catalog. supp _ id

AND parts. part _ id = catalog. part _ id

AND part. color = 'GREEN',

(*c*) Select supp _ name, color

from supplier, catalog, parts

Where supplier. supp _ id = catalog. supp _ id

AND parts. part _ id = catalog. part _ id

AND parts. color in (select color from parts)

Relational Algebra Query —

(*a*) π_{supp} – name (Supplier ∞ catalog ∞ (σ_{colar}= 'YELLOW' (parts))',

(*b*) π_{supp} – name, color (supplier ∞ catalog ∞ parts) ÷ π_{cola}r (σ_{colar} = 'Blue' or color = 'Green') (parts))

(*c*) π_{supp} – name, color (supplier ∞ catalog ∞ parts) ÷ π_{colar} (parts)

Example 3. Consider the Insurance database given below, where the primary keys are underlined:

Person (**driver _ id,** name, address)

Car (*licence*, model, year)

accident (**report _ number**, data, location)

Owns (**driver – id,** licence)

Participated (driver – id, car, report – number, damage – amount)

Construct the following SQL queries:

(*i*) Find the total number of people who owned cars that were involved in accidents in 1989

(*ii*) Find the number of accidents in which the car belonging to "Mr X" were involved.

(*iii*) Add a new accident to the database, assume any values for required attributes.

(*iv*) Delete the Santro belonging to "Mr Y".

(v) Update the damage amount for the car with licence number "AB2000" in the accident with "AB2197" to Res 25,000.

Ans. Person (**driven _ id,** name, address)

Car (**licence,** model, year)

Accident (**report _ number**, date, location)

Owns (**driven _ id,** licence)

Participated (**driver _ id**, car, report – number, damage – amount)

SQL Queries:

(*i*) Select name from person, car accident owner where date = 1989;

(*ii*) Select report number from accident participant where accident, report _ number = participant, report _ number;

(*iii*) Add report number, date, location into person, car, accident where driver _ id. person = driver _ id. owns;

(*iv*) Delete Licence, model, year from person, car, owns, where (person driver _ id = owns, driver _ id) AND name = "Mr Y";

Example 4. Consider following Scheme for PROJECT database:

Project (Project _ No, Project _ name, Project – Manager)

Employee (Employee _ No, Employee _ Name)

Assigned – To (Project _ No, Employee _ No)

(*i*) Write SQL _ DDl statement for implementation of PROJECT database. The SQL statement should clearly indicate the Primary key and foreign keys.

(*ii*) Write following queries in Relational Algebra and SQL:

- Get the detail of employees working on both projects 'P1' and 'P2'.
- List the name of employees working on project 'P1' put not on project 'P2'.
- Delete the second of employee whose Employee Number is 'E'.
- List the name of employees who are working on a project for which 'E1' is the project manager.

Ans: Project (Project _ No, Project _ Name, Project _ Manager) Employee (Employee _ No, Employee _ Name) Assigned _ To (Project _ No, Employee _ No)

(*i*) Create Table Project (Project _ No. number (3) Primary key, Project _ name varchar 2 (30) No _ null, Project Manager varchar 2 (30));

Create Table Employee (employee _ No number (4) Primary key, employee name varchar 2 (30);

Create Table Assigned _ To (Project _ No number (4) Foreign key, Employee _ No number (4) Foreign key);

(*ii*) Select employee _ No, employee name from project, employee, Assigned _ To

Where project _ No = ($P_1 \cup P_2$);

• Select employee name

from employee, project

Where project _ No = 'P_1';

• Select employee name from

Project, employee where

'E_1' = Project Manager;

• Delete employee _ No,

employee – name from employee

where employee _ No = 'E_1';

Example 5. Consider the following relations for a database that keeps track of students inrolment in courses and the books adopted for each course.

STUDENT (**SSM**, Name, Major, Dept.)

COURSE (**Course#**, Cname, Dept.)

IMROLL (**SSM, Course#, Quarter,** Grade)

BOOK–ADOPTION (Course#, Quarter, Book – ISBM)

TEXT (**Book – ISBM,** Book, Title, Publisher, Author)

The underlined the attribute form the primary key of a relation scherna. Specify the foreign keys for the above schema, stating any assumptions you make. Then specify the following queries in relational algebra.

(*i*) List the number of courses taken by all students named 'John Smith' in winter 2002 (*i.e.* Qurter = 'W_{02}')

(*ii*) Produce a list of text books (include course#, Book _ ISBM, Book _ Title) for courses offered by the 'CS' dept. that have used more than two books.

(*iii*) List any departments that has all its adopted books published by 'BC publishing'.

Ans. In above schema we have the following foreign key:

(*i*) Between STUDENT and ENROLL the foreign key is SSN which is primary key in both table.

(*ii*) Between COURSE And ENROLL the foreign key in course# it is primary key in both.

(*iii*) Between ENROLL and BOOK – APOPTION, the foreign key is course# and quarter.

Queries in relational algebra:

(*i*) π Count (*) ENROLL (σ Student. name (π Cname (σ ENROLL. SSN = STUDENT, SSN ∩ STUDENT NAME= 'John Smith ∩ ENROLL. Quarter = 'w_{02}') COURSE)))) (course)

(*ii*) π course# ∩ BOOK–ISBN, Title (σ COURSE * COURSE# = **book**. Adoption, Course # ∩ Book = Addition. BOOK – ISBN = Text. BOOK – ISBN ∩ Course. Course# 'CS' ∧ COUNT (*) > 2) (Book Adoption X TEXT)

(*iii*) π course# (σ COURSE. Course# = BOOK — ADOPTION. Course# ∩ Book — ADOPTION. BOOK — ISBN = TEXT. BOOK _ ISBM ∩ TEXT. Publisher = 'Bc') (COURSE).

Example 6. Consider the following relational detabase:

EMPLOYEE (Person _ name, street, city)

WORKS (Person – name, Company _ name, Salary)

COMPANY (Person – name, Manager – name)

(*i*) Give an SQL _ DDL definition of this database.

(*ii*) Identify referential – integrity constraints that should hold.

(*iii*) Discuss the inclusion of above constraints in DDL definition.

Ans. (i) SQL DDL definitions:

(*a*) FOR EMPLOYEE : Create table EMPLOYEE (person _ name varchar 2(30) Constraints PK Primary key, street varchar 30), city varchar 2(30);

(*b*) For WORKS : Create table WORKS (person – name varchar 2(30), Constraints PK primary key reference (EMPLOYEE (Person – name));

Cosntraint PK1 unique

Company – name, varchar (30), salary number (4);

(*c*) For COMPANY : Create table company (Company _ name varchar 2(30))

Constraint PK unique references WORKS (company _ name, city varchar 2(30));

(*d*) or MANAGERS : Create table MANAGERS

(Person _ name varchar 2(30) constraint PK3 primary key references EMPLOYEE (PERSON – NAME, Manager _ name varchar 2(30));

(*ii*) Referential Integrity Constraints are given below:

(*a*) For EMPLOYEE and WORK = Person _ name

(*b*) For WORKS and COMPANY = COMPANY _ name

(*c*) For EMPLOYEE and MANAGERS = Person _ name

(*iii*) In the given relationships, there are some referential integrity constraints such as primary key and foreign key. Now we discuss these constraints in view of given relationships.

The PRIMARY KEY clause specifies one or more attributes that make up the primary key of a relation If a CREATE TABLE EMPLOYEE (-----------)

CONSTRAINT END PK PRIMARY KEY (Person _ name)

As person _ name is the PRIMARY _ KEY in employee relation.

Now, if primary key has multiple attribute then the DDL statement will look like as below: The works relation person and company is a composite primary key.

CREATE TABLE WORKS (--------)

CONSTRAINT WORK SPK PRIMARY KEY (Person _ name, Company _ name)

Referential integrity is specified via the FOREIGH KEY Clausea A referential integity constraint can be violated when tuples are inserted or deleted or when a foreign key or primary key attribute value is modified to apply a referential integrity constraint in DDL, we use FOREIGN KEY clause as follows:

In works relation, person _ name is imported from employee relation, 50 it is a FOREIGN KEY attribute in workds relation.

CREATE TABLE WORKS (---------)

CONSTRAINT WORKEK FOREIGN KEY (Person _ name)

References EMPLOYEE (Person_name)

The default action that SQL takes for an integrity violation its to reject the update operation that will cause a violation.

Example 7. Consider the following three relation schema, S, P and SP in which S# is supplier code, P# product code and Qty is Quantity and others carry their respective meanings.

S (S#, SNAME, SLITY, TURN OVER)

P (P#, WEIGHT, COLOUR, COST, SELLING, PRICE)

SP (S#, P#, QTY)

Write the appropriate SQL and relational algebra statements for the following quereis:

(*i*) Get all details of supplier who operate from DELHI with TURNOVER = 80.

(*ii*) Get part nos weighting b/w 25 and 35.

(*iii*) Get the names of suppliers whose name begins with A.

(*iv*) For each part supplied, get part no. and names of all cities Supplying the part.

(*v*) Get the names of suppliers Who supply part no. 2.

Ans: S (S#, SNAME, SLITY, TURNOVER)

P (P#, WEIGHT, COLOUR, COST, SELLING PRICE)

SP (S#, P#, QTY)

(1) SELECT * From S where
    SCITY = 'DELHI' and Turnover = 80;

(2) SELECT SP.P# from SP
    GROUP by SP.P#
    Having weight between 25 and 35;

(3) Select SNAME from S, SP
    Where S NAME LIKE 'A%';

(4) Select SP.P# S SCITY from SP
    Group by SP.P#

(5) Select Distinct **S. Sname**
    From S Where S.S# IN
    (Select SP.S# from SP
    Where SP.P# = 'P2');

UNIT – THREE

Chapter 5

Database Design and Normalization

Chapter Outline

Functional dependencies
Normal forms (Normalization)
First normal form (INF)
Second normal form (2NT)
Third normal form (3NF)
BCNF (Boyce cold Normal Form)
Inclusion dependencies
Loss less join decompositions
(Normalization using FD (Functional dependencies), MVD (Multivalued dependencies), and JD (Join Dependencies)
Alternative approaches to dalabase design

1. Functional dependenicies

Functional dependency is denoted by $X \rightarrow Y$, between two sets of attributes X and Y.

Suppliers

S. No.	*Name*	*Status*	*City*
S1	Shyam	20	Bombay
S2	Ram	10	Calcutta
S3	Amit	30	Calcutta
S4	Chirag	20	Delhi
S5	Ramesh	30	Calcutta

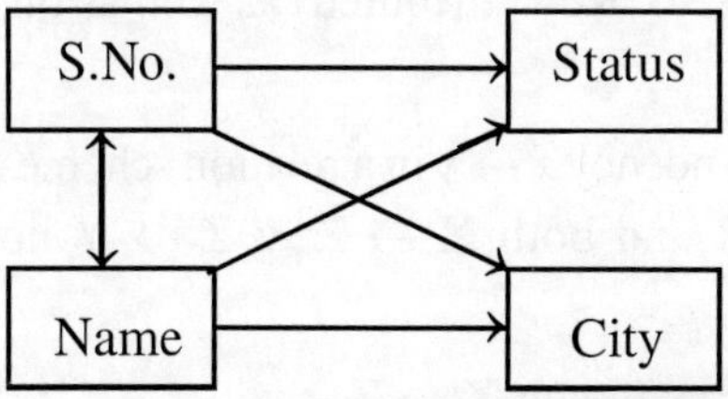

Functional dependencies in relation's

Five types of functional dependencies

(1) Full functional Dependency

(2) Partial Dependency

(3) Transitive Dependency

(4) Multivalued Dependency

(5) Join Dependency

1. **Full Functional Dependency :** When all non key attributes are dependent on the key attribute, it is called full functional dependency

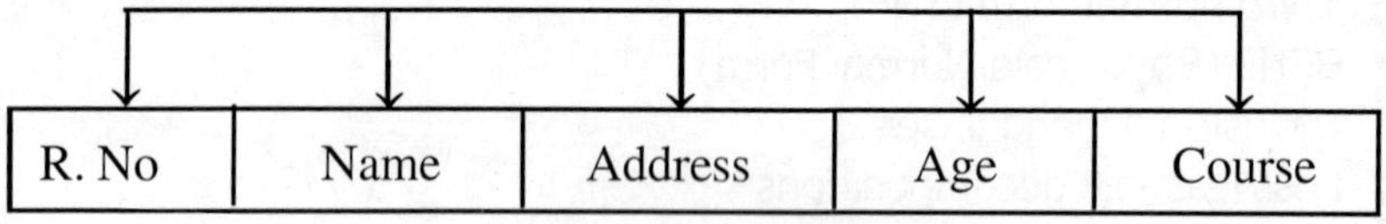

Concept of full functional dependancy

In the above example non key attributes (Name, Addr, Age and Course) are dependent on key attribute RNO, RNO stands for Roll Number.

2. Partial Dependency : All the non key attributes are not dependent on the key attribute. There is a partial dependency of non-key attributes either on the key attribute or on the non-key attribute.

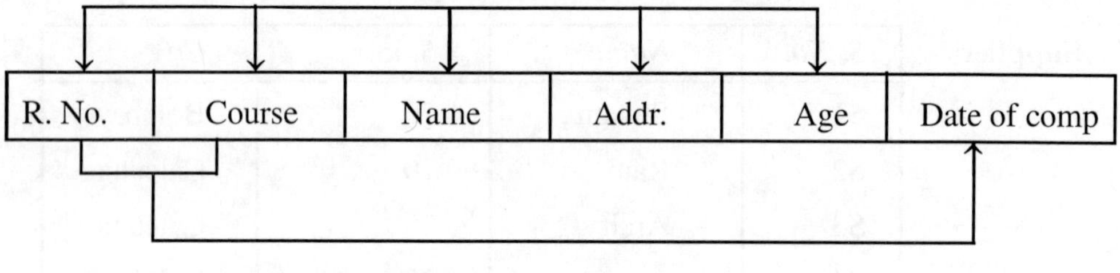

Concept of partial dependency

In Figure non key attributes name Addr and Age are dependent on R.No. and Pats of comp (Date of completion) *i.e.* non-key attribute depends on (No. Key attributed) as well as on course (non-key attribute).

3. Transitive Dependency : A functional dependency $x \rightarrow y$ in a relation scheme R, is a translative dependency if there is a set of attributes Z or R and both $X \rightarrow Z$ & $Z \rightarrow Y$ hold for transitive dependency.

$$X \rightarrow Z \ \& \ Y \rightarrow Z \text{ then } X \rightarrow Z$$

* When one non-key attribute depends on other non key attribute, it is called a transitive dependency

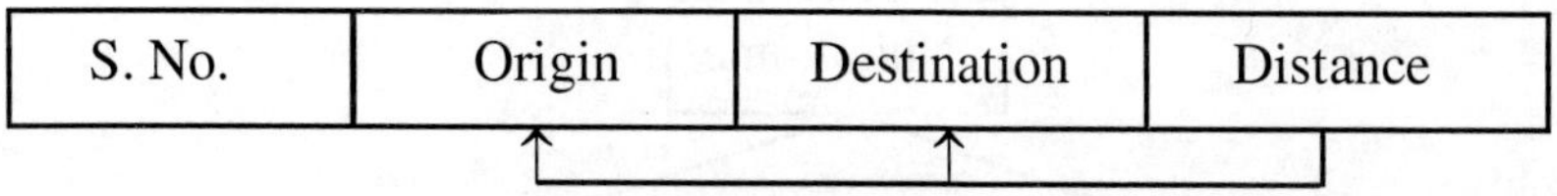

Concept of transitive dependency

Fig. (a)

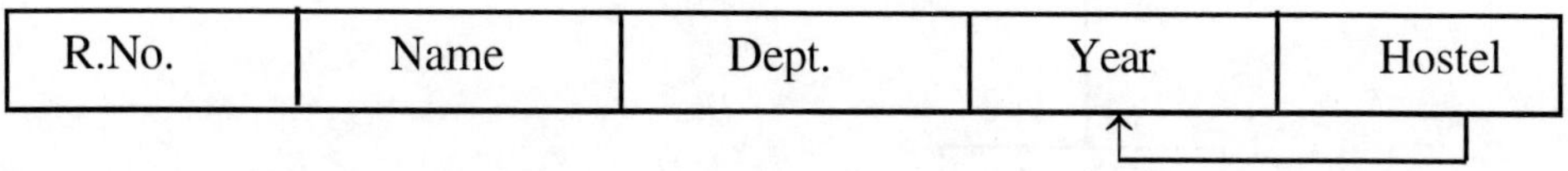

Fig (b) Concept of transitive dependency

To calculate Distance in Fig. (a) which is a non-key attribute, we must known origin & Destination which are also non-key attributes *i.e.* one non-key attribute is dependent on one or more than one non-key attributes the distance has the transitive dependency.

In Fig. (b) transitive dependency occurs because one non-key attribute is dependent on other non-key attribute i.e. if student is in Ist year then he has been assigned *Hostel Gandhi,* if he is in IInd, IIIrd year, hostel assigned is Jawahar, IIIrd year the hostel assignied is Indra. Thus Hostel assigned to a student is depondent on the year of study in the college.

4. Multivalued Dependency : Functional dependencies rule out certain tuples from being in a relation. If A → B, then we connot have two tuples with the same A value but different B values.

Ename	***Pname***	***Dname***
Smith	X	John
Smith	Y	Anna
Smith	X	Anna
Smith	Y	John

EMP

The EMP relation with two MVD

ENAME →→ PNAME and ENAME →→ DNAME

5. Join dependency : Join dependency is a constraint, similar to a functional dependency or a Multivalued Dependency. It is satisfied if and only if the relation concerned is the join of certain number of projections. And therefore, such a constraint is called a join dependency.

We now consider a special class of Join dependencies which help to capture data dependencies present in a hierarchical data structure.

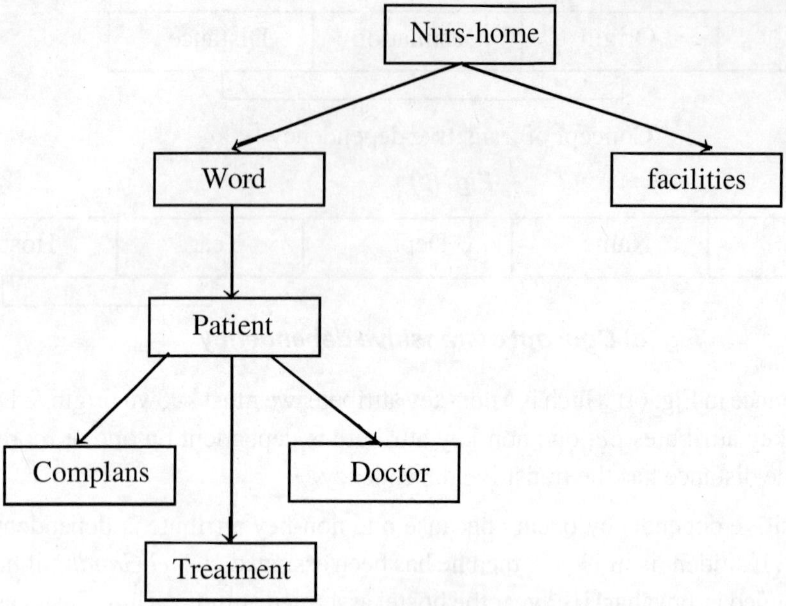

Hierarchical representation of a NURS-HOME database

(*a*) Closure of a set of functional Dependencies $\rightarrow$ (P^+)

Suppose we are given a relation schema

R = (A, B, C, G, H, I) and the set of functional dependencies F

$$A \rightarrow B$$
$$A \rightarrow C$$
$$CG \rightarrow H$$
$$CG \rightarrow I$$
$$B \rightarrow H$$

Let *f* be a set of functional dependencies.

The closure of F, denoted by F^+.

The following six rules are well known inferance rules for functional dependencies.

(1) Reflexivity rule (Trivial functional dependency)

If α is a set of attributes and $\beta \subseteq \alpha$, then $\alpha \rightarrow \beta$. holds.

Per ex. $\rightarrow$ AB $\rightarrow$ A, $\beta \subseteq \alpha$ then $\alpha \rightarrow \beta$ which is always true, so called **trivial** functional dependency.

(2) Augmentation Rule : If $\alpha \rightarrow \beta$ holds and γ is a set of attributes, then $\gamma\alpha \rightarrow \gamma\beta$ holds.

(3) Transitivity rule : If $\alpha \rightarrow \beta$ holds and $\beta \rightarrow \gamma$ holds, than $\alpha \rightarrow \gamma$ holds.

Rule 1 & Rule 2 & Rule 3 is called Arm Strong's (or rules of inference).

(4) **Decomposition or projective rule—**

If $\alpha \rightarrow \beta\gamma$ holds, then $\alpha \rightarrow \beta$ holds and $\alpha \rightarrow \gamma$ holds.

(5) **Union or Additive rule** – If $\alpha \rightarrow \beta$ holds and $\alpha \rightarrow \gamma$ holds, then $\alpha \rightarrow \beta\gamma$ holds

(6) **Pseudo transitivity rule :** If $\alpha \rightarrow \beta$ holds and $\gamma\beta \rightarrow \delta$ holds, then $\alpha\gamma \rightarrow \delta$ holds.

Another rules

(1) Determination rule

$$\alpha \rightarrow \alpha$$

(2) Composition rule

If $\alpha \rightarrow \beta$ & $\gamma \rightarrow \delta$ then $\alpha\gamma \rightarrow \beta\delta$.

Example. Given that F_2 functional dependency.

F^+ = closure of functional dependencies

relation schema R = (A, B, C, G, H, I) the set of functional dependencies

F = A → B

A → C

CG → H

CG → H

CG → I

B → H

F^+ (Closure of functional dependencies)

(1) A → B

B → H Applying transitivity rule

A → H

(2) A → B

A → C applying union rule

A → BC

(3) A → C

CG → H applying pseudo transitivity rule

(4) AG → H

A → C

CG → I applying PTR.

$AG \rightarrow I$

(5) $CG \rightarrow H$ & $CG \rightarrow I$ applying union rule

$CG \rightarrow HI$

Example 2

Given a set of functional dependences.

$A \rightarrow B, ABCD \rightarrow E$ & $EF \rightarrow G$

Is $ACDF \rightarrow G$ implied by the set of given FDs ?

Given $A \rightarrow B$ and $ABCD \rightarrow E$

Implies $ACD \rightarrow E$ (By using pseudotransitivity rule)

Now by augmentation $ACDF \rightarrow EF$

$A\ CDF \rightarrow EF$ (1) applying transistive rule

$EF \rightarrow G$

So by transistivity $ACDF \rightarrow G$

Example 3. Consider a relation R with attributes X, Y and Z and with a set of functional dependencies F such that $X \rightarrow Y$ and $Y \rightarrow Z$. Find the closure F^+ of set F. First applying trivial functional dependencies. (Reflexivity)

$X \rightarrow Y$ where $Y \subseteq X$

Using transtivity, we can generate

$X \rightarrow Y$ and $Y \rightarrow Z \Rightarrow X \rightarrow Z$.

We get the non-trivial dependencies.

from augmentation

$\{XZ \rightarrow YZ,\ XY \rightarrow XZ,\ XY \rightarrow YZ\}$

Example 4. Consider a relation R with attributes A, B, C, D, E and F with a set F of FDs_s $A \rightarrow BC$, $B \rightarrow E$ and $CD \rightarrow EF$. Find the closure set F^+ of Set F.

Given $A \rightarrow BC$

By decomposition or projective $A \rightarrow BC$ and $A \rightarrow B$

By augmentation $AD \rightarrow CD$

But given that $CD \rightarrow EF$

So by transitivity $AD \rightarrow EF$

Again By decomposition $AD \rightarrow E$

$AD \rightarrow F$

(*b*) **Equivalence of Sets of Functional Dependencies**

In this case given two sets for ex. F_1 and F_2.

Then first calculate the F^+ of F_1 to give the elements which is the element of F_2. Then F_1 and F_2 are equivalent.

Example 5. Given two sets F_1 and F_2 of FDs for a relation.

$F_1 : A \rightarrow B, AB \rightarrow C, D \rightarrow AC, D \rightarrow E$

$F_2 : A \rightarrow BC; D \rightarrow AE$

Are the two sets equivalent ?

From	F_1, $D \rightarrow$	AC implies that $D \rightarrow A$
and	$D \rightarrow$	C. Also given that $D \rightarrow E$
So	$D \rightarrow$	AE, which is a FD of set F_2,
Again	$A \rightarrow$	B and $AB \rightarrow$ C imply
		(By P seudo transitivity rule)
	$A \rightarrow$	C and so $A \rightarrow BC$, which is a. FD of set F_2.

Hence F_1 and F_2 are equivalent.

(c) **Closure of a set of Attributes (X^+)**

Read : A set of functional dependencies F

and a set of attributes X

$X^+ = X$; // initialize X^+ to X.

Closure of a set of Attributes while these is no change repeat {

if there is an FD $A \rightarrow B$ in F such that

$A \subseteq X^+$

then

Set $X^+ = X^+ \subseteq B$}

Computing the attribute closure of attribute set X

The above algorithm computes the closure of

X as follow; it starts with the set

X^+; initialized to X. For each $A \rightarrow B$ in F_1 if $A \subseteq X^+$ the algorithm modibies the X^+ by forming a union of X^+ and B. the algorithms terminates when there is no change in X^+.

Example 1. Consider a relation R with attributes A, B, C, D, E and F and a set F of FDs $A \rightarrow BC$, $E \rightarrow CF$, $B \rightarrow E$ and $CD \rightarrow EF$

Compute the closure X^+ of *the set of attributes X = (A, B)* under the given set of FDs.

Solution : We will use the algorithm given above to get the closure set of attributes. Initialize $X^+ = \{A, B\}$

Now the loap will be executed for each FD

For A → BC, since A ⊆ {A, B} so we will include BC to the closure

Now $X^+ = \{A, B, C\}$

For second FD, E → CF since E ⊆ {A, B, C},

So it will not be included in the cosure set.

For B → E, since B ⊆ {A, B, C} so E will is included in the closure set.

Now $X^+ = \{A, B, C, E\}$

Finally for FD CO → EF, again CD ⊆{A, B,C,E}

so it will not be include in the list.

Now this loop will be again executed for each FD. for first FD result. Will not be changed but for second FD (E → CF).

Since E ⊆ {A, B, C, E} the modified closure set will be

$X^+ = \{A, B, C, F, E\}$

For third and fourth FDs again X^+ will remain same. So the final closure set will be $X^+ = \{A, B, C, F, E\}$

Example 2. Consider a relation R with attributes A, B, C, D, E and F and a set F of FDs

□ A → B, BC → DE and AFE → G

Compute the closure X^+ of the set of attributes {A,C} under the given set of FDs.

Solution : $X^+ = \{ A,C\}$

for A → B, since A ⊆ {A, C} so X^+ {A, B, C}

for BC → DE, since BC ⊆ {A, B, C} so $X^+= \{A, B, C, D, E\}$

Lastly for AEF → G, AEF ⊆ {A, B, C, D, E} so it will not be included in the list.

Hence the final closure set X^+ of attributes {A, C} under the given set of FDs. is $X^+ = \{A, B, C, D, E\}$

1(*d*) **Irreducible or minimal set of Dependencies**

Let F_1 & F_2 be the two sets of FDs on a relation R. If every FD of set F_1 is implied by FD of set F_2 *i.e* if F_1^+ is a subset of F_2^+ then F_2 is called an equivalent set of F_1. Moreover if F_2 is an equivalent set of F_1 and F_1 is equivalent set if F_2 that F_1 and F_2 are called as the equivalent sets *i.e.* $F_1^+ = F_2^+$

Now a set F of FDs is said to be is irreducible set if and only if the following three conditions hold:

(*i*) The dependency of every FD (The right hand side of any FD *e.g.* B in A $\rightarrow$ B) in F involves first one attributs

(*ii*) The determinant of every FD (the left hand side) in F is irreducible.

(*iii*) No FD is F can be discarded from F without changing the F^+.

Example. Consider a relation R of attributes {A, B, C, D, E and F} with the set of FDS given as

$$AB \rightarrow C, C \rightarrow A, BC \rightarrow D, ACD \rightarrow B,$$

$$BE \rightarrow C, CE \rightarrow FA, CE \rightarrow BD \text{ and } D \rightarrow EF.$$

Find an irreducible equivalent set.

Solution : Since the dependent should involve only single attribute (Rule 1)

(*i*) AB $\rightarrow$ C

(*ii*) C $\rightarrow$ A

(*iii*) BC $\rightarrow$ D

(*iv*) ACD $\rightarrow$ B

(*v*) BE $\rightarrow$ C

(*vi*) CE $\rightarrow$ F

(*vii*) CE $\rightarrow$ A

(*viii*) CF = B

(*ix*) CF $\rightarrow$ D

(*x*) D $\rightarrow$ E

(*xi*) D $\rightarrow$ F

Now C $\rightarrow$ A implies CE $\rightarrow$ A, so we can drop CE $\rightarrow$ A

CF $\rightarrow$ B implies CF $\rightarrow$ BC by augmentation also by (iii) BC $\rightarrow$ D so by transitivity

CF $\rightarrow$ D. so we we can drop (ix)

By (viii) CF $\rightarrow$ B we will have ACF $\rightarrow$ AB

(By transitivity) and so by decomposition ACD $\rightarrow$ B. Therefore we can drop

(*iv*) also. No further reductions are possible. Hence the final minimal or irreducible set is

$$AB \rightarrow C, C \rightarrow A, BC \rightarrow D, BE \rightarrow C, CE \rightarrow F,$$

$$CF \rightarrow B, D \rightarrow E, D \rightarrow F.$$

What is normalization : Normalization is the name given to the process of simplifying the relationship among data elements in a record. Normalization replaces a collection of data in a record structure by another second design which is simple, more predictable and therefore more manageable.

The goal of a relational database design is to generate a set of relation schemes that allow is to store information without any redundant (is repeated) data. It also allow us to retrieve information easily and more efficient.

The first step towards normalization is to convert E-R model into tables and Relations. The next step is to examine the tables for redandancy and if necessary, change them to non-redund ant forms. This non-redundant model is then converted to a database definition, which achieves the objective of the database Design place.

Need for Normalization : Normalization reduces redundancy. Redundancy is the unnecassary repetition of a field. It can cause problems with storage, retrieval and updation of data. Redundancy can lead to :

(*a*) **Inconsistencies** → errors are more likely to occur when facts are repeated.

(*b*) **Update anomalies :** Inserting, modifying and deleting data may cause inconsistences. Inconsistency occurs when we perform updation of deletion of data in one relation, while for getting to make corresponding changes in other relations.

During the process of normalization we can identify dependencies which do cause problems when deleting or updating. Normalization helps in simplify the structure of the tables.

A fully normalized record consists of :

(*a*) A primary key that identifies that entity

(*b*) A set of attributes that describe that entity.

In the process of normoralizations, data are grouped in the simplest possible way so that changes can be made later with minimum impact on the data structure.

(3) **First Normal Form (INF) :** It was defined to disallow multivalued attribute. It states that the domain of an attribute must include only atomic (or indivisible values).

DEPARTMENT

(*a*)

DNAME	**DNUMBER**	DMGRSSN	DLOCATIONS

Relation schema that is not in INF

DEPARTMENT

(*b*)

DNAME	**DNUMBER**	DMGRSSN	DLOCATIONS

Research	5	333445555	{Bellaire, Sugarland, Hourton }
Administration	4	987654321	{Stafford}
Headquarters	1	888665555	{Houston}

(*b*) **Example relation Instance**

(*c*) DEPARTMENT

DNAME	**DNUMBER**	DNGRSSN	DLOCATION
Research	5	333445555	Bellaire
Research	5	333445555	Sugarland
Research	5	333445555	Houston
Administration	4	987654321	stafford
Headquarters	1	888665555	Houston

INF Relation with Redundancy Normalization into INF

4. Second Normal Form (2NF). 2NF is based on the concept of full functional dependency. A relation schema R is in 2NF if every nonprime attribute A in R is fully functionally dependent on the primary key of R.

Whose attribute is the part of primary key is called prime attribute otherwise non-prime attribute.

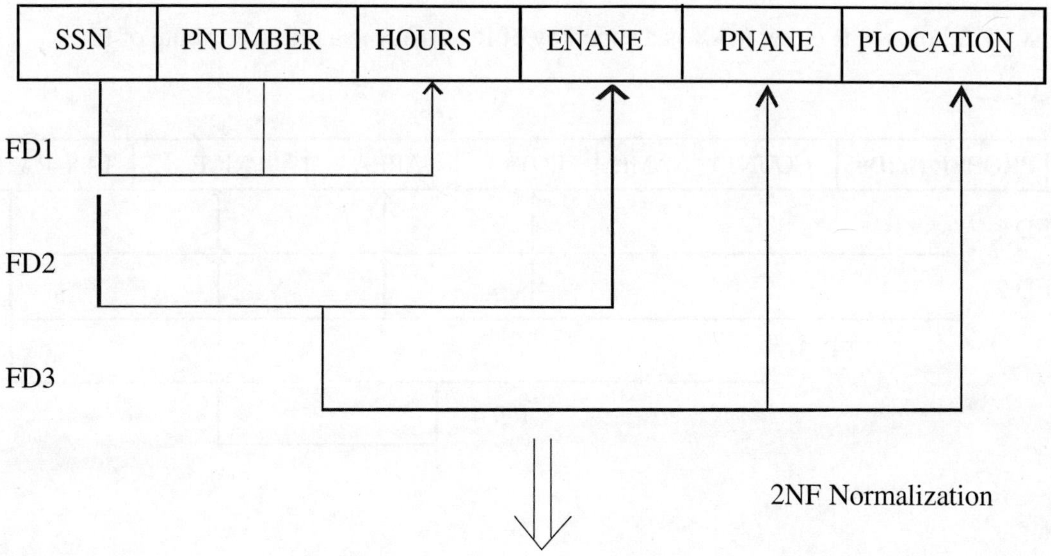

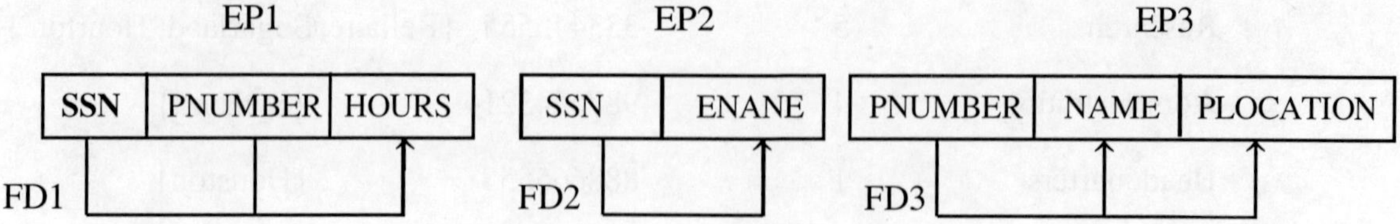

The nor_malization process

(*a*) Normalizing EMP_**PROT** into 2NF relations

(5) Thrid Normal Form (3NF) : 3 NF is based on the concept of transitive dependency. All non-prime attribute is depend on full functional depended on the prime attribute but not transtivity.

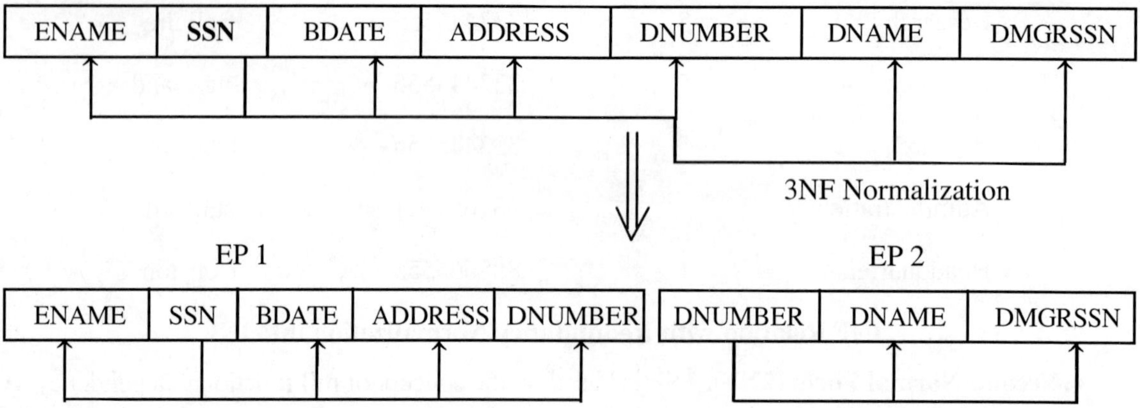

Normalizing EMP _ DEPT into 3NF relations

A relation schema R is in 3Nf if a nontrivial functional dependency

X → A holds in R either (*a*) X is a superkey of R or (*b*) A is a prime attribute of R.

(*a*)

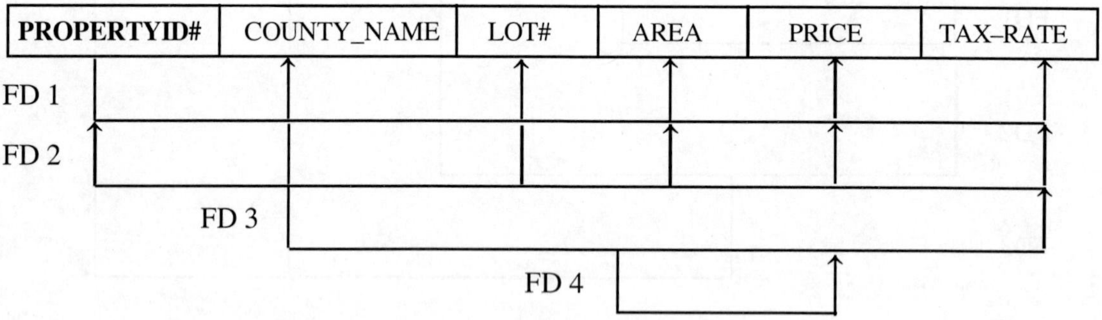

The **LOTS** relation schema and its functional dependencies FDI through FD4

(*b*) **LOTS 1**

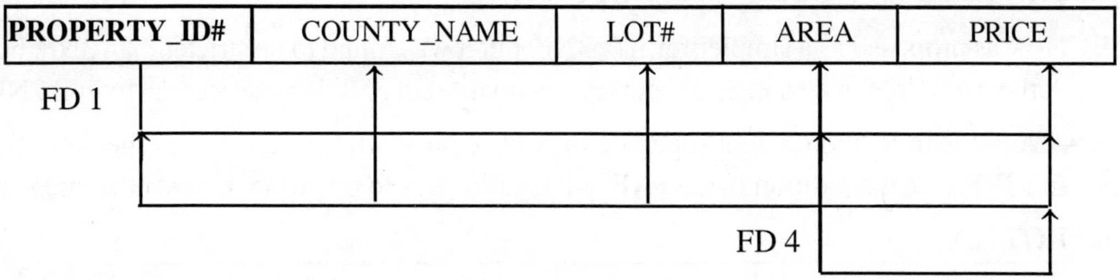

LOTS 2

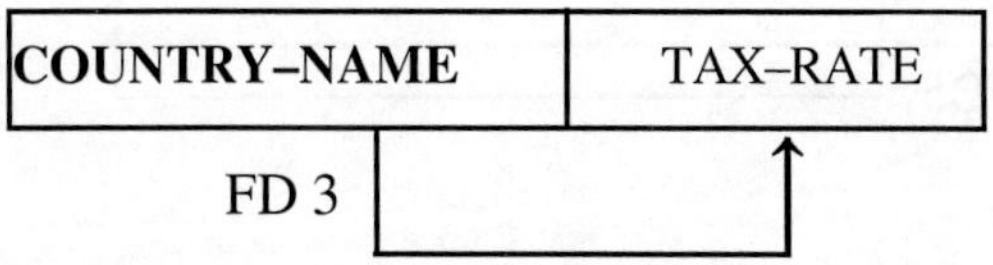

Decomposing LOTS into the 2NF relations LOTS1 and LOTS2.

(*c*) **LOTS1A**

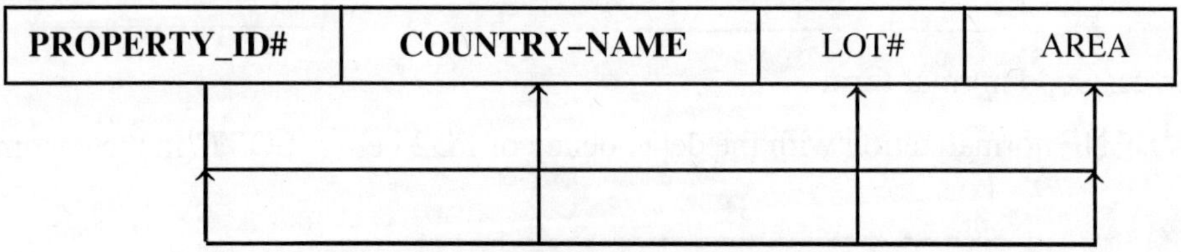

LOTS1B

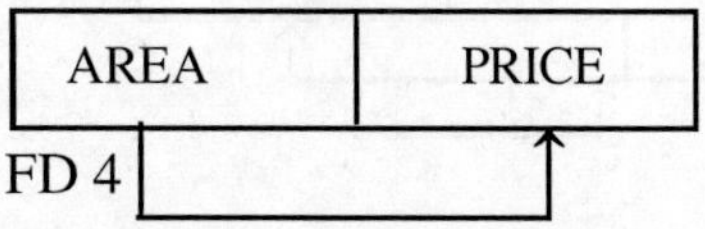

Decomposing LOTS1 into the 3NF relations LOTS1A and LOTS1 B.

(*d*)

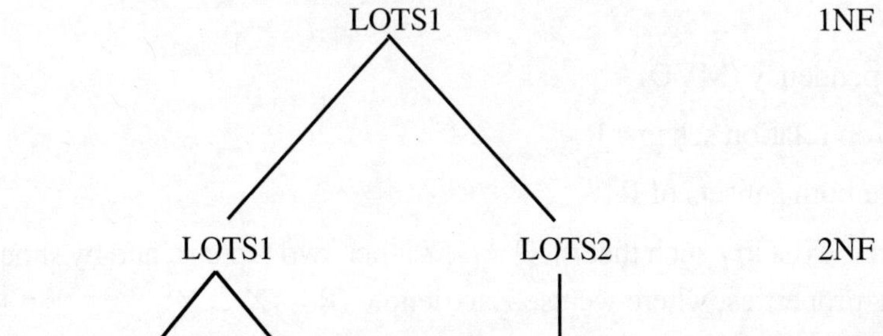

SUMMARY OF NORMALIZATION OF LOTS

(6) BCNF (Boyce _ Codd _ Normal form)

BCNF was proposed as a simpler form of 3NF, but it was found to be stricter than 3NF, because every relation in BCNF is also in 3NF, however a relation in 3NF is not necessarity in BCNF.

X → A holds in R, then X in a superkey of R. The only difference between the definitions of BCNF and 3NF is that condition (*b*) of 3NF, which allows A to be prime, is absent from BCNF.

(*a*) **LOTSIA**

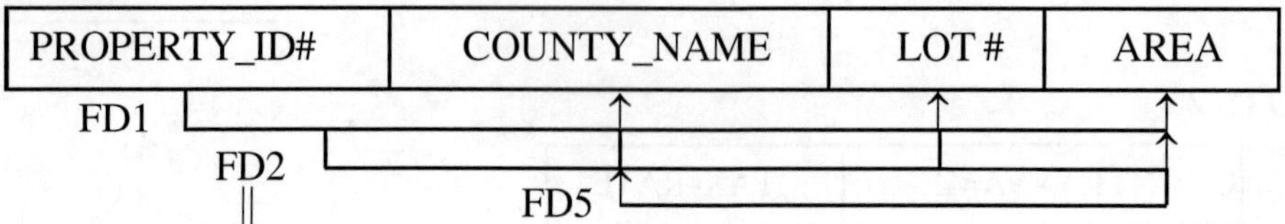

⇓

BCNF normalization

LOTSI AX **LOTSIAY**

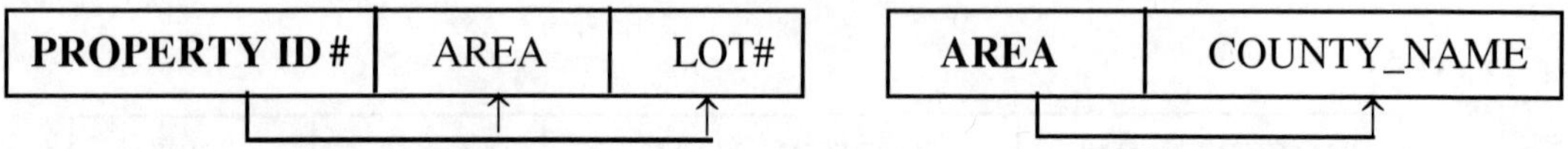

Bayce. Codd normal form

(*a*) BCNF normalization with the dependency of FD2 being 'LOST' in the decomposition

R

(*b*)

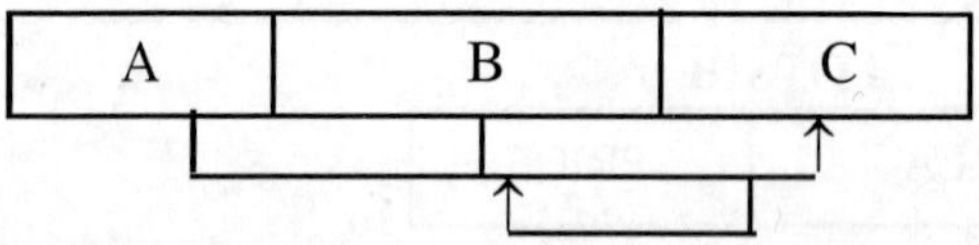

A relation R is 3NF but not in BCNF

* **Multivalued Dependencies and Fourth Normal Form**

A multivalued dependency (MVD)

X →→ Y specified on relation schema R,

Where X and Y are both subsets of R.

of two tuples t_1 and t_2 exist in *r* such that $t_1[X] = t_2 [X]$ then two tuples t_3 and by should also exist in *r* with the following properties, where we use Z to denote $(R - (X \cup Y)$

$t_3[X] = t_4[X] = t_1[X] = t_2[X]$

$t_3[Y] = t_1[Y]$ and $t_4[Y] = t_2[Y]$

$t_3[Z] = t_2[Z]$ and $t_4[Z] = t_1[Z]$

An MVD $X \rightarrow\rightarrow Y$ in R is called a trivial MVD if (*a*) $Y \subset X$ or (*b*) $X \cup Y = R$

Whenever $X \rightarrow\rightarrow Y$ holds, we say that **X** multideterminess **Y**.

***Inference Rules for functional and multivalued Dependencies.**

IR_1 (reflexive rule for FDS) : If $X \supseteq Y$, then $X \rightarrow Y$

IR_2 (augmentation rule for FDs) $\{X \rightarrow Y\} \Leftarrow$

$DZ \rightarrow YZ$

IR_3 (transitive rule for FDS): $\{X \rightarrow Y, Y \rightarrow Z\} \Leftarrow X \rightarrow Z$

IR_4 (complementation rule for MVDS) :

$\{X \rightarrow Y\} \Leftarrow \{X \rightarrow (R - (X \cup Y)\}$

IR_5 (augmentation rule for MVDs) : If $X \rightarrow Y$ and $W \supseteq Z$ then $WX \rightarrow YZ$

IR_6 (transtive rule for MVDs) : $\{X \twoheadrightarrow Y\}, \{Y \twoheadrightarrow Z) \Leftarrow X \twoheadrightarrow \{Z - Y)$

IR_7 (replication rule for FD to MVD) : $\{X \rightarrow Y\}$ and $= X \rightarrow Y$

IR_8 (Coalescence rule for FDs and MVDs) : If $X \twoheadrightarrow Y$ and their exists W with the properties that (*a*) $W \cap Y$ is empty. Relation schema R is an 4NF Y all MVD of the form $\alpha \twoheadrightarrow \beta$ R and $\beta \in$ R at least one of the following holds

(*a*) (1) $\alpha \twoheadrightarrow \beta$ is a trivial MVD

(2) α is superkey for schema R.

(*b*) $W \rightarrow Z$, and (*c*) $Y \supseteq Z$, then $X \rightarrow Z$

Fourth Normal Form : A relation schema R is in 4NF with respect to a set of dependencies *f* (that includes functional dependencies and multivalued dependencies) before every nontrivial multivalued dependency $X \twoheadrightarrow Y$ in F+, X is a superkey for R.

(*a*) EMP

ENAME	PNAME	DNAME
Smith	X	John
Smith	Y	Anna
Smith	X	Anna
Smith	Y	John

(*a*) **The EMP relation with two MVDS**

ENAME $\rightarrow\rightarrow$ PNAME and

Ename $\rightarrow\rightarrow$ DNAME

(*b*) EMP_**Projects** EMP_**Dependents**

ENAME	PNAME
Smith	X
Smith	X
Smith	Y

ENAME	DNAME
Smith	John
Smith	Anna
Smith	Anna

Recomposing EMP into two relations IMNF

Lossless : Join Decomposition into 4NF Relations

We decompose a relation schema R into R1 $(X \cup Y)$ and $R_2 = (R - Y)$ based on M V D $X \twoheadrightarrow Y$ that holds in R, the decomposition has the lossless join property.

The relation schema *s* R_1 and R_2 form a lossless join descompositon of R if and only if $(R_1 \cap R_2) \twoheadrightarrow (R_1 - R_2)$ if and only if $(R_1 \cap R_2) \twoheadrightarrow (R_2 - R_1)$

* **Join Dependencies and Fifth Normal Form**

A Join dependency (JD) denoted by JD $(R_1, R_2 - R_n)$ specified on relation schema R, specifices a constraintion the states *r* of R.

Fifth normal form which is also called project form normal form. A relation schema R is in fifth normal join (5NF) or project join normal form (PJNF) with respect to a set f of functional, multivalued, and join dependencies if for every nontrivial join dependency JD $(R_1, R_2, \text{--} R_n)$ in F^+ (that is implied by *f*), every R_1 is a superkey of R.

SPJ

S#	P#	J #
S_1	P_1	J_2
S_1	P_2	J_1
S_2	P_1	J_1
S_1	P_1	J_1

SP

S#	P #
S_1	P_1
S_1	S_2
S_2	P_1

3. JS

J#	S#
J_2	S_1
J_1	S_1
J_1	S_2

PJ

P#	J#
P_1	J_2
P_2	J_1
P_1	J_1

There exist relations that cannot be nonloss decomposed into two projection but can be non loss decomposed into three. The three briery protection (SP, JS, PJ) corresponding to the SPJ relation + Our conditional spurious tuple and the effect of the 2nd join (4 & 3) to eliminate the spurious tuple there by bringing us back to SPJ relation. In other word original SPJ relation is predecomposible

(1) and (2) Join over P#

S#	P#	J#
S_1	P_1	J_2
S_1	P_1	J_1
S_1	P_2	J_1
S_2	P_1	J_2
S_2	P_1	J_1

(3) and (4) combined

S#	P#	J#
S_1	P_1	J_2
S_1	P_1	J_1
S_1	P_2	J_1
S_2	P_1	J_1

A Relation schema R is in 5NF also called projection join NF (PJNF) is and only it every non trivial join dependency that holdes R is implied by the candidate key of R. relation SPJ is not in 5NF because 3 decomposiability is non implied by the 3 decomposiability is non implied by the fact that the combination {s#, P#, S#}; a condidate key.

The S projection (SP, PJ and JS) are each in 5NF since they do not involve any non trival join dependencies at all.

(8) **Lossless (Nonadditive join Decomposition) :** When we decompose a relation into a number of smaller relations, it is *crucial* that the decomposition be lossless. Let R be a relation schema, and let *F* be a set of functional dependencies on R. Let R_1 and R_2 form a decomposition of R. This decomposition is a lossless join decomposion of R if at least one of the following functional dependencies is in F+.

- $R_1 \cap R_2 \rightarrow R_1$
- $R_1 \cap R_2 \rightarrow R_2$

if $R_1 \cap R_2$ from a superkey of either R_1 or R_2, the decomposition is a lossless – join decomposition.

For ex. Decomposing lending schema into two schemas :

R_1 branch schema = (branch - name, beanch - city assets)

R_2

Loan info - schema = (branch - home, customer name, loan number, amount)

$R_1 \cap R_2 \Rightarrow$ Branch - Schema $\cap$ Loan info - schema

= {branch – name} it follows that our initial decompositions a lossless join decomposition.

(9) **Inclusion dependencies**: Inclusion dependencies were defined in order to formalize certain interrelational constraints. For example, the foreign key (or referential integrity) constraint cannot be specified as a functionalor multivalued dependency because it relates attributes accross relations, but it can be specified as an inclusion dependency. Moreover, inclusion dependencies can also be used to represent the constraint between two relations that represent a class/subclass relationship. An inclusion dependency R X < S . Y between two sets of attributes – X of relation schema R, and Y of relation schema S –specifies the constriant that, at any specific time when *r* is a relation state of R and *s* is a relation state of *S*, we must have

$\pi_X (r(R) \subseteq \pi_Y (s(S))$

The $\subseteq$ (subset) relationship does not necessarily have to be a proper subset obviously, the sets of attributes on which the inclusions dependency is specified X of R and Y of S – must have the some number of attributes.

Employee **F.K. (Foreign Key)**

ENAME	SSN	BDATE	ADDRESS	DNUMBER

P.K (PRIMARY KEY)

DEPARTMENT f.k.

DNAME	**DNUMBER**	DHGRSSN

P.K.

DEPT_LOCATIONS

DNUMBER	LOCATION

PROJECT F.K.

DNAME	PNUMBER	PLOCATION	DNUM

WORKS _ ON

f.k. **f.k.**

SSN	**PNUMBER**	HOURS

P.K.

Simplified Version of The Company Relational Database Schema

We can specify the following inclusion dependencies on the relational schema

DEPARTMENT. DNGRSSN < EMPLOYEE. **SSN**

WORKS_ON. ssn < EMPLOYEE . **SSN**

EMPLOYEE. DNUMBER < DEPARTMENT . DNUMBER PROJECT. DNUM < DEPARTMENT. DNUMBER WORKS ON. PNUMBER < PROJECT. PNUMBER DEPT_LOCATIONS . DNUMBER < DEPARTMEWNT DNUMBER.

All the preceding inclusion deperdencies represent referential integrity constraints. We can also use inclusion dependencies to represent class/subclass relationships. For ex., in the relational schema of Frg, we can specify the following inclusion dependencies

PERSON

SSN	Name	Birth Date Sex	Address

EMPLOYEE

SSN	Salary	Employee Type	Position	Rank	Present Time	**RAF** lag	TAF lag

Project	course

ALUMNUS **ALUMNUS DEGREES**

SSN	S. No.	Year	Degree	Major

STUDENT

SSN	Major Dept.	Area flog	Under ad flag	Degree progeam dass	Stub Assist flag

EMPLOYEE . **SSN** < PERSON. **SSN**

ALUNNUS . **SSN** < PERSON. **SSN**

STUDENT . **SSN** < PERSON. **SSN**

Examples

Example. Define limitation of all Types of Normalization.

First normal form (1NF) sets the very basic rules for an organized database:

- Eliminate duplicative columns from the same table.
- Create separate tables for each group of related data and identify each row with a unique column or set of columns (the primary key).

Second normal from (2NF) further addresses the concept of removing duplicative data:

- Meet all the requirements of the first normal form.
- Remove subsets of data that apply to multiple rows of a table and place them in separate tables.
- Create relationships between these new tables and their predecessors through the use of foreign keys.

Third normal form (3NF) goes one large step further:

- Meet all the requirements of the second normal form.
- Remove columns that are not dependent upon the primary key.

Finally, fourth normal form (4NF) has one additional requirement:

- Meet all the requirements of the third normal form.
- A relation is in 4NF if it has no multi-valued dependencies.

Example. What is normalization?

Database normalization is a design technique by which relational database tables are structured in such a way as to make them less vulnerable to certain types of logical inconsistencies and anomalies. Tables can be normalized to varying degrees: relational database theory defines "normal forms: of successively higher degrees of stringency, so, for example, a table in third normal form is less open to logical inconsistencies and anomalies than a table that is only is second normal form. Although the normal forms are often defined (informally) in terms of the characteristics of tables, rigorous definitions of the normal forms are concerned with the characteristics of mathematical constructs known as relations. Whenever information is represented relationally — that is, roughly speaking, as values within rows beneath fixed column headings — it makes sense to ask to what extent the representation is normalized.

Basically, it's the process of efficiently organizing data in a database. There are two goals of the normalization process: eliminate redundant data (for example, storing the same data in more than one table) and ensure data dependencies make sense (only storing related data in a table). Both of these are worthy goals as they reduce the amount of space a database consumes and ensure that data is logically stored.

Examples. Define Rules of Data Normalization.

1. Eliminate Repeating Groups. In the original member list, each member name is followed by any databases that the member has experience with. Some might know many, and other might not know any. To answer the question, "Who Knows DB2?" we need to perform an awkward scan of the list looking for references to DB2. This is inefficient and an extremely untidy way to store information.

Moving the known databases into a sperate table helps a lot. Separating the repeating groups of databases from the member information results in **first normal form.** The MemberID in the database table matches the primary key in the member table, providing a foreign fey for relating the two tables with a join operation. Now we can answer the question by looking in the database table for "DB2" and getting the list of members.

Member List

1. John Smith	Access, DB2, FoxPro
2. Dave Jones	dBASE, Clipper

3. Mike Beach	
4. Jerry Miller	DB2, Oracle
5. Ben Stuart	Oracle, Sybase
6. Fred Flint	Informix
7. Joe Blow	
8. Greg Brown	Access, MSSq1 Server
9. Doug Hope	

Member Table

MID	Name
1	John Smith
2	Dave Jones
3	Mike Beach
4	Jerry Miller
5	Ben Stuart
6	Fred Flint
7	Joe Blow
8	Greg Brown
9	Doug Hope

Database Table

DID	MID	Database
1	1	Access
2	3	DB2
3	1	FoxPro
4	2	dBASE
5	2	Clipper
6	4	DB2
7	4	Oracle
8	5	Oracle
9	5	Sybase
10	6	Informix
11	6	Access
12	8	MSSq1 Server

2. Eliminate Redundant Data. In the Database Table, the primary key is made up fo the MemberID and the DatabaseID. This makes sense for other attributes like "Where Learned" and "Skill Level" attributes, since they will be different for every member/database combination. But the database name depends only on the DatabaseID. The same database name will appear redundantly every time its associated ID appears in the Database Table.

Suppose you want to reclassify a database – give it a different DatabaseID. The change has to be made for every member that lists that database! If you miss some, you'll have several members with the same database under different IDs. This is an update anomaly.

Or suppose the last member listing a particular database leaves the group. His records will be removed from the system, and the database will not be stored anywhere! This is a delete anomaly, To avoid these problems, we need second normal form.

To achieve this, separate the attributes depending on both parts of the key from those depending only on the DatabaseID. This results in two tables: "Database" which gives the name for each DatabaseID, and "MemberDatabase: which lists the databases for each member.

Now we can reclassify a database in a single operation: look up the DatabaseID in the "Database" table and change its name. The result will instantly be available throughout the application.

Database Table

DID	MID	Database
1	1	Access
2	1	DB2
3	1	FoxPro
4	2	dBASE
5	2	Clipper
6	4	DB2
7	4	Oracle
8	5	Oracle
9	5	Sybase
10	6	Informix
11	8	Access
12	8	MSSq1 Server

Member Table

MID	Name
1	John Smith
2	Dave Jones
3	Mike Beach
4	Jerry Miller
5	Ben Stuart
6	Fred Flint
7	Joe Blow
8	Greg Brown
9	Doug Hope

MbrDB Table

MID	DID
1	1
1	2
1	3
2	4
2	5
4	2
4	6
5	6
5	7
6	8
8	1
8	9

Database Table

DID	Database
1	Access
2	DB2
3	Foxpro
4	dBASE

5	Clipper
6	Oracle
7	Sybase
8	Informix
9	MSS q[1] Server

3. Eliminate Columns Not Dependent On key. The Member table satisfies first normal form – it contains no repeating groups. It satisfies second normal form – Since it doesn't have a multivalued key. But the key is MemberID, and the company name and location describe only a company, not a member. To achieve third normal form, they must be moved into a separate table. Since they describe a company, CompanyCode becomes the key of the new "Company" table.

The motivation for this is the same for second normal form: we want to avoid update and delete anomalies. For example, suppose no members from the IBM were currently stored in the database. With the previous design, there would be no record of its existence, even though 20 past member were from IBM!

Member Table

MID	Name	Company	CompLoc
1	John Smith	ABC	Alabama
2	Dave Jones	MCI	Florida
3	Mike Beach	IBM	Delaware
4	Jerry Miller	MCI	Florida
5	Den Stuart	AIC	Nebraska
6	Fred Flint	ABC	Alabama
7	Joe Blow	RU Nuts	Iowa
8	Greg Brown	XYZ	New York
9	Doug Hope	IBM	Delaware

Member Table

MID	Name	CID
1	John Smith	1
2	Dave Jones	2
3	Mike Beach	3
4	Jerry Miller	2
5	Den Stuart	4
6	Fred Flint	1
7	Joe Blow	5

8	Greg Brown	6
9	Doug Hope	3

Company Table

CID	**Name**	**Location**
1	ABC	Alabana
2	MCI	Florida
3	IBM	Delaware
4	AIC	Nebraska
5	RU Nuts	Iowa
6	XYZ	New york

BCNF. Byce–Codd Normal Form

Boyce–Codd Normal Form states mathematically that:

A relation R is said to be in BCNF if whenever X → A holds in R, and A is not in X, then X is a candidate key for R.

BCNF covers very specific situations where 3NF misses inter–dependencies between non–key (but candidate key) attributes. Typically, any relation that is in 3NF is also in BCNF. However, a 3NF relation won't be in BCNF if (*a*) there are multiple candidate keys, (*b*) the keys are composed of multiple attributes, and (*c*) there are common attributes between the keys.

Basically, a humorous way to remember BCNF is that all functional dependencies are:

"The key, the whole key, and nothing but the key, so help me Codd."

4. Isolate Independent Multiple Relationships : This applies primarily to key–only associative tables, and appears as a ternary relationship, but has incorrectly merged 2 distinct, independent relationships.

The way this situation starts is by a business request list the one shown below. This could be any 2 M:M relationships from a single entity. For instance, a member could know many software tools, and a software tool may be used by many members. Also, a member could have recommended many books, and a book could be recommended by many members.

Member

Software Book

Initial business request

So, to resolve the two M:M relationships, we know that we should resolve them separately, and the would give us 4th normal form. But, if we were to combine them into a single table, it might look right (it is in 3rd normal form) at first. This is shown below, and violates 4th normal form.

Member

Software MemberSoftawreBook Book

Incorrect solution

To get a picture of what is wrong, look at some sample data, shown below. The first few records look right, where Bill knows ER Win and recommends the ER Win Bible for every one to read. But something is wrong with Mary and Steve. Mary didn't recommend a book, and Steve Doesn't know any software tools. Our solution has forced us to do strange things like create dummy records in both Book and Software to allow the record in the association, since it is key only table.

MemberSoftwareBook

MID	**SID**	**BID**
Bill	ERWin	ERWin Bible
John	VB.Net	VB for Dummies
John	Java	Java for Dummies
Mary	ERWin	N/A
Steve	N/A	PowerBuilder Bible

Sample data from incorrect solution

The correct solution, to cause the model to be in 4th normal form, is to ensure that all M:M relationships are resolved independently if they are indeed independent, as shown below.

Member

Software MemberSoftware MemberBook Book

Correct 4th normal form

NOTE : This is not to say that ALL ternary associations are invalid. The above situation made it obvious that Books and Software were independently linked to Members. If, however, there were distinct links between all three, such that we would be stating that "Bill recommends the ER Win Bible as a reference for ERWin", then separating the relationship into two separate associations would be incorrect. In that case, we would lose the distinct information about the 3-way relationship.

5. Isolate Semantically Related Multiple Relationships. Ok, now lets modify the original business diagram and add a link between the books and the software tools, indicating which books deal with which software tools, as shown below.

Member

Software Book

Initial business request

This makes sense after the discussion on Rule 4, and again we may be tempted to resolve the multiple M:M relationships into a single association, which would now violate 5th normal form.

The ternary association looks identical to the one shown in the 4th normal form example, and is also going to have trouble displaying the information correctly. This time we would have even more trouble because we can't show the relationships between books and software unless we have a member to link to, or we have to add our favorite dummy member record to allow the record in the association table.

Member

Software MemberSoftwareBook Book

Incorrect solution

The solution, as before, is to ensure that all M:M relationships that are independent are resolved independently, resulting in the model shown below. Now information about members and books, members and software, and books and software are all stored independently, even though they are all very much semantically related. It is very tempting many situations to combine the multiple M:M relationships because they are so similar. Within complex business discussions, the lines can become blurred and the correct solution not so obvious.

MemberSoftware Member MemberBook

Software SoftwareBook Book

Correct 5th normal form

6. Optimal Normal Form: At this point, we have done all we can with Entity–Relationship Diagrams (ERD). Most People will stop here because this is usually pretty good. However, another modeling style called Object Role Modelling (ORM) can display relationships that cannot be expressed in ERD. Therefore there are more normal forms beyond 5th. With Optimal Normal Form (OMF). It is defined as a model limited to only simple (elemental) facts, as expressed in ORM.

7. Domain–Key Normal Form : This level of normalization is simply a model taken to the point where there are no opportunities for modification anomalies.

❒ "If every constraint on the relation is a logical consequence of the definition of keys and domains"

❒ Constraint "a rule governing static values of attributes"

❒ Key "unique identifier of tuple"

❒ Domain "description of an attribute's allowed values":

1. A relation in DK/NF has no modification anomalies, and conversely.

2. DK/NF is the ultimate normal form; there is no higher normal form related to modification anomalies.

3. Defin: A relation is in DK/NF if every constraint on the relation is a logical consequence of the definition of keys and domains.

4. Constraint is any rule governing static values of attributes that is precise enough to be ascertained whether or not it is true.

5. E.g. edit rules, intra–relation constraints, functional and multi-valued dependencies.

6. Not including constraints on changes in data values or time–dependent constraints.

7. Key – the unique identifier of a tuple.

8. Domain: physical and a logical description of an attributes allowed values.

9. Physical description is the format of an attribute.

10. Logical description is a further restriction of the values the domain is allowed.

11. Logical consequence: Find a constraint on keys and/or domain which, if it is enforced, means that the desired constraint is also enforced.

12. Bottom line on DK/NF: If every table has a single theme, then all functional dependencies will be logical consequences of keys. All data value constraints can them be expressed as domain constraints.

13. Practical consequence: Since keys are enforced by the DBMS and domains are enforced by edit checks on data input, all modification anomalies can be avoided by just these two simple measures.

Example. Define Problems addressed by normalization.

A table that is not sufficiently normalized can suffer from logical inconsistencies of various types, and from anomalies involving data operations. In such a table:

- The same fact can be expressed on multiple records; Therefore updates to the table may result in logical inconsistencies. For example, each record in an unnormalized "DVD Rentals" table might contain a DVD ID, Member ID, and Member Address; thus a change of address for a particular member will potentially need to be applied to multiple records. If the update is not carried through successfully—if, that is, the member's address is updated on some records but not other—then the table is left in an inconsistent state. Specifically, the table provides conflicting answers to the question of what this particular member's address is. This phenomenon is known as an **Update anomaly.**

- There are circumstances in which certain facts cannot be recorded at all. In the above example, if it is the case that Member Address is held only in the "DVD Rentals" table, then we cannot record the address of a member who has not yet rented any DVDs. This phenomenon is known as an insertion anomaly.

- There are circumstances in which the deletion of data representing certain facts necessitates the deletion of data representing different facts. For example, suppose a table has the attributes Student ID, Course ID, and Lecturer ID (a given student is enrolled in a given course, which is taught by a given lecturer). If the number of students enrolled in the course temporarily drops to zero, the last of the records referencing that course must be deleted—meaning, as a side–effect, that the table no longer tells us which lecturer has been assigned to teach the course. This Phenomenon is known as a **deletion anomaly.**

Ideally, a relational database table should be designed in such a way as the exclude the possibility of update, insertion, and deletion anomalies. The normal forms of relational database theory provide guidelines for deciding whether a particular design will vulnerable to such anomalies. It is demands of the normal forms: this normalization.

Normalization typically involves decomposing an unnormalized table into two or more tables that, were they to be combined (joined), would convey exactly the exactly the same information as the original table.

Exercise

Consider the following ordering of transaction:

T2:R(X);T3:W(X);T3:commit;T1:W(Y);T1:commit;T2:R(Y);T2:W(Z);T2:commit;T4:R(X);T4:R(Y);T4:commit.

(*a*) Draw a precedence graph for.

(*b*) Is conflict–serializable according to the precedence graph?

(*a*) Draw a precedence graph for the following schedule.

(*b*) Determine if it is conflict–serializable based on the precedence graph.

Transaction

Time

T1 T2 T3 T4

1 Read(purchase)

2 Read(blance)

3 Write(tax)

4 Read(tax)

5 Write(tax)

6 Read(tax)

7 Write(balance)

8 Read(blance)

9 Write(tax)

10 Write(blance)

11 Read(blance)

12 Write(blance)

(3) Consider the following sequence of actions, listed in the order the actions are presented to the DBM. Assume that the concurrence control mechanism is trict 2PL with timestamps used for "Wait–Die" (i.e., if T i occurs before Tj, then Ti waits: otherwise T i aborts). Describe how the concurrency control mechanism handles the sequence of actions.

T1:R(X),T2W(X),T2:W(X),T3:W(Y),T1:W(Y), T1:

commit,T2:commit,T3:commit

Assume that the timestamp of transaction T i is i. Add appropriate lock and unlock requests to the sequence of actions. The DBM processes action in the order shown. If a transaction is blocked (waiting for a lock), assume that all of its actions are queued until it is resumed; the DBM continues with the next action (according to the listed sequence) of an unblocked transaction.

We assume that the DBM doesn't try to restart T2 until T1 commits. On an exam, you would be told what the abort policy was for example, a different policy might be don't restart an aborted transaction until all the other transactions have finished.

(17) Consider the following ordering of transactions:

T1:R(X), W(Y);T2:R(X),W(Y);T3:R(X),W(Y). How many schedules, if any, are conflict–equivalent to?

Soved Examples

Example – 1 Given a table as under

(*a*) Determine the primary key.

(*b*) Draw the dependency diagram.

(*c*) Is the table in 2NF? If not, correct it into 2NF, show all the table formed after decomposition the relations.

ORDER NO	TITLE	QTY	UNIT–PRICE
1	Computer Networks	1	250
1	Graphics	1	275
1	DBMS	2	295
2	Multimedia	1	300
2	Data structure	1	190
3	DBMS	1	295
3	Multimedia	2	300
3	Computer Networks	5	250

(Order)

Ans. (*a*) Primary of above relation is {order no, title}

(*b*) The following FD's exist into he relation

{order_no, litle} ⟶ QTY

{Title} ⟶ Unit price

FD diagram ⟶

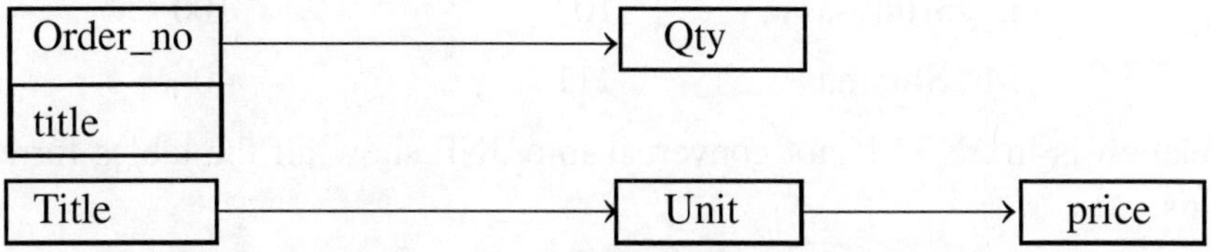

(*c*) Relation order is not in 2NF because unit price is not functionally dependent on the order no. part of the concatinated primary key, but only on the title component.

To convert into 2NF, we have to decomnpore it in two relation as follows:

Order – master (order – no, title, qty) and Book – master (title, unit–price)

ORDER–MASTER

ORDER–NO	TITLE	QTY
1	Computer Networkds	1
1	Graphics	1
1	DBMS	2
2	Multimedia	1
2	Datastructure	1
3	DBMS	1
3	Multimedia	2
3	Computer Networks	5

BOOK–MASTER

TITLE	UNIT_PRICE
Computer Networkds	250
Graphics	275
DBMS	295
Multimedia	300
Data structure	190

Example 2. Given a relation as under.

COURSE – NAME	HEAD – Dept.	ROOM – NO	ROOM – CAPACITY
B.Tech (CS)	Prof. Gupta	102	60
B.Tech (IT)	Prof. Smith	107	50
B.Tech (EC)	Dr. Sundaram	105	60
B.Tech (AI)	Dr. Srinivsasan	103	100
MCA	Mr. Sharma	111	40

Is the above relation is in 3NF? If not convert it into 3NF show all the tables formed after splitting the relations.

Ans. In the above relation, room – capacity is functionally dependent on Room – No and room – no is functionally dependent on the course name. So transitive FD exists here course – name ⟶ Room – No ⟶ Room – Capacity. So above relation is not in 3NF.

To convert into 3NF we have to decompose the given relation into two relations Course (Course – name, Head – dept., Room) and Room (Room _No, Room _ capacity)

COURSE

COURSE _ NAME	HEAD _ Dept.	ROOM _ NO.
B.Tech (CS)	Prof. Gupta	102
B.Tech (IT)	Prof. Smith	107
B.Tech (EC)	Dr. Sundaram	105
B.Tech (AI)	Dr. Srinivsasan	103
MCA	Mr. Sharma	111

ROOM

ROOM – NO	ROOM – CAPACITY
102	60
107	50
105	60
103	100
111	40

Now the above relation are in 3MF.

Example 3. Convert the following relation into BCMF and draw the modified dependency diagram.

STUD – ID	SMAME	SUBJECT	GRADE
1001	Axay	Physics	A
1001	Axay	Chemistry	C
1001	Axay	Maths	C
1002	Sparsh	Physics	A
1002	Sparsh	Chemistry	A
1002	Sparsh	Maths	B

(Student)

Ans. The given relation is in 3MF but hot in BCMF because this relation had two candidate keys (sname, subject) and stud–ed subject, which are composite keys and contain a Common attribute subject to convert it into BCNF we have to use the de composition.

In this relation following FDs exist:

SNAME, SUBJECT ⟶ GRADE

STUD_ID, SUBJECT ⟶ GRADE

SNAME ⟶ STUD–ID

STUD–ID ⟶ SNAME

The given relation is decomposited into following relation

[S grade {stud _ id, subject, grade}sid {stud _ id, SNAME}So, for above relation to be in BCMF, the decomposition will be as follows:

STUD–ID	SUBJECT	GRADE
1001	Physics	A
1001	Chemistry	C
1001	Maths	C
1002	Physics	A
1002	Chemistry	A
1002	Maths	B

(S Grade)

Ans.

STUD–ID	SNAME
1001	Axay
1002	Sparsh

FD diagram —

Stud _ id

Subject ⟶

Grade

Stude _id ⟶

Sname

(Sid)

(S Grade)

Ques 4. Consider a relation as under

Order No.	Order date	Item code	Quantity	Price unit
1456	260289	3687	52	50
1456	260289	4627	38	60
1456	260289	3214	20	17
1886	040389	4629	45	20
1886	040389	4627	30	60
1788	040489	4627	40	60

(*i*) Determine Primary key

(*ii*) Draw Dependency diagram.

(*iii*) Is the realtion in 2NF, if not convert it into 2NF.

Ans.

(*i*) Primary key in {order _ no, item _ code}

(*ii*) Dependency diagram for the given relation

Order no.

Item code

Order date

Quality

Price/Unit

(*iii*) The following dependencies exist in the relation

Item – code → Price/Unit

Order no → Order – date

{Order _ no, Order date } → QTY

The relation in NF, not in 2NF. It can be transformed to 2Nf by decomposing it into three relations.

(*a*) Orders (order no, order date)

(*b*) Order – details (Order no, Item code, QTY)

(*c*) Prices (Item code, Price/Unit)

We observe that the repetition of order date in given relation has been removed. Further if an order for an item is cancelled, the price of an item is not lost. For example if order no. 1886 for item code 4629 in cancelled in given relation them the further row will be removed and the price of the item is lost.

(*a*) Orders

Order No.	Order Date
1456	260289
1886	040389
1788	040489

(*b*) Order Details

Order No	Item Code	Qty
1456	3687	52
1456	4627	38
1456	3214	20
1886	4629	45
1886	4627	30
1788	4627	40

(*c*) Prices

Item Code	Price/Unit
3687	50.40
4627	60.20
3214	17.50
4629	20.25

(Spliting of Relation given 1 in to 2NF Relation)

These relations in 2NF form meet all the "ideal" conditions specified. Observe that the three relations obtained as self contained. There is no duplication of date within a relation.

Ques 5. Given a relation as under

Roll No.	Name	Department	Year	Hostel Name
1784	Raman	Physics		1 Ganga
1648	Krishna	Chemistry	1	Ganga
1768	Gopalan	Mathematics	2	Kaveri
1848	Raja	Botany		2 Kaveri
1682	Maya	Geology	3	Krishna
1485	Singh	Zology		4 Godavari

(Student)

Assume that all first years students are accomodated in Ganga Hostel, all second year students in Kaveri, all third students in Krishna, all fourth year students in Godavari Hostel.

(1) Draw the dependency diagram for above relation.

(2) Show that the relation is in 2NF.

(3) Convert it into 3NF and show all relation of 3NF.

Ans.

(1) Dependency diagram:

Roll no.

Name

Department

Year

Hostel name

(2) If we refer the FD diagram, Roll no. is the primary key and all other non prime attributes are functionally dependent on the primary key roll is, So it satisfy the constraints of 2NF.

(3) We observe that given he year of student his hostel in known and vice versa. The dependency of hostel on year leads to duplication of date. If it is decided to ask all first students to move to Kaveri Hostel and all second year students to Ganga hostel, this change should be made in many places given relation. Also, when a student's year of study changes, his hostel change should also. This is undesirable. A relation said to be in 3NF if it is in functionally dependent on any non _ key attribute. Thus not in 3NF. To transform it to 3NF, we should introduce another relation which includes the functionally related non key attributes.

Roll no	Name	Department	Year
1784	Raman	Physics	1
1648	Krishna	Chemistry	1

1768	Gopalan	Mathematics	2
1848	Raja	Botany	2
1682	Maya	Geology	3
1485	Singh	Zoology	4

(Department)

Year	Hostel Name
1	Ganga
2	Kaveri
3	Krishna
4	Godavari

(Hostel)

So student relation is decomposed into two relation

(1) Department (Roll No. Name department, Year)

(2) Hostel (Year, Hostel name)

Ques 6. Consider the following relation: Professor (Professor code, Department, Head of Department, Per cent time. It is assumed that

1. A Professor can work in more then one department.
2. The percentage of the time he spends in each department is given.
3. Each department has only one head of department.

Draw the dependency diagram for the above relation. Is the relation is in 3Nf.

Dependency diagram is as follows :

Department	$\longrightarrow$	Head of Department
Professor Code	$\longrightarrow$	Per cent time
Department	$\longrightarrow$	Head of Department
Head of Department	$\longrightarrow$	Department
Professor Code	$\longrightarrow$	Per cent time

If we use see the dependency diagram, these are two possible composite keys are {Professor Code, Department} and {Professor Code, Head of department} observe that department as well as Head of Department are not non-key attribute percent time is functionally dependent on candidate key. This relation satisies the 3NF constraint. So given relation is in 3NF.

7. Convert the following relation into BCNF and draw the modified depending diagram.

Professor Code	**Department**	**Head of Department**	**Per cent time**
P1	Physics	Ghosh	50
P1	Mathematics	Krishna	50
P2	Chemistry	Rao	25
P2	Physics	Ghosh	75
P3	Mathematics	Krishnan	100

(PP)

Ans: Candidate keys are {professor code, department} and {professor code, head of department} So, the given relation had two candidate key such that candidate keys are composite and had a common column a normalization is required called BCNF observe, however that the names of department and head of department are duplicated. Further, if professor P2 resigns, rows 3 and 4 are deleted. We lose the information that Rao is the Head of Department of chemistry. The normalization of the relation is done by Cleating new relation for department and Head of Department and deleting Head of Department from professor relations.

(*a*)

Professor Code	Department	Per cent Time
P1	Physics	50
P1	Mathematics	50
P2	Chemistry	25
P2	Physics	75
P3	Mathematics	100

(P1)

(*b*)

Department	Head of Department
Physics	Ghosh
Mathematics	Krishnan
Chemistry	Rao

(P2)

Dependency diagram for the decomposed relations P1 and P2 are as follows:

Department

Professor Code

Present Time

(P1)

Department Head of Department

(P2)

Quer. 8. Consider the following relation

Vendor Code	Item code	Project No.
V1	I1	P1
V1	I2	P1
V1	I1	P3
V1	I2	P3
V2	I2	P1
V2	I3	P1
V3	I1	P2
V3	I1	P2

It is assume that

- A vendor is capable of supplying many items.
- A project uses many items.
- A vendor supplies to many projects.
- An item may be supplied by many tendors.

(1) Draw the dependecy diagram of given relation.

(2) Convert it into 4NF.

Ans (1). Dependency diagram:

V

I

P

V

P

P

Here V is vendor code

I is item code

P is project no.

(2) The given relation has the following problems:

- If rendor V1 has to supply to project P2, but the item is not yet decided, then a row with a blank for item code has to be introduced.
- The information about item 1 is stored twice for vendor V3.

We observe that the given relation is in 3NF also in BCNF but not in 4NF. To convert into 4NF. We have do decompose into two relation.

(*a*) Vendor supply {vendor code, item code}

(*b*) Vendor project {vendor code, project no.)

So, decomposed relations are:

(*a*) Vendor supply (*b*) Vendor project

Vendor Code	Item code
V1	I1
V1	I2
V2	I3
V3	I1

Vendor	Project no.
V1	P1
V1	P3
V2	P1
V3	P1
V3	P2

Above relations are in 4NF.

Ques 9. Consider the relation below Employee (Employee Code, Employee name, Department, Salary, Project no. Terminations date of project)

(1) Draw the dependency diagram for the above relation.

(2) Convert it into 3NF, show modified dependency diagram.

Ans (1) Dependency diagram:

Employee code

Employee name

Department

Salary

Project no.

Termination date

(2) As can be seen from the figure the termination date of a project is dependent on the project no. Thus this relation is not in 3NF. the 3NF relations are: Employee (Employee code, Employee name, Salary, Project no.)

Project (Project no., Termenation date)

Modified dependency diagram:

Employee code

Employee name

Department

Salary

Project no.

(Employee)

Project no. $\longrightarrow$ Termination date

(Project)

EXERCISE

1. What do you mean by normalization why it is done? What are properties of normalized?
2. Explain functional dependence. Give an example.
3. What do you mean by closure of a set of dependencies? How to compute closure?
4. Suppose relation R with attributes A, B, C, D, E, F and the FD's {A $\rightarrow$ BC B $\rightarrow$ E, CD $\rightarrow$ EF} Now show that the FD AD $\rightarrow$ F holds for R and is an member of the closure of the given set.
5. Give an algorithm to compute closure of a set of attributes.
6. Relation R with attributes A, B, C, D, E' F and FD's { A $\rightarrow$ BC, E $\rightarrow$ CF, B $\rightarrow$ E, CD $\rightarrow$ EF} Compute closure $[A,B\}^+$ of the set of attribute {A,B}under this set of FD's.
7. What is 1NF? Give example to demonstrate how 1NF improves a table?
8. Discuss 2NF. Discuss the problems that can be encounted in a table, which is in 1NF, How does 2NF solve them?
9. Define 3NF. What is its need?
10. Consider a relation R with attributes A, B, C, D, E and F and a set of FD's A $\longrightarrow$ B, BC $\longrightarrow$ DE and AEF $\longrightarrow$ G compute the closure X^+ of the set of attributes {A,C} under the given set of FD's.
11. Explain Boyce Codd Normal form.
12. Explain multivalued dependency. Give an example.
13. Explain the fourth normal form (4NF).

UNIT — FOUR

Chapter 6 Transaction Processing Concepts

Chapter Outline

TRANSACTION SYSTEM

Collections of operations that form a single logical unit of work are called transactions.

Transactions access data using two operations:

(1) Read (A), which transfers the data item A from the data base to a local buffer belonging to the transaction that execute the lead operation.

(2) Write (A), which transfers the data item A from the local buffer of the transaction that executed the write back to the database.

Let T_1 be a transaction that transfers $50 from account A to account B. This transaction can be defined as

T_1: read (A)

A: = A – 50;

write (A);

read (B)

B: = B – 150;

write (B).

Transactions have four basic properties which are called ACID properties. The following are the ACID properties.

(1) **Atomicity** — A transaction is an a mix unit of processing it either performed completely or hot performed at all. The sum (A+B) is not preserved. Suppose that Transaction Ti the (2) values of

accounts A and B are $1000 and $2000, respectively. In this example power feeling is occur before write (A) value. In this case, the values of accounts A and B reflected in the database are $50 and $2000. The system destroyed $50 as a result of this failure. In particular we note that the sum A+B is no longer preserved. Thus the state is in consistent state because A = $950 and B = $2000.

(2) **Consistency —** The consistency property of a transaction implies that if database was in a consistent state before the initiation of a transaction, the at the end of transactions the database will also be in consistent state. In this ex A = $1000, A = $950, write(A) = $950, B = $2000, B = B + 50 B = $2000 + $50, B = $2050 The sum A+B = $950 + $2050 = $3000 is consistent state.

(3) **Isolation —** The isolation property of a transaction indicates that the steps or operation performed by a transaction should be isolated from other transactions. Ensuring the isolation property from other transactions. Ensuring the isolation property is the responsibility of a component of the database system called the concurrency control component.

Fo ex. Transaction T_1 transfers $50 from account A to account B.

It is definedas.

T_1: read(A)
A: = A – 50;
write(A);
read(B);
B: = B+50;
write(B)

Transaction T_2 transfers 10 percent of the balance from account A to account B. It is defined as.

T_2: read(A);
temp: A * 0.1;
A: = A– temp;
Write (A);
read(B);
B: = B + temp;
Wirte (B).

T_1	T_2
read (A); $1000	read (A); $950
A = A – 50;	temp = A * 0.1; = 65
Write (A); = $950	A = A – temp; = 950 – 95 = 855
read (B) = $2000	write(A); = $855
B = B + 50	read(B) = $2050
Write (B) $2050	B = B + temp = 2050 + 95
	write (B) $2145

Concurrent execution of serial schedule

In this ex transaction T_1 gives steps or operations isolate to other transaction T_2.

(4) **Durability** — The changes applied to the is successfully means write the value on the Harddisk, transaction must persist in the database. These changes must not be lost because of any failure.

For above ex. T_1 and T_2 executed concurrently the atomicity property in hold.

For above ex. In T_1 A = $950 then system is fail not value of A is preset not lost in 1.(a) the database.

1(*b*) **Transaction state** —

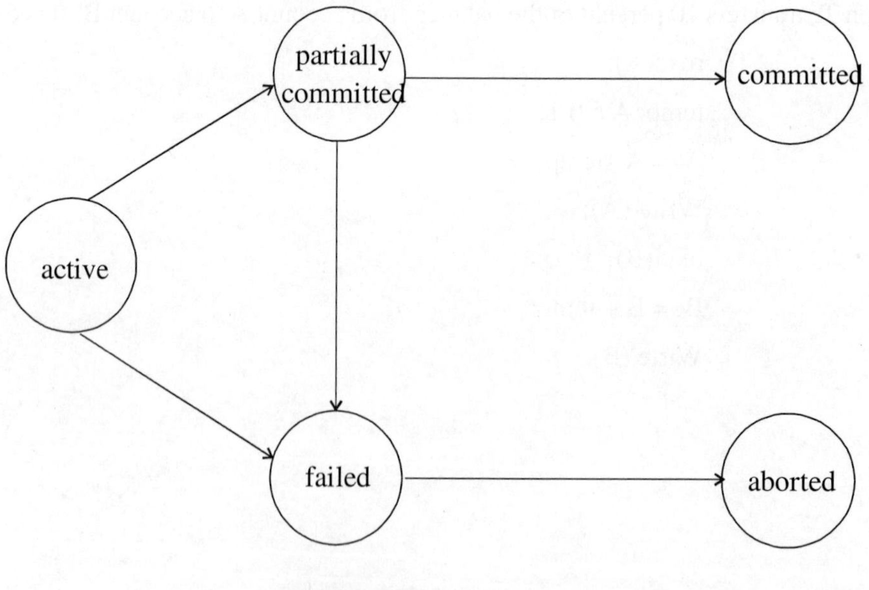

State diagram of transaction

(1) **Active state** — The initial state, the transaction stays in this state while it is executing.

(2) **Partially committed** — After the final statement has been executed.

(3) **Failed** — after the discovery that normal execute can no longer proceed.

(4) **Aborted** — after the transaction has been rolled back and the database has been restored to its state prior to the start of the transaction.

Or

A transaction may not always complete its execution successfully. Such a transaction is termed aborted.

(5) **Committed** — after successful completion.

A transaction is said to have terminated if has either committed or aborted.

SERIALIZABILITY OF SCHEDULES

Schedules

Schedules means when several transacting are excuting concurrently then the order of execution of various instructions is known as Schedule.

Let T_1 transfers \$50 from account A to account B and T_2 transfers 10 per cent of the balance from account A to account B.

	T_1	T_2	
instructions	read(A) A: = A – 50 write(A) read(B) B = B + 50 write(B)		
		read(A) temp = A * 0.1 A: = write(A) read(B) B: = B + temp write(B)	instructions

2(*a*) **Serial Schedule** —

(1) Execute all operations of Transaction T_2 than execute all operations of Transaction T_2 (in sequence)

(2) Execute all operations of transaction T_2 then execute all operations of transaction T_1 (in sequence)

T_1	T_2
read(A)	
A: = A – 50	
write(A)	
read(B)	
B: = B + 50	
write(B)	
	read(A)
	temp: = A – temp
	write(A)
	read(B)
	B: = B + temp
	write(B)

Schedule – 1 = a serial schedule in which T_1 is followed *b* T_2.

In the figure the sequence of instruction steps is in order from top to bottom, with instructions of T_1 appearing in the left column and instructions of T_2 appearing in the right column. The final values of accounts A and B, after the execution in figure takes place one \$855 and \$2145, respectively. Thus the total amount of money in accounts A and B that is the sum A + B us preserved after the execution of both transactions.

T_1	T_2
	read(A)
	A: = A – 50
	write(A)
	read(B)
	B: = B + 50
	write(B)
read(A)	
temp: = A * 0.1	
A: = A – temp	
write(A)	
read(B)	
B: = B + temp	
write(B)	

Schedule 2—a serial schedule in which T_2 is followed by T_1

Again the sum A + B is preserved and the final values of accounts A and B one $850 and $2150 respectively.

In serial Transaction (merits)—

(1) Only one transaction at a time is active.

(2) No interleaving accuse in a serial schedule.

Demerits — When transactions wait for an Input/Output operation to complete we can not switch the CPU processor the another transaction. Thus the CPU time is wasted. Committed (end of transaction successfully) means Harddisk initial value abortus (end of transaction unsuccessfully (mean to reach the initial value).

2(*b*) Non Serial Schedules — A schedule is said to be serial, if all operations of each transactions are executed consequentively, other wise it is said to be non–serial.

2(*b*) (i) Concurrent execution of serial schedule — In two transactions are executed concurrently in which several execution sequence are possible, since various instructions from both transactions may now be interleaved. Then sum (A + B) is indeed preserved. {Because concurrent execution interleaving is possible} {Because it is serial}

(1) Inter leaving may possible.

(2) Final state is an consistent state.

(3) The sum (A + B) is indeed preserved.

T_1	T_2
read(A)	
A: = A – 50	
write(A) = $ 950	read(A) = $950
	temp: = A * 0.1 = 95
	A: = A – temp = 950 – 952 = $855
read(B) = $2000	
B: = B + 50 = $2050	
write (B) = $2050	
write (A) $ 855	
read (B) = $2050	
	B: = B + temp
	= $2050 + 855 = $21.45
	write(B)

Schedule 3 — Concurrent execution of serial schedule

In this figure transactions executed serially in the order T_1 followed by T_2. The sum A + B is indeed preserved.

2(*b*) (*ii*) Concurrent execution of non serial schedule —

(1) Inter leaving is possible (Because execution is concurrent)

(2) The sum A + B is not pressured (because non serial) by the execrities of two transactions.

(3) The final state is an inconsistent state.

{Both T_1 and T_2 is non serial execution the value of T_1 does not depend upon the value of T_2.

T_1	T_2
read(A) = $1000	
A = A – 50 = $950	
	read(A) = $1000
	temp = A× 0.1 = $100
	A = temp = 1000 – 900
	write(A) = $900
	read(B) = $2000
write(A) = $950	
read(B) = $2000	
B: = B + 50 = 250	
write (B) = 2050	
	B: = B + 50 = 2000 + 900
	write (B)

Schedule 4 — Concurrent execution of non serial schedule

***2(c)* Conflict serializability** — Let us consider a schedule in which there are two consecutive instructions I_i and I_j of transaction T_i and T_j respectively (i = j). If I_i and I_j to different data items, them we can swap I_i and I_j without affecting the results of any instruction in the schedule. However, if I_i and I_j refer to the same data item Q, then the order of the two steps may matter. Since we are dealing with only read and write instructions, there are tour cases that we need to censider:

(1) I_i = read(Q), I_j = read(Q). The order of I_i and I_j does not matter.

(2) I_i = read(Q), I_j = write(Q). If I_j, than T_1 read the value of Q that is written by T_j, on I_j. Thus, the order of I_i and I_j matters.

(3) I_i = write(Q), I_j = read(Q). The order of I_i and I_j matter.

(4) I_i = write(Q), I_j = write(Q). The order of I_i and I_j does not matter.

We say that I_i and I_j conflict if they are operations by different transactions on the same data item and at least one of these instructions is a write operation.

T_1	T_2
read(A)	
write(A)	
	read (A)
	write (A)
read(B)	
write(B)	
	read(B)
	write(B)

Schedule 3 — Showing only the read and write Instructions

The write(A) instruction of T_1 conflicts with the read(A) instruction of T_2. The write(A) instruction of T_2 does not conflict with the read(B) instruction of T_1 because the two instructions access different data items. If I_i and I_j are instructions of different transactions and I_i and I_j do not conflict, then we can swap the order of I_i and I_j to produce a new schedule. Since with the read(B) instructing of T_1, re can swap these instructions to generate an equivalent schedule 5.

T_1	T_2
read (A)	
write (B)	
	read (A)
read(B)	
	write (A)
write (B)	
	read (B)
	write (B)

Schedule 5 — Schedule 3 after swapping of a pair of instructions we continue to swap nonconflicting instructions:

- Swap the read(B) instruction of T_1 with the read(A) instruction of T_2.
- Swap the write(B) instruction of T_1 with the write(A) instruction of T_2.
- Swap the write(B) instruction of T_1 with the read(A) instruction of T_2.

The final result of these swaps, schedule 6.

T_1	T_2
read (A)	
write (A)	
read (B)	
write (B)	
	read (A)
	write (A)
	read (B)
	write (B)

Schedule 6 — a serial schedule that is equivaler to schedule 3

Schedules is conflict serializable if it is conflict equivalent to a serial schedule. Thus, Schedule 3 is conflict serializable, since it is conflict equivalent to the serial Schedule 1.

2(*d*) View serializability — consider two Schedules S and S where the same set of transactions participates in both schedules. The schedule S and S' are said to be view equivalent if three conditions are met:

(1) For each data item Q_1 if transaction T_1 reads the initial value of Q in Schedule S_1 then Transaction T_1 must in Schedule S', also read the initial value of Q.

(2) For each data item Q, if transaction T_1 executes read (Q) in Schedule S and if that value was produced by write (Q) operation executed by transaction T_j, then the read(Q) operation of Transaction T_1 must in schedules also read the value of Q that was produced by the same write (Q) operation of Transaction T_j.

(3) For each data item Q, the transaction that performs the final write (Q) operation in schedules must perform the final write (Q) operation in schedules'.

We say that a schedule S is view serializable if it is view equivalent to a serial schedule.

T_1	T_2
read(A)	
A: = A – 50	
write(A)	
	read(A)
	temp = A × 0.1
	A = A – temp
	write(A)
read(B)	
B: B + 50	
write(B)	
	read(B)
	B = B + temp
	write(B)

Schedule 1 — Serial executltion

T_1	T_2
read(A) A: = A – 50 write(A) read(B) B: = B + 50 write(B)	
	read(A) temp = A × 0.1 A = A – temp write(A) read(B) B = B + temp write(B)

Schedule 2 — Serial execution

Schedule 1 and Schedule 2 are not view equivalent Since in S_1 the value of account A read by T_2 was produced by T_1 where as this case does not hold in S_2.

T_1	T_2
read(A)	
A: = A – 50	
write(A)	
	read(A)
	temp = A × 0.1
	A: = A – temp
	write(A)
read(B)	
B: = B + 50	
write(B)	
	read(B)
	B: = B + temp
	write(B)

Schedule 3 — Concurrent execution of serial Schedule S_1 and S_3 are view equivalent because values of accounts A and B read by transaction T_2 were produced by T_1.

(4) Testing of Serializability —

4(*a*) Testing for conflict Serializability — A simple and efficient method for determining conflict serializability of a schedule consider a schedule S. We construct a directed graph 1 called a precedence graph, from S. This graph consists of pair G = (V_1E) where V is a set of vertices and E is a set of edges. The set of edges consisted of all edges $T_i \rightarrow T_j$ for which one of three conditions holds.

(1) T_i executes write(Q) before T_j executes read(Q)

(2) T_i executes read(Q) before T_j executes write(Q)

(3) T_i executes write(Q) before T_j executes write(Q)

(*a*) (*b*)

Precedence graph for (*a*) schedule 1 and (*b*) schedule 2 (*a*) contains the single edge $T_1 \rightarrow T_2$, Since all the instructions of T_1 are executed before the first instructions of T_2 is executed. In (*b*) shows the precedence graph for schedules with the single edge $T_2 \rightarrow T_1$, Since all the instructions of T_2 are executed before the first instruction of T_1 is executed.

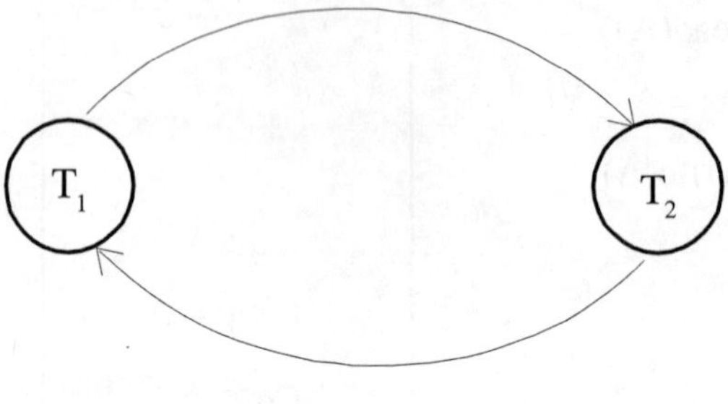

Precedence graph for schedule 4

The precedence graph for schedule 4 contains the edge $T_1 \rightarrow T_2$ because T_1 executes read(A) before T_2 executes write(A). It also contains the edge $T_2 \rightarrow T_1$ because T_2 executes read(B) before T_1 executes read(B) before T_1 executes write(B).

If the precedence graph for S has a cycle, then schedule S is not conflict serializable. If the graph contains no cycle, then the schedule S is conflict schedule.

4(b) **Testing for view serializability** — We do not have nay efficient method for testing view serializability. We shall modify prceeding graph test for conflict serializability to test for view serializability also **consider a schedule.**

T_1	T_2	T_3
read(x)		
	write(x)	
write(x)		
		write(x)

Schedule M

we shall draw a precendence graph to test conflict serializability—

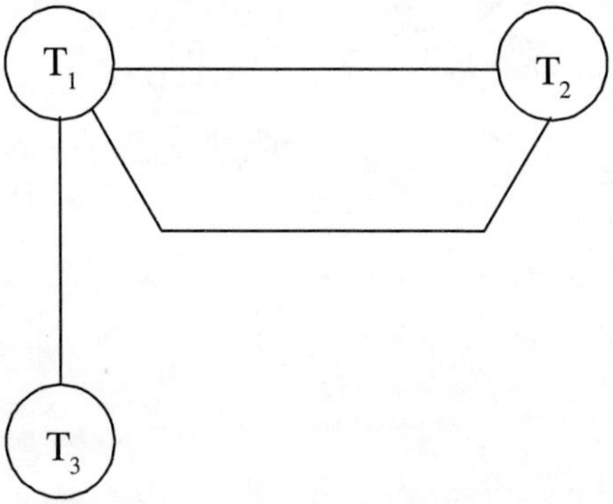

This graph contains a cycle, which indicates that schedule M is not conflict serializable. Schedule is view serializabl every conflict serializable schedule is view serializable but there one view serializable schedules that are not conflict serializable schedules that are not conflict serializable. Schedule M is not conflict serializable since every pair of consecutive instructions conflict and thus no swapping of instructions is possible. T_2 and T_3 perform write (x) operation without having performed a read(x) operation. These types of write operations are called blind writes. Blind writes appear in any view serializable schedule that is not conflict serializable. Schedule m is view serializable, Since it is view equivalent to the serial schedule <T_1, T_2, T_3>. The edge $T_2 \rightarrow T_1$ should not have been inserted in the graph, Since the value produced by T_1 and T_2 would have been used by any other transaction and T_3 produced a new final value of S. The write (X) instruction of T_1 and T_2 one called useless writes. For view serializability, we need to develop a scheme for deciding whether an edge needs to be inserted in preceding graph.

We need to expend the precedence graph to include labeled edge. We term three type of graph as labeled precedence graph.

Draw labeled precedence graph implementing following three rules:

T_b and T_f be two dummy transactions inserting T_b at the beginning of S and adding T_f at the end of S. Add an edge $T_i \rightarrow T_f$, if transaction T_i leads the value of data item X written by T_i.

(1) If $T_i = T_b$ and $T_j = T_f$ then insert the edge $T_j \rightarrow T_k$ in the labeled precedence graph.

(2) If $T_i = T_b$ and $T_j = T_b$ then insert the edge $T_c \rightarrow T_i$ in the labeled precedence graph.

(3) If $T_i = T_b$ and $T_j = T_b$ then insert the pair of edge $T_k \rightarrow T_i$ and $T_j \rightarrow T_k$ in the labeled precedence graph where p is a unique integer, which is large than 0 and not being used for libelling of edges.

Rule ≠ 1 and Rule ≠ 2.

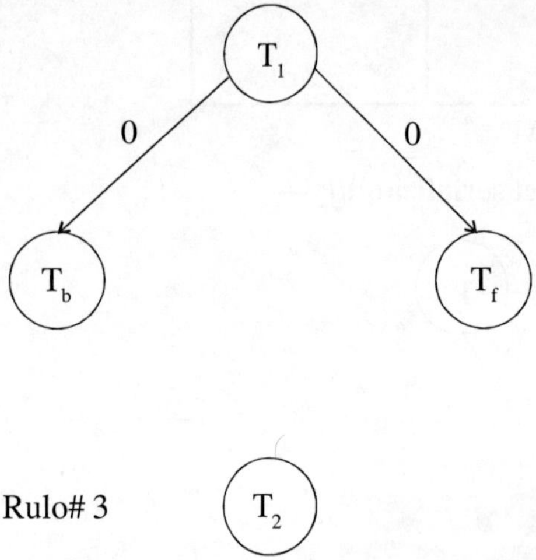

Rulo# 3

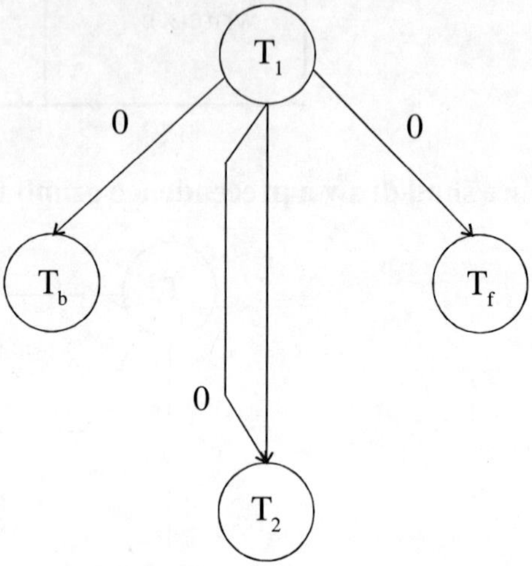

(5) **Recoverability —**

T_1	T_2
read(A)	
A: = A – 50	
write(A)	
read(B)	
B: = B + 50	
write(B)	
	read(A)
	temp = A × 0.1
	A = A – temp
	write(A)
	read(B)
	B: = B + temp
	write(B)

Consider that instruction of trasaction–1 executed successfully but transaction–2 fails, then the account will be out of balance, So, in this case the effects of instruction of transaction 1 should be written on to database. This process is called recoverability.

(5) (1) **Recovery Schemes—** There are two types of recovery schemes:

(1) Forward Error Recovery

(2) Backward Error Recovery

The data base systems use Backward Error Recovery schemes to recover from errors.

(1) Forward Error Recovery — In this scheme, when an error in the system is detected, the recovery system makes an accurate assessment of the state of the system and them makes appropriate adjustment bases on the expected results if system would be error free. The adjustment depends on the error.

The aim of adjustment is to restore the system so that the effects of the error are cancelled and the system can continue to operate. This scheme is not applicable to un-anticipated errors.

(2) Backward Error Recovery — In this scheme, no attempt is made to estimate what would be the state of the system if error had not occured. Instead, the system is reset to some previous correct state that is known to be free of any errors. The backward error recovery be free of any errors. The backward error recovery is a simulated reversal of time and does not try to anticipate the possible furture state of a system.

6. Recovery From Transaction Failure

A recovery process is an intregral part of a database system, which is responsible for detection of failures and recovery of database. Consider only two types of feutures.

The first type of feuture, loss of volatile storage can be recovered using various methods e.g.

Log based recovery, check points etc.

The second type of feuture, non–volatile storage loss, the most popular and economical scheme is to dump the entire database to a stable storage.

6 (1) Cascading Rollback —

T_1	T_2	T_3
read(A)		
read(B)		
write(A)		
	read(A)	
	write(A)	
		read(A)

In this figure Transaction T_1 writes a value of A that is read by transaction T_2. Transaction T_2 writes a value of A that is read by transaction T_3. Suppose that, at this point T_1 fails T_1 must be rolled back (means to each the initial value). Since T_2 is dependent on T_1, T_2 must be rolled back. Since T_3

is dependent on T_1, T_3 must be rolled back. This phenomenon, in which a single transaction failure leads to a series of transaction rollbacks, is called cascading rollback.

Cascading rollback is undesirable, since it leads to the undoing of a significant amount of work. It is desirable to restrict the Schedules to those where cascading rollbacks cannot occur. Such Schedules are called cascadeless schedules. Formally, a cascade schedule is one where, for each pair of Transaction T_j such that T_j reads a dataitem previously unit by T_j, the commit operation (means to write the value on the Harddisk) of T_i appears before the read operation of T_j. It is easy to verity that every cascadeless schedule is also recoverable.

T_i	T_j
read(A) data item	
A = A – 50	
write(A)	
to commute the value of a	read(A)
before read the value of A of T_J	emp = A × 0.1
	temp: = temp 50;
	write(A)

Cascadeless Schedule

6(2) Recoverable Schedules —

T_i	T_j
read(A)	
write(A)	
	read(B)
read(A)	

In this schedule T_2 is a transaction that performs only one instruction: read(A). Suppose that the system allow T_2 to commit immediately after executing the read(A) instruciton. Thus, T_2 commits (means to write the value of A on the Harddisk) before T_1 does. Suppose that T_1 fails before it commits suppose T_2 has read the value of data item A written by T_1, we must abort (to reach the initial value) to ensure transaction automatic. However, T_2 has already committed and cannot be aborted. Thus we have a situation where it is impossible to recover correctly from the failure of T_1. Schedule, with the commit happening immediately after the read(A) instance is an example of a nonrecoverable schedule which should not be allowed. Most database system require that all schedules be recoverable. A recoverable schedules is one where, for each pail of transaction T_i and T_j such the commit operation of T_i appears before the commit operation of T_j.

(7) **Log based recovery** — The most widely used structure for recording database modifications is the log. The log is a sequence of log records. It has these fields:

(1) **Transaction identifier** — TI is the unique identifies of the transaction that performed the write operation.

(2) **Data item identifier** — DI is the unique identifier of the data item written. Typically, it is location on disk of the data item.

(3) **Old value** — Old value is the value of the data item prior to the write.

(4) **New value** — New value is the value that the data item will have after the write.

We denote the various types of log records as:

- <T_i start> Transaction Ti has started.
- <T_i, $X_{j,}$ V_1, V_2> Transaction T_i has performed a write on data item X_j, X_j had value V_1 before the write and will have value V_2 after the write.
- <T_i commit> Transaction T_1 has committed.
- <T_i abort> Transaction T_i has aborted.

7(1) Deferred Database Modification — (In this case not write the old value) The deferred–modification technique ensures transaction atomicity by recording all database modifications in the log but deferring the execution of all write operations transaction until the transaction partially commits het to be a transfors that transfors $50 from account A to account B:

To:

read(A); = $1000

A: = A – 50; = $950

write(A); = $950

read(B) = $2000

B: = B – 150; = $2050

write(B) = $2050

Let T_1 be a transaction that with draws $100 from account C:

T_1: read(c) = $700

C: = C – 100; = 700 – 100 = $600

write(C)

Suppose that these transactions are executed serially in the order to followed by T_1, and that the values of accounts A, B and C before the execution took place were $ 1000, $2000 and 7000 respectively. The portion of the log containing the relevant information on these two transactions.

Appears in Fig

<T_0 start>

<T_0, A, 950>

<T_0 commit>

<T_1 start>

<T_1, C_1 600>

<T_1 commit>

Portion of the database log correrpanding to T_0 and T_1 : There are various orders in which the actual outputs can take P_8 to both the database system and the log as a result of the execution of T_0 and T_1. One such order appears in fig. Mole the value of A is changed in the database only after the record <T_0, A, 950> has been placed in the log.

Using the dog, the system can handle any failure that results in the loss of information on volatile storage. The recovery scheme uses the following recovery proceder.

(1) redo (T_i) sets the value of all data items update by transaction T_i to the new values.

Log	Database
<T_0 start>	
<T_0, A, 950>	
<T_0, B 2050>	
<T_0 commit>	
	A = 950
	B = 2050
<T_1 start>	
<T_1, C, 600>	
<T_1 commit> C = 600	

State of the log and database corresponding to T_0 and T_1

Ctrl T_1	<T_0 start>	<T_0 start>
<T_0 start>	<T_0, A, 950>	<T_0, A, 950>
<T_0, A, 950>	<T_0, B, 2050>	<T_0, B, 2050>
<T_0, B, 2050>	<To Commit>	<To commit>
	<T_1 start>	<T_1 start>
	<T_1, C, 600>	<T_1, C, 600>
		<T_1 Commit>
(*a*)	(*b*)	(*c*)

The same log as that in fig at three different times.

7(2) Immediate Database Modification — The Immediate modification technique allows database modifications to be output to the database while the transaction is still in the active state.

T_0 and T_1 is same as Deferred Database Modification

<T_0 start>

α detailed old value new value

<T_0, A, 1000, 950>

<T_0, B, 2000, 2050>

<T0 commit>

<T_1 start>

<T_1, C, 700, 600>

<T_1, commit>

Portion of the system log corresponding to T_0 and T_1

Log	Database
<T_0 start>	
<T_0, A, 1000, 950>	
<T_0, B, 2000, 2050>	
	A = 950
	B = 2050
<T_0 commit>	
<T_1 start>	
<T_1, C, 700, 600>	
	C = 600
<T_1 Commit>	

State of system log and database corresponding to T_0 and T_1

Using the log, the system can handle any failure that does not result in the loss of information in nonvolatile storage. The recovery scheme uses two recovery procedures:

- undo (T_1) restores the value of all data items up dated by transaction T_1 to the old values.
- redo (T_i) sets the value of all data items up dated by Transition T_1 to the new value.

<T0 start>	<T0 start>	<T0 start>
<T0, A, 1000, 950>	<T0, A, 1000, 950>	<T0, A, 1000, 900>
<T0, B, 2000, 2050>	<T0, B, 2000, 2050>	<T0, B, 2000, 2050>
	<To commit>	<T0 commit>
	<T_1 start>	<T_1 start>
	<T_1, C, 700, 600>	<T_1, C, 700, 600>
		<T_1, commit>
(*a*)	(*b*)	(*c*)

The same log shown at three different times.

7(3) or (8) check points — When a system failure occurs need to the log to determine those transactions the need to be redone and those that need to be undone. In principle, we need to search the entire log to determine this information. There are two major difficulties with this approach:

(1) The search process is time consuming.

(2) Most of the transactions that according to our Algorithm need to be redone have already written their updates into the database redoning them will cause no harm. To reduce these types of overhead we introduce checkpoints. During execution the system maintains the log, using one of the two techniques (1) Deffered Database modification and (2) Immediate Database modification. In addition the system periodically performs checkpoints, which require the following sequence of action to take place:

(1) O/P onto stable storage all log records currently residing in a main memory.

(2) O/P to the disk all modified buffer blocks.

(3) O/P onto stable storage a log record <checkpoint> Transactions are not allowed to perform any update actions, such as writing to a buffer block or writing a log record, While a checkpoint is in progress. The presence of <checkpoint> record in the log allow the systemless streamline its recovery procedure. For such a transaction, the <T1 commit> record appears in the log before the <check point> record, consider the set of transactions {T_0, T_1, —, T_{100}}executed in took place duling T_1 the execution in took place during T1 the execution of the transaction T_{67}. Thus, only Transactions T_{67}, T_{68}, —, T_{100} need to be committed, other wise, it needs to be undone.

(9) **Deadlock Handling —** A system is in a deadlock state if in the set is waiting a set of transactions such that every transaction in the set is waiting for another transaction in the set. There exists a set of waiting transactions {T_0, T_1, —, T_n}such that T_0 is waiting for a dataitem that T_1 holds and T_1 is waiting for a dataitems that T_{n-1} and holds T_n is waiting for a dataitem that T_n holds and T_n is waiting for a dataitem that T_0 holds. There are two principal methods for dealing with the deadlack problem. We can use a deadlock prevension protocol ensure that the system will never enter a deadlock state. We can allow the system to enter a deadlook state, and then try to recover by using a deadlook detection and deadlock recovery scheme.

9(1) **Deadlock Prevention —** There are two approaches the dead lock prevention. One approach ensures that no cyclic waits can occur by ordering the requests for locks or requiring all locks to be acquired together. The other approach is closer to deadlock recovery and perform transaction rollback. Instead of waiting for a lock, whenever the wait could potentially result in a deadlock.

Two different deadlock prevention schemes using timestsamps have been proposed.

(1) The wait die Scheme is a nonpreemptive technique. When transaction T_i requests a data item currently held by T_j, T_i is allowed to wait only is has a timestamp smaller than that of T_3 otherwise,, T_i is rolled back. For example is suppose that Transactions T_{22}, T_{23} and T_{24} have timestamps 5:10 and 15 respectively. If T_{22} requests a dataitem held by T_{23}, then T_{24} will be rolled back.

(2) The wound–wait scheme is a preemptive technique is a counterpart to the wait–die scheme. When transaction T_1 requests a dataitem currently held by T_j, T_i is allowed to wait rule is it has a timestamp larger than that of T_j otherwise T_j is rolled back. Returning to our example, with transactions T_{22}, T_{23} and T_{24} if T_{22} requests a dataitem, hold by T_{23} then the dataitem will be preempted from T_{23} and T_{24} rolled back. If T_{24} requests a data item hold by T_{23} then, T_{24} will wait.

9(2) **Timeout–Based Schemes —** Another simple approach T_1 deadlock handling is based on lock timeouts. In this approach a transaction that has requested a lock waits for at most a specified amount of time. If the lock has not been granted within that time, that transaction is said to timeout and it rolls itself back and restarts. The timeout scheme is particularly easy to implement and works will if transactions are short and if long waits are likely to be due to deadlocks.

9(3) Deadlock Detection and Recovery —

(1) **Deadlock Detection —** Deadlocks can be described precisely in terms of a directed graph called a wait–for–graph. This graph consists of pair G=(V,E), where V is a set of vertices and E is a set of edges.

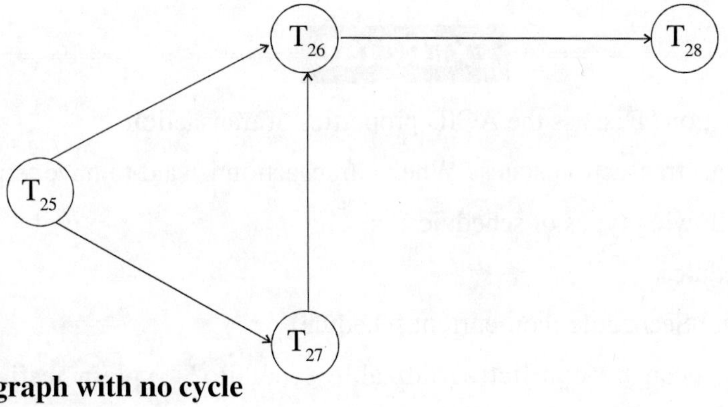

Wait–for–graph with no cycle

Consider the wait–for–graph which depicts the following situation:

- Transaction T_{25} is waiting for Transaction T_{26} and T_{27}.
- Transaction T_{27} is waiting for Transaction T_{26}.
- Transaction T_{26} is waiting for Transaction T_{28}.

Since the graph has no cycle, the system is not 1 in a deadlock state. Suppose now that transaction T_{28} is requesting an items held by T_{27}. The edge $T_{28} \rightarrow T_{27}$ is added to the wait–for–graph, resulting in the new system state in Fig. This time, the graph contain the cycle.

$T_{26} \rightarrow T_{28} \rightarrow T_{27} \rightarrow T_{26}$

Implying that transactions T_{26}, T_{27} and T_{28} are all deadlocked.

Wait–for–graph with a cycle

(2) **Recovery from Deadlock** — When a detection algoithn determines that a deadlock exists, the system must recover from the deadlock. The most common solution **is to roll back one** or more transaction to break the deadlock. Three action need to be taken:

(1) **Selection of a victim** — Given a set of deadlocked transactions, we must determine which transaction to roll back to break the deadlock. We should rollback those transactions that will incur the minimum cost. Many factors may determine the cost of a rollback including.

(*a*) How long the transaction has computed.

(*b*) How many data items the transaction has used.

(*c*) How many more data items the transaction needs for it to complete.

(*d*) How many transactions will be involved in the rollback.

(2) **Roll back** — Once we have decided that a partical or transaction must be rolled back in must determine how for this transaction should be rolled back. The simplest solution is a total rollback.

(3) **Starvation** — In a system where the selection of victims is based primarily on cost factors, it may happen that the same transaction is always picked as a victim. As a result, this transaction never completes its designated task, thus there is starvation.

EXERCISE

1. What is transaction? Discuss the ACID properties of transaction.
2. What are various transaction states? When a transaction is said to have terminated.
3. Explain the following types of schedules:

   (*i*) Serial Schedule

   (*ii*) Non – Serial Sechedule (con-current schedule)
4. What do you mean by conflict serializable schedule? Explain testing for conflict serializability.
5. What is deadlock? What are different methods for deadlock prevention?
6. What is view serializability? Which method is used to test for view serializability?

UNIT — FIVE

Chapter 7

Concurrency Control Techniques

Chapter Outline

CONCURRENCY CONTROL

One of the fundamental properties of transaction is isolation. When several transactions execute concurrently in the database may no longer be preserved. To ensure that it is the system must control the interaction among the concurrent transactions, this control is achieved through one of a variety of mechanisms called concurrency— control schemes.

LOCKING TECHNIQUES FOR CONCURRENCY CONTROL

(*a*) Locks — There are various modes in which a data item may be locked. Here consider two modes.

(1) **Shared —** If a transaction T_i has obtained a Shared mode lock (denoted by S) on item Q, then T_i can read but cannot write Q.

(2) **Exclusive —** If a transaction Ti has obtained an exclusive mode lock (denoted by X) on item Q, then T_i can both read and write Q.

	S	X
S	true	false
X	false	false

Lock compatibility matrix camp

A transacting requests a shared lock Q instruction. Similarly, a transaction and requests an exclusive lock through the lock –X(Q) instruction. A transaction can unlock a data item Q by the unlock (Q) instruction. Let A and B be two accounts that are accors by transactions T_1 and T_2. Transaction T_1 transfers $ 50 from account B to account A.

T_1:

lock – X (B);
read (B)
B: = B – 50;
write (B)
unlock (B)
lock – X (A)
read (A);
A: = A + 50;
write (A);
unlock (A).

Transaction T_1

Transaction T_2 displays the total amount of money in accounts A and B that is the Sum (A + B)

T_2:

lock – S (A);
read (A);
unlock (A);
lock – S (B);
read (B);
unlock (B);
display (A + B).

Transaction T_2

Suppose that the values of accounts A and B are $100 and $200, respectively. If these two transactions are executed serially, either in the order T_1, T_2 or the order T_2, T_1, then transaction T_2 will display the value $300.

If, however, these transactions are executed concurrently then schedule 1 Fig is possible.

T_1	T_2	Concurrency – Control Manager
lock – X (B)		
		grant – X (B, T_1)
read (B)		
B: = B – 50		
write (B)		
unlock (B)		
	lock – S (A)	
		grant – S (A, T_2)
	read (A)	
	unlock (A)	
	lock– S (B)	
		grant – S (B, T_2)
	read (B)	
	unlock (B)	
	unlock (B)	
	display (A + B)	
lock – X (A)		
		grant – X (A, T_2)
read (A)		
A: = A + 50		
write (A)		

In this case, transaction T_2 display \$250 which is incorrect. The reason for this mistake is that the transaction T_1 unlock data item B too early, as a result of which T_2 saw an inconsistent state. Suppose now that unlocking is delayed its the end of the transaction. Transaction T_3 corresponds to T_1 with unlock delayed.

T_3:

lock – X (B)
read (B)
B: = B – 50;
lock – X (A);
read (A)
A: = A + 50;
write (A);

unlock (B);

unlock (A);

Transaction T_3

Transaction T_4 corresponds to T_2 with unlocking delayed;

T_4:

lock – S (A);

read (A);

lock – S (B);

read (B);

display (A + B)

unlock (A);

unlock (B)

Transaction T_4

Consieler the partial schedule for T_3 and T_4 is holding an exclusive mode lock on B and T_4 is waiting for T_3 to unlock B. Similarly, since T_4 is holding a shared mode lock on A, T_3 is waiting for T_4 to unlock A. Thus, the have arrived at a state where neither of there transaction can ever proceed with its normal execution. This situation is called deadlock.

T_3	T_4
lock – X (B)	
read (B)	
B: = B + 50	
write (B)	
	lock – S (A)
	read (A)
	lock – S (B)

Schedule 2

(b) Granting of Locks — When a transaction requests a lock on a data item in particular mode and no other transaction has a lock on the same date item in a conflicting mode, the lock can be granted.

(c) The two phase locking (2PL) protoced — One protoced that ensures serializability is the two phase locking protocol. This protocol requires that each transaction issue lock and unlock requests in two phases:

(1) **Growing phase:** A transaction may obtain locks, but may not release any lock.

(2) **Shrinking phase:** A transaction may release locks but may not obtain any new locks.

Initially a transaction is in the growing phase. The transaction acquires locks as needed once the transaction release a lock, it enters the shrinking phase and it can issue no more lock requests.

For example transactions T_3 and T_4 are two phase on the other hand, transactions T_1 and T_2 are not two phase. Note that the unlock instructions do not need to appear at the end of the transaction. For example in the case of transaction T_3, we could move the unlock (B) instruction to just after the lock –X(A) instruction and still retain the two phase locking property. The transaction has obtained its final lock (the end of its growing phase) is called the lock point of the transaction. Two phase locking does not ensure freedom from deadlock observe that transaction T_3 and T_4 are two phase, but in schedule 2, they are deadlocked. Cascading rollback may occur under two phase locking.

T_5	T_6	T_7
lock – X (A) read (A) lock – S (B) read (B) write (A) unlock (A)		
	lock – X (A) read (A) write (A) unlock (A)	
		lock – S (A) read (A)

Partial schedule under two phase locking

In this Schedule each transaction observes the 2PL protocol, but the fewline of T_5 after the read (A) step of T_7 leads to cascading rollback of T_6 and T_7.

Cascading rollbacks can be avoided by a modification of two phase locking called the strict two phase locking protocol. This protocol requires not only that locking be two phase, but also that all exclusive — mode locks taken by a transaction be held until that transection commits. This requirement ensures that any data written by an uncommitted transaction one locked in exclusive mode until the translation commits — preventing any other transaction from reading the data.

Another Variant of two phase locking is the stick or rigorous two phase locking protocol. Which requires that all locks be held until the transacting commits.

Consider the following two transactions for which we have shown only some of the significant read and write operations:

T_8 :

read (a_1);
read (a_2);
read (a_n);
write (a_1);

T_9 :

read (a_1);
read (a_2);
display ($a_1 + a_2$);

Refinement of the basic two phase locking protocol 1 in which lock conversions are allowed. We shall provide a mechanism for upgrading a shared lock to an exclusive lock and downglading an exclusive lock to a shared lock. We devote conversion from shared to exclusive modes by upgrade and from exclusive to shared by downgrade.

TIMESTAMPING PROTOCOL FOR CONCURRENCY CONTROL

For determining the serializability order is to select an ordering among transactions in advance. The most common method for doing so is to use a timestamp–ordering scheme.

(*a*) **Timestamps :** With each transaction T_i in the system we associate a unique fixed timestamp, denoted by TS(Ti). This timestamp is assigned by the database system before the transaction T_i starts execution. If a transaction T_i has been assigned timestamp $TS(T_i)$ and a new transaction T_j enter the system, then $TS(T_j) < TS(T_j)$. There are two simple methods for implementing this scheme:

(1) Use the value of the system clock as the timestamp that is, a transaction's timestamp is equal to the value of the clock when the transaction enters the system.

(2) Use a logical counter that is intermarried after a new timestamp has been assigned. That is a transaction is timestamp is equal to the value of the counter when the transaction enters the system.

To implement this scheme, we associate with each data item Q two timestamp values:

- W — timestamp (Q) denotes the largest timestamp of any transaction that executed write (Q) successfully.
- R — timestamp (Q) denotes the largest timestamp of any transaction that executed read(Q) successfully.

(*b*) **The timestamp ordering Protocol :** This protocol operates as follows.

(1) Suppose that transaction T_i issues read (Q)

(*a*) If $TS(T_i) <$ W — timestamp (Q), then T_i needs to read a value of Q that was already over written. Hence, the read operation is rejected and T_i is rolled back.

(2) Suppose that transaction T_i issues write (Q)

(*a*) If $TS(T_i) <$ R—timestamp (Q), then the system rejects this write operation and rolls T_i back.

(*b*) If TS(T_i) < W—timestamp (Q), then the system rejects this write operation and rolls T_i back.

(*c*) Otherwise the system executes the write operation and sets W—timestamp (Q) to TS(T_i),

T_1	T_2
read (B)	
	read (B)
	B: = B – 50
	write (B)
read (A)	
	read (A)
display (A+B)	
	A: = A + 50
	write (A)
	display (A + B)
schedule	

TS (T_1) < TS (T_2) and the schedule is possible under the timestamp protocol.

(c) Thomas Write Rule : The modification to the timestamp ordering protocol called Thomas write rule, is this suppose that transaction T_1 issues write (Q).

(1) If IS(Ti) < R — timesstamp (Q), then the value of Q the T_i is producing was previously needed and it had been assumed that the value would never be produced. Hence, the system rejects the write operation and rolls T_i back.

(2) If TS(T_i) < W — timestamp (Q), then T_i is attempting to write an obsolete value of Q. Hence with is write operation can be ignored size.

(3) Otherwise the system executes the write operation and sets W — timestamp (Q) to TS(T_i)

VALIDATION BASED PROTOCOLS

It is based open three phases. (1) Read phase (2) validation phase (3) write phase

(1) **Read phase** — During this phase, the system executes transaction T_i. It reads the values of the various date items and stores them in variables local to T_i. It performs all write operations on temporary local variables without updates of the actual database.

(2) **Validation phase** — Transaction T_1 performs a validation test to determine whether it can copy to the database the temporary local variables that hold the results of write operations without causing a violation of serializability.

(3) **Write phase** — It transaction T_i succeeds in validation then the system applies the actual updates to the database otherwise the system rollsback T_i.

To perform the validation test three different timestamps with transaction T_i.

(1) Start (T_i), the time when T_i started its execution.

(2) Validation (T_i), the time when T_i finished its read phase and started its validation phase.

(3) Finish (T_i), the time when T_i finished its write phase.

T_1	T_2
read (B)	
	read (B)
	B: = B – 50
	read (A)
	A: =A + 50
read (A)	
<validate>	
display (A + B)	
	<validate>
	write (B)
	write (A)

Schedule produced by using validation

The validation Test for transaction T_j requires that, for all transactions T_i with TS (T_i) < TS (T_j), one of the following two conditions must hold:

(1) Finish (T_i) < Start (T_j), Since T_i completes its execution before T_j started the serializability order is indeed maintained.

(2) The set of date items written by T_i does not intersect with the set of data items read by T_j and T_i completes its write phase before T_j starts its validation phase (Start (T_j) < Finish (T_1) < validation (T_j)). This condition ensures that the writes of T_i and T_j do not overlap. Since the writes of T_j, and since T_j cannot affect the read of T_i, the serializability order is indeed maintained.

MULTIPLE GRANULARITY

The multiple granularity locking protocol which ensures serializability is this: Each transaction T_1 can lock a node Q by following these rules:

(1) **It must observe the lock** — Compatibility function of fig

	IS	IX	S	SIX	X
IS	true	true	true	true	false
IX	true	true	false	false	false
S	true	false	true	false	false
SIX	true	false	flase	flase	false
X	false	false	flase	flase	false

Compatibility matrix (IS/Intention Read)

(It explicitly applies a shared lock on some descendant modes

IS → Intention shared mode

IX → Intention–exclusive mode

S → Shared mode

SIX → Shared and intention exclusive (SIX) mode

X → Exclusive mode

If a mode is locked in intention shared (IS) mode, explict locking is being done at a lower level of the tree, but with only shand mode locks. Similarly, if a mode is locked in intention exclusive (IX) mode, then explicit locking is being done at a lower level, with exclusive mode or shened mode locks. Finally, if a mode is locked in shared and intention exclusive (SIX) mode, the subtlee rooted by that mode is locked explicitly in shared mode and that explict locking is being done at a lower level with exclusive mode locks.

(2) It must lock the loot of the tree first and can lock it in any mode.

(3) It can lock a mode Q in S or IS mode only if it currently has the parent of Q locked in either IX or IS mode.

(4) It can lock a mode Q in X, SIX or IX mode only it currently has the parent of Q locked in either IS or SIX mode.

(5) It can lock a mode only if it has not previously unlock any mode.

(6) It can unlock a node Q only if it currently has none of the children of Q locked multiple — granularity protocol requires that locks be acquired in top own (root – to leaf) order, whereas locks must be released in bottom (leaf – to – root) order.

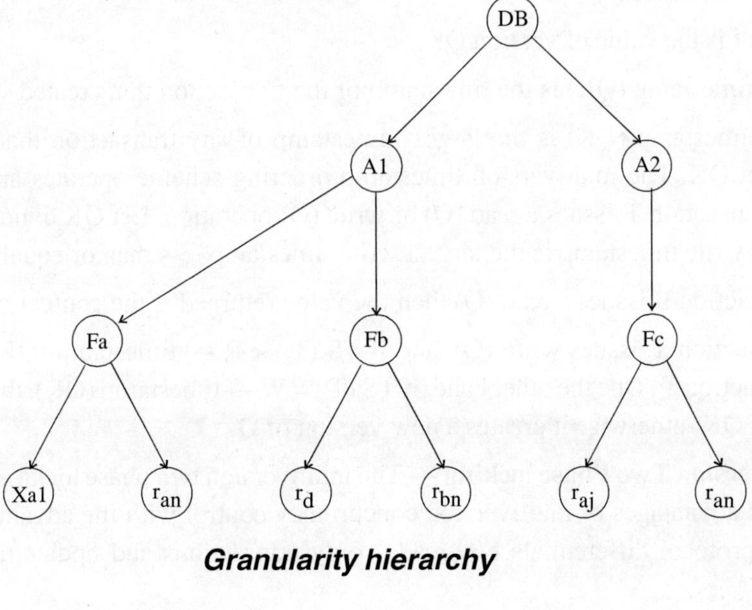

Granularity hierarchy

Consider the tree which consiste of four levels of nodes. The highest level represent the entire database. Below it are nodes of type area; the database consists of exactly these areas. Each area in turn has nodes if type file as its children. Each area contains exactly those files that are its child nodes. No file is in more than one area each file has nodes of type record. The file consists of exactly those records that are its child nodes and no record can be present in more than one file consider the tree and these transactions. Suppose that transaction T_{18} reads record ra_2 in the file Fa. Then, T_{18} needs to lock the database, are A_1 and Fa in IS mode (and in that order) and finally to lock ra_2 in S mode.

Suppose that transaction T_{19} modifies record has in file Fa. Then, T_{19} needs to lock the database, area A_1 and file Fa in IX mode, and finally to lock ra_9 in X mode. Suppose that transaction T_{20} reads all the record in file Fa. Then, T_{20} needs to lock the database and area A_1 (in that order) in IS mode and finally to lock FA in S mode.

Suppose that transaction T_{21} reads the entire database. It can do so after locking the can do so after locking the database in S mode.

We note that transactions T_{18}, T_{20} and T_{21} can access the database concurrently. Transaction T_{19} can execute concurrently with T_{18}, but not with either T_{20} or T_{21}.

MULTIVERSION SCHEMES

In multiversion concurrency control schemes each write (Q) operation creates a new version of Q. When a transaction issues a read (Q) operation, the concurrency — control manager selects one of the versions of Q to Be read.

***(a)* Multiversion timestamp ordering —** The most common transaction ordering technique used by multiversion schemes is timestamping with each date item Q, a sequence of versions QK contains three date fields:

- Content is the value of version QK.
- W — timestamp (QK) is the timestamp of the transaction that created version QK.
- R — timestamp (QK) is the largest timestamp of any transaction that successfully read version QK. The multiversion timestamp ordering scheme operates are follows suppose that transaction T_i issues a read (Q) or write (Q) operation. Let QK donote the version of Q whose write timestamp is the largest write timestamp less than or equal to $TS(T_i)$.

(1) If transaction II issues a read (Q) then the value returned is the content of version QK.

(2) If transaction T_i issues write (Q), and if TS $(T_i) <$ R — timestamp (QK), then the system rollsback transaction T_i. One the other hand, if TS $(T_i) =$ W — timestamp (QK), the system overwrite the contents of QK, otherwise it creates a new version of Q.

***(b)* Multiversion Two Phase locking —** The multiversion two phase locking protocol attempts to combine the advantages of multiversion concurrency control with the advantages of two phase locking. This protocol differentials b/w read – only transactions and update transactions update transactions perform strict two phase locking, read only transactions are assigned a timestamp by reading the current value of TS counter before they start execution; the follow the multiversion timestamp ordering protocol for performing reads.

RECOVERY WITH CONCURRENCY TRANSACTIONS

Recovery in an environment where only a single transaction at a time is executing.

(1) Interaction with Concurrency Control — The recovery scheme depends greatly on the Concurrency Control scheme that is used. To roll back a failed transaction, we must undo the updates performed by the transaction.

(2) Transaction Rollback — We rollback a failed transaction, T_i by using the log. The system scans the log backward for every log record of the form <T_i, X_j, V_1, V_2> found in the log the system restores the data item S_j to its old value V_1 **scanning of the log** terminates when the log record <T_i, start> is found.

(3) Check points — We used checkpoints reduce the number of log records that the system must scan when it recovers from a clash. Since we assumed no concurrancy, it was necessary to consider only the following transactions during recovery.

- Those transactions that started after the most recent checkpoint.
- The one transaction, if any, that was active at the time of the most recent check point.

(4) Restart Recover — When the system recovers from a clash, it constracts two lists: The undo list consists of transaltions to be undone and the redo— list consists of transactions to be the system constructs the two lists as follows: Initially, they are both empty. The system scans the log backward, examining each record until it tends the first < checkpoint> record.

- For each record found of the form <T_i commit>, it adds Ti to redo– ist.
- For each record found of the form <T_i start> if T_i is not in redo–list then it adds T_i to undo–list. Once the redo list and undo–list have been constructed, the recovery proceeds as follows:
  (1) The system rescans the log from the most recent record backward and performs an undo for each log record that belong transaction T_i on the undolist.
  (2) The system locates the most recent <checkpoint 1> record on the log.
  (3) The system scans the log forward from the most recent <checkpoint 1> record and performs redo for each log record that belongs to a transaction T_i that is on the redo for each log record that belongs to a transaction T_i that is on the redo list.

TRANSACTION PROCESSING IN DISTRIBUTED SYSTEM

Transaction in a distributed database system access records by issuing read and write operations each distributed database Mgt system consists of a Transaction Manager (TM), a data Manager (DM) and a Schedules. Transactions Commini cate with TMS, TMS talks to schedulers regarding each row and write of the transaction; schedulers comminicate among themselves and also with DMS; and the DMS manage the date.

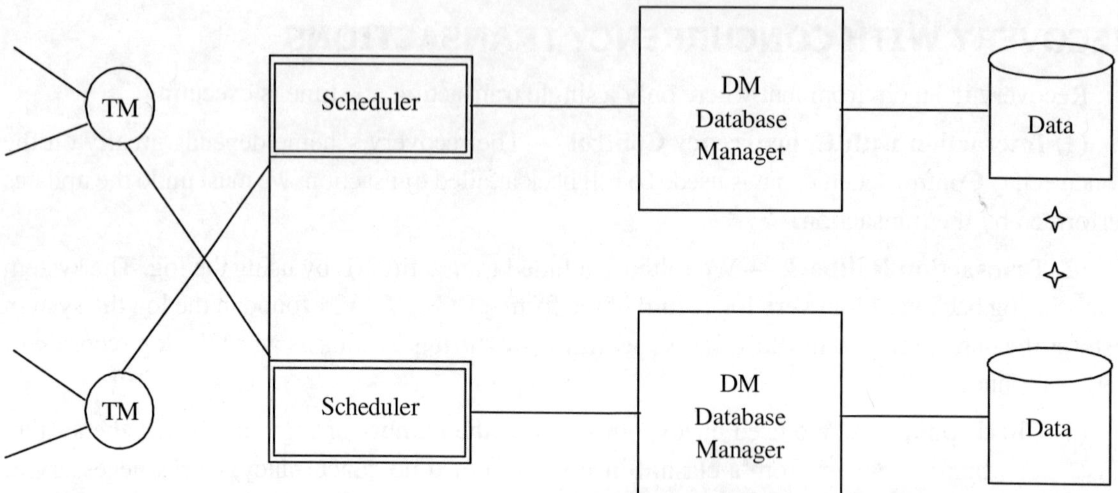

The major advantages of DD BMS —

(1) New sites can be added to the systems anytime with no or little efforts.

(2) DD BMS allows each site to store and maintain its own database, causing the immediate and efficient access to data.

DATA FRAGMENTATION

Data fragmentation is a method in which different relations of selational data base system can be subdivided and distributed among different **Network sites suppose we have a relation S and it is** fragmented, it means it is divided into subsets (fragments) S_1, S_2, S_3 $-S_n$. The union of these fragments re–constructs the original relation S.

There are two types of fragments:

(1) Horizontal Flagmentation

(2) Vertical Fragmentation

In horizontal fragmentation tuples are divided into subsets (fragments), whereas in vertical fragmentation attributes are divided into subsets.

(1) Horizontal freagmentatin — In horizontal fragmentation tuples of relation are divided into no of subsets. For example consider a relation EMP, this relation can be subdivided into different fragments each of which contains tuples belonging to a particular dept. no. If above relation has two Departments 1 and 2, then there may be two different fragments.

Emp–no	Emp–name	Resignation	Salary	Dept–no
1001	Akilesh	Clerk	5000	1
1002	Ashish	Sales Person	5500	1
1003	Sohan	Sales Person	6000	2
1004	Mohan	PRO	6500	2
1005	Ram	PRO	10500	2
1006	Rahul	Manager	1000	2

Relation – EMP

EMP1 = 'Dept–no = "1" (Emp)

EMP2 = 'Dept–no = "2" (Emp)

These two fragment in Fig 1 and Fig 2, can now be stored **on different Networks.**

Emp–no	Emp–name	Resignation	Salary	Dept–no
1001	Akilesh	Clerk	5000	1
1002	Ashesh	Sales Person	5500	1

Relation EMP 1

Emp–no	Emp–name	Designation	Salary	Dept–no
1003	Sohan	Sales person	6000	2
1004	Mohan	PRO	6500	2
1005	Ran	PRO	10500	2
1006	Rahul	Manager	11000	2

Relation EMP 2

The reconstruction of relation EMP can be obtained by taking the union of all fragmentatins that is:

EMP = EMPI U EMP2

(2) Vertical Fragmentation — Vertical fragmentation is very much similar to horizontal fragmented. In horizontal fragmentation tuples of a relation are divided into has of subsets whereas in vertical fragmentation attributes are divided into member of subsets vertical fragmentation its accomplished by adding a special attribute called tuple–id. A tuple–id is a logical address for every tuple. Since each tuple in any relation must have a unique address, which is achieved by adding tuple–id attribute.

Emp–no	Emp–name	Resignation	Salary	Dept–no	Tuple–id
1001	Akilesh	CEO	500	1	1
1002	Ashish	Sales Person	5001	1	2
1003	Sohan	Sales Person	5002	2	3
1004	Mohan	PRD	5003	2	4
1005	Ram	PRD	1001	2	5
1006	Rahul	Manager	1002	2	6

Suppose we want to make two fragments of this relation EMP, EMP 1 and EMP 2.

Then each fragment can be defined as:

EMP 1 = Π Emp–no, Emp–name, Designation, tuple–id (Emp)

EMP 2 = Π Salary, Dept–no, tuple–id (Emp)

Which are shown in Fig 1 and Fig 2.

Emp–no	Emp–name	Designation	Tuple–id
1001	Akilesh	CEO	1
1002	Ashish	Sales Person	2
1003	Suhan	Sales Person	3
1004	Mohan	PRO	4
1005	Ram	PRO	5
1006	Rahul	Manager	6

Relation EMP 1

Salary	Dept–no	Tuple–id
5000	1	1
5001	1	2
5002	2	3
5003	2	4
10001	2	5
10002	2	6

Relation EMP 2

(3) **Mixed Fragmentation —** Horizontal (or vertical fragmentation) of a relation, followed by further vertical (or horizontal) fragmentation is a called the mixed feagmentation.

For example one mixed fragmentation is Π Emp–name, Designation (emp–no > 1003 (Emp)) The result shown in Fig.

Emp–name	Designation
Mohan	PRO
Ram	PRO
Rahul	Manager

REPLICATION

Replication is a key to providing high availability and fault tolerance in distributed systems, high availability is of increasing interest with the tendency towards mobile computing.

Replication

(1) Introduction

(2) System model and group communication

(3) Fault tolerant services

(4) Highly available services

(5) Transactions with replicated data

(2) System model —

Distributed Data Storage — Consider a relation that is to be stored in the database. There are two approaches to storing this relation in the distributed database:

• **Replication —** The system maintains several identical replicas (copies) of the relation and stores each replica at a different **site. The alternative to replication is to store only one copy of relation.**

• **Fragmentation —** The system partitions the relation into several fragment, and stores each fragment at a different site. Fragmentation and replication can be combined. A relation can be partitioned into several fragments and there may be several replicas of each fragment.

(1) **Data Replication —** If relation *r* is replicated a copy of relation *r* is stored in two or more sites. In the most extreme case, we have full replication in which a copy is stored in every site in the system.

There are a number of advantages and disadvantages to replication.

(1) **Availability —** If one of the sites containing relation *r* fails, then the relation *r* can be found in another sites queries involving *r*, despite the failure of one site.

(2) **Increased parallelism —** In the case where the majority of accesses to relation r result in only the reading of the relation, then several sites can process queries involving *r* in parallel. The more replicas of *r* there are the greater the chance that the needed date will be found in the site where the transaction is executing. Hence, date replication minimizes movement of data b/w sites.

(3) **Increased Overhead on update** — The system must ensure that all replic as of a relation *r* are consistent, whenever *r* is updated, the update must be propagated to all sites containing replicas. The result is increased overhead. In general replication enhances the performance of read operations and increases the availability of data read only transactions.

ALLOCATION TECHNIQUES FOR DISTRIBUTED SYSTEMS

In a distributed database system, the database is stored on several computers. The computers in a distributed system communicate with one another through various communication media, such as high speed N/WS or telephone lines. They do not share main memory or disk S. The computers in a distributed system many vary in size and function, changing from work stations up to mainframe systems. The computers in a distributed system are referred to by a member of different names, such as sites or nodes. In distributed database system, we differentiate b/w local and global transactions. A local transaction is one that accesses data only from sites where the transaction was initiated. A global transaction, on the other hand is one that either accesses data in a site different from the one at which the transaction was initiated accesses data in several There are several reasons for building distributed databases systems, including sharing of data autonomy and availability.

(1) **Sharing Data** — The major advantage in building a distributed database system is the provision of an envirorm where users at one site may be able to access the date residing at other sites.

(2) **Autonomy** — The primary advantage of sharing date by means of data distribution is that each site is able to retain a degree of control over data that are stored locally.

(3) **Availability** — If one site fails, in distributed, the remaining sites may be able to continue operating. In particular, if data items are replicated (copies) in several sites a transaction needing particular data item may find that item in any of several sites.

OVERVIEW OF CONCURRENCY CONTROL AND RECOVERY IN DISTRIBUTED DATABASE

(1) **Locking Protocols** — We used the shared and exclusive lock modes.

(*a*) **Single Lock Manager Approach** — In the single lock manager approach, the system maintains a single lock manager that resides in a single chosen site.

The scheme has these advantages:

• **Simple implementation** — This scheme requires two messages for handling lock requests and one message for handling unlock requests.

• **Simple deadlock handling** — Since all lock and unlock requests are made at one site.

The disadvantages of the scheme are:

(1) **Bottleneck** — The site S_i becomes a bottleneck, since all requests must be processed there.

(*b*) **Distributed Lock manager** — Each site maintains a local lock manager whose function is to administer the lock and unlock requests for those data items that are stored in the site.

The distributed lock manager scheme has the advantage of simple implementation and reduces the degree to which the coordinator is a bottleneck.

(*c*) **Primary Copy** — When a system uses data replication, we can choose one of the replicas as the primary copy. Thus, for each item Q, the primary copy of Q must reside in precisely one site, which We call the primary site of Q.

(*d*) **Majority Protocal** — The majority protocol works this way: If data item Q is replicated in n different sites, than a lock request message must be sent to more than one–half of the n sites in which Q is stored. However, it suffers from these disadvantages:

• **Implementation** — The majority protocol is more complicated to implement than are the previous schemes. It requires messages for handling lock requests, and messages for handling unlock request.

(2) **Deadlock handling** — In addition to the problem of global deadlocks due to the use of a distributed lock manager approach, it is possible for a deadlock to occur even if only one data item is being locked.

SOLVED EXAMPLES

Example 1. Define strict two–phase locking

In computer science, **strict two–phase locking (Strict 2PL)** is a locking method used in concurrent systems.

The two rules of Strict 2PL are:

1. If a transaction T wants to read/write an object, it must request a shared/exclusive lock on the object.
2. All **exclusive** locks held by transaction T are released when T commits (and not before).

Here is an example of Strict 2PL in action with interleaved action.

D =

T1	T2
S(A)	
R(A)	
	S(A)
	R(A)
	X(B)
	R(B)
	W(B)
	Commit
X(C)	
R(C)	
W(C)	
Commit	

Or in text form:

T1: S(A), R(A); T2:S(A), R(A), X(B), R(B), W(B), commit; T1:X(C), R(C), W(C), commit

Where

- S(O) is a shared lock action on an object O
- X(O) is an exclusive lock action on an object O
- R(O) is a read action on an object O
- W(O) is a write action on an object O

Strict 2Pl prevents transactions reading uncommitted data, overwriting uncommitted date, and unrepeatable reads. Thus, it prevents cascading rollbacks, since exclusive locks (for write privileges) must be held until a transaction commits.

Strict 2PL does not guarantee a deadlock–free schedule

Avoiding deadlocks can be important in real time systems, and may additionally be difficult to enforece in distributed data bases, or fault tolerant systems with multiple redundancy.

A deadlock schedule allowed under strict 2PL:

G =

T1	T2
X(A)	
	X(B)
X(B)	
	X(A)

Text: T1: X(A) T2: X(B) T1: X(B) T2: X(A)

T1 is waiting for T2's lock on b to be released, while T2 is waiting for T1's lock on A to be released. These transactions cannot proceed and both are deadlocked.

There is no general solution to the problem of deadlock in computing systems, so they must be anticipated and dealt with accordingly. Nonetheless, several solutions such as the Banker's algorithm or the imposition of a partial ordering on lock acquisition exist for avoiding deadlocks under certain conditions.

Even more strict than strict two–phase locking is rigorous two–phase locking, in which transactions can be serialized by the order in which they commit. Under rigorous 2PL, **all locks (shared and exclusive)** must be helod until a transaction commits. Most database systems use strict 2PL.

Example 2. What is non–strict two–phase locking

In computer science, **non–strict two–phase locking,** also 2PL, is a locking method used in concurrent systems.

The rules for 2PL are similar to those of Strict 2PL:

1. If a transaction T wants to read/ write an object, it must request a shared/exclusive lock on the object.
2. A transaction cannot request additional locks on any object once it releases any lock, and it can release locks at any time (not only at commit time, as in strict 2PL)

So, every transaction has a growing phase (it acquires locks) and a shrinking phase (it releases locks). 2PL allows only conflict serializable schedules, but doesn't guarantee that deadlocks will be avoided.

2PL is one scheduling algorithm, sometimes used instead of:

- Simultaneous locking and unlocking (Disadvantage: redundant locking, no interactive transactions)
- Incremental lock, simultaneous release (Disadvantage: Deadlock)
- Simultaneous locking, incremental release (Disadvantage: rollback, redundant locking)
- Incremental locking, incremental release (Disadvantage: deadlock, rollback)

Example 3. What is conservative two–phase locking.

In computer science, **conservative two–phase locking (C2PL)** is a locking method used in DBNS and relational databases.

Conservative 2PL *prevents* deadlock.

The difference between 2PL and C2PL is that C2PL's transactions obtain all the locks they need before the transactions begin. This is to ensure that a transaction that already holds some locks will not block waiting for other locks.

In heavy lock contention, C2PL reduces the time locks are held on average, relative to 2Pl and Strict 2PL, because transactions that hold locks are never blocked.

In light lock contention, C2PL holds more locks than is necessary, because it is hard to tell what locks will be needed in the future thus leads to higher overhead.

Also, a transaction will not even obtain any locks if it cannot obtain all the locks it needs in its initial request. Furthermore, each transaction needs to declare its read and write set (data items to be read/written during transaction), which is not always possible. Because of these limitations, C2PL is not used very frequently.

Example 4. Define Index locking clearly with example.

Index locking is a procedure in which running one task on a database table blocks all access by other tasks to the entire table. With index locking it may be necessary to lock the index build for a column, not just the data items themselves. Index locking prevents conflicts between functions by ensuring that a table is not modified while a function is attempting to use it.

The circumstances where it is necessary to index lock include:

- Adding a new level to the root page
- Shrinking the root page
- Splitting or shrinking the immediate child of the root page, causing an update on the root page

Circumstances where it is not necessary to Index lock include where:

- Small tables with index levels no higher than 3 are being use.
- Possible modifications to the root page of an index are envisioned.

Example 5. What is multiple granularity locking and give some example.

In computer science, **multiple granularity locking** (MGL), sometimes called the **John Rayner locking method,** is a locking method used in database management systems(DBMS) and relational databases.

In MGL, locks are set on objects that contain other objects. MGL exploits the hierarchical nature of the *contains* relationship. For example, a database may have files, which contain pages, which further contain records. This can be through of as a tree of objects, where each node contains its children. A lock a node and its descendants.

Multiple granularity locking us usually used with Non–strict two–phase locking to guarantee serializability. MGL uses lock excalation to determine granularity lock on a node and its ancestors.

Example 6. Define Lock Modes with suitable figures and example.

In addition to shared (s) locks and exclusive (A) locks from other locking schemes, like Strict Two–phase locking, MGL also uses *intention shared* and *intention exclusive* locks. IS locks conflict with X locks, while IX locks conflict with S and X locks.

To lock a node in S (or X), MGL has the transactin locks all of its ancestors with IS (or IX), so if a transaction locks a node in S (or X), no other transaction can access its ancestors in X (or S and X).

MGL locking modes are compatible with each other as defined in the following matrix.

	IS	**IX**	**S**	**SIX**	**X**
IS	YES	YES	YES	YES	NO
IX	YES	YES	NO	NO	NO
S	YES	NO	YES	NO	NO
SIX	YES	NO	NO	NO	NO
X	NO	NO	NO	NO	NO

Example 7. Define non–lock concurrency control.

In computer science, in the field of databases, non–lock **concurrency control** is concurrency control method used in relatinal databases without using locking.

There are several non–lock concurrency control methods:

- Optimistic concurrency control
- Timestamp–based concurrency control
- Multiversion concurrency control

Example 8. Define optimistic concurrency control and pahses in an OCC transaction.

In computer science, in the field of databases, **optimistic concurrency control,** (OCC) is a concurrency control method used in relational databases without uing locking. It is commonly referred to as **optimistic locking,** a misnomer.

Optimistic Concurrency Control is based on the assumption that database transactions mostly don't conflict with other transactions, and that allow OCC to be as permissive as possible in allowing transactions to exectue.

There are three phases in an OCC transaction:

1. **READ:** The client read values from the database, storing them to a private sandbox orcache that the client can then edit.

2. **VALIDATION:** When the client has comnpleted editing of the values in its sandbox or cache, it initiates the storage of the changes back to the database. During validation, an algorithm checks if the changes to the data would conflict with either.

- Already–committed transactions in the cqase of *Backward Validatin schemes, or*
- Currently exectuing transactions in the case of *Forward Validation Schemes.*

If a conflict exists, a Conflict Resolution Algorithm must be used to resolve the conflict somehow (ideally by minimizing the number of changes made by the use) or, as a last resort, the entire transactin can be aborted (resutlting in the loss of changes made by the user).

3. **WRITE:** If there is no possibility of conflict, the transaction commits.

If thereare few confllicts, validatin can be done efficiently, and leads to better performance than other concurrency control methods. Unfortunately, if there are many conflicts, the cost of repeatedly restarting transactions, hurts performance significantly–other non–lock concurrency control methods have better performance when there aremany conflicts.

Example 9. Define timestamp–based concurency control.

In computer science, in the field of databases, **timestamp–based concurrency control** is a non–lock concurrency control method, used in relational databasesto dafely handle transactions, using timestamps.

Assumptions :

- Every timestamp value is unique and accurately represents an instant in time. No two timestamps can be the same.

Formal

Each tansaction can be assigned a timestamp at startup, so we can ensure that if an action A_i fo a transaction T_i conflicts with actin A_j of a transaction T_j, action A_i occurs before action A_j if TS(transaction T_i) < TS(transaction T_j), where TS(x)means the timestamp of x. If an action violates the order, the transaction is aborted and restarted.

Every database object O is given a **read timestamp** RTS(O) and a **write timestamp** WTS(O).

If a transaction T wants to read O, and TS(T) < WTS(O), the order of the read with respect to the most recent write on O would violate the timestamp order between transaction and writer. So, T is aborted and restarted with a new, larger timestamp. If a transaction T wants to read O, and TS(T) > WTS(O), T reads O, RTS(O) is set to max {RTS(O), TS(T)].

If a transaction T wants to write O, if TS(T) < RTS(O), the write action would conflict with the read action of O and T is aborted and restarted.

If a transaction T wants to write O, if TS(T) < WTS(O), we use the Thomas Write Rule and ignore this write to O and continue.

Otherwise, T writes to O, and WTS(O) is set to TS(T)

Informal

Whenever a transaction starts, it is given a timestamp. This is so we can tell which order that the transactions are suppose to be applied in. So given two transactions that affect the same object, the transacion that has the earlier timestamp is meant to be applied before the other one. However, if the wrong transaction is actually presented first, it is aborted and must be restarted.

Every object in the database has **read timestamp,** which is update whenever the objects data is read, and a **write timestamp,** which is update whenever the object's data is changed.

If a transaction wants to read an object,

- But the transaction started *before* the object's **write timestamp** it means that something changed the object's data after the transaction started. In this case, the transaction is cancelled and must be restarted.
- And the transaction started *after* the object's **write timestamp,** it means that it is safe to read the object. In this case, if the transactin timestamp is after the object's **read timestamp,** the read timestamp is set to the transaction timestamp.

If a transaction wants to write to an object,

- But the transactin started before the object's **read** timestamp it means that something has had a look at the object and we assume it took a copy of the object's data. So we can't write to the object as the would make any copied data invalid, so the transaction is aborted and must be restarted.

- And the transaction started *before* the object's **write timestamp** it means that something has changed the object since we started our transaction. In this case we use the Thomas Write Rule and simply cancel our transaction and continue as normal; it does not have to be restarted.
- Otherwise, the transaction writes to the object, and the object's write timestamp is set to the transaction's timestamp.

Recoverability

For an explanation of the terms **recoverable** (RC), **avoids cascading aborts** (ACA) and **strict** (ST) see Schedule (computer science).

Note that timestamp ordering in its basic form does not produce recoverable histories. Consider for example the following history with transaction T_1 and T_2.

$W_1(x)\ R_2(x)\ W_2(y)\ C_2\ R_1(z)\ C_1$

This could be produced by a TO schedule, but is not recoverable, as T_2 commits even though having read from an uncommitted transaction. To make sure the it produces recoverable histories, a scheduled can keep a list of other transactions each transaction has *read from,* and not let a transaction commit before this list consisted of only committed transactions. To avoid cascading aborts, the schedule could tag data written by uncommitted transactions as dirty, and never let a read operation commence on such a data item before it was untagged. To get a strict history, the scheduled should not allow any operations on dirty items.

Implementation Issues

Timestamp Granularity : If the granularity of the timestamp is too large, the possibility of two or more timestamps being equal is increased and thus enabling some transaction to commit out of correct order.

Timestamp Locking : Even though this technique is a non–locking one, in as much as the Object is not locked from concurrent access for the duration of a transaction, the act of recording each timestamp against the Object requires an extremely short duration lock on the Object or its proxy.

Example 10. Explain clearly multiversion concurrency control with example.

In computer science, in the field of databases, **multiversion concurrency control** (abbreviated **MCC** or **MVCC**) is a concurrency control method commonly used by data base management systems to provide concurrent access to the database.

From the perspective of the client, MVCC provides each user connected to the database with a "snapshot" of that person to work with. Any changes made will not be seen by other users of the database until the transactin has been committed.

Implementation : MCC uses timestamps or increasing transaction IDs to achieve serializable. Mcc ensures a transaction never has to wait for a database object and to maintain several versions of an object. Each version would have a write timestamp and it would let a transaction T_i read the most recent version of an object which precedes timestamp $TS(T_i)$

If Ti wants to write to an object, and if there was another transaction Tj, the timestamp order must be $TS(T_i) < TS(T_j)$ for the object write to succeed.

Every object would also have a read timestamp, and if T_i wanted to write to object P, and $TS(T_i) < RTS(P)$, T_i is aborted and restarted. Otherwise, T_i creates a new version of P and sets the read/write timestamps of P to $TS(T_i)$

The obvious drawback to this system is the cost of storing multiple versions of objects in the database. On the other hand, reads are never blocked, which can be important for workloads mostly involving reading values from the database. MCC is particularly adept at implementing true snapshot isolation, something which other methods of concurrency control frequently do either incompletely or with high performance cost.

History

Multiversion concurrency control is described in some detail in sections 4.3 and 5.5 of the 1981 paper "Concurrency Control in Distributed Database Systems" by Philip Bh\ernstein and Nathan Goodman – then employed by the computer corporation of America. Bernstein and Goodman's paper cites a 1978 dissertation by D.P. Reed which quit clearly describes MVCC and claims it as an original work.

Jim Starkey was working at DEC on their Datatrieve network database product when he came up with an idea for a system to manage concurrent changes by many users. The idea dramatically simplified the existing problems of locking which were proving to be a serious problem for the new relational database systems being developed at the time. He started working on the system at DEC, but at the time DEC had just started a relational database effort which led to the Rdb/VMS product. When they found out about his project a turf war broke out (although the product was released as Rdb/ELN), and Starkey eventually decided to quit.

He had heard the local workstation vendor Apollo Computer was looking for a database offering on their Unix machines, and agreed to fund development. With their encouragement he formed Groton Database Systems (named after the town, Groton, Massachusetts, where they were located) on September 3rd, 1984 (Labor Day in the United States) and started work on what would eventually be released as **InterBase** in 1986.

Although InterBase's implementation is much more similar to the system described by Reed in his MIt dissertation than any other database that existed at the time and starkey knew Bernstein from his previous position at the Computer Corporation of America and his previous position at the Computer Corporation of America and later at DEC, Starkey has stated that he arrived at the idea of multiversion concurrency control independently. In the same comment, Starkey says:

The inspiration for multi–generational concurrency control was a database system done by Prime that supported page level snapshots. The intention of the feature was to give a reader a consistent view of the database without blocking writer. The idea intrigued me as a very useful characteristic of a database system.

Example 11. Explain Concurrency Control in RDBMS.

Concurrency control is the mechanism required to manage multiple users accessing the same resource (in the case, tables and rows). In general the goal is to implement this with the least possible overhead, optimized for what you're trying to accomplish. Every approach has pros and cons. Also, this talk is not specific to MySQL at all.

Without any rules, obviously you're going to run into rules. Connection A and B do a select, then an update, but they're a little behind on B, so someone's update gets lost. Whatever concurrency control does, it has to prevent this sort of situation.

You must also avoid "uncommitted dependencies." When one person does something, then another does something using the result of the first person, then the first person issues a rollback. This is similar to something called "inconsistent analysis", which is someone who's working on rows that have changed, and then you end up with bad data.

One big concept here is locking granularity. You want to lock things, but hos low level do you want to go? SQLite does it on the database level, MySQL/MyISAM and MySQL/MEMORY do it at the table, Berkeley DB and Ingres do it at the page level, and pretty much every body uses row level locking.

Once you've got granularity, you have types of locks. Shared read locks allow other people to read rows, as long as they don't change them. Update locks mean you intend to update the row. Nobody else get an update lock while you've got one. Exclusive locks mean it's just you. All you!

Then, after locking is implemented, you want transactions. It's certainly not always necessary, but it's definitely something that needs supporting. It allows multiple commands to execute within a safe area where they cann't get run over. This is usisng the ACID rules...

Atomicity — One or more operatins are a single unit of work, and indivisible. Either all or nothing.

Consistency – The database must always move from one consistent state to another. Inconsistencies may exist during a transaction, but must not after you commit or rollback.

Isolation — Changes in flight (in an uncommitted transaction) must not be visible to other transactions.

Durabiltiy — Once committed, data must persist somewhere/somehow.

(This is all stuff I know/am familiar with. The talk is a bit geared towards never people and reminds me a lot about the database courses at school...)

There are now four isolation levels. Not all of these are implemented by every database server, but of them are. For completeness her they are:

Read Uncommitted — Doesn't solve isolation, you acn see data that is coming from other transactions that are in flight. You can get bad data/dairty reads this way.

Repeatable Read — You only see data that is committed, and you don't see uncommitted transactions. This can cause non–repeatable reads, which is where you're reading data, someone commits a transaction, and you do the same read again, getting new data.

Repeateable Read — You only see committed transactins that were committed *before* you started you transaction. Except for phantoms. Which is where you select data that doesn't exist, then someone inserts the row, and you select again – now you get the row. (InnoDB prevents this by locking the gap on the rows that don't exist.)

Serializable — Transactions are *completely* isolated from eachother. The problem is that every single select requires a shared lock. Prevents phantoms, regardless of the database you use. Can be very slow.

So, higher isolatin level is more correct, but hurts concurrency. It's a huge trade off to make. If you don't implement every isolation level, then you database should escalate to a level higher if you don't implement one they're asking for. (Unfortunately, some databases don't do this)

When doing locking, escalate to the next higher level if you're starting to do a lot of it. If you're starting to lock a ton of rows, lock pages. Lots of pages? Lock tables. This is not stuff that the end user decides, this is all dictated by the database. Set it up to save memory as appropriate.

There are two types of locking... optimistic, and pessimistic. The former is to only take actin when necessary, the latter assumes that you're going to run into problems, so lock things all the time just to make sure we don't have problems. (At this point he's skimming through things, as we're 5 minutes to the end of the session.)

Tgere are other concepts here, such as two–phase locking, multiversioned concurrency control (MVCC), and deadlock. The latter mean you have to rollback transactions.

most databases also support explicit locking – you can tell it to lock something. Not all databases support this, and it's not defined in the SQL standards. (Interesting – a community standard? Among databases.

EXERCISE

1. Explain the concurrency control schema based on timestamping protocol.
2. What are the different locking techniques for concurrency control?
3. How is the concurrency control performed in distributed database? Discuss various validation techniques.
4. Discuss the precedence graph. How will you design it?
5. What is a lock? Defferentiate between exclusive lock and shared lock, give suitable examples.

6. Explain two phase locking with suitable example. Also explain the advantages of two phase locking over single phase locking?
7. What is deadlock? Explain with example how deadlock occurs. How will you recover from deadlock and how you can avoid deadlock?
8. Why concurrency control?
9. What are the varions Locking Techniques for concurrency control?
10. What is time stamping?
11. Write the Time Stamp Ordering Algorithm.
12. What is validation Based Protocol? Discuss it.
13. How to recover date with Concurrent Transaction?
14. Waht is Multiple Granularity?
15. Discuss two multiversion techniques per concurrency control.

UNIT — SIX

Chapter 8 Data Mining and Data Warehousing

Chapter Outline

DATA MINING

What is data mining?

The past two decades has seen a dramatic increase in the amount of information or data being stored in electronic format. This accumulation of data has taken place at an explosive rate. It has been estimated that the amount of information in the world doubles every 20 months and the size and number of databases are increasing even faster. The increase in use of electronic data gathering devices such as point-of-sale or remote sensing devices has contributed to this explosion of available data. Figure 1 from the Red Brick company illustrates the data explosion.

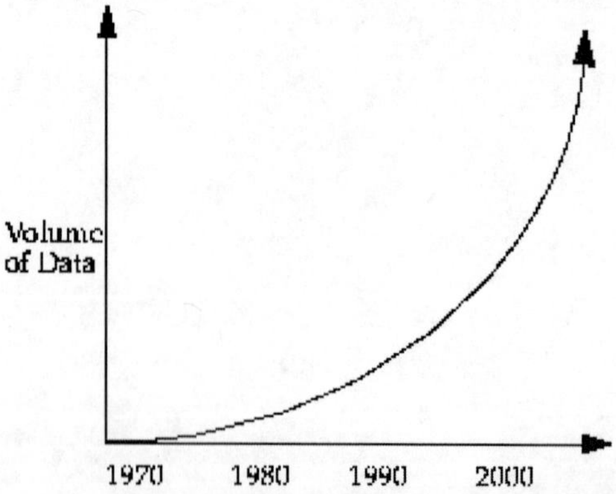

Figure 1: The Growing Base of Data

Data storage became easier as the availability of large amounts of computing power at low cost ie the cost of processing power and storage is falling, made data cheap. There was also the introduction of new machine learning methods for knowledge representation based on logic programming etc. in addition to traditional statistical analysis of data. The new methods tend to be computationally intensive hence a demand for more processing power.

Having concentrated so much attention on the accumulation of data the problem was what to do with this valuable resource? It was recognised that information is at the heart of business operations and that decision-makers could make use of the data stored to gain valuable insight into the business. Database Management systems gave access to the data stored but this was only a small part of what could be gained from the data. Traditional on-line transaction processing systems, OLTPs, are good at putting data into databases quickly, safely and efficiently but are not good at delivering meaningful analysis in return. Analysing data can provide further knowledge about a business by going beyond the data explicitly stored to derive knowledge about the business. This is where Data Mining or Knowledge Discovery in Databases (KDD) has obvious benefits for any enterprise.

The term data mining has been stretched beyond its limits to apply to any form of data analysis. Some of the numerous definitions of Data Mining, or Knowledge Discovery in Databases are:

Data Mining, or Knowledge Discovery in Databases (KDD) as it is also known, is the nontrivial extraction of implicit, previously unknown, and potentially useful information from data. This encompasses a number of different technical approaches, such as clustering, data summarization, learning classification rules, finding dependency net works, analysing changes, and detecting anomalies.

William J Frawley, Gregory Piatetsky-Shapiro and Christopher J Matheus

Data mining is the search for relationships and global patterns that exist in large databases but are 'hidden' among the vast amount of data, such as a relationship between patient data and their medical diagnosis. These relationships represent valuable knowledge about the database and the objects in the database and, if the database is a faithful mirror, of the real world registered by the database.

Marcel Holshemier & Arno Siebes (1994)

The analogy with the mining process is described as:

Data mining refers to "using a variety of techniques to identify nuggets of information or decision-making knowledge in bodies of data, and extracting these in such a way that they can be put to use in the areas such as decision support, prediction, forecasting and estimation. The data is often voluminous, but as it stands of low value as no direct use can be made of it; it is the hidden information in the data that is useful"

Clementine User Guide, a data mining toolkit

Basically data mining is concerned with the analysis of data and the use of software techniques for finding patterns and regularities in sets of data. It is the computer which is responsible for finding the patterns by identifying the underlying rules and features in the data. The idea is that it is possible to strike gold in unexpected places as the data mining software extracts patterns not previously discernable or so obvious that no-one has noticed them before.

Data mining analysis tends to work from the data up and the best techniques are those developed with an orientation towards large volumes of data, making use of as much of the collected data as possible to arrive at reliable conclusions and decisions. The analysis process starts with a set of data, uses a methodology to develop an optimal representation of the structure of the data during which time knowledge is acquired. Once knowledge has been acquired this can be extended to larger sets of data working on the assumption that the larger data set has a structure similar to the sample data. Again this is analogous to a mining operation where large amounts of low grade materials are sifted through in order to find something of value.

The following diagram summarises the some of the stages/processes identified in data mining and knowledge discovery by Usama Fayyad & Evangelos Simoudis, two of leading exponents of this area.

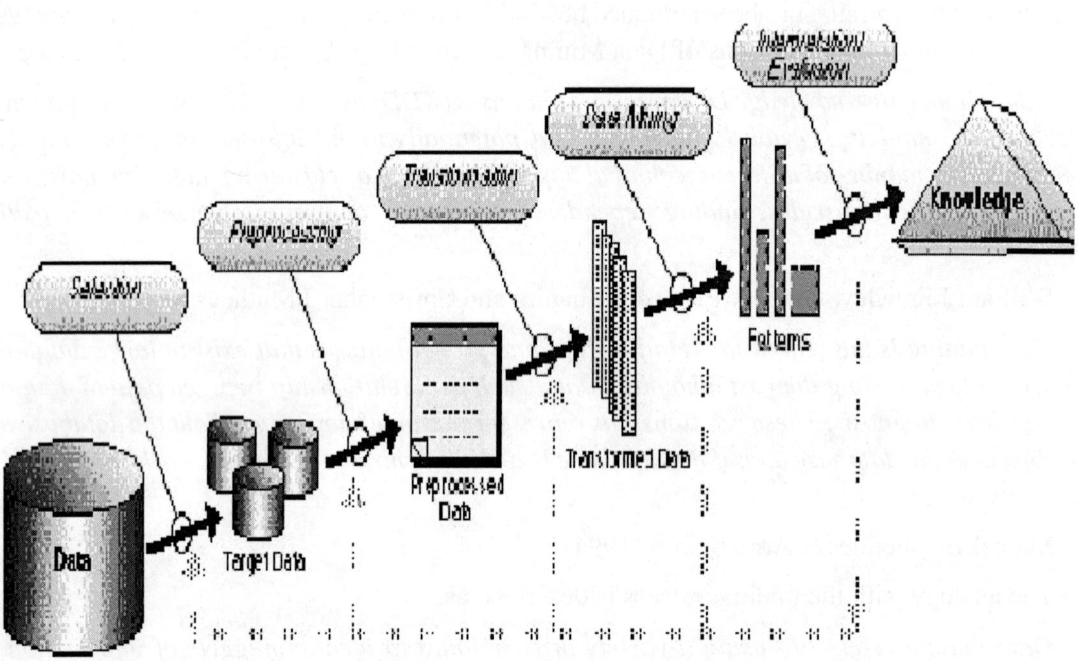

The phases depicted start with the raw data and finish with the extracted knowledge which was acquired as a result of the following stages:

- Selection - selecting or segmenting the data according to some criteria e.g. all those people who own a car, in this way subsets of the data can be determined.
- Preprocessing - this is the data cleansing stage where certain information is removed which is deemed unnecessary and may slow down queries for example unnecessary to note the

sex of a patient when studying pregnancy. Also the data is reconfigured to ensure a consistent format as there is a possibility of inconsistent formats because the data is drawn from several sources e.g. sex may recorded as f or m and also as 1 or 0.

- Transformation - the data is not merely transferred across but transformed in that overlays may added such as the demographic overlays commonly used in market research. The data is made useable and navigable.
- Data mining - this stage is concerned with the extraction of patterns from the data. A pattern can be defined as given a set of facts(data) F, a language L, and some measure of certainty C a pattern is a statement S in L that describes relationships among a subset Fs of F with a certainty c such that S is simpler in some sense than the enumeration of all the facts in Fs.
- Interpretation and evaluation - the patterns identified by the system are interpreted into knowledge which can then be used to support human decision-making e.g. prediction and classification tasks, summarizing the contents of a database or explaining observed phenomena.

DATA MINING BACKGROUND

Data mining research has drawn on a number of other fields such as inductive learning, machine learning and statistics etc.

Inductive learning

Induction is the inference of information from data and inductive learning is the model building process where the environment i.e. database is analysed with a view to finding patterns. Similar objects are grouped in classes and rules formulated whereby it is possible to predict the class of unseen objects. This process of classification identifies classes such that each class has a unique pattern of values which forms the class description. The nature of the environment is dynamic hence the model must be adaptive i.e. should be able learn.

Generally it is only possible to use a small number of properties to characterise objects so we make abstractions in that objects which satisfy the same subset of properties are mapped to the same internal representation.

Inductive learning where the system infers knowledge itself from observing its environment has two main strategies:

- supervised learning - this is learning from examples where a teacher helps the system construct a model by defining classes and supplying examples of each class. The system has to find a description of each class i.e. the common properties in the examples. Once the description has been formulated the description and the class form a classification rule which can be used to predict the class of previously unseen objects. This is similar to discriminate analysis as in statistics.

- unsupervised learning - this is learning from observation and discovery. The data mine system is supplied with objects but no classes are defined so it has to observe the examples and recognise patterns (i.e. class description) by itself. This system results in a set of class descriptions, one for each class discovered in the environment. Again this similar to cluster analysis as in statistics.

Induction is therefore the extraction of patterns. The quality of the model produced by inductive learning methods is such that the model could be used to predict the outcome of future situations in other words not only for states encountered but rather for unseen states that could occur. The problem is that most environments have different states, i.e. changes within, and it is not always possible to verify a model by checking it for all possible situations.

Given a set of examples the system can construct multiple models some of which will be simpler than others. The simpler models are more likely to be correct if we adhere to Ockhams razor, which states that if there are multiple explanations for a particular phenomena it makes sense to choose the simplest because it is more likely to capture the nature of the phenomenon.

Statistics

Statistics has a solid theoretical foundation but the results from statistics can be overwhelming and difficult to interpret as they require user guidance as to where and how to analyse the data. Data mining however allows the expert's knowledge of the data and the advanced analysis techniques of the computer to work together.

Statistical analysis systems such as SAS and SPSS have been used by analysts to detect unusual patterns and explain patterns using statistical models such as linear models. Statistics have a role to play and data mining will not replace such analyses but rather they can act upon more directed analyses based on the results of data mining. For example statistical induction is something like the average rate of failure of machines.

Machine Learning

Machine learning is the automation of a learning process and learning is tantamount to the construction of rules based on observations of environmental states and transitions. This is a broad field which includes not only learning from examples, but also reinforcement learning, learning with teacher, etc. A learning algorithm takes the data set and its accompanying information as input and returns a statement e.g. a concept representing the results of learning as output. Machine learning examines previous examples and their outcomes and learns how to reproduce these and make generalisations about new cases.

Generally a machine learning system does not use single observations of its environment but an entire finite set called the training set at once. This set contains examples i.e. observations coded in some machine readable form. The training set is finite hence not all concepts can be learned exactly.

Differences between Data Mining and Machine Learning

Knowledge Discovery in Databases (KDD) or Data Mining, and the part of Machine Learning (ML) dealing with learning from examples overlap in the algorithms used and the problems addressed.

The main differences are:

- KDD is concerned with finding understandable knowledge, while ML is concerned with improving performance of an agent. So training a neural network to balance a pole is part of ML, but not of KDD. However, there are efforts to extract knowledge from neural networks which are very relevant for KDD.
- KDD is concerned with very large, real-world databases, while ML typically (but not always) looks at smaller data sets. So efficiency questions are much more important for KDD.
- ML is a broader field which includes not only learning from examples, but also reinforcement learning, learning with teacher, etc.

  KDD is that part of ML which is concerned with finding understandable knowledge in large sets of real-world examples. When integrating machine learning techniques into database systems to implement KDD some of the databases require:

- more efficient learning algorithms because realistic databases are normally very large and noisy. It is usual that the database is often designed for purposes different from data mining and so properties or attributes that would simplify the learning task are not present nor can they be requested from the real world. Databases are usually contaminated by errors so the data mining algorithm has to cope with noise whereas ML has laboratory type examples i.e. as near perfect as possible.
- more expressive representations for both data, e.g. tuples in relational databases, which represent instances of a problem domain, and knowledge, e.g. rules in a rule-based system, which can be used to solve users' problems in the domain, and the semantic information contained in the relational schemata.

Practical KDD systems are expected to include three interconnected phases

- Translation of standard database information into a form suitable for use by learning facilities;
- Using machine learning techniques to produce knowledge bases from databases; and
- Interpreting the knowledge produced to solve users' problems and/or reduce data spaces. Data spaces being the number of examples.

DATA MINING MODELS

IBM have identified two types of model or modes of operation which may be used to unearth information of interest to the user.

Verification Model

The verification model takes an hypothesis from the user and tests the validity of it against the data. The emphasis is with the user who is responsible for formulating the hypothesis and issuing the query on the data to affirm or negate the hypothesis.

In a marketing division for example with a limited budget for a mailing campaign to launch a new product it is important to identify the section of the population most likely to buy the new product. The user formulates an hypothesis to identify potential customers and the characteristics they share. Historical data about customer purchase and demographic information can then be queried to reveal comparable purchases and the characteristics shared by those purchasers which in turn can be used to target a mailing campaign. The whole operation can be refined by 'drilling down' so that the hypothesis reduces the 'set' returned each time until the required limit is reached.

The problem with this model is the fact that no new information is created in the retrieval process but rather the queries will always return records to verify or negate the hypothesis. The search process here is iterative in that the output is reviewed, a new set of questions or hypothesis formulated to refine the search and the whole process repeated. The user is discovering the facts about the data using a variety of techniques such as queries, multidimensional analysis and visualization to guide the exploration of the data being inspected.

Discovery Model

The discovery model differs in its emphasis in that it is the system automatically discovering important information hidden in the data. The data is sifted in search of frequently occurring patterns, trends and generalisations about the data without intervention or guidance from the user. The discovery or data mining tools aim to reveal a large number of facts about the data in as short a time as possible.

An example of such a model is a bank database which is mined to discover the many groups of customers to target for a mailing campaign. The data is searched with no hypothesis in mind other than for the system to group the customers according to the common characteristics found.

DATA WAREHOUSING

Data mining potential can be enhanced if the appropriate data has been collected and stored in a data warehouse. A data warehouse is a relational database management system (RDMS) designed specifically to meet the needs of transaction processing systems. It can be loosely defined as any centralised data repository which can be queried for business benefit but this will be more clearly defined later. Data warehousing is a new powerful technique making it possible to extract archived operational data and overcome inconsistencies between different legacy data formats. As well as integrating data throughout an enterprise, regardless of location, format, or communication requirements it is possible to incorporate additional or expert information. It is, the logical link between what the managers see in their decision support EIS applications and the company's operational activities

John McIntyre of SAS Institute Inc

In other words the data warehouse provides data that is already transformed and summarized, therefore making it an appropriate environment for more efficient DSS and EIS applications.

Characteristics of a data warehouse

According to Bill Inmon, author of Building the Data Warehouse and the guru who is widely considered to be the originator of the data warehousing concept, there are generally four characteristics that describe a data warehouse:

- subject-oriented: data are organized according to subject instead of application e.g. an insurance company using a data warehouse would organize their data by customer, premium, and claim, instead of by different products (auto, life, etc.). The data organized by subject contain only the information necessary for decision support processing.
- integrated: When data resides in many separate applications in the operational environment, encoding of data is often inconsistent. For instance, in one application, gender might be coded as "m" and "f" in another by 0 and 1. When data are moved from the operational environment into the data warehouse, they assume a consistent coding convention e.g. gender data is transformed to "m" and "f".
- time-variant: The data warehouse contains a place for storing data that are five to 10 years old, or older, to be used for comparisons, trends, and forecasting. These data are not updated.
- non-volatile: Data are not updated or changed in any way once they enter the data warehouse, but are only loaded and accessed.

Processes in data warehousing

The first phase in data warehousing is to "insulate" your current operational information, ie to preserve the security and integrity of mission-critical OLTP applications, while giving you access to the broadest possible base of data. The resulting database or data warehouse may consume hundreds of gigabytes - or even terabytes - of disk space, what is required then are efficient techniques for storing and retrieving massive amounts of information. Increasingly, large organizations have found that only parallel processing systems offer sufficient bandwidth.

The data warehouse thus retrieves data from a variety of heterogeneous operational databases. The data is then transformed and delivered to the data warehouse/store based on a selected model (or mapping definition). The data transformation and movement processes are executed whenever an update to the warehouse data is required so there should some form of automation to manage and execute these functions. The information that describes the model and definition of the source data elements is called "metadata". The metadata is the means by which the end-user finds and understands the data in the warehouse and is an important part of the warehouse. The metadata should at the very least contain;

- the structure of the data;

- the algorithm used for summarization;
- and the mapping from the operational environment to the data warehouse.

Data cleansing is an important aspect of creating an efficient data warehouse in that it is the removal of certain aspects of operational data, such as low-level transaction information, which slow down the query times. The cleansing stage has to be as dynamic as possible to accommodate all types of queries even those which may require low-level information. Data should be extracted from production sources at regular intervals and pooled centrally but the cleansing process has to remove duplication and reconcile differences between various styles of data collection.

Once the data has been cleaned it is then transferred to the data warehouse which typically is a large database on a high performance box either SMP, Symmetric Multi-Processing or MPP, Massively Parallel Processing. Number-crunching power is another important aspect of data warehousing because of the complexity involved in processing ad hoc queries and because of the vast quantities of data that the organisation want to use in the warehouse. A data warehouse can be used in different ways for example it can be used as a central store against which the queries are run or it can be used to like a data mart. Data marts which are small warehouses can be established to provide subsets of the main store and summarised information depending on the requirements of a specific group/department. The central store approach generally uses very simple data structures with very little assumptions about the relationships between data whereas marts often use multidimensional databases which can speed up query processing as they can have data structures which are reflect the most likely questions.

Many vendors have products that provide one or more of the above described data warehouse functions. However, it can take a significant amount of work and specialized programming to provide the interoperability needed between products from multiple vendors to enable them to perform the required data warehouse processes. A typical implementation usually involves a mixture of products from a variety of suppliers.

Another approach to data warehousing is Parsaye's Sandwich Paradigm put forward by Dr. Kamran Parsaye, CEO of Information Discovery, Hermosa Beach, CA. This paradigm or philosophy encourages acceptance of the probability that the first iteration of a data-warehousing effort will require considerable revision. The Sandwich Paradigm advocates the following approach:

- pre-mine the data to determine what formats and data are needed to support a data-mining application;
- build a prototype mini-data warehouse i.e the meat of the sandwich, with most of the features envisaged for the end product;
- revise the strategies as necessary;
- build the final warehouse.

Data warehousing and OLTP systems

A database which is built for on line transaction processing, OLTP, is generally regarded as unsuitable for data warehousing as they have been designed with a different set of needs in mind ie maximising transaction capacity and typically having hundreds of tables in order not to lock out users etc. Data warehouses are interested in query processing as opposed to transaction processing.

OLTP systems cannot be repositories of facts and historical data for business analysis. They cannot quickly answer ad hoc queries and rapid retrieval is almost impossible. The data is inconsistent and changing, duplicate entries exist, entries can be missing and there is an absence of historical data which is necessary to analyse trends. Basically OLTP offers large amounts of raw data which is not easily understood. The data warehouse offers the potential to retrieve and analyse information quickly and easily. Data warehouses do have similarities with OLTP as shown in the table below.

Table 1 : Similarities and Differences in OLTP and Data Warehousing

	OLTP	**Data Warehousing**
Purpose	Run day-to-day operations	Information retrieval and analysis
Structure	RDBMS	RDBMS
Data Model	Normalised	Multi-dimensional
Access	SQL	SQL plus data analysis extensions
Type of Data	Data that runs the business	Data that analyses the business
Condition of Data	Changing, incomplete	Historical, descriptive

The data warehouse serves a different purpose from that of OLTP systems by allowing business analysis queries to be answered as opposed to "simple aggregations" such as `what is the current account balance for this customer?' Typical data warehouse queries include such things as `which product line sells best in middle-America and how does this correlate to demographic data?'

The Data Warehouse model

Data warehousing is the process of extracting and transforming operational data into informational data and loading it into a central data store or warehouse. Once the data is loaded it is accessible via desktop query and analysis tools by the decision makers.

The data warehouse model is illustrated in the following diagram.

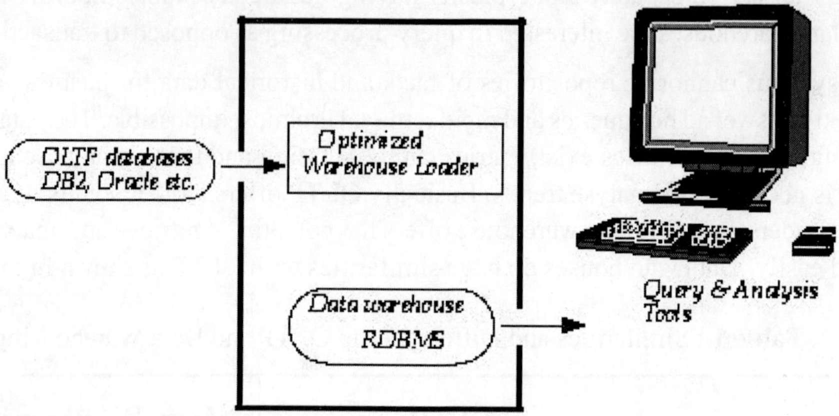

Figure 2: A data warehouse model

The data within the actual warehouse itself has a distinct structure with the emphasis on different levels of summarization as shown in the figure below.

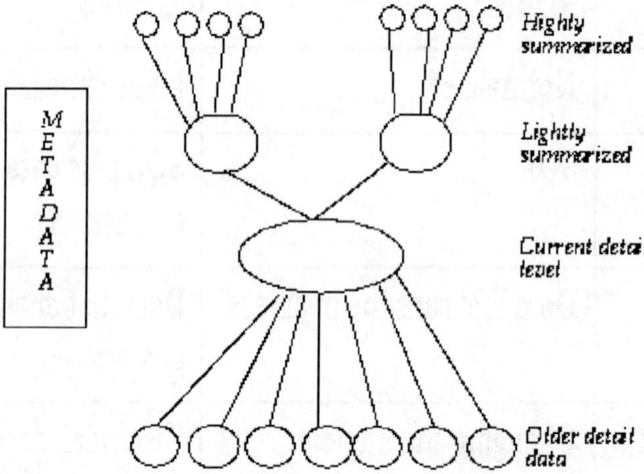

Figure 3: The structure of data inside the data warehouse

The current detail data is central in importance as it:

- reflects the most recent happenings, which are usually the most interesting;
- it is voluminous as it is stored at the lowest level of granularity;
- it is always (almost) stored on disk storage which is fast to access but expensive and complex to manage.

Older detail data is stored on some form of mass storage, it is infrequently accessed and stored at a level detail consistent with current detailed data.

DATA MINING FUNCTIONS

Data mining methods may be classified by the function they perform or according to the class of application they can be used in. Some of the main techniques used in data mining are described in this section.

Classification

Data mine tools have to infer a model from the database, and in the case of supervised learning this requires the user to define one or more classes. The database contains one or more attributes that denote the class of a tuple and these are known as predicted attributes whereas the remaining attributes are called predicting attributes. A combination of values for the predicted attributes defines a class.

When learning classification rules the system has to find the rules that predict the class from the predicting attributes so firstly the user has to define conditions for each class, the data mine system then constructs descriptions for the classes. Basically the system should given a case or tuple with certain known attribute values be able to predict what class this case belongs to.

Once classes are defined the system should infer rules that govern the classification therefore the system should be able to find the description of each class. The descriptions should only refer to the predicting attributes of the training set so that the positive examples should satisfy the description and none of the negative. A rule said to be correct if its description covers all the positive examples and none of the negative examples of a class.

A rule is generally presented as, if the left hand side (LHS) then the right hand side (RHS), so that in all instances where LHS is true then RHS is also true, are very probable. The categories of rules are:

- exact rule - permits no exceptions so each object of LHS must be an element of RHS
- strong rule - allows some exceptions, but the exceptions have a given limit
- probablistic rule - relates the conditional probability P(RHS|LHS) to the probability P(RHS)

Other types of rules are classification rules where LHS is a sufficient condition to classify objects as belonging to the concept referred to in the RHS.

Associations

Given a collection of items and a set of records, each of which contain some number of items from the given collection, an association function is an operation against this set of records which return affinities or patterns that exist among the collection of items. These patterns can be expressed by rules such as "72% of all the records that contain items A, B and C also contain items D and E." The specific percentage of occurrences (in this case 72) is called the confidence factor of the rule.

Also, in this rule, A,B and C are said to be on an opposite side of the rule to D and E. Associations can involve any number of items on either side of the rule.

A typical application, identified by IBM, that can be built using an association function is Market Basket Analysis. This is where a retailer run an association operator over the point of sales transaction log, which contains among other information, transaction identifiers and product identifiers. The set of products identifiers listed under the same transaction identifier constitutes a record. The output of the association function is, in this case, a list of product affinities. Thus, by invoking an association function, the market basket analysis application can determine affinities such as "20% of the time that a specific brand toaster is sold, customers also buy a set of kitchen gloves and matching cover sets."

Another example of the use of associations is the analysis of the claim forms submitted by patients to a medical insurance company. Every claim form contains a set of medical procedures that were performed on a given patient during one visit. By defining the set of items to be the collection of all medical procedures that can be performed on a patient and the records to correspond to each claim form, the application can find, using the association function, relationships among medical procedures that are often performed together.

Sequential/Temporal patterns

Sequential/temporal pattern functions analyse a collection of records over a period of time for example to identify trends. Where the identity of a customer who made a purchase is known an analysis can be made of the collection of related records of the same structure (i.e. consisting of a number of items drawn from a given collection of items). The records are related by the identity of the customer who did the repeated purchases. Such a situation is typical of a direct mail application where for example a catalogue merchant has the information, for each customer, of the sets of products that the customer buys in every purchase order. A sequential pattern function will analyse such collections of related records and will detect frequently occurring patterns of products bought over time. A sequential pattern operator could also be used to discover for example the set of purchases that frequently precedes the purchase of a microwave oven.

Sequential pattern mining functions are quite powerful and can be used to detect the set of customers associated with some frequent buying patterns. Use of these functions on for example a set of insurance claims can lead to the identification of frequently occurring sequences of medical procedures applied to patients which can help identify good medical practices as well as to potentially detect some medical insurance fraud.

Clustering/Segmentation

Clustering and segmentation are the processes of creating a partition so that all the members of each set of the partition are similar according to some metric. A cluster is a set of objects grouped together because of their similarity or proximity. Objects are often decomposed into an exhaustive and/or mutually exclusive set of clusters.

Clustering according to similarity is a very powerful technique, the key to it being to translate some intuitive measure of similarity into a quantitative measure. When learning is unsupervised then the system has to discover its own classes i.e. the system clusters the data in the database. The system has to discover subsets of related objects in the training set and then it has to find descriptions that describe each of these subsets.

There are a number of approachs for forming clusters. One approach is to form rules which dictate membership in the same group based on the level of similarity between members. Another approach is to build set functions that measure some property of partitions as functions of some parameter of the partition.

IBM - Market Basket Analysis example

IBM have used segmentation techniques in their Market Basket Analysis on POS transactions where they separate a set of untagged input records into reasonable groups according to product revenue by market basket i.e. the market baskets were segmented based on the number and type of products in the individual baskets.

Each segment reports total revenue and number of baskets and using a neural network 275,000 transaction records were divided into 16 segments. The following types of analysis were also available, revenue by segment, baskets by segment, average revenue by segment etc.

DATA MINING TECHNIQUES

Cluster Analysis

In an unsupervised learning environment the system has to discover its own classes and one way in which it does this is to cluster the data in the database as shown in the following diagram. The first step is to discover subsets of related objects and then find descriptions e.eg D1, D2, D3 etc. which describe each of these subsets.

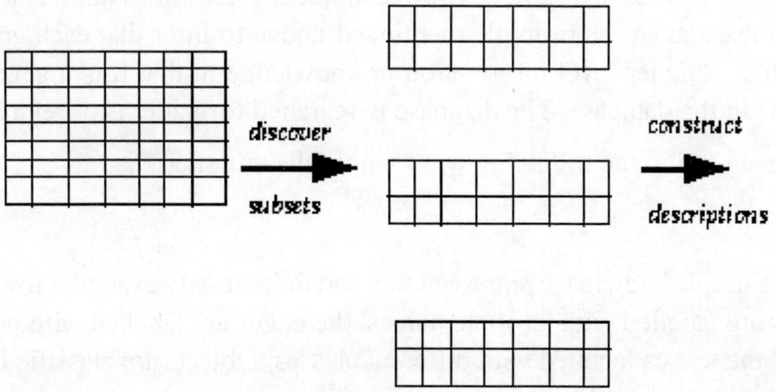

Figure 5: Discovering clusters and descriptions in a database

Clustering and segmentation basically partition the database so that each partition or group is similar according to some criteria or metric. Clustering according to similarity is a concept which appears in many disciplines. If a measure of similarity is available there are a number of techniques for forming clusters. Membership of groups can be based on the level of similarity between members and from this the rules of membership can be defined. Another approach is to build set functions that measure some property of partitions ie groups or subsets as functions of some parameter of the partition. This latter approach achieves what is known as optimal partitioning.

Many data mining applications make use of clustering according to similarity for example to segment a client/customer base. Clustering according to optimization of set functions is used in data analysis e.g. when setting insurance tariffs the customers can be segmented according to a number of parameters and the optimal tariff segmentation achieved.

Clustering/segmentation in databases are the processes of separating a data set into components that reflect a consistent pattern of behaviour. Once the patterns have been established they can then be used to "deconstruct" data into more understandable subsets and also they provide sub-groups of a population for further analysis or action which is important when dealing with very large databases. For example a database could be used for profile generation for target marketing where previous response to mailing campaigns can be used to generate a profile of people who responded and this can be used to predict response and filter mailing lists to achieve the best response.

Induction

A database is a store of information but more important is the information which can be inferred from it. There are two main inference techniques available ie deduction and induction.

- Deduction is a technique to infer information that is a logical consequence of the information in the database e.g. the join operator applied to two relational tables where the first concerns employees and departments and the second departments and managers infers a relation between employee and managers.
- Induction has been described earlier as the technique to infer information that is generalised from the database as in the example mentioned above to infer that each employee has a manager. This is higher level information or knowledge in that it is a general statement about objects in the database. The database is searched for patterns or regularities.

Induction has been used in the following ways within data mining.

Decision trees

Decision trees are simple knowledge representation and they classify examples to a finite number of classes, the nodes are labelled with attribute names, the edges are labelled with possible values for this attribute and the leaves labelled with different classes. Objects are classified by following a path down the tree, by taking the edges, corresponding to the values of the attributes in an object.

The following is an example of objects that describe the weather at a given time. The objects contain information on the outlook, humidity etc. Some objects are positive examples denote by P and others are negative i.e. N. Classification is in this case the construction of a tree structure, illustrated in the following diagram, which can be used to classify all the objects correctly.

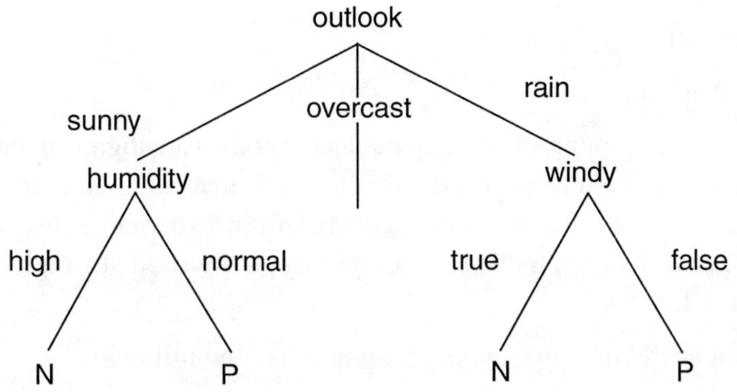

Figure 5: Decision tree structure

Rule induction

A data mine system has to infer a model from the database that is it may define classes such that the database contains one or more attributes that denote the class of a tuple ie the predicted attributes while the remaining attributes are the predicting attributes. Class can then be defined by condition on the attributes. When the classes are defined the system should be able to infer the rules that govern classification, in other words the system should find the description of each class.

Production rules have been widely used to represent knowledge in expert systems and they have the advantage of being easily interpreted by human experts because of their modularity i.e. a single rule can be understood in isolation and doesn't need reference to other rules. The propositional like structure of such rules has been described earlier but can summed up as if-then rules.

Neural networks

Neural networks are an approach to computing that involves developing mathematical structures with the ability to learn. The methods are the result of academic investigations to model nervous system learning. Neural networks have the remarkable ability to derive meaning from complicated or imprecise data and can be used to extract patterns and detect trends that are too complex to be noticed by either humans or other computer techniques. A trained neural network can be thought of as an "expert" in the category of information it has been given to analyse. This expert can then be used to provide projections given new situations of interest and answer "what if" questions.

Neural networks have broad applicability to real world business problems and have already been successfully applied in many industries. Since neural networks are best at identifying patterns or trends in data, they are well suited for prediction or forecasting needs including:

- sales forecasting
- industrial process control
- customer research
- data validation
- risk management
- target marketing etc.

Neural networks use a set of processing elements (or nodes) analogous to neurons in the brain. These processing elements are interconnected in a network that can then identify patterns in data once it is exposed to the data, i.e the network learns from experience just as people do. This distinguishes neural networks from traditional computing programs, that simply follow instructions in a fixed sequential order.

The structure of a neural network looks something like the following:

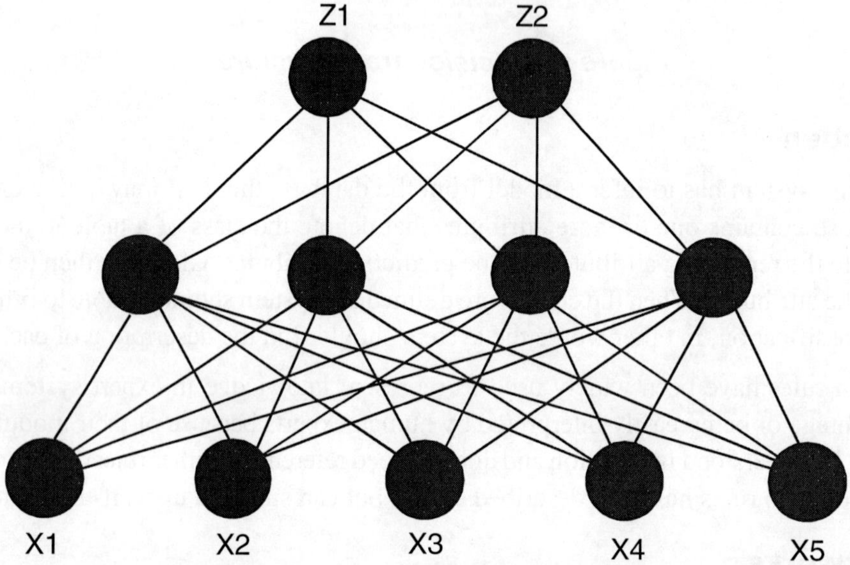

Figure 6: Structure of a neural network

The bottom layer represents the input layer, in this case with 5 inputs labels X1 through X5. In the middle is something called the hidden layer, with a variable number of nodes. It is the hidden layer that performs much of the work of the network. The output layer in this case has two nodes, Z1 and Z2 representing output values we are trying to determine from the inputs. For example, predict sales (output) based on past sales, price and season (input).

Each node in the hidden layer is fully connected to the inputs which means that what is learned in a hidden node is based on all the inputs taken together. Statisticians maintain that the network can pick up the interdependencies in the model. The following diagram provides some detail into what goes on inside a hidden node.

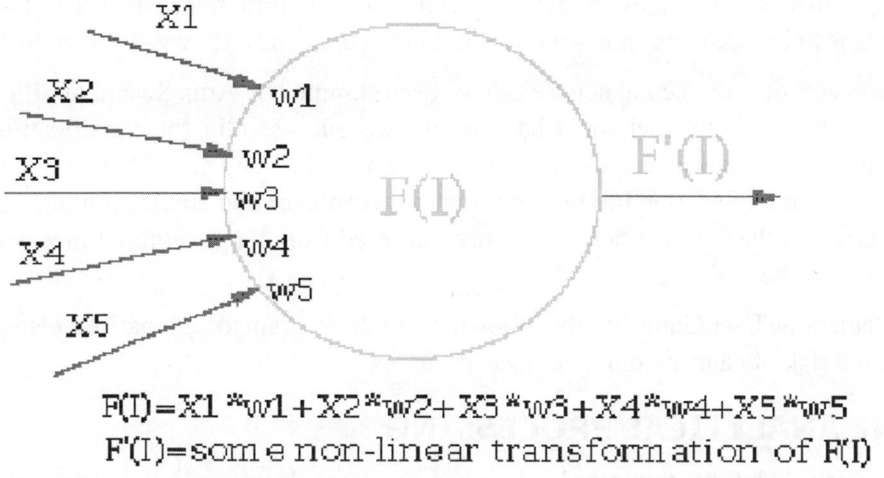

Figure 8: Inside a Node

Simply speaking a weighted sum is performed: X1 times W1 plus X2 times W2 on through X5 and W5. This weighted sum is performed for each hidden node and each output node and is how interactions are represented in the network.

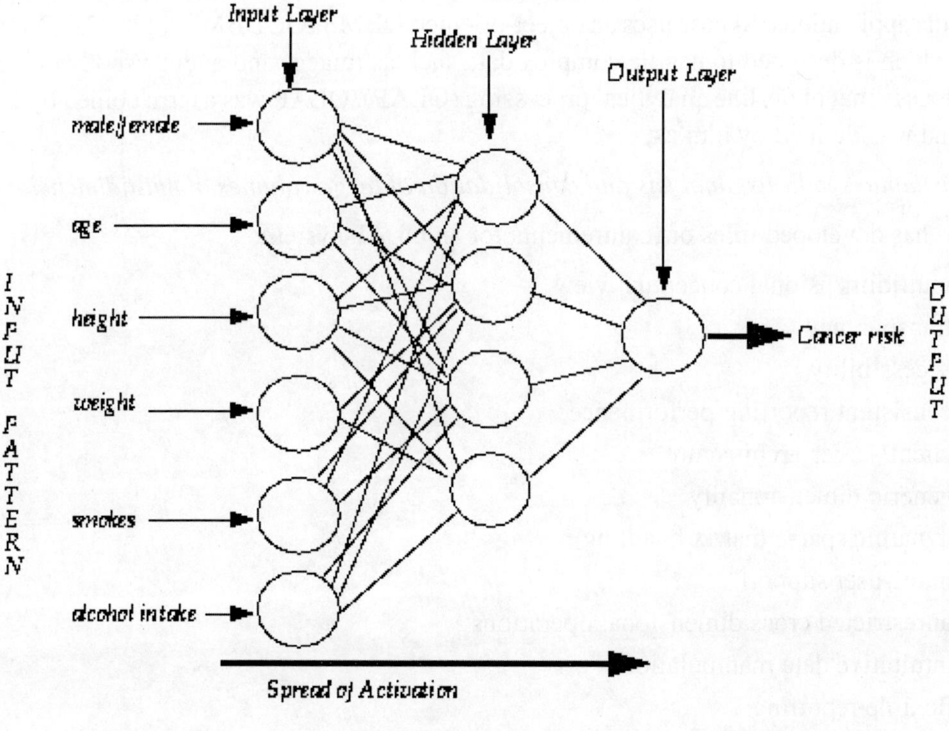

Figure 9: Example Neural network from Clementine User Guide

The issue of where the network get the weights from is important but suffice to say that the network learns to reduce error in it's prediction of events already known (*i.e*, past history).

The problems of using neural networks have been summed by Arun Swami of Silicon Graphics Computer Systems. Neural networks have been used successfully for classification but suffer somewhat in that the resulting network is viewed as a black box and no explanation of the results is given. This lack of explanation inhibits confidence, acceptance and application of results. He also notes as a problem the fact that neural networks suffered from long learning times which become worse as the volume of data grows.

The Clementine User Guide has the following simple diagram to summarise a neural net trained to identify the risk of cancer from a number of factors.

ON-LINE ANALYTICAL PROCESSING

A major issue in information processing is how to process larger and larger databases, containing increasingly complex data, without sacrificing response time. The client/server architecture gives organizations the opportunity to deploy specialized servers which are optimized for handling specific data management problems. Until recently, organizations have tried to target relational database management systems (RDBMSs) for the complete spectrum of database applications. It is however apparent that there are major categories of database applications which are not suitably serviced by relational database systems. Oracle, for example, has built a totally new Media Server for handling multimedia applications. Sybase uses an object-oriented DBMS (OODBMS) in its Gain Momentum product which is designed to handle complex data such as images and audio. Another category of applications is that of on-line analytical processing (OLAP). OLAP was a term coined by E F Codd (1993) and was defined by him as;

the dynamic synthesis, analysis and consolidation of large volumes of multidimensional data

Codd has developed rules or requirements for an OLAP system;

- multidimensional conceptual view
- transparency
- accessibility
- consistent reporting performance
- client/server architecture
- generic dimensionality
- dynamic sparse matrix handling
- multi-user support
- unrestricted cross dimensional operations
- intuitative data manipulation
- flexible reporting
- unlimited dimensions and aggregation levels

An alternative definition of OLAP has been supplied by Nigel Pendse who unlike Codd does not mix technology prescriptions with application requirements. Pendse defines OLAP as, Fast Analysis of Shared Multidimensional Information which means;

Fast in that users should get a response in seconds and so doesn't lose their chain of thought;

Analysis in that the system can provide analysis functions in an intuitative manner and that the functions should supply business logic and statistical analysis relevant to the users application;

Shared from the point of view of supporting multiple users concurrently;

Multidimensional as a main requirement so that the system supplies a multidimensional conceptual view of the data including support for multiple hierarchies;

Information is the data and the derived information required by the user application.

One question is what is multidimensional data and when does it become OLAP? It is essentially a way to build associations between dissimilar pieces of information using predefined business rules about the information you are using. Kirk Cruikshank of Arbor Software has identified three components to OLAP, in an issue of UNIX News on data warehousing;

- A multidimensional database must be able to express complex business calculations very easily. The data must be referenced and mathematics defined. In a relational system there is no relation between line items which makes it very difficult to express business mathematics.
- Intuitative navigation in order to 'roam around' data which requires mining hierarchies.
- Instant response i.e. the need to give the user the information as quick as possible.

Dimensional databases are not without problem as they are not suited to storing all types of data such as lists for example customer addresses and purchase orders etc. Relational systems are also superior in security, backup and replication services as these tend not to be available at the same level in dimensional systems. The advantages of a dimensional system are the freedom they offer in that the user is free to explore the data and receive the type of report they want without being restricted to a set format.

OLAP Example

An example OLAP database may be comprised of sales data which has been aggregated by region, product type, and sales channel. A typical OLAP query might access a multi-gigabyte/multi-year sales database in order to find all product sales in each region for each product type. After reviewing the results, an analyst might further refine the query to find sales volume for each sales channel within region/product classifications. As a last step the analyst might want to perform year-to-year or quarter-to-quarter comparisons for each sales channel. This whole process must be carried out on-line with rapid response time so that the analysis process is undisturbed. OLAP queries can be characterized as on-line transactions which:

- Access very large amounts of data, e.g. several years of sales data.

- Analyse the relationships between many types of business elements e.g. sales, products, regions, channels.
- Involve aggregated data e.g. sales volumes, budgeted dollars and dollars spent.
- Compare aggregated data over hierarchical time periods e.g. monthly, quarterly, yearly.
- Present data in different perspectives e.g. sales by region vs. sales by channels by product within each region.
- Involve complex calculations between data elements e.g. expected profit as calculated as a function of sales revenue for each type of sales channel in a particular region.
- Are able to respond quickly to user requests so that users can pursue an analytical thought process without being stymied by the system.

Comparison of OLAP and OLTP

OLAP applications are quite different from On-line Transaction Processing (OLTP) applications which consist of a large number of relatively simple transactions. The transactions usually retrieve and update a small number of records that are contained in several distinct tables. The relationships between the tables are generally simple.

A typical customer order entry OLTP transaction might retrieve all of the data relating to a specific customer and then insert a new order for the customer. Information is selected from the customer, customer order, and detail line tables. Each row in each table contains a customer identification number which is used to relate the rows from the different tables. The relationships between the records are simple and only a few records are actually retrieved or updated by a single transaction.

The difference between OLAP and OLTP has been summarised as, OLTP servers handle mission-critical production data accessed through simple queries; while OLAP servers handle management-critical data accessed through an iterative analytical investigation. Both OLAP and OLTP, have specialized requirements and therefore require special optimized servers for the two types of processing.

OLAP database servers use multidimensional structures to store data and relationships between data. Multidimensional structures can be best visualized as cubes of data, and cubes within cubes of data. Each side of the cube is considered a dimension.

Each dimension represents a different category such as product type, region, sales channel, and time. Each cell within the multidimensional structure contains aggregated data relating elements along each of the dimensions. For example, a single cell may contain the total sales for a given product in a region for a specific sales channel in a single month. Multidimensional databases are a compact and easy to understand vehicle for visualizing and manipulating data elements that have many inter relationships.

OLAP database servers support common analytical operations including: consolidation, drill-down, and "slicing and dicing".

- Consolidation - involves the aggregation of data such as simple roll-ups or complex expressions involving inter-related data. For example, sales offices can be rolled-up to districts and districts rolled-up to regions.

- Drill-Down - OLAP data servers can also go in the reverse direction and automatically display detail data which comprises consolidated data. This is called drill-downs. Consolidation and drill-down are an inherent property of OLAP servers.
- "Slicing and Dicing" - Slicing and dicing refers to the ability to look at the database from different viewpoints. One slice of the sales database might show all sales of product type within regions. Another slice might show all sales by sales channel within each product type. Slicing and dicing is often performed along a time axis in order to analyse trends and find patterns.

OLAP servers have the means for storing multidimensional data in a compressed form. This is accomplished by dynamically selecting physical storage arrangements and compression techniques that maximize space utilization. Dense data (i.e., data exists for a high percentage of dimension cells) are stored separately from sparse data (i.e., a significant percentage of cells are empty). For example, a given sales channel may only sell a few products, so the cells that relate sales channels to products will be mostly empty and therefore sparse. By optimizing space utilization, OLAP servers can minimize physical storage requirements, thus making it possible to analyse exceptionally large amounts of data. It also makes it possible to load more data into computer memory which helps to significantly improve performance by minimizing physical disk I/O.

In conclusion OLAP servers logically organize data in multiple dimensions which allows users to quickly and easily analyse complex data relationships. The database itself is physically organized in such a way that related data can be rapidly retrieved across multiple dimensions. OLAP servers are very efficient when storing and processing multidimensional data. RDBMSs have been developed and optimized to handle OLTP applications. Relational database designs concentrate on reliability and transaction processing speed, instead of decision support need. The different types of server can therefore benefit a broad range of data management applications.

Data Visualisation

Data visualisation makes it possible for the analyst to gain a deeper, more intuitive understanding of the data and as such can work well along side data mining. Data mining allows the analyst to focus on certain patterns and trends and explore in-depth using visualisation. On its own data visualisation can be overwhelmed by the volume of data in a database but in conjunction with data mining can help with exploration.

SIFTWARE - PAST AND PRESENT DEVELOPMENTS

This section outlines the historic background or the evolution of database systems in terms of parallel processing and data mining with reference to the part played by some of the main vendors and their successes.

New architectures

The best of the best commercial database packages are now available for massively parallel processors including IBM DB2, INFORMIX-OnLine XPS, ORACLE7 RDBMS and SYBASE System 10. This evolution, however, has not been an easy road for the pioneers.

HPCwire by Michael Erbschloe, contributing editor Oct. 6, 1995

The evolution described by Michael Erbschloe is detailed and expanded on in the following sections.

Obstacles

What were the problems at the start?

- the typical scientific user knew nothing of commercial business applications and gave little attention or credence to the adaptation of high performance computers to business environments.
- the business database programmers, who, although well versed in database management and applications, knew nothing of massively parallel principles.

The solution was for database software producers to create easy-to-use tools and form strategic relationships with hardware manufacturers and consulting firms.

The key

The key is the retooling database software to maspar environments. Parallel processors can easily assign small, independent transactions to different processors. With more processors, more transactions can be executed without reducing throughput. This same concept applies to executing multiple independent SQL statements. A set of SQL statements can be broken up and allocated to different processors to increase speed.

Multiple data streams allow several operations to proceed simultaneously. A customer table, for example, can be spread across multiple disks, and independent threads can search each subset of the customer data. As data is partitioned into multiple subsets performance is increased. I/O subsystems then just feed data from the disks to the appropriate threads or streams.

An essential part of designing a database for parallel processing is the partitioning scheme. Because large databases are indexed, independent indexes must also be partitioned to maximize performance. There are five partitioning methods used to accomplish this:

1. Hashing, where data is assigned to disks based on a hash key
2. Round-robin partitioning, which assigns a row to partitions in sequence.
3. Allocating rows to nodes based on ranges of values.
4. Schema partitioning (Sybase Navigation Server), which lets you tie tables to specific partitions.
5. User-defined roles (Informix).

Oracle was first

Oracle was the first to market parallel database packages with their flagship product, ORACLE7 RDBMS having been installed at over 100 user sites. Oracle began beta support for the IBM SP platform in July 1994.

Ease of use is an important factor in the success of any commercial application and by design the Oracle Parallel Server hides the complexities of data layout from the users. Users who wish to add disks or processor nodes can do so without complex data reorganization and application re-partitioning. In addition, Oracle Parallel Server software uses the same SQL interface as the Oracle7 database. Since no new commands or extensions to existing commands are needed, previously developed tools and applications will run unchanged.

The Oracle Parallel Server technology performs both the parallelization and optimization automatically, eliminating the need to re-educate application developers and end users. It is also easy for user organizations to deploy because it eliminates many traditional implementation burdens.

Reference - http://www.oracle.com.

Red Brick has a strong showing

Red Brick Systems, based in Los Gatos, Calif., specializes in software products used for fast and accurate business decisions where large client/server databases, usually tens to hundreds of gigabytes in size with hundreds of millions of records, are the norm. These applications require historical context, but timely analysis of complex data relationships for both consolidated and detailed business information.

Red Brick Warehouse VPT, (Very large data warehouse support, Parallel query processing, Time based data management), is a DBMS tuned for data warehouse applications. It employs specialized indexing techniques which are designed to facilitate data warehousing. The join accelerator STARjoin uses a special index to multiple tables that participate in a join. With its parallel capability it can run applications that can handle up to 500 GB or more of data It is a parallel database product that significantly improves the organization, availability, administration, and performance of data warehouse applications.

Unlike RDBMS products optimized for on-line transaction processing, Red Brick Warehouse VPT allows business management applications to be developed and deployed quickly;

- to query very large databases of information gathered from disparate sources;
- to provide the best access to both consolidated and detailed business information;
- and to simply run fast.

Red Brick's server-based relational engine is accessible by several popular front-end client application environments which support Microsoft ODBC, Sybase Open Client, and Information Builders, Inc. EDA/SQL interfaces.

Reference - http://www.redbrick.com.

IBM is still the largest

IBM is the world's largest producer of database management software. Eighty percent of the FORTUNE 500, including the top 100 companies, rely on DB2 database solutions to manage data on mainframes, minicomputers, RISC workstations and personal computers. The availability of the new DB2 Parallel Edition, extends the functionality and reliability of the DB2 to IBM's high-performance parallel systems SP2. With DB2 Parallel Edition running on the SP2, users can access very large databases, process huge amount of data, and perform complex queries in minutes.

DB2 Parallel Edition is packaged with the SP2 running AIX and a set of services to help users speed their transactions and quickly and easily derive the benefits of parallel computing. The turnkey solution, called POWERquery, provides a relatively cost-effective, large-scale decision support.

DB2 Parallel Edition is a member of the IBM DB2 family of databases, therefore users do not have to rewrite any applications or retrain their staffs. To a user, the database appears to be a single database server, only faster. It is faster because all functions are performed in parallel, including data and index scans, index creation, backup and restore, joins, inserts, updates and deletes.

Reference - http://www.ibm.com.

Informix is online with 8.0

Informix has been supporting SMP with Informix Parallel Data Query (PDQ) as part of its Dynamic Scalable Architecture (DSA) and through DSA/XMP by extending PDQ functions to work in loosely coupled parallel environments, including clusters. Online 8.0 is the latest high-performance, scalable database server based on Informix's industry-leading DSA. OnLine XPS extends DSA to loosely coupled, shared-nothing computing architectures including clusters of symmetric multiprocessing (SMP) systems and (MPP) systems.

One key to Informix's success on SMP is a joint development agreement with Sequent Computer Systems (Beaverton, Ore. that resulted in a rebuild of the core of Informix OnLine to a multithreaded system with small-grained, lightweight threads. Virtual processors are pooled and the DBMS allocates them dynamically to CPUs, based on processing requirements. OnLine XPS' high availability, systems management based on the Tivoli Management Environment (TME), data partitioning, enhanced parallel SQL operations, and other features are designed to simplify and economize VLDB applications. OnLine XPS also offers a significant improvement in performance for mission-critical, data-intensive tasks associated with data warehousing, decision support, imaging, document management and workflow, and other VLDB operational environments.

Although Informix databases, such as OnLine XPS and INFORMIX-OnLine Dynamic Server, are at the heart of data warehousing solutions, other products and services must integrate with the databases to ensure a successful data warehouse implementation, a critical component of a data warehouse architecture is online analytical processing (OLAP).

Informix delivers relational multidimensional capabilities through strategic partnerships with Information Advantage, MicroStrategy, and Stanford Technology Group. Informix also has proven partnerships with technology providers, such as Business Objects, Coopers & Lybrand, Evolutionary

Technologies, KPMG, Price Waterhouse, Prism, and SHL Systemhouse, to provide capabilities such as data modelling, data extraction, data access, multidimensional analysis, and systems integration.

Reference - http://www.informix.com.

Sybase and System 10

Sybase has improved multithreading with System 10 which has been designed to handle interquery and transaction parallelizing on SMP computers with very large, heavyweight threads. Up to 64 processors can be utilized as SQL servers configured into a single system image. This was accomplished in part by the use of the Sybase Navigation server which takes advantage of parallel computers. Parallelism is achieved by an SQL Server on a processor and control servers, which manages parallel operations. Sybase's Navigation Server partitions data by hashing, ranges, or schema partitioning. Reports indicate that the partitioning scheme and keys chosen impact parallel performance.

Sybase IQ was delivered to 24 beta customers in July, providing predictable interactive access to large amounts of data directly in the warehouse. While offering up to 100-fold query performance improvement over standard relational databases, Sybase IQ slashes warehouse query costs by orders of magnitude, requiring up to 80 percent less disk, up to 98 percent less I/O, and utilizing existing hardware, according to Sybase.

An optional extension for the SYBASE SQL Server, SYBASE IQ includes patent-pending Bit-Wise indexing that allows significantly more data to be processed in each instruction, resulting in up to thousands of times faster performance without adding hardware. Beyond simple bit maps, Bit-Wise indexing makes it possible to index every field in the database —including character and numeric fields not supported by other bit-map indexing schemes — in less than the size of the raw data, substantially reducing disk costs. SYBASE IQ indexes provide a complete map of the data, eliminating table scans and directly accessing just the information required, reducing I/O by up to 98 percent and resulting in fast, predictable answers to any query.

Reference - http://www.sybase.com.

Information Harvester

Information Harvester software on the Convex Exemplar offers market researchers in retail, insurance, financial and telecommunications firms the ability to analyse large data sets in a short time.

The flexibility of the Information Harvesting induction algorithm enables it to adapt to any system. The data can be in the form of numbers, dates, codes, categories, text or any combination thereof. Information Harvester is designed to handle faulty, missing and noisy data. Large variations in the values of an individual field do not hamper the analysis. Information Harvester claims unique abilities to recognize and ignore irrelevant data fields when searching for patterns. In full-scale parallel-processing versions, Information Harvester can handle millions of rows and thousands of variables.

The Exemplar series, based on HP's high performance PA-RISC processors, is the first supercomputer-class family of systems to track the price/performance development cycle of the desktop. They are being used for a range of applications including automotive, tire and aircraft design, petroleum research and exploration, seismic processing, and university, scientific and biomedical research.

Reference - http://www.convex.com

VENDORS AND APPLICATIONS

This section examines some of the major vendors of siftware with supporting case studies.

4.2.1 Information Harvesting Inc

The problem of deriving meaningful information from enormous amounts of complex data is being handled by the data mining software produced by Information Harvesting Inc. (IH), founded in 1994 and based in Cambridge, Mass. It makes use of conventional statistical analysis techniques by building upon a proprietary tree-based learning algorithm similar to CART, ID3 and Chaid that generates expert-system-like rules from datasets, initially presented in forms such as numbers, dates, categories, codes, or any combination.

The proprietary Information Harvesting algorithm operates by creating a set of bins for each field in the data, with groups of values within a field ultimately determining the rules. According to the distribution of values the algorithm delineates bin boundaries via fuzzy logic to determine where a given value falls within a bin and thus how the values may be grouped.

A binary tree then generates rules from the data. At the uppermost node the algorithm analyses all data rows, and at each lower level subsets created by the node above are analysed. Each node arrives at a set of rules categorizing the data reviewed at that level. Each rule may include multiple variables (combined with ANDs) or multiple clauses (combined with ORs) and derives from the way variables fall into various bins. A prediction can be based on one or more rules.

Rule quality, the amount of error for each rule, and importance, how often each rule is used for making predictions, are also assessed by the software. This avoids the effect of simply memorizing historical data or misunderstanding the relevance of a given rule. Design rows are used to extract the rules per se, but test rows are utilized to determine the rules level of accuracy.

In addition, the program is set to optimize results by running over the same datasets again and again while adjusting the internal parameters for the best result. Optimization can be achieved with either a rapid hill-climbing algorithm or completely with a modified genetic algorithm.

The data mining modules are written in ANSI C and thus can be ported to a wide range of platforms: on client/server architecture (where the application uses TCP/IP), parallel processing machines, or mainframe supercomputers.

Two examples of companies using the software are:

Healthcare - Michael Reese Medical Associates (MRMA) employed data mining software from Information Harvesting and Vantage Point as a tool for gaining advantage in contract negotiations. The 28-doctor group had to predict trends in type, price, location, and use of service, since they must negotiate with insurance companies to provide certain services at a set monthly fee, doctors must accurately predict their per member/per month cost to break even or make a profit. Normally physicians could only make an intuitive estimate roughly based on after-the-fact evaluations of prior estimates when determining this critical figure whereas data mining offered a new approach.

Finance - The Philadelphia Police and Fire Federal Credit Union (PFFCU) used data mining to maximize their membership base by cultivating multiple relationships (e.g. consumer loans, annuities, credit cards, etc.) with members. Because the membership base is extremely homogeneous (police and fire dept. employees and their families), data had to be deeply drilled to identify segmented groups. Used in conjunction with software such as InterGlobal Financial Systems' Credit Analyzer, Information Harvester identified members most and least profitable to the organization as well as those who would make attractive loan candidates. Data mining often led PFFCU to accurate but counter-intuitive results. For example, members who had filed for bankruptcy were more inclined to clear debts with the Credit Union than outside lenders. Thus, PFFCU identified members with imperfect credit histories but a strong tendency to pay, whereas these individuals would be ignored by large conventional lenders.

Red Brick

Red Brick have a number of cases to present in support of the use of their data mining technology, two of which are H.E.B. of San Antonio, and Hewlett-Packard.

H.E.B.- Category management in retailing

H.E.B. of San Antonio, Texas (sales of approx. $4.5 billion, 225 stores, 50,000 employees) was able to bring a category management application from design to roll out in under nine months because it kept the requirements simple and had database support from Red Brick and server support from Hewlett-Packard Company.

Previously, the marketing information department would take ad hoc requests for information from users, write a program to extract the information, and return the information to the user a week or so later - not timely enough for most business decisions and in some cases not what the user really wanted in the first place.

The organizational change to category management was implemented in 1990. The category manager is characterized as the "CEO" of the category with profit and loss responsibilities, final decision over which products to buy and which to delete, and where the products are to be located on the shelves. The category manager also decides which stores get which products. Although H.E.B. stores are only within the state of Texas, it is a diverse market where some stores near Mexico are 98% Hispanic while suburban Dallas stores may be only 2% Hispanic. The change to category management centralized all merchandising and marketing decisions, removing these decisions from the stores.

As category managers built up their negotiating skills, technical skills, and partnering skills over three years, the need for more timely decision-support information grew. An enterprise-wide survey of users to determine requirements took until September 1993. The company then benchmarked three database management systems - Red Brick, Teradata and Time Machine - and picked Red Brick. The group leased the hardware, a Hewlett-Packard 9000 model T500 (2-processor, with 768M of RAM, and 100GB of disk space—the system now has 200 GB). For a user interface, the company contracted for a custom graphical front-end based on Windows. Also, a COBOL programmer was used to write data extraction programs to take P.O.S. data from the mainframe, format the data properly, and transfer the data to the Red Brick database.

The model was delivered in March 1994 and the application has been up and running without problems since then. The company maintains two years of data by week, by item (257,000 UPCs), by store. This is about 400 million detail records. Summary files are only maintained by time and total company, which can be an advantage.

The goal was to have all queries answered in 4 seconds, but some trends reports with large groups of items over long time periods take 30 - 40 seconds. The users are not always technically oriented, so the design intentionally aimed for simplicity. The system is ad hoc to the extent that the user can specify time, place, and product.

H.E.B. feels that category managers are now making fact-based decisions to determine which products to put in which stores, how much product to send to a store, and the proper product mix. Historically, buyers usually were promoted from the stores and had considerable product knowledge whereas now category managers are coming from other operational areas such as finance and human resources. This is possible because the system give people with limited product knowledge the equivalent of years experience.

Hewlett-Packard: "Discovering" Data To Manage Worldwide Support

Hewlett-Packard, a premier, global provider of hardware systems is known for manufacturing high quality products but to maintain its reputation they depended on delivering service and support through and after product delivery.

The Worldwide Customer Support Organization (WCSO) within Hewlett-Packard is responsible for providing support services to its hardware and software customers. For several years, WCSO has used a data warehouse of financial, account, product, and service contract information to support decision making. WCSO Information Management is responsible for developing and supporting this data warehouse.

Until 1994, WCSO Information Management supported business information queries with a data warehouse architecture based on two HP3000/Allbase systems and an IBM DB2 system. This was a first attempt at collecting, integrating, and storing data related to customer support for decision-making purposes. As they increasingly relied upon the data warehouse, they began to demand better performance, additional data coverage, and more timely data availability.

The warehouse architecture did not keep pace with the increased requirements from WCSO users. Users wanted to get information quickly. Both load and query performance were directly impacted as more data was added. It was to decided to investigate other warehouse alternatives with the aim of finding a new data warehouse that would significantly improve load/query performance, be more cost effective, and support large amounts of data without sacrificing performance. To help select the best combination of hardware and software for the new warehouse, benchmarks were conducted using Red Brick and two other RDBMS products. They did not look at Oracle or Sybase because they were promoting OLTP data functionality and weren't focused upon data warehousing.

Benchmarks included tests simulating some of HP's most demanding user queries, testing the load times for tables in the five to eight million row range. Tests also were conducted to verify that performance did not degrade as data was added into the warehouse. "The Red Brick product performed head and shoulders above the rest," recalls Ryan Uda, Program Manager for WCSO's Information Management Program. Benchmark results showed Red Brick loading data in one hour against ten hours for other systems. Red Brick's query performance was consistently five to ten times faster. Red Brick returned consistently superior performance results even when large amounts of data were added to the warehouse.

HP chose to use Red Brick software on an HP9000 and the project began with the consolidation of the existing three databases into a single data warehouse named "Discovery." This downsizing provided significant cost savings and increased resource efficiencies in managing and supporting the warehouse environment. Today, Discovery supports approximately 250 marketing, finance, and administration users in the Americas, Europe, and Asia-Pacific regions. They pull query results into their desktop report writers, load information into worksheets, or use the data to feed Executive Information Systems. User satisfaction has risen dramatically due to Discovery's vastly improved performance and remodelled business views.

Oracle

For large scale data mining, Oracle on the SP2 offers customers robust functionality and excellent performance. Data spread across multiple SP2 processor nodes is treated as a single image affording exceptionally fast access to very large databases. Oracle Parallel Query allows multiple users to submit complex queries at the same time. Individual complex queries can be broken down and processed across several processing nodes simultaneously. Execution time can be reduced from overnight to hours or minutes, enabling organizations to make better business decisions faster.

Oracle offers products that help customers create, administer and use their data warehouse. Oracle has a large suite of connectivity products that provide transparent access to many popular mainframe databases. Through the use of these products, customers can move data from legacy mainframe applications into the data warehouse on the SP2.

Some of the examples of their technology at work are as follows:

John Alden Insurance based in Miami, Fla., is using Oracle Parallel Query on the SP2 to mine healthcare information and they have seen orders-of-magnitude improvements in response time for typical business queries.

ShopKo Stores, a $2 billion, Wisconsin-based mass merchandise chain which operates 128 stores throughout the Midwest and Northeast, chose the SP2 to meet their current and projected needs for both data mining and mission-critical merchandising applications.

Pacific Bell and U.S. West, both telecommunications providers, have are using the Oracle Warehouse to improve their ability to track customers and identify new service needs. The solutions are based on the Oracle Warehouse, introduced in June, 1995.

- Pacific Bell's data warehouse provides a common set of summarized and compressed information to base decision support systems. The first system is designed to analyse product profitability, and similar decision support systems are in development for marketing, capital investment and procurement, and two additional financial systems.
- U.S. West has implemented a warehousing system to analyse intra-area code calling data from its three operating companies. Running Oracle7 Release 7.2 on a 9-CPU symmetric multiprocessing system from Pyramid, US West's initial centralized architecture supports use by 20 executives and marketing specialists. The next phase will deliver warehouse access to more than 400 service representatives, which will ultimately be expanded up to 4,500 service representatives.

Informix - Data Warehousing

As a major player in the field of data mining Informix have a number of success stories to quote some of which are:

Informix and Associated Grocers (retail example)

Associated Grocers, one of the leading cooperative grocery wholesalers in the northwest United States, with revenues of $1.2 billion, is replacing its traditional mainframe environment with a three-tiered client/server architecture based on Informix database technology. The new system's advanced applications have cut order-fulfilment times in half, reduced inventory carrying costs, and enabled the company to offer its 350 independent grocers greater selection at a lower cost. The details are -

- Hardware: Hewlett-Packard, IBM, AT&T GIS
- Partners: Micro Focus and Lawson Associates
- Applications: Inventory management, post billing, radio frequency, POS scanning, and data warehousing
- Key Informix Products: INFORMIX-On Line Dynamic Server

In 1991, Associated Grocers embarked on a phased transition from its mainframe-based information system to open systems. The company initially used IBM RS/6000 hardware, and has since included Hewlett-Packard and NCR. In evaluating relational database management systems, Associated Grocers developed a checklist of requirements including education/training, scalability, technical support, solid customer references, and future product direction.

After selecting Informix as its company wide database standard, Associated Grocers then assembled the rest of its system architecture using a three tier model. On tier one, the "client" presentation layer, graphical user interfaces are developed using Microsoft(R) Windows(TM) and Visual Basic(TM). Tier two, based on Hewlett-Packard hardware, runs Micro Focus COBOL applications on top of the OEC Developer Package from Open Environment Corporation. This helps Associated Grocers develop DCE-compliant applications. The third layer, the data layer, is the INFORMIX-OnLine database.

Associated Grocers' pilot Informix-based application provides real-time inventory information for its deli warehouse. In the past, merchandise was received manually, and pertinent product information was later keyed into Associated Grocers' financial system. In contrast, the new system recognizes merchandise right at the receiving dock. Hand-held radio frequency devices allow merchandise to be immediately scanned into the Informix database. Product is assigned to a warehouse location and its expiration date is noted. When orders are filled, products with the earliest expiration dates are shipped first.

An extension to the deli warehouse system is a new post billing system, which is the ability to separate physical and financial inventory. Previously, merchandise could not be released for sale until the financial systems had been updated, which typically occurred over night. The new Informix-based system allows for immediate sale and distribution of recently received merchandise.

A third Informix-based application enables Associated Grocers to economically sell unique items-slow moving merchandise which is ordered monthly versus daily. Rather than incurring the high cost to warehouse these items, Associated Grocers created a direct link to outside speciality warehouses to supply the needed items on demand. Independent stores simply order the merchandise from Associated Grocers. The order goes into Associated Grocers' billing system then gets transmitted to the speciality warehouse, which immediately ships the merchandise to Associated Grocers. The speciality items are loaded onto Associated Grocers' delivery trucks and delivered along with the rest of an independent store's order.

Host Marriott (retail example)

Host Marriott has revenues of $1.1 billion and is a leading provider of food, beverage, and merchandise concession outlets located at airports, travel plazas, and toll roads throughout the United States. The company is streamlining its information systems to develop better cost controls and more effectively manage operations. To accomplish this, Host Marriott selected Informix database technology as its strategic IS foundation, which includes the development of a data warehouse using INFORMIX-OnLine Dynamic Server(TM) and INFORMIX-NewEra(TM). The new system will deliver valuable information throughout the organization, from field operators to corporate analysts. Details of the solution are:

- Hardware: IBM, Hewlett-Packard
- Applications: Sales and marketing, inventory management, labor productivity, and data warehousing
- Informix Products: INFORMIX-OnLine Dynamic Server, INFORMIX-NewEra, INFORMIX-ESQL/C

The company split into two separate companies; Host Marriott and Marriott International, and as the company grew more diverse, so did its computer systems. Unique and more advanced information systems were coupled with inadequate ones. As a result, financial consolidation was primarily done manually, with sales information from each outlet keyed into individual computer systems every night. The information was then sent to Host Marriotts corporate office, where it was posted to the mainframe accounting system, which had no analysis capabilities. Any analysis had to be completed via a second system, proving to be a labor-intensive and slow process.

In an effort to streamline operations and improve system flexibility, Host Marriott is replacing its manually-intensive system with a series of new client/server-based applications using Informix development tools and relational database products running on an IBM RS/6000 and Hewlett-Packard Vectra PCs.

The first of Host Marriotts new Informix-based applications automates its sales and marketing functions. It was developed using INFORMIX-HyperScript(R) Tools—a visual programming environment used to create client/server applications for Windows(TM), UNIX(R), and Macintosh(R) systems, and INFORMIX-ESQL/C—a database application development tool which is used to embed SQL statements directly into C code. Instead of waiting for individual end-of-day reports, the system automatically polls sales data from the point-of-sale terminals at each outlet and consolidates it in the INFORMIX-SE relational database.

This information is used to consolidate and speed up end-of-day reporting, analyse sales, and monitor regulatory compliance. It has reduced a 10 hour process to less than one hour, and enables corporate and concession management to perform the kind of in-depth analysis that allows them to fine tune their product mix, reduce administrative overhead, and ultimately increase profit margins.

Focus is now on a data warehouse to leverage its existing businesses and generate new growth opportunities in the future. The data warehouse is a separate database that Host Marriott is designing explicitly for its data-intensive, decision-support applications. Building a data warehouse will allow them to optimize query times and eliminate impact on the company's production systems. The warehouse is being developed with INFORMIX-NewEra, an open, graphical, object-oriented development environment especially suited for creating enterprise wide client/server database applications.

The foundation of Host Marriotts data warehouse will be INFORMIX-OnLine Dynamic Server, which takes advantage of multiprocessing hardware to perform multiple database functions in parallel. The data warehouse will help the company determine which brands will succeed in which market. It will also help Host Marriott develop more proprietary brands, and deliver better products and services at lower cost.

By pooling sales data, market research, customer satisfaction ratings, etc., Host Marriott will be able to perform detailed analysis in order to eliminate unnecessary costs from operations, and fully leverage new business opportunities. Relying on Informix products and services is enabling Host Marriott to make the important shift from simple data processing to strategic business analysis.

Sybase

There is a lot of interest and activity in data warehousing, recent surveys show that more than 70 percent of Fortune 1000 companies have Data Warehousing projects budgeted or underway at an average cost of $3 million and a typical development time of 6 to 18 months (Meta Group Inc.).

Conventional warehousing applications today extract basic business data from operational systems, edit or transform it in some fashion to ensure its accuracy and clarity, and move it by means of transformation products, custom programming, or "sneaker net" to the newly deployed analytical database system. This extract, edit, load, query, extract, edit, load, query system might be acceptable if business life were very simple and relatively static but that is not the case, new data and data structures are added, changes are made to existing data, and even whole new databases are added.

Sybase Warehouse WORKS

Sybase Warehouse WORKS was designed around four key functions in data warehousing:

- Assembling data from multiple sources
- Transforming data for a consistent and understandable view of the business
- Distributing data to where it is needed by business users
- Providing high-speed access to the data for those business users

The Sybase Warehouse WORKS Alliance Program provides a complete, open, and integrated solution for organizations building and deploying data warehouse solutions. The program addresses the entire range of technology requirements for data warehouse development, including data transformation, data distribution, and interactive data access. The alliance partners have made commitments to adopt the Warehouse WORKS architecture and APIs, as well as to work closely with Sybase in marketing and sales programs.

SG Overview

The advances in data analysis realized through breakthroughs in data warehousing are now being extended by new solutions for data mining. Sophisticated tools for 3D visualization, coupled with data mining software developed by Silicon Graphics, make it possible to bring out patterns and trends in the data that may not have been realized using traditional SQL techniques. These "nuggets" of information can then be brought to the attention of the end user, yielding bottom-line results.

Using fly-through techniques, you can navigate your models on consumer purchasing and channel velocity to follow trends and observe patterns. In response to what you see, you can interact directly with the data, using visual computing to factor critical "what-if" scenarios into your models. By making it possible to go through many such iterations without resorting to over-burdened IS staff for analytical assistance, you can eliminate days - even months - from the review process.

IBM Overview

IBM provides a number of decision support tools to give users a powerful but easy-to-use interface to the data warehouse. IBM Information Warehouse Solutions offer the choice of decision support tools that best meet the needs of the end users in keeping with their commitment to provide open systems implementations.

IBM has announced, a Customer Partnership Program, to work with selected customers to gain experience and validate the applicability of the data mining technology. This offers customers the advantage of IBM's powerful new data mining technology to analyse their data looking for key patterns and associations. Visa and IBM announced an agreement on 30 May 1995 signalling their intention to work together. This will change the way in which Visa and its member banks exchange information worldwide. The proposed structure will facilitate the timely delivery of information and critical decision support tools directly to member financial institutions' desktops worldwide.

IBM Visualizer provides a powerful and comprehensive set of ready to use building blocks and development tools that can support a wide range of end-user requirements for query, report writing, data analysis, chart/graph making, business planning and multimedia database. As a workstation based product, Visualizer is object-oriented and that makes it easy to plug-in additional functions such as those mentioned. And, Visualizer can access databases such as Oracle and Sybase as well as the DB2 family.

There are a number of other decision support products available from IBM based on the platform, operating environment and database with which you need to work. For example, the IBM Application System (AS) provides a client/server architecture and the widest range of decision support functions available for the MVS and VM environments. AS has become the decision support server of choice in these environments because of its capability to access many different data sources. IBM Query Management Facility (QMF) provides query, reporting and graphics functions in the MVS, VM, and CICS environments. The Data Interpretation System (DIS) is an object-oriented set of tools that enable end users to access, analyse and present information with little technical assistance. It is a LAN-based client/server architecture that enables access to IBM and non-IBM relational databases as well as host applications in the MVS and VM environment. These and other products are available from IBM to provide the functions and capabilities needed for a variety of implementation alternatives.

DATA MINING EXAMPLES

5.1 Bass Brewers

Bass Brewers is the leading beer producer in the UK and has a 23% of the market. The company has a reputation for great brands and good service but realised the importance of information in order to maintain a lead in the UK beer market.

We've been brewing beer since 1777, with increased competition comes a demand to make faster, better informed decisions.

Mike Fisher, IS director, Bass Brewers

Bass decided to gather the data into a data warehouse on a system so that the users i.e. the decision-makers could have consistent, reliable, online information. Prior to this users could expect a turn around of 24 hours but with the new system the answers should be returned interactively.

For the first time, people will be able to do data mining - ask questions we never dreamt we could get the answers to, look for patterns among the data we could never recognise before.

Nigel Rowley, Information Infrastructure manager

This commitment to data mining has given Bass a competitive edge when it comes to identifying market trends and taking advantage of this.

Northern Bank

A subsidiary of the National Australia Group, the Northern Bank has a major new application based upon Holos from Holistic Systems now being used in each of the 107 branches in the Province. The new system is designed to deliver financial and sales information such as volumes, margins, revenues, overheads and profits as well as quantities of product held, sold, closed etc.

The application consists of two loosely coupled systems;

- a system to integrate the multiple data sources into a consolidated database,
- another system to deliver that information to the users in a meaningful way.

The Northern is addressing the need to convert data into information as their products need to be measured outlet by outlet, and over a period of time.

The new system delivers management information in electronic form to the branch network. The information is now more accessible, paperless and timely. For the first time, all the various income streams are attributed to the branches which generate the business.

Malcolm Longridge, MIS development team leader, Northern Bank

TSB Group PLC

The TSB Group are also using Holos supplied by Holistic Systems because of

its flexibility and its excellent multidimensional functionality, which it provides without the need for a separate multidimensional database

Andrew Scott, End-User Computing Manager at TSB

The four major applications which have been developed are:

- a company-wide budget and forecasting model, BAF, for the finance department - has 50 potential users taking information out of the Millennium general ledger and enables analysts to study this data using 40 multidimensional models written using Holos
- a mortgage management information system for middle and senior management in TSB Homeloans;

- a suite of actuarial models for TSB Insurance; and
- Business Analysis Project, BAP, used as an EIS type system by TSB Insurance to obtain a better understanding of the company's actual risk exposures for feeding back into the actuarial modelling system.

BeursBase, Amsterdam

BeursBase, a real-time on-line stock/exchange relational data base (RDB) fed with information from the Amsterdam Stock Exchange is now available for general access by institutions or individuals. It will be augmented by data from the European Option Exchange before January, 1996. All stock, option and futures prices and volumes are being warehoused.

BeursBase has been in operation for about a year and contains approximately 1.8 million stock prices, over half a million quotes and about a million stock trade volumes. The AEX (Amsterdam EOE Index) or the Dutch Dow Jones, based upon the 25 most active securities traded (measured over a year) is refreshed via the database approximately every 30 seconds.

The RDB employs SQL/DS on a VM system and DB2/6000 on a AIX RS/6000 cluster. A parallel edition of DB2/6000 will soon be ready for data mining purposes, data quality measurement, plus a variety of other complex queries.

The project was founded by Martin P. Misseyer, assistant professor on the faculty of economics, business administration and econometrics at Vrije Universiteit. More information about BeursBase can be found on the World Wide Web at, http://www.econ.vu.nl.

BeursBase unique in its kind is characterized by the following features: first BeursBase contains both real time and historical data. Secondly, all data retrieved from ASE are stored, rather than a subset, all broadcasted trade data are stored. Thirdly, the data, BeursBase itself and subsequent applications form the basis for many research, education and public relations activities. A similar data link with the Amsterdam European Option Exchange (EOE) will be established as well.

Delphic Universities

The Delphic universities are a group of 24 universities within the MAC initiative who have adopted Holos for their management information system, MIS, needs. Holos provides complex modelling for IT literate users in the planning departments while also giving the senior management a user-friendly EIS.

Real value is added to data by multidimensional manipulation (being able to easily compare many different views of the available information in one report) and by modelling. In both these areas spreadsheets and query-based tools are not able to compete with fully-fledged management information systems such as Holos. These two features turn raw data into useable information.

Michael O'Hara, chairman of the MIS Application Group at Delphic

J.P. Morgan

This leading financial company was one of the first to employ datamining/forecasting applications using Information Harvester software on the Convex Examplar and C series.

The promise of data mining tools like Information Harvester is that they are able to quickly wade through massive amounts of data to identify relationships or trending information that would not have been available without the tool.

THE SCOPE OF DATA MINING

Data mining derives its name from the similarities between searching for valuable business information in a large database — for example, finding linked products in gigabytes of store scanner data — and mining a mountain for a vein of valuable ore. Both processes require either sifting through an immense amount of material, or intelligently probing it to find exactly where the value resides. Given databases of sufficient size and quality, data mining technology can generate new business opportunities by providing these capabilities:

• **Automated prediction of trends and behaviors**. Data mining automates the process of finding predictive information in large databases. Questions that traditionally required extensive hands-on analysis can now be answered directly from the data — quickly. A typical example of a predictive problem is targeted marketing. Data mining uses data on past promotional mailings to identify the targets most likely to maximize return on investment in future mailings. Other predictive problems include forecasting bankruptcy and other forms of default, and identifying segments of a population likely to respond similarly to given events.

• **Automated discovery of previously unknown patterns**. Data mining tools sweep through databases and identify previously hidden patterns in one step. An example of pattern discovery is the analysis of retail sales data to identify seemingly unrelated products that are often purchased together. Other pattern discovery problems include detecting fraudulent credit card transactions and identifying anomalous data that could represent data entry keying errors.

Data mining techniques can yield the benefits of automation on existing software and hardware platforms, and can be implemented on new systems as existing platforms are upgraded and new products developed. When data mining tools are implemented on high performance parallel processing systems, they can analyze massive databases in minutes. Faster processing means that users can automatically experiment with more models to understand complex data. High speed makes it practical for users to analyze huge quantities of data. Larger databases, in turn, yield improved predictions.

Databases can be larger in both depth and breadth:

• **More columns**. Analysts must often limit the number of variables they examine when doing hands-on analysis due to time constraints. Yet variables that are discarded because they seem unimportant may carry information about unknown patterns. High performance data mining allows users to explore the full depth of a database, without preselecting a subset of variables.

- **More rows**. Larger samples yield lower estimation errors and variance, and allow users to make inferences about small but important segments of a population.

A recent Gartner Group Advanced Technology Research Note listed data mining and artificial intelligence at the top of the five key technology areas that "will clearly have a major impact across a wide range of industries within the next 3 to 5 years."2 Gartner also listed parallel architectures and data mining as two of the top 10 new technologies in which companies will invest during the next 5 years. According to a recent Gartner HPC Research Note, "With the rapid advance in data capture, transmission and storage, large-systems users will increasingly need to implement new and innovative ways to mine the after-market value of their vast stores of detail data, employing MPP [massively parallel processing] systems to create new sources of business advantage (0.9 probability)."3

The most commonly used techniques in data mining are:

- **Artificial neural networks**: Non-linear predictive models that learn through training and resemble biological neural networks in structure.

- **Decision trees**: Tree-shaped structures that represent sets of decisions. These decisions generate rules for the classification of a dataset. Specific decision tree methods include Classification and Regression Trees (CART) and Chi Square Automatic Interaction Detection (CHAID) .

- **Genetic algorithms**: Optimization techniques that use processes such as genetic combination, mutation, and natural selection in a design based on the concepts of evolution.

- **Nearest neighbor method**: A technique that classifies each record in a dataset based on a combination of the classes of the k record(s) most similar to it in a historical dataset (where k ³ 1). Sometimes called the k-nearest neighbor technique.

- **Rule induction**: The extraction of useful if-then rules from data based on statistical significance.

Many of these technologies have been in use for more than a decade in specialized analysis tools that work with relatively small volumes of data. These capabilities are now evolving to integrate directly with industry-standard data warehouse and OLAP platforms. The appendix to this white paper provides a glossary of data mining terms.

ARCHITECTURE FOR DATA MINING

To best apply these advanced techniques, they must be fully integrated with a data warehouse as well as flexible interactive business analysis tools. Many data mining tools currently operate outside of the warehouse, requiring extra steps for extracting, importing, and analyzing the data. Furthermore, when new insights require operational implementation, integration with the warehouse simplifies the application of results from data mining. The resulting analytic data warehouse can be applied to improve business processes throughout the organization, in areas such as promotional campaign management, fraud detection, new product rollout, and so on. Figure 1 illustrates an architecture for advanced analysis in a large data warehouse.

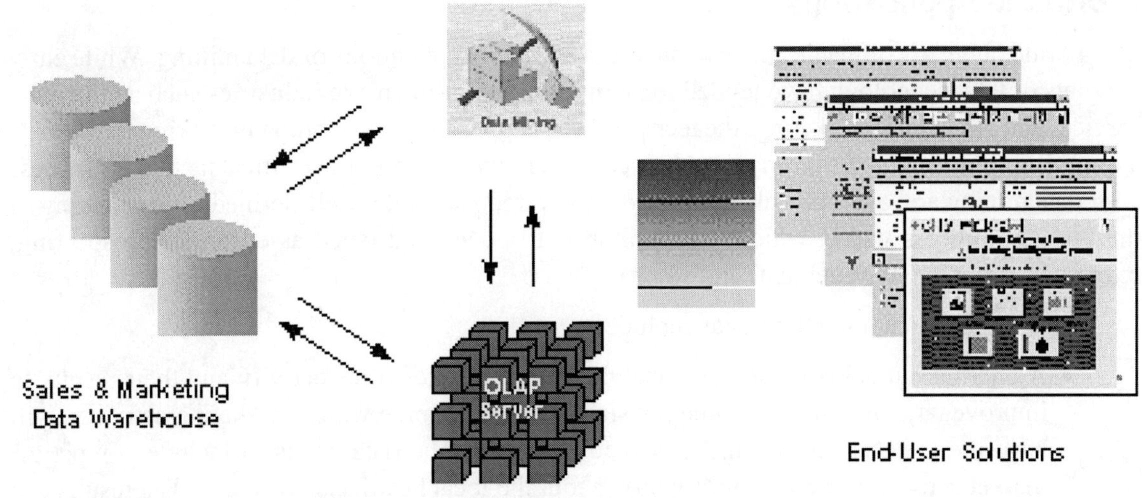

Figure 9. Integrated Data Mining Architecture

The ideal starting point is a data warehouse containing a combination of internal data tracking all customer contact coupled with external market data about competitor activity. Background information on potential customers also provides an excellent basis for prospecting. This warehouse can be implemented in a variety of relational database systems: Sybase, Oracle, Redbrick, and so on, and should be optimized for flexible and fast data access.

An OLAP (On-Line Analytical Processing) server enables a more sophisticated end-user business model to be applied when navigating the data warehouse. The multidimensional structures allow the user to analyze the data as they want to view their business – summarizing by product line, region, and other key perspectives of their business. The Data Mining Server must be integrated with the data warehouse and the OLAP server to embed ROI-focused business analysis directly into this infrastructure. An advanced, process-centric metadata template defines the data mining objectives for specific business issues like campaign management, prospecting, and promotion optimization. Integration with the data warehouse enables operational decisions to be directly implemented and tracked. As the warehouse grows with new decisions and results, the organization can continually mine the best practices and apply them to future decisions.

This design represents a fundamental shift from conventional decision support systems. Rather than simply delivering data to the end user through query and reporting software, the Advanced Analysis Server applies users' business models directly to the warehouse and returns a proactive analysis of the most relevant information. These results enhance the metadata in the OLAP Server by providing a dynamic metadata layer that represents a distilled view of the data. Reporting, visualization, and other analysis tools can then be applied to plan future actions and confirm the impact of those plans.

Profitable Applications

A wide range of companies have deployed successful applications of data mining. While early adopters of this technology have tended to be in information-intensive industries such as financial services and direct mail marketing, the technology is applicable to any company looking to leverage a large data warehouse to better manage their customer relationships. Two critical factors for success with data mining are: a large, well-integrated data warehouse and a well-defined understanding of the business process within which data mining is to be applied (such as customer prospecting, retention, campaign management, and so on).

Some successful application areas include:

- A pharmaceutical company can analyze its recent sales force activity and their results to improve targeting of high-value physicians and determine which marketing activities will have the greatest impact in the next few months. The data needs to include competitor market activity as well as information about the local health care systems. The results can be distributed to the sales force via a wide-area network that enables the representatives to review the recommendations from the perspective of the key attributes in the decision process. The ongoing, dynamic analysis of the data warehouse allows best practices from throughout the organization to be applied in specific sales situations.
- A credit card company can leverage its vast warehouse of customer transaction data to identify customers most likely to be interested in a new credit product. Using a small test mailing, the attributes of customers with an affinity for the product can be identified. Recent projects have indicated more than a 20-fold decrease in costs for targeted mailing campaigns over conventional approaches.
- A diversified transportation company with a large direct sales force can apply data mining to identify the best prospects for its services. Using data mining to analyze its own customer experience, this company can build a unique segmentation identifying the attributes of high-value prospects. Applying this segmentation to a general business database such as those provided by Dun & Bradstreet can yield a prioritized list of prospects by region.
- A large consumer package goods company can apply data mining to improve its sales process to retailers. Data from consumer panels, shipments, and competitor activity can be applied to understand the reasons for brand and store switching. Through this analysis, the manufacturer can select promotional strategies that best reach their target customer segments.

Each of these examples have a clear common ground. They leverage the knowledge about customers implicit in a data warehouse to reduce costs and improve the value of customer relationships. These organizations can now focus their efforts on the most important (profitable) customers and prospects, and design targeted marketing strategies to best reach them.

Examination Papers

B. TECH **CS-502**

FIFTH SEMESTER EXAMINATION, 2002-03

DATA BASE MANAGEMENT SYSTEM

Time : 2 Hours *Total Marks : 50*

Note : Attempt **ALL** *the questions.*

Q. 1. Attempt any FOUR of the following :— **(3 × 4 = 12)**

1. (a) Distinguish between a file-processing system and a DBMS.

Ans. File pocessing system : The typical file-processing system is supported by a conventional operating system. Permanent records are stored in various (lies and different application program are written to extract records form and to add records to the appropriate files. Before the advent of DBMS, organizations typically stored information using such system. Keeping orginizational information in a file—processing system has a number of major disadvantages :

(a) Data redundancy and inconsistency

(b) Difficulty in accessing data

(c) Data isolation

(d) Integrity problems

(e) Atomicity problems

(f) Concurrent-access anonalies

(g) Security problems.

DBMS—Data base management system is a collection of programs, that enables you to enter, organise and select data in a database. The advantage of DBMS are :

(a) Redundancy can be reduced

(b) Inconsistency can be avoided (to some extent)

(c) The data can be shared

(d) Standards can be enforced

(e) Security restrictions can be applied

(f) Conflicting requirements can be balanced.

1. (b) What is the role of database administrator?

Ans. Database administrator : The database administrator (DBA) is the person (or group of persons) responsible for overall control of the database system. The role of DBA is as following:

(i) Deciding the information content of the database.

(ii) Deciding the storage structure and access strategy.

(iii) Liaising with users.

(iv) Defining a strategy for backup and recovery.

(v) Defining authorization checks and validation procedures.

(vi) Monitoning performance and responding to change in requirements.

1. (c) Construct an E-R diagram for a hospital with a set of patients and a set of medical doctors. Associate with each patient, a log of the various tests and examinations conducted.

Ans.

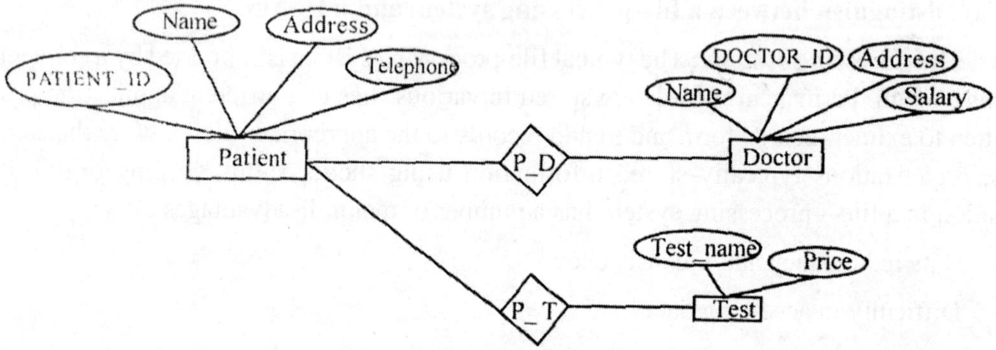

1. (d) Explain the distinction among the terms, primary key candidate key and super key.

Ans. Super key : A super key is a set of one or more attributes that, taken collectively, allows us to identify uniquely an entity in the entity set. For example, the social-security attribute of the entity set **customer** is sufficient to distinguish one customer entity from another. Thus, social-security is a super key. Similary, the combination of customer-name and social-security is a super key for the entity set customer.

Candidate key : Super keys for which no proper subset is a super key. Such minimal **superkeys** are called candidate key. Social-security is a candidate key.

Primary key : A candidate key that is chosen by the database designer as the principal means of identifying entities within an entity set. Social security is primary key.

1. (e) We can convert any weak entity set to a strong entity set by adding appropriate attribute. Why, then, do we have weak entity sets?

Ans. Weak entity sets are those sets, which are least frequently used, are of least concern, so they are not binded with appropriate attribute to form strong entity. In case of strong entities, the system operation have to take care of most of the strong entities, thus the complexity of system processes will be increased.

1. (f) What is the role of data independence in DBMS?

Ans. Data independence : The ability to modify a schema definition in one level without affecting a schema definition in the next higher level is called data independence. There are two levels of data independence :

(i) Physical data independence—It is the ability to modify the physical schema without causing application programs to be rewritten. Modification at the physical level are occasionally necessary to improve performance.

(ii) Logical data independence—It is the ability to modify the logical schema without causing application programs to be rewritten. Modification at the logical level are necessary whenever the logical structure of the database is altered.

Q. 2. This question contains two sections 'A' and 'B', each containing parts (a), (b) and (c). Attempt any FOUR parts, two each from sections 'A' and 'B':— (3 × 4=12)

2.(A) Consider the following set of requirements for a bank database:—"A large bank has several branches at different places. Each branch maintains the account details of the customers. The customers may open joint as well as single accounts. The bank also provides loan to the customer for different purposes. Bank keeps record of each trnasaction by the customer to his account. AH of the branches have employees and some employees are managers."

Draw an E-R diagram that captures this information.

Ans.

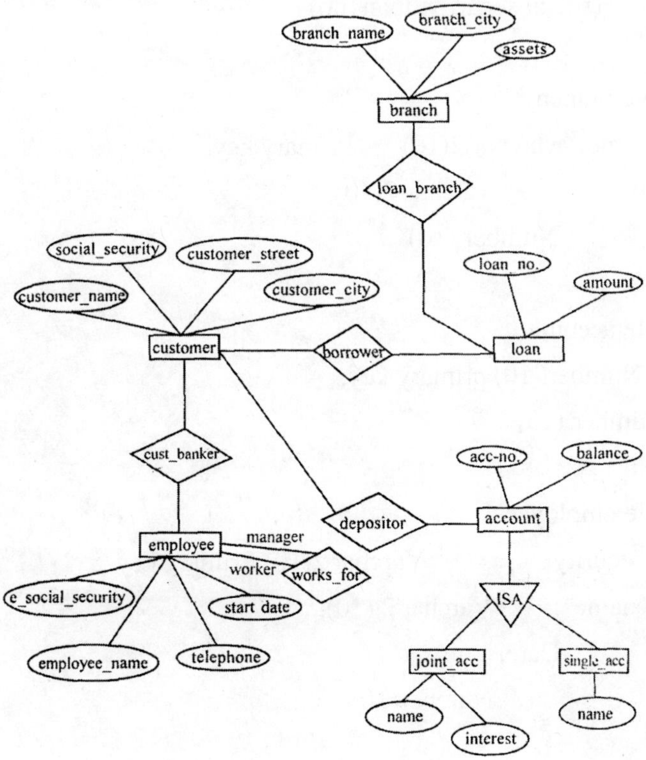

joint (acc_no, name, interest)

single (acc_no, name)

2. (A), **(c) Write SQL-DDL statement to implement bank database schema.**

Ans. (i) Create table loan

```
( loan_no "Number (10) primary key,
Amount Number (10)
);
```

(ii) Create table customer

```
(customer_name varchar2 (20)
social_security varchar 2(5), Primary key,
customer_street varchar 2(20),
customer-city varchar 2(10)
}
```

(iii) Create table borrower

```
(social_security varchar 2(5),
loan_no Number(10)
Primary key) (social security, loan_no)
}
```

(iv) Create table branch

```
( branch_name varchar 2(10) Primary key,
branch_city varchar 2(10),
assets Number (10)
);
```

(v) Create table account

```
( Acc_no, Number( 10) primary key,
balance Number (15)
)
```

(vi) Create table employee

```
(e_social_security Varchar 2(10) Primary key,
employee_name Varchar 2 (20),
Start date Date,
telephone Number(10)
)
```

(vii) Create table loan_branch

{branch name Varchar2 (10) references branch (branch_name),

loan no. Numbcr(10) references loan (loan_no),

primery key (branch_name, loan _no)

)

(viii) Create table depositor

(social_security varchar2 (5) references customer (social_security)

acc_no (10) references Account (acc_no)

primary key (social_security, acc_no)

(ix) Create table joint

(Acc_no, Number(10) references Account (acc_no),

Name Varchar2(20),

interest Number (5),

)

(x) Create table single

(acc_no. Number (1-) references Account (acc_no),

Name varchar2(20),

)

2(B) Consider the following scheme:—

SUPPLIER (<u>SUPPLIER ID</u>, SUPPLIER_NAME, SUPPLIER_ADDRESS)

PARTS (<u>PART ID</u>, PART NAME, COLOR)

CATALOG (<u>SUPPLIER ID, PART ID</u>, COST)

Write the following queries in relational algebra and SQL:—

(a) Find the name of the suppliers who supply yellow parts.

(b) Find the name of suppliers who supply both blue and green parts.

(c) Find the name of suppliers who supply all parts.

Ans. SQL

(a) Select supplier_name from supplier when supplier_id in (select supplier_id from catalog where part_id in (select part_d from parts where color = 'yellow')).

(b) Select supplier_name from supplier where supplier_id in (select supplier_id from catalog where part_id in (select part_id from parts where color = 'blue' and color = 'green')).

(c) Select supplier_name from supplier where supplier_id in (select supplier_id from catalog where, part_id in (select part_id from parts)).

Relational algebra :

(a) Π supplier_name (Supplier ∞ (Catalog ∞ 8 color = 'yellow' (Catalog ∞ Parto)));

(b) Π supplier_name (Supplier ∞ Catalog ∞ color ∞ 'Blue' AND 5 color = 'Green' (Catalog ∞ parts)));

(c) Π supplier_name (Supplier ∞ (Π supplier_id, part_id (catalog) ÷ Π partid (Parts)));

Q. 3. Answer any TWO of the following :— (6 × 2=12)

3. (a) What does unnormalized relation refer to? Define Boyce-Codd normal form. How does it differ from third normal form?

Ans. An unnormalized relation refer to a relation, which have redundancy and have insert, update and delete anomalies.

Boyce-codd normal form : A relation is in BCNF if and only if every determinant have candidate key.

or

A relation is in BCNF if and only if every nontivial left-irreducible functional dependency has a candidate key as its determinant.

For example, suppose that in the Supplier relation

S(SNO, SNAME, STATUS, CITY)

attribute S # and SNAME are both candidate key (e.g. SNO and SNAME is unique for every supplier). This relation S is in BCNF.

BCNF differ from third normal form that is 3NF is successive normalization based on a predefined primary key in each relation. BCNF is stronger from of 3NF. Every BCNF is in 3NF, but every 3NF is not necessarily in BCNF.

3. (b) Consider the scheme R=(V,W,X,Y,Z). Suppose, the following functional dependencies hold:—

$$Z \rightarrow V$$
$$W \rightarrow Y$$
$$XY \rightarrow Z$$
$$V \rightarrow WX$$

State whether the following decomposition of scheme R is loss less_join decomposition. Justify your answer.

(i) $R_1 = (V,W,X)$

$R_2 = (V,Y,Z)$

(ii) $R_1 = (V,W,X)$

$R_2 = (X,Y,Z)$

Ans. (i) Loss less_join decomposition: — Let R be a relation schema and let F be a set of PD on R. Let R_1 and R_2 form a decomposition of R. This decomposition is a lossless_join decomposition, of R if at least one of the following FD are in Ft:

* $R_1 \wedge R_2 \rightarrow R_1$
* $R_1 \wedge R_2 \rightarrow R$.

Case (i) $R_1 \wedge R_2 = (V, W, X) \wedge (V, Y, Z) \rightarrow V$

Since $V \rightarrow WX$

$V \rightarrow VWX = R_1$ (by augmentation rule)

hence

$R_1 \wedge R_2 \rightarrow R_1$

So, that decomposition into R_1 and R_2 of R are loss less_Join decomposition.

Case (ii) $R_1 \wedge R_2 = (V, W, X) \wedge (X, Y, Z) \rightarrow X$

$XY \rightarrow Z$

$XY \rightarrow V$ $(Z \rightarrow V)$

$XY \rightarrow WX(V \rightarrow WX)$

$VXY \rightarrow VWX$ (by augmentation rule)

but $X \rightarrow VWX$

hence $R_1 \wedge R_2 \not\rightarrow R_1$ or $R_1 \wedge R_2 \not\rightarrow R_2$

So, that decomposition into R_1 and R_2 of R are not loss less_Join decomposition.

3. (c) Consider the universal relation R = (A, B, C, D, E, F, G, H, I, J) and the set of functional dependencies F as given below:—

$$F = \{AB \rightarrow C, A \rightarrow DE, B \rightarrow F, F \rightarrow GH, D \rightarrow IJ\}$$

(i) Determine the Key for R.

Ans. $AB \rightarrow C$

$AB \rightarrow ABC$ (by augmentation rule).

$AAB \rightarrow AABC$

$AB \rightarrow ABCDE$ $(A \rightarrow DE)$

$ABB \rightarrow ABCDEB$

$AB \rightarrow ABCDEF$ $(B \rightarrow F)$

ABD → ABCDEFD

ABD → ABCDEFIJ (D → IJ)

hence the key of R is ABD.

(ii) Decompose R into second normal form.

Ans. R_1, R_2 and R_3 are the decomposition of R is second normal form such that

R_1 = (A, B, C, D, E) having primary key AB

R_2 = (B, F, G, H) having primary key B

R_3 = (D,I,J) having primary key D.

Q. 4. Answer any TWO of the following : (7 × 2=14)

4. (a) Consider the following two transactions :—

T_1 = read (A)

read (B)

if A = 0 then B : = B + 1

Write (B)

T_2 : read (B)

read (A)

if B = 0 then A: = A + 1

Write (A)

Let the consistency requirement be

A= 0 V B = 0

with A = B = 0 the initial values.

(i) Show that every serial execution involving these two transactions preserves the consistency of the database.

(ii) Show a concurrent execution of T_1 and T_2 that produces a non-serializable schedule.

(iii) Is there a concurrent execution of T_1 and T_2 that produces a serializable schedule?

Ans. (i) Serial execution of transaction T_1 followed by T_2 = 1 and A = 0, which preserves consistent of the database and another serial execution of transaction T_2 followed by T_1 produces B = 0 and A = 1. which preserves consistent of the database.

(ii) Consider following schedule which have concurrent execution of T_1 and T_2.

T_1	T_2
Read.(A)	
	Read (B)

Read (B)

ifA = 0 then

B = B+1

Write (B)

Read (A)

If B = 0 then A : = A + 1

Write (A)

If all instruction of T_2 swapping before Read (A) instruction of T_1 then write (A) of T_2 is conflicting Read (A) of T_1 so that we are not able to produce serial schedule T_2 followed by T_1 as well as if all instruction of T_1 swapping before Read(B) instruction of T_1 then write (B) of T_1 is conflicting Read(B) of T_2 so that we are not able to produce serial schedule T_1 followed by T_2. Hence above concurrent execution of T_1 and T_2 produce a non-serializable schedule.

(iii) No, there are no concurrent execution of T_1 and T_2that produces a serializable schedule, because it does not produce serial schedule.

4. (b) What is a recoverable schedule? Why is recoverability of schedules desirable? Are there any circumstances, under which it would be desirable to allow non-recoverable schedules?

Ans. Recoverable schedule : Consider following schedule, in which T_2 is a transaction

T_1	T_2
Read (A)	
Write (A)	
	Read (A)
Read (B)	

that performs only one instruction : Read (A). Suppose that the system allow T_2 to commit immediately after executing the Read(A) instruction. Thus, T_2 commits before T_1 does. Now suppose that T. fails before it commits. Since T_2 has read the value of data item A written by T_1, we must abort T_2 to ensure transaction atomicily. However, T_2 has already committed and cannot be aborted. Thus, we have a situation where it is impossible to recover correctly from the failure of T_1

Schedule above, with the commit happening immediately after the Read (A) instruction, is an example of a ron_recoverable schedule, which should be not allowed. Most database system require that all schedules be recoverable. A recoverable schedule is one where, for each pair of transaction T_i and T_j and that T_j reads a data items previously written by T_i, the commit operation of T_i appears before the commit operation of T_j.

Recoverability of schedule is desirable to provide consistency of the database, assuming that there are no transaction failures. This effect of transaction failures during concurrent execution is also applied.

No, there is no any circumstances, under which it would be desirable to allow non-recoverable schedules, because due to this consistency of database is violated.

Since it is, in general, not possible to distinguish between network link failures and site failures, any reconfiguration scheme must be designed to work correctly in case of a partitioning of the network. In particular, the following situations must be avoided ;

* Two or more central servers are elected in distinct partitions.
* More than one partition updates **a** replicated data item.

Reintegration of a repaired site or link into the system also requires care. When a failed site recovers, it must initiate a procedure to update its system tables to reflect changes made while it was down. If the site had replicas of any data items, it must obtain the current values of these data items and ensure that it receives all future updates. Reintegration,of a site is more complicated than it may seem to be at first glance, since there may be updates to the data items processed during the time that the site is recovering. An easy solution is temporarily to halt the entire system while the failed site rejoins it. In most applications, however, such a temporary halt is unacceptably disruptive. Techniques have been developed to allow failed sites to reintegrate while allowing concurrent updates to data items. If a failed link recovers, two or more partitions can be rejoined. Since a partitioning of the network limits the allowable operations by some or all sites, it is desirable to inform all sites promptly of the recovery of the link. See the bibliographic notes for more information on recovery in distributed systems.

4. (c) Explain the commit protocol with reference to distributed database. How does the 2PC protocol respond to various types of failures?

Ans. Commit protocols : If we are to ensure atomicity, all the sites in which a transaction T executed must agree on the final outcome of the execution. T must either commit at all sites, or it must abort at all sites. To ensure this property, the transaction coordinator of T must execute a *commit protocol.*

The widely used commit protocol is the two-phase commit protocol (2PC).

Two-phase commit :

Let T be a transaction initiated at site "S_1 and let the transaction coordinator at S_i be C_i

The commit protocol :

When 1 completes its execution—that is. when all the sites at which 7 has executed inform C_i that T has completed—C_i starts the 2PC protocol.

* **Phase 1 :** C adds the record **<prepare** T > to the log and forces the log executed. On receiving such a message, the transaction manager at that site determines whether it is willing to commit its portion of T. If the answer is no, it adds a record **<no** T > to the log and then responds by sending an **abort** T message to C_i. If the answer is yes, it adds a record **<ready** T> to the log and forces the log (with all the log records corresponding to T*)* onto stable storage. The transaction manager then replies with a **ready** T message to C_i.

* **Phase 2** : When C_i receives responses to the **prepare** T message from all the sites or when a prespecified interval of time has elapsed since the **prepare** T message was sent out, C_i can determine whether the transaction T can be committed or aborted. Transaction T can be commited if C received a **ready** T message from all the participating sites. Otherwise, transaction Tmust be aborted. Depending on the verdict, either a record **<commit** T > or a record **<abort** T> is added to the log and the log is forced onto stable storage. At this point, the fate of the transaction has been sealed. Following this point, the corrdinator sends either a **commit** T or an **abort** T message to all participating sites. When a site receives that message, it records the message in the log.

A site at which executed can unconditionally abort T at any time prior to its sending the message **ready** T to the coordinator. The **ready** T message is, in effect, a promise by a site to follow the coordinator's order to commit to abort T. The only means, by which a site can make such a promise is if the needed information is stored in stable storage. Otherwise, if the site crashes after sending **ready** T, it may be unable to make good on its promise.

Since unanimity is required to commit a transaction, the fate of T is sealed as soon as at least one site responds **abort** T. Since the coordinator site, S_i is one of the sites at which T executed, the coordinator can decide unilaterally to abort T. The final verdict regarding T is determined at the lime that the coordinator writes that verdict (commit or abort) to the log and forces that verdict to stable storage. In some implementations of the 2PC protocol, a site sends an **acknowledge** T message to the coordinator at the end of the second phase of the protocol. When the coordinator receives the **acknowledge** T message from all the sites, it adds the record **<completc** T > to the log. **Respond to various types of failure** :

We now examine in detail how the 2PC protocol responds to various types failures

- **Failure of a participating site** : If the coordinator C_i detects that a site has failed, it takes the following actions. If the site fails before responding with a **ready** T message to C_i it is assumed to have responded with an **abort** T message. If the site fails after the coordinatore has received the ready T message from the site, the rest of the commit protocol is executed in the normal fashion, ignoring the failure of the site.

When a participating site S_k recovers from a failure, it must examine its log to determine the fate of therefore of execution when the failure occurred. Let T be one such transaction. We consider each of the possible cases:

- The log contains a <**commit** T> record. In this case, the site executes **redo** *(*T*),*

- The log contains an<**abort** T> record. In this case, the site executes **undo** *(*T*)*.

- The log contains a <**ready** 7> record. In this case, the site must consult C_i to determine the fate of T. If C is up, it notifies, S_k regarding whether T committed or aborted. In the former case, it executes **redo** (T)**;** in the latter case, it executes **undo**(T)- If C_i is down. S_k must try to find the fate of T from other sites. It does so by sending a **query-status** T message to all the sites in the system. On receiving such a message, a site must consult its log to determine whether 7'has executed there, and if T has, whether T committed or aborted. It then notifies, S_k about this outcome. If no site has the appropriate information (that is, whether T committed or aborted), then S_k can neither abort nor commit T. The decision concerning T is postponed until S_k can obtain the needed information. Thus, S_k must periodically resend the **query-status** message to the other sites. It continues to do so until a site recovers that contains the needed information. Note that the site at which C_i resides always has the needed information.

□ The log contains no control records **(abort, commit, ready)** concerning T. Thus, we know that S_k failed before responding to the **prepare** T message from C_t. Since the failure of S precludes the sending of such a response, by our algorithm C_i must abort T. Hence, S_k must execute **undo**(T).

□ **Failure of the coordinator :** If the coordinator fails in the midst of the execution of the commit protocol for transaction T, then the participating sites must decide the fate of T. We shall see that, in certain cases, the participating sites cannot decide whether to commit or abort T and therefore these sites must wait for the recovery of the failed coordinator.

□ If an active site contains a **<commit** T> record in its log, then T must be committed.

□ If an active site contains an **<abort** T> record in its log, then T must be aborted.

□ If some active site does *not* contain a <ready T> record in its log, then the failed coordinator C cannot have decided to commit T, because a site that does not have a **<ready** T> record in its log cannot have sent a ready T message to C . However, the coordinator may havee decided to abort T. but not to commit T. Rather than wait for C_i to recover, it is preferable to abort T.

□ If none of the preceding cases holds, then all active sites must have a **<ready** T> record in their logs, but no additional control records (such as **<abort** T> or **<commit** T>). Since the coordinator has failed, it is impossible to determine whether a decision has been made, and if one has, what that decision is, until the coordinator recovers. Thus, the active sites must wait for C_i to recover. Since the fate of T remains in doubt, T may system. For example, if locking is used. T may hold locks on data at active sites. Such a situation is undesirable, because it may be hours or days before C_i is again active. During this time, other transactions may be forced to wait for T. As a result, data items may be unavailable not only on the failed site (C_i), but on active sites as well. This situation is called the *blocking* problem, because T is blocked pending the recovery of site C_i .

□ **Network partition** : When a network partitions, two possibilities exist:

1. The coordinator and all its participants remain in one partition. In this case, the failure has no effect on the commit protocol.

2. The coordinator and its participants belong to several partitions. From the viewpoint of the sites in one of the partitions, it appears that the sites in other partitions have failed. Sites that are not in the partition containing the coordinator simply execute the protocol to deal with failure of the coordinator. The coordinator and the sites that are in the same partition as the coordinatore follow the usual commit protocol, assuming that the sites in the other partitions have failed.

Thus, the major disadvantage of the 2PC protocol is that coordinator failure may result in blocking, where a decision either to commit or to abort T may have to be postponed unti, C_i recovers.

B. TECH **CS-502**

FIFTH SEMESTER EXAMINATION, 2003-04

DATA BASE MANAGEMENT SYSTEM

Time : 2 Hours *Total Marks : 50*

Note : **1. The question paper contains FOUR questions.**

2. Attempt ALL questions.

Q. 1. Attempt any FOUR parts :— **(3x4=12)**

1. (a) What are main differences between a file processing system and a database management system?

Ans. Pl. See Q.1 (a) of 2002-2003

1. (b) What do you mean by data abstraction? Explain the difference between physical level, conceptual leval and view level of data abstraction.

Ans. Data abstraction : For the system to be unable, it must retrive data efficiently. This concern has led to the design of complex data structure for the representation of data in the database. Since many database systems users are not computer trained developers hide the complexity from users through several levels of abstraction, to simplify user's interaction with the system:

Physical level : The lowest level of abstraction describes how the data are actually stored. At the physical level, complex low level data structures are described in detail.

Conceptual Level (Logical-level) : The next higher level of abstraction describes what data are stored in the database and what relationships exist among those data. The entire database is thus described in term of a small number of relatively simple structures. Although implementation of the simple structures at the logical level may invlove complex physical-level structures, the user of the logical level docs not need to be aware of this complexity. The logical level of abstraction is used by database administrators, who must decide what information is to be kept in the database.

View level : The highest level of abstraction describes only part of the entire database. Despite the use of simpler structures at the logical level, some compexity remains, because of the large size of the database. Many users of the database system will not be concerned with all this information. Instead, such users need to access only a part of the database. So that their interaction with the system is simplified, the view-level of abstraction is defined. The system may provide many view for the same database.

1. (c) What is data independence? What are the differences between logical data independence and physical data independence?

Ans. Pl. See Q. 1(f) of 2002-2003.

1. (d) What are the differences between super key, candidate key and primary key? Explain with a suitable example.

Ans. Pl. see Q. 1 (d) of 2002-2003

1. (e) What are the differences between data definition language and data manipulation language? Explain with example.

Ans. Data definition language (DDL): Once the design of a database is completed and a DBM **is** chosen to implement the database, the first order of the day is to specify conceptual and internal schemes for the database and any mapping between the two. In many DBMS where no strict seperation of levels is maintained, one language, called the **data definition language (DDL),** is used by database designers to define both schema. The DBMS will have a DDL compiler, whose function is to process DDL statements in order to identify descriptions of the schema constructs and to store the schema description in the DBMS catalog.

Data manipulation language (DML) : Once the database schemas are compiled and the database is populated with data, users must hare some means to manipulate the database. Typical manipulations include retrieval, insertion, deletion and modification of the data. The DBMS provides a **data manipulation language** (DML) for these purposes.

1. (f) What do you mean by entity and relationship in ER model? Explain how a relationship set is defined.

Ans. Entity : An entity is a "thing" or "object" in the real word that is distinguishable from all other objects. For example, each person in an enterprise is an entity. An entity has a set of properties and the values for some set of properties may uniquely identify an entity. For example, the social-security number uniquely identifies one particular person in the enterprise.

Relationship : A relationship is an association among several entities. For example, we can define a relationship that associates customer Raman with loan L-15. This relationship specifies that Raman is a customer with loan number L-15.

Relationship set : A relationship set is a set of relationships of the same type. Formally, it is a mathematical relation on $n \geq 2$ (possibly nondistinct) entity sets. If E_1 $E_2 ... E_n$ are entity, then **a** relationship set R is a subset of $\{(e_1, e_2,...e_n)$ I $e_1 \in E_1, e_2 \in E_2 ... e_n \in E_n\}$ Where $(e_1, e_2,...e_n)$ is a relationship.

Q. 2. Attempt any TWO parts :— **(6x2=12)**

2. (a) Design an E-R diagram for airline reservation system consisting of flights, aircrafts, airports, fares, reservations, tickets, pilots, crew and passengers. Clearly highlight the entities, relationship, primary keys and mapping constraints. Transform this E-R diagram to relational database schemas. Clearly mention the generalization, aggregation, weak entity and referential integrity in your design.

Ans. Please see the diagram on page no. 256.

2. (b) Consider following scheme for PROJECT database :—

Project (Project_No, Project_Name, Project_Manager)

Employee (Employee_No, Employee_Name)

Assigned_To, (Project_No, Employee_No)

(i) Write SQL-DDL statement for implementation of PROJECT database. The SQL statement should clearly indicate the primary key and foreign keys.

Ans. (i) * Create table Project

(Project_No Number(6) Primary Key,

Project_Name Varchar2 (20),

Project_Manager Varchar2 (20)

);

* Create table Employee

(Employee_No Number (6) Primary key,

Employee_Name Varchar2 (20)

)

* Create table Assigned_To

(Project_No Number (6) references project (Project_No),

Employee_No Number (6) references Employee (Employee_No),

Primary key (Project_No, Employee.No)

);

(ii) Write following queries in relational algebra and SQL :—

- **Get the detail of employees working on both projects 'P1' and 'P2'.**

Ans. 2 (a) E-R diagram

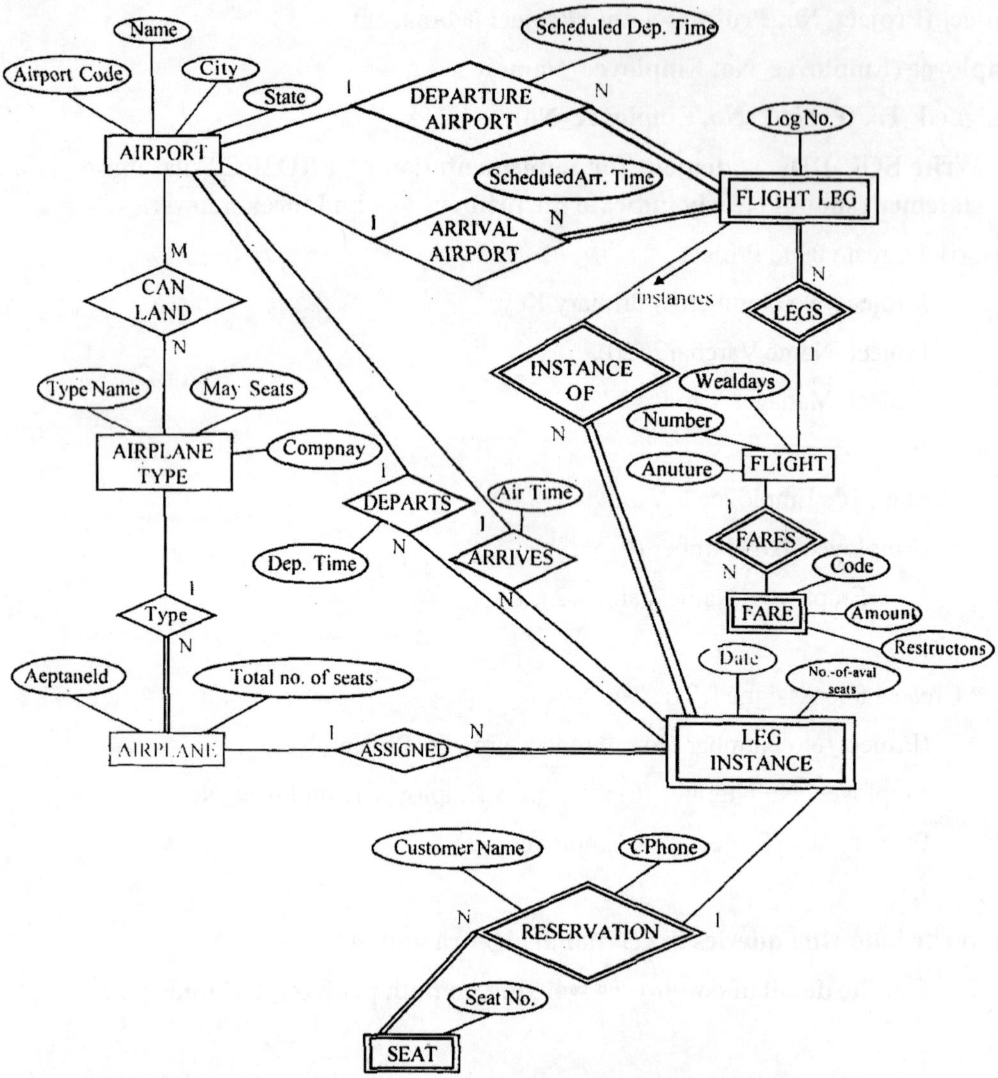

- **List the name of employees working on prject 'P1' but not on project 'P2'.**
- **Delete the record of employee whose Employee Number is 'E1'.**
- **List the name of employees who are working on a project for which 'E1' is the project manager.**

Ans. (a) SQL : Select * from Employee where Employee__No in (Select Employee_No from Assigned_To where Project_No = 'P1' AND Project_No = 'P2');

(b) Select Employee_Name from Employee where Employee_No in (Select Employee_No from Assigned To where Project_No = 'P1 AND Project_No ! = 'P2').

(c) Delete from employee where Employee_No = 'El' cascade Delete,

(d) Select Employee_No in (Select Employee_No from Assigned_To where project_No in (Select Project_No from Project where Project_Manager = 'El'));

Relational algebra :

(a) Employee ∞ (Assigned_To ÷ π Project_No

(δ Project_No = 'P1' AND Project_No = 'P2' (Assigned_To)));

(b) Employee ∞ (Assigned_To ÷ π Project_No.

(δ Project_No = 'P1' AND Project_No = 'P2' (Assigned_To)));

(c) Employee—(δ Employee_No ÷ 'El' (Employee));

(d) π Employee_Name (Employee ∞ (Assigned_To ÷ π project_No (δ Project_Manager = 'E1' (Project))));

2. (c) Answer the following :—

(i) What are views? How is view defined? Explain with a suitable example. Discuss the problems of insert, delete and update through the views.

Ans. A VIEW is a database object that contains no data of its own. It is a virtual table, whose contents are taken from other tables through the execution of a query. The changes in the tables are automatically reflected in the VIEWs. A VIEW is created with the CREATE VIEW command. A VIEW is queried just like querying a table. A user can not distinguish between a table and a VIEW. Most of the operations on a table can also be carried out with VIEWs, with some restrictions. The advantages of a VIEW are as follows :

* Any updation of rows in the table will automatically reflect in the VIEWs.
* As a VIEW does not store any data, the redundancy problem does not arise.
* Critical data in the base table is safeguarded as access to such data can be controlled using VIEWs.
* Complicated queries are simplified using VIEWs.

For example :

```
CREATE VIEW empdept AS
SELECT empno, ename, deptno
FROM emp
WHERE deptno = 30,
```

* Attempts to insert values into the base table through a VIEW that violate the integrity constraint, will be rejected.
* A modification is permitted through a view only if the view in question is defined in terms of one relation of the actual relational database — that is, of the logical-level database.

Under this constraint, the update, insert and delete operations would be forbidden.

(ii) What do you mean by referential integrity? Define foreign key and discuss the concept behind declaration of foreign keys.

Ans. Referential integrity : Let D be a primary domain and let R_1 be a relation with an attribute A, that is defined on D. Then, at any given time, each value of A in R_1 must be either (a) null, or (b) equal to V, say, where V is the primary key talue of some tuple in some relation R_2 (R_1 and R_2 not necessarily distinct) with primary key defined on D.

Foreign key : Foreign key represent relationships between tables. A foreign key is a column (or a group of columns), whose values are derived from the primary/unique key of the same or some other table.

Declaration of foreign keys :

```
Create table emp
(empno char(10) primary key,
    deptno char (10),
    constraint dept-f key
    Foreign key (deptno) References dept).
```

(iii) What are triggers? How are they different from the assertions? Discuss the cases where the triggers and assertions are used.

Ans. Triggers : A database trigger is a stored PL\SQL program unit associated with a specific database table. Triggers implicitly get fired (executed) whenever the table is affected by any SQL operation.

Assertion : An assertion is a predicate expressing a condition that we wish the database always to satisfy. Domain constraints and referential-integrity constraints are special forms of assertions. We have paid substantial attention to these forms of assertion because they are easily tested and apply to wide range of database applications. However, there are many constraints that we cannot express using only these special form.

In assertion, there is only condition we have to specify, but in triggers, there are both condition and actions.

Q. 3. Attempt any TWO parts :— (6½ × 2=13)

3. (a) What are normal forms? What is the motivation behind normalizing a database? Discuss the first and second normal forms. Define and explain the functional dependency with a suitable example.

Ans. Normal form : A relation is said to be in a particular normal form if it satisfies a certain specified set of constraints. The normal forms are of following types : 1NF, 2NF, 3NF, BCNF, 4NF & 5NF. The motivation behind normalizing a database is as follows :

(i) To reduce the redundancy so that the space is saved,

(ii) To minimize the insertion, deletion and update anomalies.

First normal form : A relation is in 1NF if and only if all underlying domain contains atomic values only.

Second normal form : A relation is in 2NF if and only if it is in 1NF and every non-key attribute is fully functionally dependent on primary key.

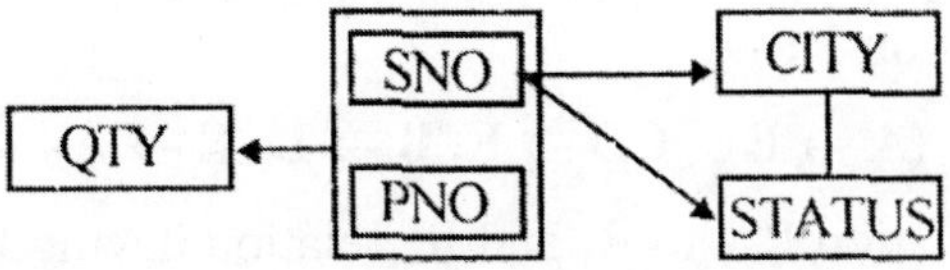

above functional dependencies is in 1NF

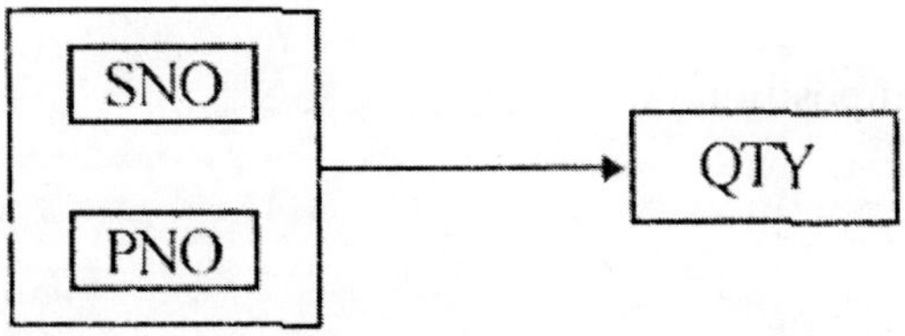

and

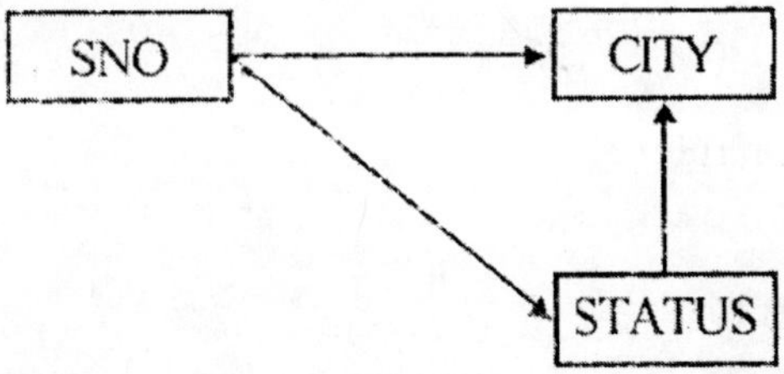

above functional dependencies are in 2NF.

Functional dependency : Given a relation R, attribute Y of R is functonally dependent on attribute X of R if and only if each x-vaiue in R has associated with it precisely one Y-value in R (at any one time)

For example :

In the supplier-and-parts database, attribute; SNAME, STATUS and CITY of relation S are each functionally dependent on attribute SNO because given a particular value for SNO, there exists precisely one correspondence value for each of SNAME, STATUS and CITY. In symbols, we have

SNO $\rightarrow$ SNAME

SNO $\rightarrow$ STATUS

SNO $\rightarrow$ CITY

or

SNO $\rightarrow$ (SNAME, STATUS, CITY)

3. (b) Suppose a relational scheme R = (A,B,C,D,E) is decomposed into following scheme :—

(A,B,C)

(A,D,E)

Prove that this decomposition is a lossless join decomposition, if the following set of functional dependencies holds on R:—

$$(A \rightarrow BC, CD \rightarrow E, B \rightarrow D, E \rightarrow A)$$

Ans. If we decompose a relation R into R_1 and R_2 relation having FDF the decomposition is lossless join decomposition if and only if it have at least one FD in FT as follows :

* $R_1 \cap R_2 \rightarrow R_1$
* $R_1 \cap R_2 \rightarrow R_2$

From the following decomposition

(A,B,C) and (A,D,E)

We have

$(A,B,C) \cap (A,D,E) \rightarrow A$

by using FDs given

$A \rightarrow BC$

$A \rightarrow ABC$ (by augmentation rule)

i.e.

$(A.B,C) \cap (A,D,E) \rightarrow (A,B.C)$

hence we can say that above decomposition is loosless join decomposition.

3. (c) Define fourth normal form. Consider a relational scheme R = (A,B,C,D,E). Let M is the following set of multivalued dependencies :—

$$M = (A \rightarrow\rightarrow BC, B \rightarrow\rightarrow CD, E \rightarrow\rightarrow AD)$$

Give a lossless join decomposition of scheme R into fourth normal form. Justify your answer.

Ans. Fourth normal form (4NF) : A relation schema R is in 4NF with respect to a set D of functional and multivalued dependencies if, for all multivalued dependencies in D^+ of the form $A \rightarrow\rightarrow B$, Where $A \subseteq R$ and $B \subseteq R$, at least one of the following holds:

* $A \rightarrow\rightarrow B$ is a trivial multivalued dependency
* A is a superkey for schema R.

Given

$A \rightarrow\rightarrow BC$

$A \rightarrow\rightarrow C\,D$ $(B \rightarrow CD)$

$A \rightarrow\rightarrow BCD$ (by union rule)

$E \rightarrow\rightarrow AD$

Since

R = (A.B,C,D,E)

and

$A \rightarrow\rightarrow BCD$

and

$E \rightarrow\rightarrow A,D$

hence we replace R by

(A,B,C,D) and (A,E,D)

$(ABCD) \cap (A,E,D) \rightarrow\rightarrow AD$

$A \rightarrow\rightarrow BC$

$A \rightarrow\rightarrow ABC$ (by augmentation rule)

$AD \rightarrow\rightarrow ABCD$ (by augmentation rule)

hence

$(ABCD) \cap (A,E,D) \rightarrow\rightarrow ABCD$

Now, we can say that schema R can be decomposed into (ABCD) and (A,E,D), which are lossless join decomposition and are in 4NF.

Q. 4. Attempt any TWO parts : (6½ × 2 = 13)

4. (a) What is log? How is it maintained? Discuss the salient features of deferred database modification and immediate database modification strategies in brief.

Ans. Log : The most widely used structure for recording database modifications is the **log.** The log is a sequence of log records and maintains a record of all the update activities in the database. There are several types of log records. An update log record describes a single database write and has the following field :

* Transaction identifier
* Data-item identifier
* Old value
* New value.

We denote the various types of log records as follows :

* $< T_i$ start> Transaction T_i has started
* $<T_i, X_i, V_i, V_2>$ Transaction T_i has performed a write on data item X_J . X_J had value V_1 before the write and will have value V_2 after the write.

* <T_i commit>. Transaction T_i has committed
* <T_i abort>. Transaction T_i has aborted.

For log records to be useful for recovery from system and disk failures, the tog must reside in stable storage.

There are two techniques for using the log to ensure transaction atomicity despite failures. They are as follows:

(i) Deferred database modification

(ii) Immediate database modification.

(i) Deferred database modification : The deferred modification technique ensures transaction atomicity by recording all database modifications in the log, but deferring the execution of all write operations of a transaction until the transaction partially commits. A transaction is said to be partially committed once the final action of the trnasaction has been executed. For deferred modification technique, we assume that transactions are executed serially.

Let us consider simplified banking system. let I_0 be transaction that transfers Rs 50 from account A to account B. This transaction is defined as follows :

To:

Read (A)

A: = A –50

Write (A)

Read (B)

B : = B + 50

Write (B)

Let T_1 be a transaction that withdraws Rs. 100 from account C. This transaction is defined as:

T_1 :

Read (c)

C: = C–100

Write (c)

Suppose that these trensaction are executed serially, in the order to follow by T. and the value of accounts A, B and C before the execution took place were Rs 1000. Rs 2000 & Rs 700 respectively. The recovery schemes uses the following recovery procedure that is redo (T_i). The portion of the log & its database for above two transactions is as follows :

Log **Database**

< To start>

<To, A, 950>

<To, B.2050>

< To commit>

A = 950

B = 2050

<T_1 start>

<T_1 C,600>

<T_1 commit>

C = 600

(ii) Immediate database modification : The immediate update technique allows database modifications to be output to the database while the transaction is still in the active state. Database modification written by active transaction are called uncommitted modification. In the event of a crash or a transaction failure, the system must use the old-value field of the log records, to restore the modified data item to the value they had prior to the start of the transaction, This restoration is accomplished through the undo operation.

Using the log, the system can handle any failure that does not result in the loss of information on nonvolatile storage. The recovery uses two recovery procedures that is undo (T_1) or redo (T_1). The portion of log and database for above two transaction (T_0 & T_1) is as fallows :

Log **Database**

< To start>

<To, A, 1000, 950>

<To, B, 2000, 2050>

A = 950

B = 2050

< To commit>

< T_1 Start >

<T_1,C, 700,600>

C = 600

<T_1 Commit>

4. (b) What are schedules? Define conflict and view serializable schedules. State whether the following schedule is conflict serializable or not. Justify your answer :—

T_1	T_2
Read (A)	
Write (A)	

	Read (B)
	Write (B)
Read (B)	
Write (B)	
	Read (A)
	Write (A)

Ans. Schedules : The execution sequences of different transaction are called schedules. They represent the chronological order, in which instructions are executed in the system.

Conflict serializable schedules : A schedule S is **conflict serializable** if it is conflict equivalent to a serial schedule. If a schedule S can be transformed into a schedule S' by a series of swaps of nonconflicting instructions, we say that S and S' are **conflict equivalent.**

We say that instruction I_i and I_j **conflict** if they are aperations by different transactions on the same item, and at least one of these instruction is a **write** operation.

View serializable schedules : Consider two schedules S and S', where the same set of transaction participates in both schedules. The schedules S and S' are said to be view equivalent if the following three conditions are met :

1. For each data item Q, if transaction $T_i$reads the initial value of Q in schedule S, then transaction T_i must in schedule S' also read the initial value of Q.
2. For each data item Q, if transaction T_j execute read (Q) in schedule S and that value was produced by transaction T_j (if any), then transaction T_j must in schedule S', also read the value of Q that was produced by transaction T_j.
3. For each data item Q, the transaction (if any) that performs the final write (Q) operation in schedule S must perform the final write (Q) operation in schedule S'.

A schedule is view serializable if it is view equivalent to a serial schedule.

Given

T_1	T_2
Read (A)	
Write (A)	
	Read (B)
	Write (B)
Read (B)	
Write (B)	
	Read (A)
	Write (A)

Since swapping of Read (B) of T_1 and Write (B) of T_2 is conflicting, hence we are not able to get serial schedule by swapping and thus we can say that above schedule is not equivalent to serial schedule. Finally we say that above schedule is not conflict serializabie schedule.

4. (c) What are locks? Differentiate shared mode and exclusive mode locks. How can a serializability be ensured by using lock based protocols? With reference to two phase locking protocol, explain how the upgrading and downgrading of locks takes place. Explain with a suitable example.

Ans. Locks : One way to ensure serializability is to require that access to data item be done in a mutually exclusive manner: that is, while one transaction is accessing a data item, no other transaction can modify thai data item. The most common method used to implement this requirement is to allow a transaction to access a data item only if it is currently holding a lock on that item. There are various modes, in which a data item may be locked. There are two modes of locks :

(a) **Shared mode** : If a transaction T_i has obtained a shared mode lock (denoted by S) on item Q, then T_1 can read, but cannot write, Q.

(b) Exclusive mode : If a transaction T_i has obtained an exclusive mode lock (denoted by X) on item Q. then T_i can both read and write Q.

Two phase locking protocol : One protocol that ensures serializability is the two phase locking protocol. This protocol requires that each transaction issue lock and unlock requests in two phases:

1. **Upgrading phase** : A transaction may obtain locks, but may not release any lock.

2. **Downgrading phase** : A transaction may release locks, but may not obtain any new locks..'

Initially, a transaction is in the upgrading phase. The transaction acquires locks as needed. Once the transaction releases a lock, it enters the downgrading phase and it can issue no more lock requests.

For example, the following transaction follows two phase locking protocol :

T_1 :

Lock-X(B);

Read (B):

B : = B -50;

Write (B);

Lock -X (A);

Read (A);

A : = A + 50;

Write (A)

Unlock (B)

Unlock (A).

B. TECH CS-502

FIFTH SEMESTER EXAMINATION, 2004-05

DATA BASE MANAGEMENT SYSTEM

Time : 2 Hours *Total Marks : 50*

Note : Attempt **ALL** *the questions.*

1. Attempt any FOUR of the following: (5×2=10)

1. (a) Define following terms:

Data, Database, Database System.

Ans. (a) Data: It refer to value its physically recorded in the database.

Database: A database is a collection of stored operational.data used by the application systems of some particular enterprise.

Database System: A database system is a computerized record-keeping system. It perform following operation. For example, insert, update, delete and retrieval of the data.

1. (b) What do you mean by External Schema, Conceptual Schema and Internal Schema?

Ans. External Schema: It consists of definitions of the each the various types of external record in that external view.

Conceptual Schema: It consist of definitions of each of the various types of conceptual record.

Internal Schema: It defines the various types of stored record, and specifies what indexes exist, how stored fields are represented what physical sequence the stored records are in.

1. (c) What is the difference between logical data independence and physical data independence?

Ans. Logical Data Independence: It is the ability to modify the logical schema without causing application programs to be rewritten.

Physical Data Independence: It is the ability to modify the physical schema without causing application programs to be rewritten.

1. (d) Discuss briefly the conventions for displaying an ER Schema as an ER diagram.

Ans. The following components in ER diagram are used to represents the ER schema.

(i) Entity sets — Rectangles

(ii) Attributes — Ellipses

(iii) Relationship sets — Diamonds

(iv) Link attributes to entity set and entity sets to relationship sets. — Lines

(v) Multivalued attributes — Double ellipses

(vi) Derived attributes — Dashed ellipses

1. (e) What is the Specialization and Generalization with respect to Database?

Ans. Specialization: The process of designating subgroupings within an entity set is specialization. The specialization of account allows us to distinguish among accounts based on the type of account. The specialization of ACCOUNT is SAVING-ACCOUNT and CHECKING-ACCOUNT.

Generalization: The design process in which multiple entity sets are synthesized into a higher level entity set based on common features. The account is the generalization of SAVING-ACCOUNT and CHECKING-ACCOUNT:

Example:

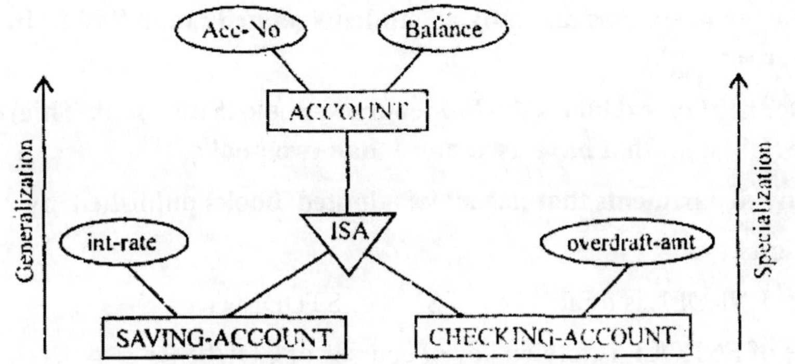

1. (f) Explain difference between a weak and a strong entity set.

Ans. Weak Entity Set: An entity set which have no primary key is called weak entity set; It has a discriminator which is a set of attributes that allows this distinction to be made.

Strong Entity Set; An entity set which have primary key is called strong entity set. Primary key is a key which uniquely identify the entity set.

Example:

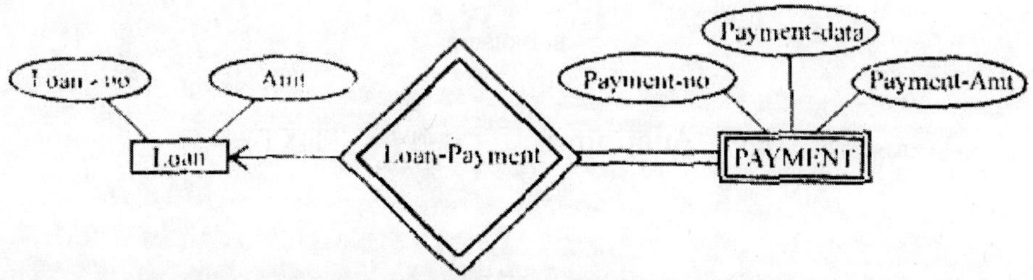

Above loan is strong entity set and payment is weak entity set.

2. This question contains two sections 'A' and 'B' each pontaining parts (a), (b) and (c). Attempt any four parts, two each from sections 'A' and 'B'.

2. (a) Consider the following relations for a database that keeps track of students enrollment in courses and the books adopted for each courses.

STUDENT (SSN, Name, Major, Bdate)

COURSE (Course#, Cname, Dept.)

ENROLL (SSN, Course//, Quarter, Grade)

BOOK-ADOPTION (Course#, Quarter, Book ISBN)

TEXT (Book-ISBN Book, Title, Publisher, Author)

The underlined attributes form the primary key of a relational schema.

Specify the foreign keys for the above schema, stating any assumptions you make.

Then specify the following queries in relational algebra.

(i) List the no. of courses taken by all students named 'John Smith' in Winter 2002 (i.e. Quarter = 'W_{02}').

(ii) Produce a list of text books (include courses, Book-ISBN, Book-Title) of courses offered by the 'CS' dept that have used more than two books.

(iii) List any departments that has all its adopted books published by 'BC Publishing'.

Ans. Foreign key:

(i) SNN of ENROLL is foreign key of SNN of STUDENT.

(ii) Course of ENROLL is foreign key of course# of COURSE.

(iii) BOOK-ISBN of BOOK-ADOPTION is foreign key of BOOK-ISBN of TEXT.

(iv) Course#, Quarter of ENROLL is foreign key of course# Quarter of BOOK-ADOPTION.

$$G_{count(course\#)} \quad {}_{course\#} \quad {}_{\substack{Name='John\ Smith' \\ AND\ S.SSN = E.SNN \\ AND\ Quarter = 'Wo_2'}} (student \times Enroll)$$

$$BOOK\text{-}ISBN$$

$$_{course\#.Book\text{-}ISBN} (Book\text{–}Adoption) \qquad {}_{\substack{publisher \\ = 'BC\ Pub'}} (TEXT)$$

$$X = \quad {}_{Dept} \quad {}_{course.course\# = y.course} (course\ XY)$$

2. **(b) Consider the following relational database:**

EMPLOYEE (Person-name, Street, City)

WORKS (Person-name, Company-name, Salary)

COMPANY (Company-name City)

MANAGES (Person-name, Manager-name)

(i) Give an SQL DDL definition of this database.

(ii) Identify referential - integrity constraints that should hold.

(iii) Discuss the inclusion of above constraints in DDL definition,

Ans. (i) & (ii) & (iii)

Create table EMPLOYEE

(. Person-name	varchar 2(20) Primary Key,
Street	varchar 2(15)
City	varchar 2(10)
)	

Create table WORKS

(Person-name	varchar 2(20) references EMPLOYEE (Person-name),
Company-name Varchar 2(25)	reference COMPANY (Company-name)
Salary	Number (5)
)	

Create table COMPANY

(Company-name	Varchar 2 (25) Primary key
City	Varchar 2 (10).

3. Answer any TWO of the following: **(6×2 = 12)**

3. (a) Discuss lossless join and dependency preservation.

Ans. Lossless Join: Let R be a relation, and let F be a set of functional dependencies on R. Let R_1 and R_2 form a decomposition of R. This decomposition is a lossless join decomposition of R if at least one of the following functional dependencies are in F^+ :

(i) $R_1 \cap R_2 \rightarrow R_1$

(ii) $R_1 \cap R_2 \rightarrow R_1$

Example: Consider Leading-schema

Lending-schema = (branch_name, branch_ city, assets, customer_ name, loan_no, amount)

Following decomposition of above schema are loss-less join decomposition:

Branch-schema = (branch name, branch_city, assets)

Loan-info-schema = (branch_name, customer_ name, loan_no, amount)

The set F of functional dependencies that we require to hold on lending-schema are

branch_name → assets, branch city

loan no → amount, branch_name

Consider above functional dependencies as

branch_name → assets, branch_city by augmentation rule

branch_name → branch_name, assets, branch_city

Since Branch_schema ∩ Loan_infor_schema = {branch_name} it follows that our initial decomposition is a lossless join decomposition.

Dependency preservation : When an update is made to the database, the system should be able to check that the update will not create an illegal relation - that is, one that does not satisfy all the given functional dependencies. If we are to check updates efficiently, we should design relational-database schemas that allow update validation without the compulation of joins.

The set of restrictions $F_1, F_2, \ldots F_n$ is the set of dependencies that can be checked efficiently. We now must ask whether testing only the restrictions is sufficient. Let $F^1 = F_1 \cup F_2 = \cup F^r$. F^+ is a set of functional dependencies on schema R, but, in general F = F. However, even if $F^+ = F^+$ it may be that $F^+ \# F^+$. If the latter is true, then every dependency Is F is logically implied by F, and, if we verify that F is satisfy, we have verified that F is satisfied. We say that a decomposition having the property $F'^+ = F^+$ is a dependency - preserving.

3. (b) Let R = {A, B, C, D, E} be a schema and let M be a set of following multivalued dependencies A →→ BC, B →→ CD, E →→ AD. List the nontrivial dependencies in M⁺.

Ans. By Decomposition rule

A →→ BC then

A →→ B ∩ C

A →→ B – C

A →→ C – B

We have MVD

A →→ BC, B →→ CD, E →→ AD

hence A →→ B, A →→ C

B →→ C, B →→ D

E →→ A, E →→ D

by transitivity

A →→ C, A →→ D

E →→ B, E →→ C

Hence nontrivial dependencies in M^+ are

A →→ B, A →→ C

$B \rightarrow\rightarrow C$, $B \rightarrow\rightarrow D$

$E \rightarrow\rightarrow A$, $E \rightarrow\rightarrow D$

$E \rightarrow\rightarrow B$, $E \rightarrow\rightarrow C$

$A \rightarrow\rightarrow D$.

3. (c) **Discuss join dependency and fifth normal form (5NF). Why is 5NF also called projection join normal form?**

Ans. Join Dependency: Let R be a relation schema and R_1, R_2...R_n be a decomposition of R. The join dependency * (R_1 R_2, ... R_n) is used to restrict the set of legal relations to those for which R_1, R_2...R_n is a lossless join decomposition of R. Formally, if $R = R_1 \cap R_2 \cap ... \cap R_n$, we say that a relation r(r) satisfies the join dependency * (R_1, R_2, R_3 ... R_n) if

$$r \quad _{R_{1(r)}} \bowtie \;_{R_2}(r) \bowtie ... \;_{R_n}(r)$$

A_{join} dependency is trivial if one of the R_t is R itself.

Fifth Normal Form: A 5 NF is defined as **a** relation schema. R is in 5NF with respect to a set D of functional, multivalued, and join dependencies if, for all join dependencies in D^+ of the form *(R_1, R_2...R_n), each R_i, $\subseteq$ R and $R = R_1 \cap R_2 \cap ... \cap R_n$, at least one of the following holds:

1. *(R_1, R_2...R_n) is a trivial join dependency.
2. Every R_i is a superkey for R.

In some of the literature on database normalization the SNF is also called projection join normal form (PJKNF).

4. Answer any TWO of the following: **(7x2=14)**

(a) Consider the following graph-based locking protocol that allows only exclusive lock modes, and that operates on data graphs that are in the form of a rooted directed a cyclic graph.

- **A transaction can lock any verte first.**
- **To lock any other verte, the transaction must have visited all the parents on that vertex, and must be holding a lock on one of the parents of the vertex. Show that the protocol ensures serializability and dead lock freedom.**

Ans. To illustrate the protocol, consider the database graph of following:

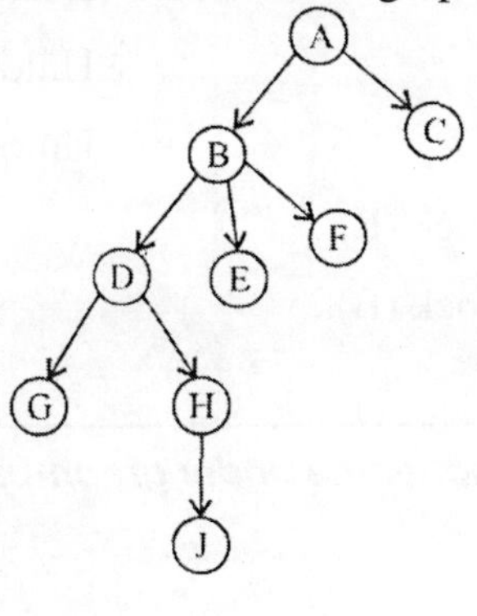

Now Consider following four transaction based on given graph-based locking protocol on above graph. The transactions, are

T_1 : Lock - X(B): lock- X(E). lock- X(D);
Unlock (B); unlock (E), lock - X(G):
Unlock (D), unlock (G)

T_2 : Lock-X(D); lock-X(H): unlock (D): unlock (H)

T_3 : Lock -X(B); lock - X(E); unlock (E); unlock (B)

T_4 : Lock- X(D): lock.- X(H); unlock (D): unlock (H)

One possible schedule in which above four transactions participated is as follows:

T_1	T_2	T_3	T_4
Lock-X(B)			
	Lock-X(D)		
	Lock-X(H)		
	Unlock (D)		
Lock-X(E)			
Lock-X(D)			
Lock (B)			
Lock (E)			
		Lock-X(B)	
		Lock-X(E)	
	Unlock (H)		
Lock-X(G)			
Unlock (D)			
		Lock-X(D)	
		Lock-X(H)	
		Unlock (D)	
		Unlock (H)	
	Unlock (E)		
	Unlock (B)		
Unlock (G)			

Fig. Serializable schedule under graph-based locking protocol.

After observing above schedule we find that the above schedule is a conflict serializable. It means that given protocol ensures conflict serializability, and it also ensures dead lock freedom.

4. (b) Which of the following schedules is conflict serializable? For each serializable schedule, determine the equivalent serial schedules:

(i) $r_1(X)$; $r_3(X)$; $w_1(X)$; $r_2(X)$; $w_3(X)$;

(ii) $r_1(X)$; $r_3(X)$; $w_3(X)$; $w_1(X)$; $r_2(X)$;

(iii) $r_3(X)$; $r_2(X)$; $w_3(X)$; $w_1(X)$; $w_1(X)$;

Ans. (i)

T_1	T_2	T_3
$r_1(X)$		
		$r_3(X)$
$w_1(X)$		
	$r_2(X)$	
		$w_3(X)$

It is non-conflict serializable because we cannot swap to its serial schedules.

(ii)

T_1	T_2	T_3
$r_1(X)$		
		$r_3(X)$
		$w_3(X)$
$w_1(X)$		
	$r_2(X)$	

It is non-conflict serializable schedule because we cannot swap to its serial

(iii)

T_1	T_2	T_3
		$r_3(X)$
	$r_2(X)$	
		$w_3(X)$
$r_1(X)$		
$w_1(X)$		

by swaping we have

T_1	T_2	T_3
	$r_2(X)$	
		$r_3(X)$
		$w_3(X)$
$r_1(X)$		
$w_1(X)$		

It is serial schedule T_1, T_2, T_3 that is $r_2(X)$, $r_3(X)$, $w_3(X)$, $r_1(X)$, $w_1(X)$ hence the given schedule is conflict serializable.

4. (c) Consider the three transactions T_1, T_2 and T_3 and the schedules S_1 and S_2 given below. Draw the scrializability (precedence) graph for S_1 and S_2.

T_1 : $r_1(X)$; $r_1(Z)$; $w_1(X)$;

T_2 : $r_2(Z)$; $r_2(Y)$; $w_2(Z)$; $w_2(Y)$;

T_3 : $r_3(X)$; $r_3(Y)$; $w_3(Y)$;

S_1 : $r_1(X)$; $r_2(Z)$; $r_1(Z)$; $r_3(x)$; $r_3(Y)$; $w_3(Y)$; $r_2(Y)$; $w_2(Z)$; $w_2(Y)$;

S_2 : $r_1(X)$; $r_2(Z)$; $r_3(X)$; $r_1(Z)$; $r_2(Y)$; $r_3(Y)$; $w_1(X)$; $w_2(Z)$; $w_3(Y)$; $w_2(Y)$;

Ans. For schedules S_1

T_1	T_2	T_3
$r_1(X)$		
	$r_2(Z)$	
$r_1(Z)$		
		$r_3(X)$
		$r_3(Y)$
		$w_3(Y)$
	$r_2(Y)$	
	$w_2(Z)$	
	$w_2(Y)$	

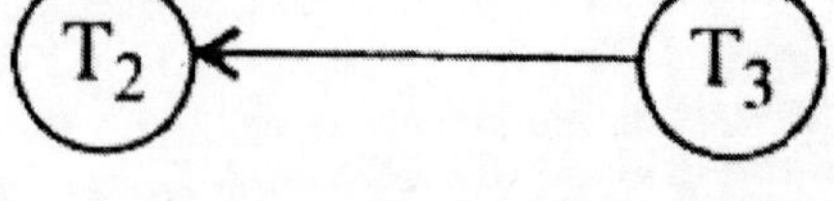

(Precedence Graph) for S_1

For schedules S_2

T_1	T_2	T_3
$r_1(X)$		
	$r_2(Z)$	
		$r_3(X)$
$r_1(Z)$		
	$r_2(Y)$	
		$r_3(Y)$
$w_1(X)$		
	$w_2(Z)$	
		$w_3(Z)$
	$w_2(Y)$	

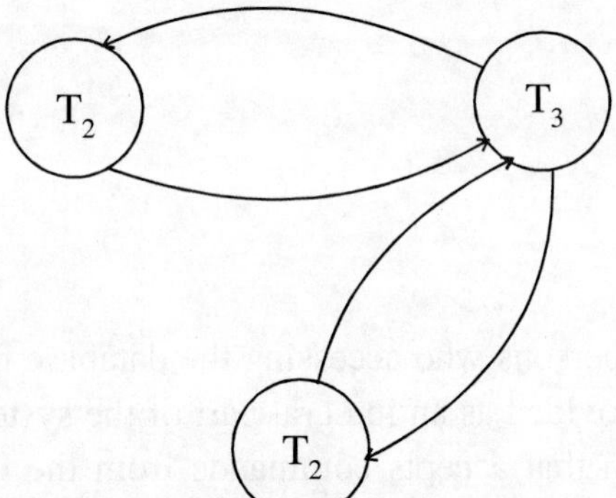

(Precedence Graph) for S_2

B. TECH CS-502

FIFTH SEMESTER EXAMINATION, 2005-06

DATA BASE MANAGEMENT SYSTEM

Time : 3 Hours *Total Marks : 100*

Note : Attempt ALL *the questions.*

Q.1. Attempt any four of the following questions: (3 × 4=12)

***(a)* Define the following terms:**

(i) Database System

(ii) End User

(iii) DML

(iv) DDL

Ans. (a) (i) Data Base System : It is a computerised record-keeping system which have following component :

- Data
- Software
- Hardware
- End user.

(ii) End User : End user is persons who accessing the database from a terminal. An end user any employ a query language provided as an integral part of the system. He or She may invoke a user-written application program that accepts commands from the terminal and in times issues requests to the DBMS on the end-users behalf. Either way the user may again perform all the functions of retrieval, creation, detection and modifications.

(iii) DML : It is Data Manipulation Language. In this language we perform the operation of retrieval, insertion, deletion and updation.

(iv) DDL : It is Data Definition Language, in this language, we define scheme. We create table, view, users, alter table, drop table, view.

Q. 1. (b) Distinguish between a file processing system and DBMS.

Ans. Please see Q. 1 *(a)* of 2002-03

Q. 1. (c) What is the difference between logical data independence and physical data independence?

Ans. Please see Q. 1 (f) of 2002-03

Q. 1. (d) Construct an E-1 diagram for a hospital with, set of patients and set of medical doctors. Associate with each patient a log of the various tests and examination conducted.

OR

Draw E-R relationship diagram showing the cardinality for the following:

A operator can work on many machines and each machine has many operators. Each machine belongs to one department but a department can have many machines.

Ans.

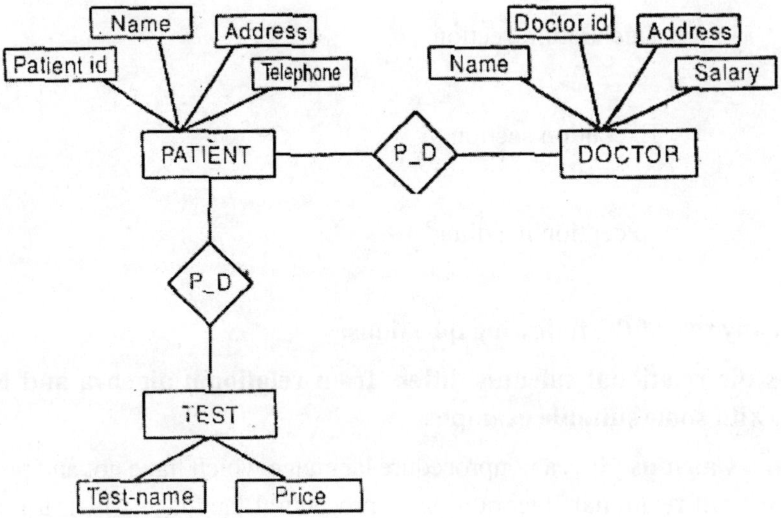

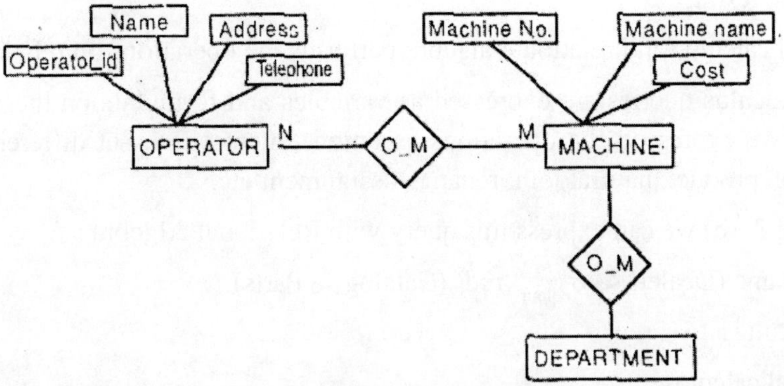

Q.1. (e) When is the concept of a weak entity useful in data modelling? Define the terms: owner entity type and weak entity type.

Ans. A weak entity set may be more appropriately modeled as an attribute if it participate in only the identifying relationship, and if it has attributes. A weak entity set may participate as owner in an identifying relationship with another weak entity set. Even though a weak entity set is always existence dependent on a dominant entity. Weak entity set that depend on one particular strong entity.

Owner Entity Type : An entity set which have primary key is called owner entity type.

Weak Entity Type: An entity set which have no. primary key is called weak entity type.

Q.1. (*f*) What is the difference between procedural and non procedural DMLs.

Ans. Procedural DML extends SQL by adding constructs found in a procedural languages, resulting in a structural language that is more powerful than SQL. The basic unit of procedural DML is a block. All procedural DML programs are made up of blocks which can be nested within each other. Each block performs a logical action in the programs. A block has the following structure:

Declare

Declaration section

Begin

Execution section

Exception

Exception handling

end.

Q.2. Attempt any two of the following questions: (7×2 = 14)

(a) How does the relational calculus differs from relational algebra and how they are similar? Explain with some suitable example.

Ans. Relational Calculus : It is a nonprocedure language which have not any procedure to get the result. But in case of relational algebra it has a procedural language which follow the certain procedure to get the result.

Both relational calculus and relational algebra performs the operations on relations.

In relational calculus queries are expressed as variables and formula's on these variables. In relational algebra we expressed the operations as union, intersection, set difference, selection, projection, cartision product, natural join, rename, assignment etc.

By considering 2. (b) we can express this query with Relational Algebra :

The detector-name (Dealer $\bowtie \sigma_{colour}$ 'red' (Catalog $\bowtie$ Parts)

Relational calculus:

Tuple relational calculus

{+ [dealer_name]| * e Dealer A

Q.2. (*b*) Consider the following scheme:

DEALER (DEALER_ID, DEALER_NAME, DEALER_ADDRESS)

PARTS (PART_ID, PART_NAME, COLOUR) CATALOG (DEALER_ID, PART_ID, COST)

Write the following query in Relational Algebra, and SQL:

(i) Find the name of the Dealers who supply red parts.

(ii) Find the name of Dealers who supply yellow and green parts.

(iii) Find the name of the Dealers who supply all parts.

Ans. Relational Algebra:

(i) $\Pi_{\text{dealer name}}$(Dealer ⋈ $\sigma_{\text{colour='red'}}$) (Parts ⋈ Catalog)

(ii) X ← scolor = yellow color = 'green' (Parts ⋈ Catalog)

(iii) $\gamma \leftarrow \Pi_{\text{dealer\_id, part\_id}}$ (Catalog) ÷ Πpart_id(parts) Π_{dealer}, name (Dealer ⋈ γ)

SQL

```
(i) SELECT      dealer_name
    FROM        DEALER
    WHERE       dealer_id in  (SELECT dealer_id)
                              FROM CATALOG
                              WHERE part_id in
                              (SELECT part_id)
                              FROM PARTS
                              WHERE color_red)

(ii) SELECT     dealer_name
     FROM       DEALER
     WHERE      dear_id in' (SELEC dealer_id
                              FROM CATALOG
                              WHERE part_id in
                              (SELECT part_id)
                              FROM  PARTS WHERE
                              color_'yellow' AND colors _'green')

(iii) SELECT    dealer_name
      FROM      Dealer D
      WHERE     NOT EXISTS
                (SELECT*
                FROM PARTS P
                WHERE NOT EXISTS
                (SELECT*
                FROM CATALOG C
                WHERE P. part id = C - part id
                AND C deafer _id = D, dealer_id).
```

Q.2. (c) Discuss the various update operations on relations and the type of integrity constraint that must checked for each update operation.

Ans. Various update operations on relations is insert, delete and update. In SQL, the insert are done as

INSERT INTO (table_name)

In SQL, the delete operations are done as

```
DELETE    FROM (table_name)
WHERE     (condition)
```

In SQL, the update operations are done as

```
UPDATE    (table_name)
SET       Col 1 = new-values 1
          Col 2 = new-values 2
          Col n = new-values n
WHERE     (condition)
```

there are three integrity constraint that must be checked for each update operation.

(i) Domain constraint

(ii) Entity constraint

(iii) Referential integrity constraint

(i) Domain Constraints: Domain constraints are the most elementary form of integrity constraint. They are tested easily by the system when end a new data item is entered into the database. It is possible for several attributes to have the same domain.

(ii) Entity Constraints : No component of primary key may be null. They are tested when there is primary key in the table during insert and update operations.

(iii) Referential Integrity Constraint: A value that appears in one relation for a given set of attributes also appears for a certain set of attributes in another relations. The foreign key of one table must reference to the primary key or unique key of same table or another table.

Q.3. Attempt any two of the following questions: **(6×2=12)**

(a) Write notes on the following:

(i) Functional Dependency or 4NF

(ii) Normal Forms

Ans. Functional Dependency: Let R be a relation A and B be the attribute of R.

If $A \rightarrow B$ (B is functionally dependent on A if and only if each A value in R has associated with it precisely one B-value in R.

For example, In relation S.

S (SNO, S name, Status, City)

the following FD exists.

S NO $\rightarrow$ S name

S NO $\rightarrow$ Status

S NO $\rightarrow$ City

There is two types of FD : trivial and nontrivial dependencies. A dependencies are trivial if it cannot possibly not be satisfied.

{SNO,PNO} $\rightarrow$ SNO.

In fact, an FD is trivial if and only if the right-hand side is a subset of left-hand side. The non-trivial FD.

S NO $\rightarrow$ S name

4NF: A relation scheme R is in 4NF with respect to a set D of functional and multivalued dependencies if, for all multivalued dependencies in D^+ of the form $\alpha \rightarrow \beta$, where $\beta \subseteq R$ and $\beta \subseteq R$, at least one of the following holds.

* $\alpha \rightarrow \beta$ is a trivial multivalued depending.

* α is a super key for schema R.

Multivalued Dependencies: Let R be arelation schema and let $\alpha \subseteq R$ and $\beta \rightarrow R$. The multivalued dependency $\alpha \rightarrow \beta$ holds on R if, in any legal relation r (R), for all pairs of tuple t_1 and t_2 in r such that $t_1 [\alpha] = t_2 [\alpha]$, there exists tuples t_3 and t_4 in r such that

$$t_1 [\alpha] = t_2 [\alpha] = t_3 [\alpha] = t_4 [\alpha]$$

$$t_3 [\beta] = t_1 [\beta]$$

$$t_4 [\beta] = t_2 [\beta]$$

$$t_3 [R - \alpha - \beta] = t_2 [R - \alpha - \beta]$$

$$t_4 [R - \alpha - \beta] = t_1 [R - \alpha - \beta]$$

Example

We consider the following stable which is not in 4NF.

ename	pname	dname
Smith	X	Jonh
Smith	Y	Anna
Smith	X	Anna
Smith	Y	John

In above following MVD holds.

e name $\rightarrow$ p name

e name $\rightarrow$ d name.

Now we decompose it into two table which is in 4NF.

ename	pname
Smith	X
Smith	Y

ename	dname
Smith	Jonh
Smith	Anna

Q. 3. (a) (ii) Normal Forms: A relation is said to be in a particular normal form if it satisfies a certain prescribed set of condition. There is different Normal Forms: 1NF, 2NF, 3NF, BCNF, 4NF and F NF/.

1 NF : A relation is in I'NF if and only if all the underlying domain contains atomic values only.

2 NF : A relation is in 2 NF if and only it it is in 1 NF and every non key attributes fully dependent on the primary key.

3 NF : A relation is in 3 NF if and only it is in 2 NF and every non-key attributes are non transitively dependent on the primary key.

BCNF : A relation is in BCNF if and only if the only determinants are candidate keys.

4 NF : A relation schema R is in 4 NF with respect to a set D of functional and multivalued dependencies if, for all multivalued dependencies in D^+ of the form $\alpha \rightarrow \beta$, where $\alpha \subseteq R$ and $\beta \subseteq R$, at least one of the following holds.

* $\alpha \rightarrow \beta$ is a trivial multifluid dependency.

* α is a super key for schema R.

5 NF : A relation schema R is in 5 NF (PJNF) with respect to a set D of functional, multivalued, and join dependencies if, for all join dependencies in D^+ of the form * $(R_1, R_2, \ldots\ldots R_n)$. Where each $R_1 \subseteq R$ and $R = R_1 \cup R_2 \cup R_3 \ldots\ldots R_v$, at least one of the following holds.

* $(R_1, R_2, \ldots\ldots\ldots R_n)$ is a trivial join dependency.

* Every R_i is a super key for R.

Q.3. (b) Consider the scheme S = (V, W, X, V, Z). Suppose, the following functional dependencies hold:

$$Z \rightarrow V$$

$$W \rightarrow Y$$

$$WY \rightarrow Z$$

$$V \rightarrow MX$$

State whether the following decomposition of scheme S is loss less join decomposition. Justify your answer:

(i) $S_1 = (V,W,X)$

$S_2 = (V,Y,Z)$

(ii) $S_1 = (V,W,X)$

$S_2 = (X,Y,Z)$

Ans. Please see Q.3(b) of 2002-03.

Q.3. (c) What do you understand by fifth normal forms? Explain with some suitable example.

Ans. 5 NF : A relation schema R is in 5 NF (PJNF) with respect to a set D of functional, multivalued and join dependencies if, for all join dependencies in D^+ of the form * $(R_1, R_2 \ldots\ldots\ldots R_n)$, where each $R_i \subseteq R$ and $R = R_1 \cup R_2 \cup \ldots\ldots\ldots\ldots R_n$, at least one of the following holds:

* * $(R_1, R_2 \ldots\ldots\ldots R_n)$ is a trivial join dependency.

* Every R_1 is a super key for R.

Join Dependency: Let R be a relation schema and R_1, R_2 ......R_n be a decomposition of R. The join dependency *$(R_1, R_2 \ldots\ldots R_n)$ is use to restrict the set of legal relations to those for which R_1, R_2, ...R_n is a loss-less-join decomposition of R. Formally if $R = R_1 \cup R_2 \cup \ldots\ldots\ldots \cup R_n$, we say that a relation r (R) satisfies the join dependency * $(R_1, R_2 \ldots\ldots\ldots R_n)$ if

$$r = \Pi_{R_1}(r) \bowtie \Pi_{R_1}(r) \bowtie \ldots\ldots \bowtie \Pi_{R_1,(r)}$$

A join depending is trivial if one of the R_i is R itself.

These exist relation that cannot be lossless decomposition into two projection but when we decomposed into three or more then it is loss-less decomposition.

For example

Consider following table SPJ:

S#	P#	J#
S1	P1	J2
S1	P2	J1
S2	P1	J1
S1	P1	J1

If we decompose above into two projection then it is loose. So we decompose it into three projection as follows:

SP

S#	P#
S1	S2
S2	P1
S2	P1

PJ

P#	J#
P1	P2
P2	J1
P1	J1

JS

J#	S#
J2	S1
J1	S2
J1	S2

If we join SP and PJ

SP1

	S#	P#	J#
	S1	P1	J2
	S1	P2	J1
	S2	P1	J1
Spurious ⟶	S2	P1	J2
	S1	P1	J1

then it produce one spurious tuple but if we join SP, PJ and JS it will produce original relation.

Q.4. Attempt any two of the following questions: (6 × 2 = 12)

Q.4. (a) Write notes on the following:

(i) Dead lock; *(it)* Two phase locking protocol.

Ans. (i) Dead lock: A system is in a deadlock state if there exists a set of transactions such that every transaction in the set is waiting for another transaction in the set. More precisely, there exists a set of waiting transaction $\{T_0, T_1 ......T_n\}$ such that T_0 is waiting for a data item that is held by T_1 and T_1, is waiting for a data item that is held by T_2, and ...... and T_{n-1} is waiting for a data item that is held by T_n, and T_n is waiting for a data item that is held by T_0. None of the transactions can make progress in such a situation. The only remedy to this undesirable situation is for the system to invoke some drastic action, such as rolling back some of the transactions involved in the deadlock.

There are two principal methods for dealing with the deadlock problem.

(i) Deadlock - prevention

(ii) Deadlock -detection and dead lock-recovery.

Deadlock-Prevention: In Deadlock-Prevention protocol to ensure that the system will never enter a deadlock state. There are two approaches to deadlock prevention. One approach ensures that no cyclic waits can occur by ordering the request for lock, or requiring all locks to be acquired together. The other approach in lower to deadlock recovery, and performs transaction rollback instead of waiting for a lock, whenever the wait could potentially result in a deadlock. Two different deadlock-prevention schemes using time stamps have been proposed.

(i) Wait-die

(ii) Wound-wait

Deadlock Detection and Recovery: If a system does not employ some protocol that ensures deadlock freedom, then a detection and recovery scheme must be used. An algorithm that examines the state of the system is invoked periodically to determine whether a deadlock has occurred. If one-has, then the system must attempt to recover from the deadlock.

Deadlock Detection : Deadlock can be described in the terms of a directed graph called a wait-for graph. If a wait for graph has acycle then a deadlock occur. If a wait for graph has no cycle then system is not in a deadlock state.

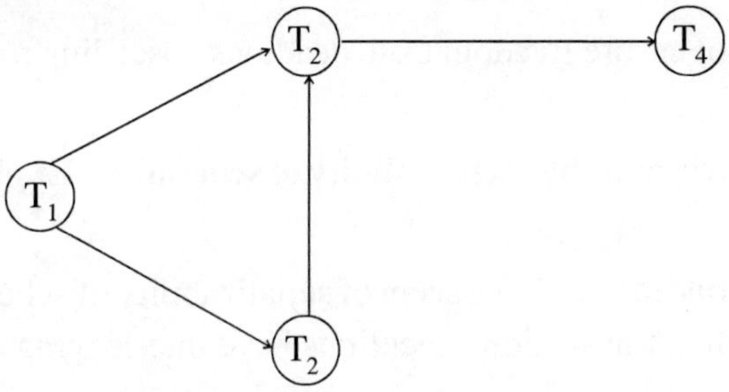

Fig. Wait-for graph with no cycle.

On above wait for graph there is no cyclic so there is no deadlock state.

Recovery from Deadlock: When a detection algorithm determines that a deadlock exists, the system must recover from the deadlock. The most common solution is to rollback one or more transactions to break the deadlock. Three actions need to be taken :

(i) Selection of a victim

(ii) Rollback

(iii) Starvation.

Q.4. (a) (ii) Two Phase Locking Protocol : One protocol that ensures serviceability is the two-phase locking protocol. This protocol requires that each transaction issue lock and unlock requests in two phases :

(i) Growing Phase : A transaction may obtain locks, but may not release any lock.

(ii) Shrinking Phase: A transaction may release locks, but may not obtain any new locks.

Initially, a transaction is in the growing phase.. The transaction acquires locks as needed. Once the transaction releases a lock, it enters the shrinking phase, and it cannot no more lock requests.

For example, the following transaction follows two phase locking protocol.

T_1 : lock-X(B)	T_2 : lock-S(A)
Read(B)	Read (A)
B : B-50	lock-S(B)
Write (B)	Read(B)
lock-X (A)	display (A+ B)
Read (A)	unlock (A)
A:A + 50	unlock(B)
	Write (A)

unlock (B)

unlock (A)

Two phase locking does not ensure freedom from deadlock cascading rollback may occur under two-phase locking.

Q.4. (b) What do you understand by serializability of schedules? Explain with some suitable example.

Ans. Serializability of Schedules : The concept of serializability of schedules is used to identify which schedules are correct when transaction executions have interleaving of their operation in the schedules.

There are two types of serializability:

(i) Conflict serializability

(ii) View serializability

(i) Conflict Serializability: A schedule is conflict serialized, if it is conflict equivalent to a serial schedule conflict equivalent.

If a schedule S can be transformed into a schedule S by a series of swaps of non-conflicting instructions , we say that S and S′ are conflict equivalent.

We say that I_i and I_j conflict if they are operations by different transactions on the same data item, and at least one of those instruction is a WRITE operation. For example. We have Transaction T_1 and T_2.

T_1	T_2	T_1 Read (A)
Read (A)		A = A – 50
A = A-50		Write (A)
Write (A)		Read (B)
Read (B)		B = B + 50
B = B + 50		Write (B)
Write (B)	T_2	Read (A)
	Read (A)	temp: A-0.1
	temp : = A × 0.1	A = A - temp
	A = A - temp	Write (A)
	Write (A)	Read(B)
	Read(B)	B = B + temp
	B = B + temp	Write (B)
	Write (B)	

(Schedule-1)

T_1	T_2
Read(A)	
Write (A)	
	Read (A)
	Write (A)
Read(B)	
Write (B)	
	Read (B)
	Write (B)

(Schedule-3)

schedule - 1 and schedule - 3 is conflict serialized because (B) and write (B) instruction of T, can be swapped with the Read (A) and Write (A) instruction of T_2 schedule - 1 is serial schedule of schedule - 3.

View Serializability : Consider two schedules S and S′, where the same set of transactions participates in both schedules. The schedules S and S′ are said to be **view equivalent** if the following three conditions are met:

(i) For each data item Q, if transaction T_i reads the initial value of Q in schedule S, then transaction T_i must, in schedule S, also need the initial value of Q.

(ii) For each data item Q. if transaction T_i executes read (Q) in schedule S, and that value was produced by transaction T_j (if any), then transaction T_i must, in schedule S′ also read the value of Q that was produced by transaction T_j.

(iii) For each data item Q, the transaction (if any) that performs the final write (Q) operation in schedule S must perform the final write (Q) operation in schedule S.

The concept of view equivalence leads to the concept of view serializability. We say that a schedule S is view serialized if it is view equivalent to a serial schedule.

For example, Schedule 1 is view equivalent to schedule 3, because the values of recent A and B read by transaction T_2 were produced by T_1 in both schedules.

Q.4. (c) What is the transaction system? How would you make recovery from transaction failures? Explain with some suitable examples.

Ans. ***(c)*** **Transaction :** Collections of operations at form a single logical unit of work are called Transactions a database system must ensure proper execution of transactions despite failure either. The entire transaction executes, or none of it does.

We can make recovery from transaction failures by using a log-based recovery.

Log-based Recovery : The most widely used structure for recording database modifications is the log. The log is a sequence of log records and maintains a record of all the separate activities in the database. There are several types of log records. An update log record describes a single database write, and has the following fields:

* Transaction identifier
* Data-item identifier
* Old value
* New value

We denote the various types of log records as follows:

* $<T_i$ start$>$ Transaction T_i has started.
* $<T_i, X_j, V_1, V_2>$ Transaction T_1 has performed a write on data item X_j, X_j had value V_1 before the write, and will have value V_2 after the write.
* $<T_i$ commit$>$ Transaction T_i has committed.
* $(T_i$ abort) Transaction T_i has aborted.

Whenever a transaction performs a write, it is essential that the log record for that write; be created before the database is modified. Once a log records, exists, we can output the modification to the database if that is desirable.

For log records to be useful for recovery from system and disk failures, the log must reside in stable storage.

There are two techniques for using the log to ensure transaction atomicity despite failures. They are as follows :

(i) Deferred Database Modification

(ii) Immediate Database Modification.

(i) Differed Database Modification: The deferred modification technique ensures transaction atomicity by recording all database modifications in the log, but deferring the execution of all write operations of a transaction until the transaction partially commits. A transaction is said to be partially committed one the final action of the transaction has been executed. For deferred-modification technique, we assume, that transactions are executed serially.

(ii) Immediate Database Modification : The immediate-update technique allows database modifications to be output to the database while the transaction is still in the active state. Data modification written by active transactions are called uncommitted modifications. In the event of a crash or a transaction failure, the system must use the old value field of the log records, to restore the rnodified data items to the value they had prior to the start of the transaction. This restoration is accomplished through the undo operation.

For example: Let us consider simplified banking system base. To be a transaction that transfers Rs. 50 from account A to account B. Thus transaction is defined as follows, let T_1 be a transaction that withdraws Rs. 100 from account C.

This transaction is defined as follows :

T_0 :	T_1 :
Read(A)	Read(C)
A = A – 50	C = C– 100
Write (A)	Write (C)
Read(B)	
Write (B)	

Suppose that these transaction are executed serially in order to follow by T_1, initially A = 1000, B = 7000 and C = 700.

The portion of the log containing the database for above two transaction is as follows :

For Deferred Database Modification		For Immediate Database Modification	
Log	Database	Log	Database
<To start>		(To start)	
<To, AA, 950>		<To, A, 1000,950>	
<To, B, 2050>		<To, B, 2000, 2050>	
<To Commit>			A = 950
	A = 900		B = 2050
	B = 50	<To commit>	
<To start>		<T_1 start>	
<T_1, C, 600>		<T_1, C, 600>	
<T_1, commit>			C = 600
	C = 600	<T_1 commit>	

Suppose the crash occurs after the log record for the step.

Deferred Database Modification	Immediate Database Modification
Case a:	**a:**
<To start>	<To start>
<To, A, 950>	<To, A, 1000, 95.0>
<To, B, 2050>	<To, B, 2000,2050>
Case b:	**b:**
<To start>	<To start>

<To, A, 950>	<To, A, 1000, 950>
<To, B, 2050>	<To B, 2000, 2050>
<To commit>	<To Commit>
<To start>	<T_1 start>
<T_1, C. 600>	<T_1,c,700, 600>
Case c :	**c :**
<To start>	<To start>
<To, A, 950>	<To, A, 1000, 950>
<To, B, 2050>	<To B, 2000, 2050>
<To commit>	<To Commit>
<T_1, start>	<T_1,c,700, 600>
<T_1 C,600>	<T_1,c,700, 600>
(T_1, commit)	(T_1, commit)

We perform following operation

* Redo (T_i) → there is <T_i start> and <T_i commit>

*Delete log when there is any <T_i start>

In above case Recovery occurs

a : delete log record of T_0

b : Redo (T_0 but delete log second of T_1).

c : Redo (T_0) and Redo (T_1).

We perform following operation

* Redo (Ti) → there is <Ti start> and <Ti commit>

In above case recovery occuring undo (T_0)

a : undo (T_0)

b : Redo (T_0), undo (T_1)

c : Redo (T_0) & Redo (T_1)

With Recovery scheme uses the following recovery scheme:

Undo (T_i) restores the value of all data items update by transaction T_i to the old values.

Redo (T_i) set the value of all data items updated by transactionT_i to the new values.

B. TECH **TCS-402**

FOURTH SEMESTER EXAMINATION, 2005-06

DATA BASE MANAGEMENT SYSTEM

Time : 3 Hours *Total Marks : 100*

Note : (i) Attempt ALL *the questions.*

(ii) All questions carry equal marks.

(iii) In case of numerical problems assume data wherever not provided,

(iv) Be precise in your answer.

Q.1. Attempt any Four parts : **(5×4=20)**

(a) Define the following terms :

(i) Data abstraction (ii) Data independency (iii) Database schema (iv) Data redundancy (v) DDL& DML.

Ans. (i) Data Abstraction : A major purpose of a database system is to provide users with an abstract view of the data. That is the system hides certain details of how the data are stored and maintained. It does so by defining three level of obstruction at which may be viewed . physical love, logical level and view level.

(ii) **Data Independency**: The ability to modify a schema definition in one-level without affecting a schema definition in next higher level is called data independence.

(iii) **Database Schema** : The overall design of the database is called data base schema.

(iv) **Data Redundancy** : Some information may be duplicated in several places (files) due to file and application are created by the different programmer over a long period, various files are likely to have different formats and program may be written In several programming language.

(v) **DDL;** A database schema is specified by a set of definition that are expressed By a data-definition language.

DHL : A data manipulation language is a language that enables users to access or manipulated data.

Q.1. (b) **Discuss the rule of the Data Base Administrator (DBA) in Data Base Management System.**

Ans. Please See Q. 1 *(b)* of 2002-2003.

Q.1. (c) Explain three level architecture of DBMS in detail.

Ans. The three level of architecture of DBMS are physical, logical and view. For detail See Q. 1 (b) of 2003-04.

Q.1. *(d)* **Define the terms Generalization, Specialization and Aggregation with a suitable example.**

Ans. Specialization : It is the result of taking a subset of a higher level entity set to form a lower level entity set.

Generalization : It is the result of taking the union of two or more disjoint entity sets to product a higher level entity set.

Aggregation : It is used to find the relationship among the relationship.

Example :

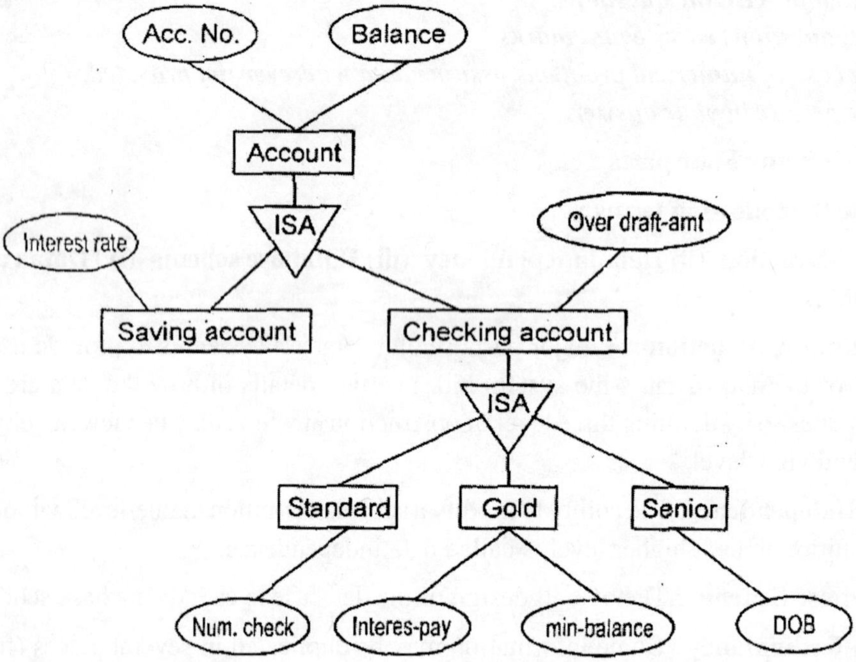

Q. 1 *(e)* Draw the E-R diagram of the registration process of the student in a particular course. Convert the E_R diagram into tables also.

Ans. E_R diagram of the registration process of a student in a particular course.

(1) Student no, stname, stprequalification

(2) Course, course name, course id, fee, dob, doj.

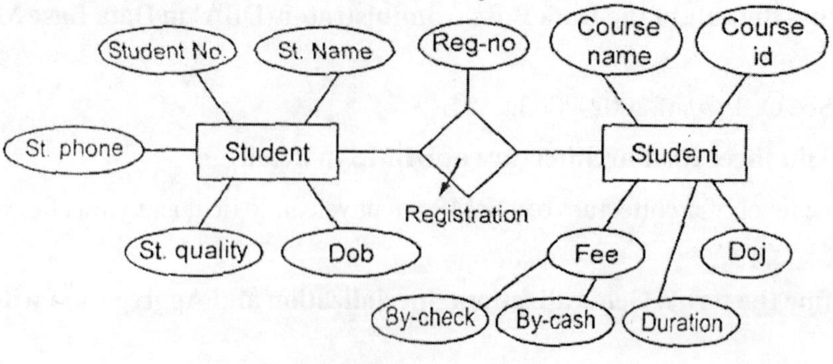

Registration (coursed, stno, fee, doj, Reg_no)

Student {st_no., stname, st_quali, dob, coursed, st_phone no.)

Course (coursed, stno, course name, duration,

Fee (course id, by-cheque, by-cash)

Q.2. Attempt any Two parts : (10 × 2=20)

(a) Consider the following three relation schema S, P and SP in which S# is supplier code, P# product code and Qty is Quantity and others carry their respective meanings.

S (S#, SNAME, SCITY, TURNOVER)

P (P#, WEIGHT, COLOR, COST, SELLING PRICE)

SP (S#, P#, QTY)

Write the appropriate SQL and relational algebra statements for the following queries.

(i) Get all details of supplier who operate from DELHI with TURNOVER = 80.

(ii) Get part nos. weighting between 25 and 35.

(iii) Get the names of suppliers whose name begins with A.

(iv) For each part supplied, get part no. and names of all cities supplying the part.

(v) Get the names of suppliers who supply part no. 2.

Ans. The SQL statement for a given problem :

(i) Select*

from S

where scity = Delhi and turnover = 80 ;

(ii) Select P# form P

where weight ≥ 25 and weight ≤ 35 ;

(iii) Select Sname

from S

where Sname like "A%".

(iv) Select P . P# , S.xity

from P, S, SP

where P. P# = SP. P# and S.S# = SP. S# ;

(v) Select Sname

from S, SP

where S . S# = SP . S# and SP . P# = 2;

and the relational algebra for given/problem.

(i) $\{t/t \in s \wedge u \in S \wedge t[s] = u[s] \wedge u[s] = \text{'Delhi'}\}\ u[s] = 80$

Q. 2 (b) A university has many departments. Each department may have many full-time and part-time students. Each department may float multiple courses for its own students. Each department has staff members who may be full time or part-time. Design a generalization, specialization hierarchy for the university.

Ans.

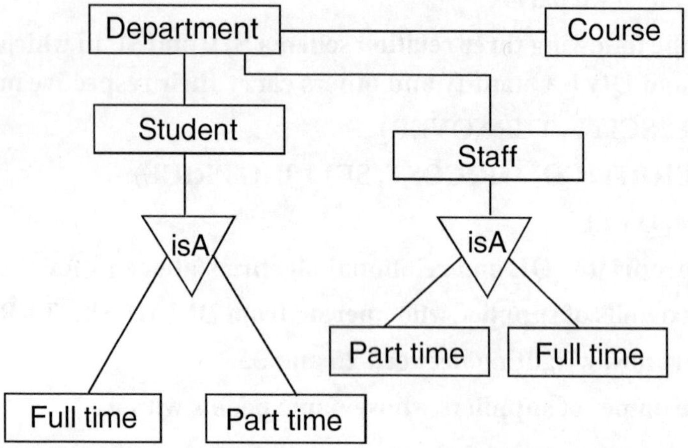

Q. 2 (c) Define the following terms :

(i) Integrity Constraints.

(ii) Foreign Key

(iii) Primary Key

(iv) Super Key

(v) Candidate Key.

Ans. (i) Integrity Constraints : The data value in the database must satisfied some constraints. For example the number of hours of an employee may work in one weak may not exceed a specified limit (say hours).

(ii) Foreign Key: A foreign key is an attributed or set of attributes of a relation which is used to find a relationship among table.

(iii) **Primary Key:** Primary key is key which is used to d ist inguish the two or more instances having same value.

(iv) Super Key: When we see some additional key in with primary key then the resulting key is a super key. A primary key is a minimum super key.

(v) Candidate Key : Two or more distribution or combination of attributes that uniquely identify an instance of an entity set. The attributes or combination of attributes are called candidate key.

Q. 2 (d) Consider the following tables :

P

A	B	C
a	b	c
b	c	a
c	a	b

Q

A	B	C
c	b	a
b	a	c
b	c	a

R

J
J_1
J_2
J_3

Perform the following relational algebra operations.

(i) P ∪ Q

(ii) P ∩ Q

(iii) P – Q and Q – P

(iv) P × R and Q × R

Ans. (i)

A	B	C
a	b	c
b	c	a
c	a	b
c	b	a
b	a	c

P ∪ Q

(ii)

A	B	C
b	a	c

P ∩ Q

(iii)

A	B	C
a	b	c
c	a	b

P – Q

and

A	B	C
c	b	a
b	a	c

Q – P

(iv)

A	B	C	R
a	b	c	J
b	c	a	J
c	a	b	J
a	b	c	J_1
b	c	a	J_1
c	a	b	J_1
a	b	c	J_2
b	c	a	J_2
c	a	b	J_2
a	b	c	J_3
b	c	a	J_3
a	b	c	J_3

P × R

and

A	B	C	R
c	b	a	J
b	a	c	J
b	c	a	J
c	b	a	J_1
b	a	c	J_1
b	c	a	J_1
c	b	a	J_2
b	a	c	J_2
b	c	a	J_2
c	b	a	J_3
b	a	c	J_3
b	c	a	J_3

Q × R

Q.2. (e) What do you mean by View ? Discuss the advantages and disadvantages of View in detail.

Ans. A view is a database object that contains no data of its own. It is a virtual table whose contains are taken from other table through the execution of query. The changes in the table are automatically rejected in the view. It is created with the create view command. A view is queried just like querying a table a user can't distinguish between a view and table :

The advantage of view are :

- Any updation of row in the table will automatically reflect in the view. .
- As a view does not store any data, the redundancy problem does not arise.
- Critical data in the database table is safeguarded as access to such data can be controlled using view.
- Compatible queries are simplified using view.

Disadvantage :

On the view level it is not possible to update, insert and delete the data.

Q.3. Attempt any Two parts : (10 × 2=20)

(a) (i) Discuss the various anomalies associates with relational database management system by giving suitable examples.

Ans. Database Anomalies : Basically three, types of database anomalies are present in RDBMS.

(i) Insert

(ii) Update

(iii) Delete

(i) Insert: It is radiational annually for inserting rewards in the database.

```
SQL syntax for insert anomaly
Sql > insert into < table name >
(coll. col 2, ... col n)
values (val 1, val 2, ..., val 2) ;
```

(ii) Update : For updation of record this anomaly always used.

```
Sql syntax for update anomaly.
Sql > update < table name > set
< col name > = value [where < condition > ]
```

(iii) Delete : This anomaly used for deletion of record from the database.

SQL syn tax for delete anamoly :

Sql > delete from < table name >

[where = condition >]

So, there are the basic anomalies for RDBMS.

Q.3. (a) (ii) Consider the following relational schema :

R(A, B, C, D, E, F, G, H) with the FDs

AB→C, BC→D, E→F, G→F, H→A, FG→G

Is the decomposition of R into R_1 (A, B, C, D), R_2 (A, B, C, E, F), R_3 (A, D, F,G, H) lossless ? Is it dependency preserving ?

Ans. The given relation is lossless because, after the decomposition data will remains unchanged *i.e.*,

R_1 :	AB → C
	BC → D
R_2 :	E → F
R_3 :	H → C
	G → F
	FG → H
and	$R = R_1 \cup R_2 \cup R_3$

So it is lossless and also dependency pressing.

Q.3. (b) What is join dependency ? How is it different to that of Multivalued and Functional dependency? Give an example each of join and multivalued dependency. Discuss the Fourth Normal Form (4NF) also in detail.

Ans. Join dependencies: Let R be a relation scheme and R_1 R_2,..., R_n be a decomposition of R. The join dependency (R_1 R_2,..., R_n) is used to restrict the set of legal relation to those for which R_1 R_3, ..., R_n is a lossless. Join decomposition of R formally of R = R_1 U R_2d ... U R_n, we say true a relation r(R) satisfies the join dependency *(R_1 R_2 ..., R_n) if

$$r = \pi R_1(r) \text{ U } \pi R_2, (r) \text{ U} \ldots \text{U } \pi R_n| \, r)$$

Functional dependencies are a generalization of key dependencies. They require that the value for a certain set of attributes determines uniquely the value for another set of attributes.

So, functional dependency rule out certain types from being in a relation. If A → B then we can not have two types with the same A value bit different B values.

While the multivalued dependency do not rule out the existence of certain tuples instead, they require that other tuples of a certain form be present in the relation. For this reason, functional dependencies sometimes are referred to as equality generating dependencies and multivalued dependencies are referred to as tuple-generating dependencies.

Q.3. (c) What do you mean by Functional Dependency? Explain BCNF with a suitable example. "A decomposition in BCNF may be lossless and dependency preserving." Is this statement correct ? Justify your answer with a suitable example.

Ans. Boyce-Codd Normal Form: One of the more desirable normal forms that we can obtain in *Bpyce- **Codd** normal form (BCNF).* A relation schema *R* is in BCNF with respect to a set *F* of functional dependencies if for all functional dependencies in F^+ of the form $\alpha \rightarrow \beta$, where $\alpha \subseteq$ Rand $\alpha \subseteq$ R, at least one of the following holds :

- $\alpha \rightarrow \beta$ is a trivial functional dependency (that is, $\beta \subseteq \alpha$)
- α is a super key for schema *R.*

A database design is in BCNF if each member of the set of relation schemes that constitutes the design is in BCNF.

As an illustration, let us consider the following relation schemas, and their respective functional dependencies.

- *Customer-schema = (customer-name, customer-street, customer-city) customer-name → customer-street customer-city.*
- *Branch-schema = (branch-name, assets, branch-city)*

  branch-name → assets branch-city.
- *Loan-info-schema = (branch-name, customer-name, loan-number, amount loan-number → amount branch-name).*

We note that a candidate key for the schema is *customer-name.* The only nontrivial functional dependencies that hold on *Customer-scheme have customer-name* on the left side of the arrow. Since *customer-name* is a candidate key, functional dependencies with *customer-name* on the left side do not violate the definition of BCNF. Similarly, it can be shown easily that the relation schema. *Branch-schema* is in BCNF.

The schema, *Loan-info-schema,* however, is not in BCNF. First, note that *loan-number* is not a super key for *Loan- info-schema,* since we could have a pair of tuples representing a single loan made to two people— for example

(Downtown, Mr. Bell, L-44, 1000)

(Downtown, Ms. Bell, L-44, 1000)

Because we did not list functional dependencies that rule out the preceding case *loan-number* is not a candidate key. However, the functional dependency *loan-number → amount is* nontrivial. Therefore, *Loan-info-schema* does not satisfy the definition of BCNF.

We claim that *Loan-info-schema* is not in a desirable ffom, since it suffers from the problem of *repetition of information.* If there are several customer names associated with a loan, in a relation on *Loan-info-schema,* then we are forced to repeat the branch name and the amount once for each customer. We can eliminate this redundancy by redesigning our database such that all schemes are in BCNF. One approach to this problem is to tak the existing non-BCNF design as a starting point, and to decompose those schemas that are not in BCNF. Consider the decomposition of *Loan-info-schema* into two schemas:

Loan-schema = (branch-name, loan-number, amount)

Borrower-schema = (customer-name, load-number)

This decomposition is a lossless-join decomposition.

To determine whether these schemas are in BCNF, we need to determine what functional dependencies apply to them. In this example, it is easy to see that

loan-number→ amount branch-name

applies to *Loan-schema,* and that only trivial functional dependencies apply to *Borrower-schema.* Although *loan-number* is not a super key for *Loan-info-schema,* it is a candidate key for *Loan-schema.* Thus, both schemas of our decomposition are in BCNF.

It is now possible to avoid redundancy in the case where there are several customers associated with a loan. There is exactly one tuple for each loan in the relation on *Loan-schema,* and one tuple for each customer of each loan is the relation in *Borrower-schema.* Thus, we do not have to repeat the branch name and the amount once for each customer associated with a loan.

We are now able to state a general method to generate a collection of BCNF schemas. if R is not in BCNF, we can decompose R into a tollection of BCNF schemas R_1, R_2, ..., R_n which generates not only a BCNF decomposition, but also a lossless-join decomposition. We replace a schema R_t with $(R_i - \beta)$ and $(\alpha \rightarrow \beta)$, the dependency $\alpha \rightarrow \beta$ holds, and $(R_i - \beta) \cap (\alpha, \beta) = \alpha$.

Let us apply the BCNF decomposition algorithm to the *Lending-schema* schema that we used in example of a poor database design :

Lending-schema = (branch-name, branch-city, assets, customer, name, loan-number, amount)

The set of functional dependencies that we require to hold on *Landing-schema* are

branch -name → assets branch-city

branch-name → amount branch-name

A candidate key for this schema is (*loan-number, customer-name*).

We can apply the algorithm of Figure to the Lending schema example as follows :

- The functional dependency

  branch-name → assets branch-city

  holds on *Lending-schema*, but *branch-name* is not a super key. Thus, *Lending-schema* is not in BCNF. We replace *Lending-schema* by

  Branch-schema = (*branch-name, branch-city, assets*)

  Loan-info-schema = (*branch-name, customer-name, loan-number, amount*)

- The only nontrivial functional dependencies that hole on *Branch-schema* include *branch-name* on the left side of the arrow. Since *branch-name* is a key for *Branch-schema,* the relation *Branch-schema* is in BCNF.
- The functional dependency

  loan-number → amount branch-name

  holds on *Loan-info-schema,* but *loan-number* is not a key for *Loan-info-schema.* We replace *Loan-info-schema* by

  Loan-Schema = (*branch-name, loan-number, amount*).

  Borrower-schema = (*customer-name, loan-number*)
- *Loan-schema* and *Borrower-schema,* are in BCNF.

Thus, the decomposition of Lending-schema results in the three relation schemas *Branch-schema, Loan-scheme* and *Borrower-schema,* each of which is in BCNF. The resulting decomposition is both a lossless-join decomposition and a dependency-preserving decomposition.

Not every BCNF decomposition is dependency preserving. As an illustration consider the relation schema.

Banker-schema = (branch-name, customer-name, banker-name)

which indicates that a customer has a "personal banker" in a particular branch. The set F of functional dependencies that we require to hold on the *Banker-schema* is

banker-name → branch-name

branch-name customer-name → banker-name

Q.4. Attempt any Two parts : (10×2 = 20)

(a) What is deadlock ? When does it occur ? How is it detected in data base system ? How can it be avoided ? Discuss in detail.

Ans. Please See Q. 4 (a) (i) of 2005-06.

Q. 4 (A) What do you mean by Transaction system? List the ACID properties of transaction. Discuss the recovery from transaction failures also.

Ans. A transaction is a unit of program execution that accesses and possibly update various data items. The transaction consists of all operations executed between the begin and end of the transaction. To ensure integrity of the data, we require that the database system maintains the following properties of the transactions.

- **Atomicity :** Either all operations of the transaction are reflected property in the database.
- **Consistency :** Execution of a transaction in isolation (that is, with no other transaction execution concurrently) preserves the consistency of the database.
- **Isolation:** Even though multiple transactions may execute concurrently.the system guarantees

that, for every pair of transactions T_i and T_j it appears to T_i that either T_j. finished execution before T_i started, or T_j started execution after T_i finished. Thus, each transaction is unaware of other transaction executing concurrently in the system.

• **Durability :** After a transaction completes successfully, the changes it has made to the database persist, even if there are system failures.

• **Recoverability :** So far, we have studied what schedules are acceptable from the viewpoint of consistency of the database, assuming implicitly that there are no transaction failures. We now address the effect of transaction failures during, concurrent execution.

If a transaction T_i fails, for whatever reason, we need to do the effect of this transaction to ensure, the atomicity property of the transaction. In a system that allows, concurrent execution, it is necessary also to insure that any transaction T_i, that is dependent on T_i (that is, T_i has read data written by T_i) is also aborted. To achieve this surety, we need to place restrictions on the type of schedules permitted in the system.

Q. 4. *(c)* What do you mean by Serializability ? Discuss the Conflict and view serializability with suitable example. Discuss the testing of serializability also.

Ans. Please See Q. 4 *(b)* of 2004-05.

Q. 5. Attempt any Two parts : (10 × 2=20)

(a) What is multi-version schemes of Concurrency Control? Describe with the help of an example. Discuss the various time stamping protocols for concurrency control also.

Ans. Multiversion Schemes : The concurrency control schemes discussed thus far ensure serializability by either delaying an operation or aborting the transaction that issued the operation. For sample, a road operation may be delayed because the appropriate value has not been written yet; or it may be rejected. These difficulties could be avoided if old copies of each data item were kept in a system.

In *multiversion* database systems, each **write** (Q) operation creates a new version of Q. When a read (Q) operation is issued, the system selects one of the versions of Q to be read. The concurrency-control scheme must ensure that the selection of the version to be read is done in a manner that ensures serializability. It is also crucial, for performance reasons, that a transaction be able to determine easily and quickly v.'hich version of the data item should be read.

Multiversion Timestamp Ordering : The most common technique used among multiversion schemes in timestamping. With each transaction T_i in the system, we associate a unique static timestamp, denoted by TS (T_i). This timestamp is assigned before the transaction starts execution.

With each data item Q, a sequence of versions $< Q_1, Q_2 ..., Q_m >$ is associated. Each version Q_k contains three data fields :

- **Content** is the value of version Q.
- **W-timestamp** (Q_k) is the timestamp of the transaction that created version Q_k.

- **R-timestamp** (Q_k) is the largest timestamp of any transaction that successfully read version Q_k

A transaction—say, T_i—creates a new version Q_k of data item Q by issuing a write (Q) operation. The content field of the version holds the value written by T_i. The W-timestamp and R-timestamp are initialized to TS(T_i). The R-timestamp value is updated whenever a transaction T_j reads the content of Q_k, and R-timestamp (Q_k) < TS (T_j).

The multiversion timestamp scheme presented next ensures serializability. The scheme operates as follows. Suppose that transaction T_i issues a **read** (Q) or **write** (Q) operation. Let Q_k denote the version of Q whose write timestamp is the largest write timestamp less than or equal to TS (T_i).

1. If transaction T_i issues a **read** (Q), then the value returned is the content of version Q_k
2. If transaction T_i issues a **write** (Q), and TS (T_i) < R-timestamp (Q_k), then transaction T_i is rolled back. Otherwise, if TS(T_i) = W-timestamp (Q_k), the content of Q_k are overwritten, otherwise a new version of Q is created.

The justification for rule 1 is clear. A transaction reads the most recent version that comes before it in time. The second rule forces a transaction to abort if it is "too late" in doing a write. More precisely, if T_i attempts to write a version that some other transaction would have read, then we cannot allow that write to succeed.

Versions that are no longer needed are removed based on the following rule. Suppose that there are two versions, Q_k and Q_j, or a data mite, and that both the system. Then, the older of the two'versions Q_k and Q_j will not be used again, and can be deleted.

The multiversion timestamp-ordering scheme has the desirable property that a read request never fails and is never made to wait. In typical database systems. where reading is a more frequency operation than is writing, this advantage may be of major practical significance.

The scheme, however, suffers from two undesirable properties. First, the reading of a data item also requires the updating of the R-timestamp field, resulting in two potential disk accesses, rather than one. Second, the conflicts between transactions are resolved through rollbacks, rather than through waits. this alternative may be expensive.

Q.5. (b) What do you mean by Multiple Granularity ? Discuss with a suitable example. Discuss the validation based protocols also with a suitable example.

Ans. Multiple Granularity : In the concurrency control schemes we have used each individual data item until on which synchronization is performed.

There are circumstances, however, where it would be advantageous to group several data items, and to treat them as one individual synchronization unit. For example, it a transaction T_i needs to access the entire database, and a locking protocol is used, then T_i must lock each item in the database. Clearly, executing these locks is time consuming. It would be better if T_i could issue a *single* lock request to lock the entire database. On the other hand, if transaction T_i needs to access only a few data items, it should not be required to lock the entire database since otherwise concurrency is lost.

What is needed is a mechanism to allow the system to define multiple levels of *granularity.* We can make one by allowing data items to be of various sizes and defining a hierarchy of data granualarities, where the small granularities are nested within larger ones. Such a hierarchy can be represented graphically as a tree. Note that the tree is significantly different from that used by the tree protocol. A non leaf node of the multiple-granularity tree represents the data associated with its descendants. In the tree protocol, each node is an independent data item.

As an illustration, consider the tree of Figure, which consists of four levels of nodes. The highest level represents the entire database. Below it are nodes of type *area;* the database consists of exactly these areas. Each area in turn has nodes of type *file* as its children. Each area contains exactly those files that are its child nodes. Finally, each file has nodes of type record, the file consists of exactly those records that are its child nodes, and no record can be present in more than one file.

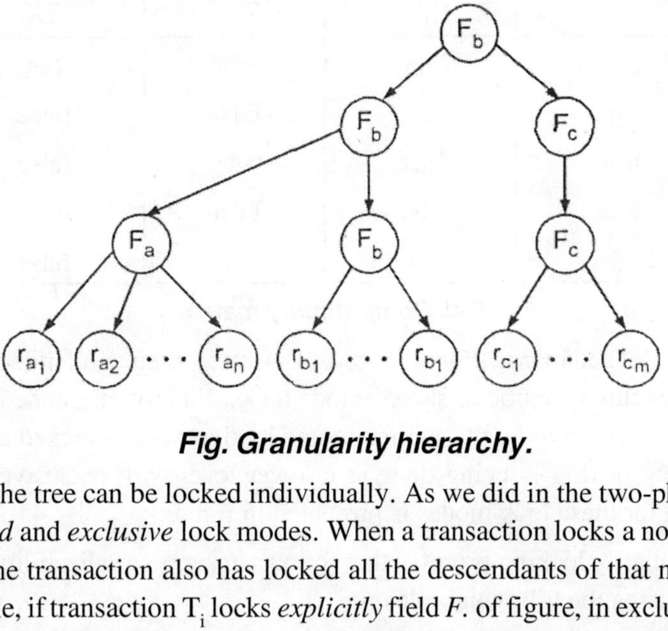

Fig. Granularity hierarchy.

Each node in the tree can be locked individually. As we did in the two-phase locking protocol, we shall use *shared* and *exclusive* lock modes. When a transaction locks a node, in either *shared* or exclusive mode, the transaction also has locked all the descendants of that node in the same, lock mode,. For example, if transaction T_i locks *explicitly* field *F.* of figure, in exclusive mode, then it has locked *implicitly* in exclusive mode all the records belonging to that file. It does not need to lock the individual records of F_c *explicitly.*

Suppose that transaction T_j wishes to lock record T_{b6} of the F_b Since T_i has locked F_h explicitly, it follows that $r_{b6'}$ is also locked (implicitly). But, when T_j issues a lock request for r_{b6} , $r_{b6'}$ is not explicitly locked ! How does the system determine whether T_j can lock r_{b6} ? T_j must traverse the tree from the root of record r_{b6} . If any node in that path is locked in an incompatible mode, then T_j must be delayed.

Suppose now that transaction T_k wishes to lock the entire database. To do so, it simply must lock the root of the hierarchy. Note, however, that T_k should not succeed in locking the root node, since T_i is currently holding a lock on part of the tree (specifically, on file F_b). But how does the system determine if the root node can be locked ? One possibility is for it to search the entire tree.

This solution, however, defeats the whole purpose of the multiple granularity locking scheme. A more efficient way to gain this knowledge is to introduce a new class of lock modes, called *intention* lock modes. If anode is locked in an intention mode, explicit locking is being done at a lower level of the tree (that is, at a finer granularity). Intention locks are put on all the ancestors' of a node before that node is locked explicitly. Thus, a transaction does not need to search the entire tree to determine whether it can lock a node successfully. A transaction wishing to lock a node— say. Q— must traverse a path in the tree from the root to *Q*. While traversing the tree, the transaction locks the various nodes in an intention node.

There is an intention mode associated with *shared* mode, and there is one with *exclusive* mode. If a mode is locked in *intention-shared* (IS) mode, explicit locked is being done at a lower level of the tree, but with only shared-mode locks.

	IS	IX	S	SIX	X
IS	true	true	true	true	false
IX	true	true	false	false	false
S	true	false	true	false	false
SIX	true	false	false	false	false
X	false	false	false	false	false

Fig. Compatibility matrix.

Similarly, if a node locked in *intention-exclusive* (IX) mode, then explicit locking is being done at a lower level, with exclusive-mode or shared-mode locks. Finally, if a node is locked in shared and intension-exclusive (SIX) mode, the subtree rooted by that node is locked explicitly in shared mode, and that explicit locking is being done at a lower level with exclusive mode locks. The compatibility function for these lock modes is presented in figure.

The multiple-granularity locking protocol that follows ensures serializability. Each transaction T_i can lock a node Q, using the following rules ;

1. The lock-compatibility function of Figure must be observed.
2. The root of the tree must be locked first, and can be locked in any mode.
3. A node Q can be locked by T_i in S or IS mode only if the parent of Q is currently locked by T_i in either IX or IS mode.
4. A node Q can be locked by T_i in X, SIX or IX mode only ifthe parent of Q is currently locked by T_i in either IX or SIX mode.
5. T_i can lock a node only if it has not previously unlocked any node (that is, T_t is two-phase).
6. T_i can unlock a node Q only if none of the children of Q are currently locked by T_r

Observe that the multiple-granularity protocol requires that locks be acquired in top-down (root-to-leaf) order, whereas locks must be released in bottom-up (leaf-to-root) order.

As an illustration of the protocol, consider the tree of Figure and the following transactions:

- Suppose that transaction T_{18} reads record r_{a2} in file F_a. Then, T_{18} needs to lock the database, area A_1, and F_a in IS mode (and in that order), and finally to lock r_{a2} in S mode.
- Suppose that transaction T_{19} reads record r_{a9} in file F_a. Then, T_{19} needs to lock the database, area A_1 and F_a in IX mode and finally to lock r_{a9} in X mode.
- Suppose that transaction T_{20} reads all the records in file F_a. Then, T_{20} needs to lock the database and area A_1 (in that order) in IS mode and finally to lock F_a in S mode.
- Suppose that transaction T_{21} reads the entire database. It can do so after locking the database in S mode.

We note that transaction T_{18}, T_{20} and T_{21} can access the database currently. Transaction T_{19} can execute concurrently with T_{18}, but not with either T_{20} or T_{21}.

This protocol enhances concurrency and reduces lock overhead. It is particularly useful in applications that include a mix of

- Short transactions that access only a few data items.
- Long transactions that produce reports from an entire file or set of files.

There is a similar locking protocol that is applicable to database system in which data granularies are organized in the form of a directed acyclic graph. See the bibliographic notes for additional references. Deadlock is possible in (he protocol that we have, as it is in the two-phase locking protocol. There are techniques to reduce deadlock frequency in the multiple-granularity protocol, and also to eliminate deadlock entirely. These techniques are references in the bibliographic notes.

Q. 5 (c) What is two phase locking ? Describe with the help of an example. Will two phase locking result in deadlock ? Justify your answer with the help of an example. Discuss the Recovery with concurrent transactions also.

Ans. The Two-Phase Locking Protocol : One protocol that ensures serialization is the *two-phase locking protocol.* This protocol requires that each transaction issue lock and unlock request in two phases.

1. **Growing phase :** A transaction may obtain locks, but may not release any lock.
2. **Shrinking phase:** A transaction may release locks, but may obtain any new locks.

Initially, transaction is in the growing phase. The transaction acquires locks as needed. Once the transaction releases a lock, it enters the shrinking phase, and it can issue no more lock requests.

For example, transactions T_3 and T_4 are two phase. On the other hand, transaction T_1 and T_2 are not two phase. Note that the unlock instructions do not need to appear at the end of the transaction. For example, in the case of transaction T_3 we could move the **unlock** (B) instruction to just after the **lock-X**(A) instruction, and still retain the two-phase locking property.

We can show that the two-phase locking protocol ensures conflict serializability. Consider any transaction. The point in the schedule where the transaction has obtained its final lock (the end of its growing phase) is called the *lock point* of the transaction. Now, transactions can be ordered according to their lock points — this ordering is, in fact, a serializability ordering for the transactions.

Two-phase locking does *not* ensure freedom from deadlock. Observe that transactions T_3 and T_4 are two-phase, but. they are deadlocked.

It is desirable that schedules be cascade less. Cascading rollback may occur under two-phase locking. As an illustration, consider the partial schedule of Figure. Each transaction observes the two-phase locking protocol, but the failure of T_5 after the. read (A) step of T_7 leads to cascading rollback of T_6 and T_7.

Cascading rollback can be avoided by a modification of two-phase locking called the *strict two-phase locking* protocol. The strict two-phase locking protocol, requires, that in addition to locking being two-phase, all exclusive-mode locks taken by a transaction must be held until that transaction commits. This requirement ensures that any data written by an uncommitted transaction are locked in exclusive mode until the transaction commits, preventing any other transaction from reading the data.

T_5	T_6	T_7
lock-X(A)		
read (A)		
lock-S(B)		
read(B)		
write(A)		
unlock(A)		
	lock-X(A)	
	read (A)	
	write(A)	
	unlock(A)	
		lock-S(A)
		read (A)

Fig. *Partial schedule under two-phase locking.*

Another variant of two-phase locking is the *rigorous two-phase* locking protocol, which requires all locks to be held until the transaction commits. It can be easily verified that, with-rigorous two-phase locking, transaction can be serialized in the order in which they commit. Most database systems implement either strict or rigorous two-phase locking.

Consider the following two transactions for which we have shown only some of the significant read and write operations. Transaction T_s is defined as :

T_8 : **read** (a_1) ;

read (a_2);

. . .

read (a_n);

write (a_1).

Transaction T_9 is defined as

T_9 : **read** (a_1);

read (a_2);

display ($a_1 + a_2$).

If we employ the two-phase locking protocol, then T_8 must lock a_1 in exclusive mode. Therefore, any concurrent execution of both transaction amounts to a serial execution. Notice, however, that T_8 needs an exclusive lock on a_1 only at the end of its execution, when it writes a_1 Thus, if T_8 could initially lock a_1 in shared mode, and then could later change the lock to exclusive mode, we could get more concurrency, since T_8 and T_9 could access a_1 and a_2 simultaneously.

This observation leads us to a refinement of the basic two-phase locking protocol, in which lock *conversions* are allowed. We shall provide a mechanism for upgrading a shared lock to an exclusive lock, and downgrading an exclusive lock to a shared lock. We denote conversion .from shared to exclusive modes by **upgrade,** and from exclusive to shared by **downgrade.** Lock conversion cannot be allowed to occur arbitrarily. Rather, upgrading can take place in only the growing phase, whereas downgrading can take place in only the shrinking phase.

Transactions T_8 and T_9 can run concurrency under the refined two-phase locking protocol as shown in the incomplete schedule of Figure, where only some of the locking instructions are shown.

Note that a transaction attempting to upgrade a lock on an item Q may be forced to wait. This enforced wait occurs if Q is currently locked by another transaction in shared mode.

Just like the basic two-phase locking protocol, two-phase locking with lock conversion generates only conflict serializable schedules, and transactions can be serialized by their lock points. Further, if exclusive locks-are held, until the end of the transaction, the schedules are cascade less.

When a transaction T_i issues a read (Q) operation, the system issues a **lock-S**(Q) instruction followed by the **read**(Q) instruction. When T_i issues **a write**(Q) operation, the system checks to see whether T_i already holds a shared lock on Q. If it does, then the system issues an **upgrade**(Q) instruction, followed by the **write**(Q) instruction. Otherwise, the system issues a **lock-X(g)** instruction, followed by the **write**(Q) instruction. All locks obtained by a transaction are unlocked after that transaction commits or aborts.

T_8	T_9
lock-S(a_1)	lock-S(a_1)
lock-S(a_2)	lock-S(a_2)
lock-S(a_3)	
lock-S(a_4)	unlock(a_1)
	unlock(a_2)
lock-S(a_n)	
ungrade(a_1)	

Fig. Incomplete schedule with a lock conversion.

For a set of transactions, there may be conflict-serializable schedules that cannot be obtained through the two-phase locking protocol. However, to obtain conflict-serializable schedules through non-two-phase locking protocols, we need either to have additional information about the transactions or to impose some structure or ordering on the set of data items in the database. In the absence of such information, two-phase locking is necessary for conflict serializability—-if T_i is a non-two-phase transaction, it is always possible to find another transaction T. that is two-phase such that there is a schedule possible for T_i and T_j that is not conflict serializable.

Strict two-phase locking and rigorous two-phase locking (with lock conversions) are used extensively in commercial database systems.

B. TECH TCS-402

FOURTH SEMESTER EXAMINATION, 2006-07

DATABASE MANAGEMENT SYSTEM

Time : 3 Hours *Total Marks : 100*

Note : (i) Attempt ALL *the questions.*

(ii) All questions carry equal marks.

1. Answer any two parts : **(10 × 2 = 20)**

(a) Describe the three schema architecture and explain the need of mapping between schema levels.

Ans.

View (Sub Schema) → Top level - it changes frequency

Logical Schema → Middle level -schema can be change but not so frequently as of view level.

Physical Schema → Lowest level at this level schema is changed rarely.

* A Database System Support one physical schema, on logical schema and several sub (view) schema. It is partitioned according to the level of Abstraction.

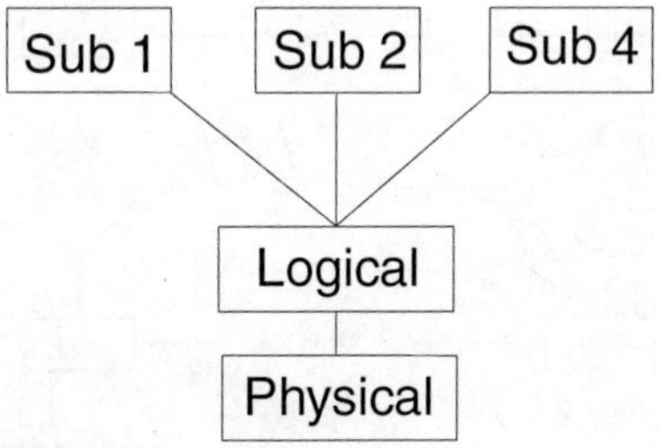

(b) Differentiate between the following clearly :

(i) Weak entity and Strong types

(ii) Primary key and Super key

(iii) Database and File system

Ans.

(i) Weak ⇒ No primary key exist

Name/D.O.B

Strong ⇒ Primary key exist

Roll No./Name/D.O.B.

(ii) Primary key ⇒ Not null and no subset (only one column or Attribute)

Super key ⇒ Subset can be there (set of more than one attribute)

(iii) Database ⇒ Data in Tabular form

File system ⇒ • Data Redundancy
- Data Inconsistency
- Difficulty in accessing data
- Data isolation
- Integrity
- Atomicity
- Security
- Concurrent Access

(c) What is purpose of the E-R diagram. Construct an E-R diagram for a University system which should include information about students, departments, professors, courses, which students are enrolled in which course, which professors are teaching in which courses, student grades, which course a department offers. Make suitable assumptions wherever required.

Ans. E-R Diagram ⇒ Entity Relationship Diagram

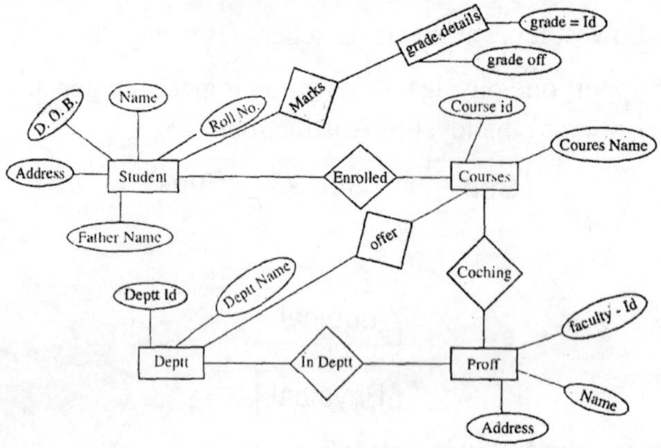

2. Answer any two parts **(10×2 = 20)**

(a) Consider the database given below, where primary keys are underlined :

employee (person name, street city)

works_for (person name, company name, salary)-

company (company name, city)

managers (person _ name. manager_name)

Give an expression in relation algebra to express each of the following queries :

Ans. Employee (person name, street city)

Works_for (person name, company name, salary)

Company (company name, city)

Managers (person name, manager_name)

(i) Find the names of all employees who live in the same city and on the same street as do their managers.

Ans. r ← Employee × Managers

r × (r)
k

r.manager_name = k.person_name ^
r.city = k. city ^ r.short = k.short

r-person-name, K. parson-name.

(ii) Find the names of all employees who do not work for company X.

Ans. p (employee) ⊞ π (σ (works-for) coper-Name = 'X').

Person-Name Person Name

(iii) Find the names and addresses of all employees of company Y.

Ans. Max-Salary-Y ← G(s (works-For) couper-Name = 'Y'
Max (Salary)

(work-iov)
Salary > Max – Salary – Y ⋈ employee

Person-Name, Start, city

(iv) Update the address of employee E.

Ans. temp ← π (s (employer) person-Name = "E") person-Name, start = "Now start". City - "New-City"

employee ← (employee - σ(employee) person -name = "E") Utemp

(v) Update salary of all managers by 10%.

Ans. temp II ← π (σ (employer & manager)
person-name, manager-name
person-name, couper-name. salary

Empolyer ← (employee-lap 1) Vπ (tap 1)
employee-name, couper-name salary * 1.1

(b)) (i) Given the relational schema R = (A, IS, C) and S = (D, E, F) and relations r(R) and s(S). Give equivalent SQL statements for each of the following expressions :

(1) $\pi_A(r)$

(2) $\sigma_B = {}_{17}(r)$

(3) **r X s**

(4) $\pi_{A, F}(\sigma_{C = D}(r \times s))$

Ans. R = (A,B,C).

S = (D,E,F)

1. $\pi_A(r)$

SQL. Select A

from r;

2. $\sigma_B = {}_{17}(r)$

SQL. Select *

from r

where B = 17;

3. $r \times s$

SQL. Select k.*, p.*

from r k, s p;

4. $\pi_{A, F}(s_{C = D}(r \times s))$

SQL. Select A, F

from r, s

where C = D;

(ii) Discuss the various types of inner join operations. Why is theta join required? Explain with suitable examples.

Ans. Types of inner join :

1. Equijoin → Equijoin is special type ??, ?? show - condition
2. Cartesian Join → 'X' contains all the combinations of tuples
3. Natural Join → Natural join is a equijoin followed by removal of superfluous attribute

Equijoin

Select e. cname, d. deptno from emp e, dept a

where e. deptno = d. deptno

Cartesian

Select * from emp, dept

$\pi_{\text{emp name' balance Amm}}$ (emp ∞ balance)

We need Theta join because Tuples whose join attributes are null do not appear in the result. In that sense, the join operation does not necessarily preserve all of the information in the participating relations.

Eg. $\pi_{\text{emp name}}$ ($\sigma_{\text{salary} > 200}$ $^{(\text{emp} \infty \text{balance})}$)

(c) (i) Define and explain the following terms briefly :

Domain constraints, Referential - integrity.

Ans. Domain Constraints : It is the most elementary form of integrity constraint. They are easily tested by the system whenever a new data item is entered into the database. It is possible for several attributes to have the same domain.

Referential Integrity : To ensure that a value that appears in one relation for a given sel of attributes also appears for a certain set of'attributes in another relation. This condition is called as referential integrity.

(ii) List the data types that are allowed for SQL attributes and give the complete syntax for SQL statements including all clauses.

Ans. Data Types : (1) numeric (2) character-string (3) bit-string (4) Date and time

1. CHAR
2. Integer

VARCHAR	INT
VARCHARZ	

3. BIT
4. DATE
5. Year, Month

1.	select	[attribute-list]
	from	[Table-name]
	where	[condition]
2.	select	[all-name]
	from	[table-name]
	Group by	all-names
	having	condition
	order by	[all-name]

3. Answer any two parts : (10×2 = 20)

(a) Define multi-valued dependencies. What type of constraints does it specify? When does it arise?

Ans. MVD (Multi Valued Dependency)

$X \to\to Y$

indicates that for each value of X there are many values of Y.

and if $X \to\to Y$ holds in a relation R then for all pairs of t_1 and t_2, in r such that $t_1[X] = t_2[X]$ then there exists t_3, and t_4 so that

$t_1[X] = t_2[X] = t_3[X] = t_4[X]$

$t_3[Y] = t_1[Y]$

$t_3[R - Y] = t_2[R - Y]$

$t_4[Y] = t_2[Y]$

$t_4[R - Y] = t_2[R - Y]$

$X \to\to Y$ is needed when we have a relation between X and Y is independent of relationships between X and R - Y.

Specify following constraints :

1. Constraint on set of legal relations *i.e.* relations that satisfy some FDs or MVDs.
2. To lest relations.to determine whether they are legal relations under a set of FDs and MVDs.

(b) Suppose we decompose the schema R = (A, B, C, D, E) into R_1 and R_2 defined follows :

R_1(A,B,C)

R_2(C,D,E)

Justify whether it is a lossless decomposition or not.

Ans. = (A,B,C,D,E)

R_1(A,B,C)

R_2 (C. D, E)

Decomposition of R into R_1 and R_2 will be lossless decomposition

if $C \to AB$

or

$C \to DE$

Else it is toss.

(c) (i) Why are normal forms alone insufficient as a condition for a good schema design? Explain.

Ans. Normal forms refers to the desirable properties of a relation schema. Process of normalization includes analysis of relations to meet more desirable properties. But normal forms alone do not guarantee a good database design. It is not sufficient to check separately that each relation schema in the database is i n BCNF or BNF or in some desirable NF. Rather, it must also confirm the existence of additional properties that schemas takes together *e.g.*

1. **lossless join** 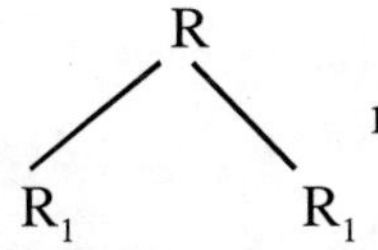

must be achieved

2. **dependency preservation:** Sometimes needed more over [he constraints on which NF has been defined are hard to defect and understand sometimes. And relations generally are not normalized to higher degree.

(ii) Define join dependencies and fifth normal form. Why is 5 NS also called project join normal form.

Ans. JD : A scheme R is said to have JD* (R_1R_2, ...R_n) if each legal relative r(R) satisfies

$$r(R) = \pi_{R_1}(r) \qquad \pi_{R_2}(r) \qquad \pi_{R_a}(r)$$

The reason is that if r(R) is pointed into $\pi_{R_1}(r)$, $\pi_{R_2}(r)$ .... $\pi_{R_a}(r)$ and then projection are join then we must get the original relation r(R).

4. Answer any two parts : **(10 × 2 = 20)**

(a) Discuss the procedures of deadlock detection and recovery in transactions.

Ans. Deadlock Detection :

- Create a wait for graph G = (V, E)
- Deadlock exists off wait for Graph contains a cycle

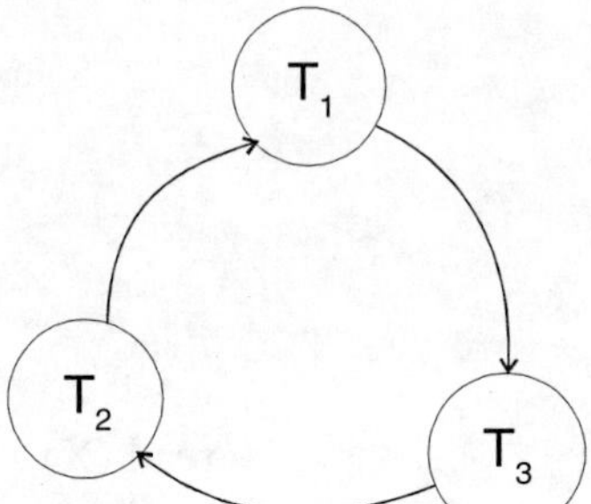

Recovery :

1. Selection of a victim
2. Rollback
3. Starvation

(b) What is the system log used for? What is the typical kinds of records in a system log? What are transaction commit point and why are they important?

Ans. Log File : Contains into regarding which transactions has executed of which OP. which failed etc. such entries all called log records, for *e.g.*

1. start [T]
2. abort [T]
3. write [T, X, O, N]
4. read [T, X]
5. check point

A check point is the last safe state to which Ds will be restored incase system fails or transaction fails.

(c) Consider a database with objects X and Y and assume that there are two transactions T_1 and T_2 The transaction T_1 reads object X and Y then writes objects X. The transaction T_2 reads X and Y then writes objects X and Y. Give examples of schedules with actions of T_1 and T_2 on X and Y that results in :

(i) write-read conflict.

(ii) read-write conflict.

(iii) write-write conflict.

Ans.

T_1	T_2
read (X)	read (X)
read(Y)	read(Y)
write (X)	write (X)
	write (Y)

(i) write-read conflict

T_1	T_2
read (X)	
read (Y)	
write (X)	
	read (X)

(ii) read-write conflict

T_1	T_2
read (X)	
read (Y)	read (X)
write (X)	

(iii) write-write conflict

read (X)	
read (Y)	
	read (X)
	read (Y)
	write (X)
write (X)	

5. Answer any two parts : **(10×2 = 20)**

(a) Explain the working of locking technique in concurrency control. What benefit does rigorous two-phase locking provide? How does it compare with other forms of two-phase locking?

Ans. Locking : To ensure serializability *i.e.* at one time only one X-action can access the data item locking is used.

Concurrency control can be done with the help of locking techniques.

Shared (S) (read but not write)

Exclusive (X) (read and write both)

Two phase locking protocol:

1. Growing Phase : A transaction way obtain locks but may not release any lock.

2. Shrinking Phase : A transaction may release locks but may not obtain any new lock.

(b) State the multi-version timestamp based protocol. Suggest a scheme to avoid the phanton phenomenon.

Ans. In multiversion scheme, many versions of a data base object/item X exist (created on each write (X) request). Whenever a transaction requests read (X), the—Latest version is made a read and when it requests write (X) a new version of X is created and updation is made over it.

1. Multiversion timestamp ordering : With each version Q_K we attach 3 fields.

1. Content
2. W-Timestamp (Q_K)
3. R-timestamp(Q_K)
   1. if T_1 issues read (Q)—value returned is that of latest version,
   2. if it issues write (Q)— if T_s (T_i) < R-timestamp (Q_K) then T= is rolled back.

      $T_s(T_i)$ = W-times (Q_K)—ones write otherwise—Create a new version.

2. Multiversion 2 phase locking : Each data item has a single timestamp and it is a counter.

Whenever a T_x issues a Read Queue, latest version is made read.

Write Queue, first it take lock on data item and set its time stop = 0 for new created version.

Then makes updation then updates value of ts-counter by one and assigns it to new.

(c) What is a recoverable schedule? Why is recoverability of schedules desirable? Are there any circumstances under which it would be desirable to allow non-recoverable schedules? Explain your answer.

Ans. Schedule : The chronological order in which instructions are executed in the system is called as schedule.

A schedule for a set of transactions must consist of all instruction of these transaction.,

→ Serial schedule

→ Concurrent schedule

Recoverability : If any transaction fails due to any reason then we need to undo the effect of this X-action to ensure the atomicity property of the X-action. This is called as recoverability. No, in any circumstances non-recoverable schedules are not allowed.

Because it will Break the ACID property and Data base will be inconsistent.